Policing and Race
in America

Policing and Race in America

Economic, Political, and Social Dynamics

Edited by
James D. Ward

LEXINGTON BOOKS
Lanham • Boulder • New York • London

Published by Lexington Books
An imprint of The Rowman & Littlefield Publishing Group, Inc.
4501 Forbes Boulevard, Suite 200, Lanham, Maryland 20706
www.rowman.com

Unit A, Whitacre Mews, 26–34 Stannary Street, London SE11 4AB

British Library Cataloguing in Publication Information Available

Library of Congress Cataloging-in-Publication Data

Names: Ward, James D. (James Dale), 1959- editor.
Title: Policing and race in America : economic, political, and social
    dynamics / edited by James D. Ward.
Description: Lanham : Lexington Books, [2017] | Includes bibliographical
    references and index.
Identifiers: LCCN 2017044239 (print) | LCCN 2017056385 (ebook) | ISBN
    9781498550925 (Electronic) | ISBN 9781498550918 (cloth : alk. paper)
Subjects: LCSH: Discrimination in law enforcement—United States. |
    Police—United States.
Classification: LCC HV8141 (ebook) | LCC HV8141 .P 2017 (print) | DDC
    363.2/308900973—dc23
LC record available at https://lccn.loc.gov/2017044239

Printed in the United States of America

Contents

List of Figures   vii

List of Tables   ix

Acknowledgments   xi

Introduction   1
James D. Ward

PART I: POLITICAL CHALLENGES   **15**

1 What to Do When the Yelling Stops: How Black Lives Matter Can
     Have Lasting Impact   17
     Domonic A. Bearfield, Robert Maranto, and Ian Kingsbury

2 Contemporary Police and Minorities in the United States: Causes,
     Theories, and Solutions   31
     John A. Eterno and Christine S. Barrow

3 Leveraging the Intersection of Politics, Problem, and Policy in
     Organizational and Social Change: An Historical Analysis of the
     Detroit, Los Angeles, and Atlanta Police Departments   55
     Andrew J. Grandage, Britt S. Aliperti, and Brian N. Williams

4 Policy Feedback: Government Skepticism Trickling
     from Immigration to Matters of Health   85
     Vanessa Cruz Nichols, Alana M. W. LeBrón, and Francisco I. Pedraza

PART II: ECONOMIC REALITIES   109

5   What Have We Learned about Incarceration and Race? Lessons
    from Thirty Years of Research   111
    Samuel L. Myers, Jr.

6   Should More Law Enforcement be the Answer to Crime?   123
    Ronald Zullo

7   Punishing Members of Disadvantaged Minority
    Groups for Calling 911   141
    Barry D. Friedman and Maria J. Albo

PART III: SOCIAL RAMIFICATIONS   163

8   Check Your Bubble! Mindful Intersections of
    Trauma and Community Policing   165
    Sharlene Graham Boltz

9   Assessing Racial and Ethnic Differences in the
    Consequences of Police Use of Force   181
    Jared Ellison and Benjamin Steiner

10 Bridging the Safety Divide through Technology to
    Improve the Partnership between Students and Campus
    Law Enforcement: An "App" Opportunity   207
    Edward C. Dillon, Brian N. Williams, Seong C. Kang,
    Juan E. Gilbert, Julian Brinkley, and Dekita Moon.

11 Community Policing as a Solution: What is the Evidence?   221
    Lauren Hamilton Edwards and Ian Klein

12 Developing a Comparativist Ethics for the Evaluative Study of
    Racialized Police Violence   241
    Mario A. Rivera and James D. Ward

Conclusion: Reflections on Realities, Challenges, and Ramifications   263
James D. Ward

Appendix 1   273

Appendix 2   279

Index   281

About the Editor and Contributors   285

List of Figures

Figure 1.1   Sources of Variables   23
Figure 3.1   Police Departments Operate with
             an Open System   59
Figure 3.2   Representation Ratios by City for Black Officers   62
Figure 3.3   Percentage of Black Population by City   63
Figure 3.4   Representation Ratios by City, 2013   63
Figure 4.1   Secure Communities Enforcement 2011, Exposure among
             HINTS 4, Cycle 1 Participants   94
Figure 4.2   Predicted Probability of Immigration Enforcement
             on Trust in Government as a Source of
             Health Information by Race and Ethnicity   98
Figure 5.1   Countries with Largest Number of Prisoners
             per 100,000 of the National Population,
             as of June 2014   112
Figure 5.2   Total Incarcerations, Blacks and Whites, 1978–2013   113
Figure 5.3   Unemployment versus Incarceration   115
Figure 5.4   Black-White Differences in Arrests Rates, 1960–2013   117
Figure 5.5   Disparity in Incarcerations Greater than
             in the Disparity in Arrests   118
Figure 5.6   Effects of Drug Arrests on Incarceration Rates   118
Figure 10.1 Conceptual Framework of Co-Production   209
Figure 10.2 Police Confidence (Overall)   211
Figure 10.3 Police Confidence (by Race and Location)   211
Figure 10.4 Emergent Perceptions   213
Figure 10.5 Application (Example Scenario)   216

List of Tables

Table 2.1   2012 Survey Findings   43
Table 2.2   2012 Survey Findings   44
Table 4.1   Summary Statistics   93
Table 4.2   Logistic Regression Estimates of Trust in
            Government as a Source of Health Information   95
Table 4.3   Split-Sample Logistic Regression Estimates of
            Trust in Other Source of Health Information Such
            as the Internet, Charities, Physicians, Family Members,
            Religious Leaders, Radio, Magazine, and Television   97
Table 5.1   Prisoners Under State and Federal Jurisdiction
            1974, 1980, 1990, 2000, and 2010   113
Table 6.1   Variables, Definitions, and Descriptive Statistics   128
Table 6.2   Violent Crime and Public Service, US Counties,
            2002–2011   130
Table 6.3   Property Crime and Public Service,
            US Counties, 2002–2011   132
Table 6.4   Violent and Property Crime Components and
            Public Service, US Counties 2002–2011   134
Table 6.5   Interactions between Public Jobs and Demographics
            across Violent and Property Crimes,
            US Counties, 2002–2011   136
Table 9.1   Description of Sample and Measures   188
Table 9.2   Inmate Effects on Assaults   190
Table 9.3   Inmate Effects on Nonviolent Offenses   191
Table 9.4   Description of Outcomes and Main
            Predictor Variables by Racial Group   192

Table 9.5	Relationship between Use of Force and Assaults by Race/Ethnicity	193
Table 9.6	Relationship between Use of Force and Nonviolent Offenses by Race/Ethnicity	195
Table 11.1	Findings for Reducing Crime	227
Table 11.2	Findings for Holding Offenders Accountable	228
Table 11.3	Reducing Fear	229
Table 11.4	Citizen Satisfaction	230
Table 11.5	Citizen Engagement	231
Table 11.6	Police Force	232
Table A1	OLS Estimates of Determinants of Racial Differences in Incarceration Rates	274
Table A2	OLS Estimates of Coefficients in Model of Black Incarceration Rates	275
Table A3	OLS Estimates of Coefficients in Model of White Incarceration Rates	276

Acknowledgments

I wish to thank all contributors who worked diligently to help make this volume a reality. I must especially give thanks to the chapter reviewers who contributed their time and effort to enhancing the quality of this volume. Reviewers include Thomas Barth, James Brunet, Charles Epp, Alfred Ho, Cryshanna Jackson-Leftwich, Mario A. Rivera, and Meghan Rubado.

Introduction

James D. Ward

- August 26, 1998. A young assistant professor is pulled over at gunpoint in Las Cruces, New Mexico after he allegedly changed lanes without signaling. He is Black. The police officer is Hispanic. No citation was issued.
- July 17, 2014. Eric Garner dies from a chock hold in NYC after being detained for selling loose cigarettes. He repeatedly states, "I can't breathe," after the officer subdued him to the ground. Garner was Black. The officer is White. There was no indictment.
- April 12, 2015. Freddie Gray dies from a spinal cord injury after an alleged "rough (van) ride" by six Baltimore police officers (three White and three Black). There is no conviction. Gray was Black.
- June 18, 2016. Antwun "Ronnie" Shumpert is allegedly mauled by a police K-9 and shot four times in Tupelo, Mississippi after he fled from a police officer during a traffic stop. Police say Shumpert came out from hiding and attacked the dog and the police officer. Witnesses say Shumpert was attempting to surrender when he was attacked by the K-9. Shumpert, who was Black and unarmed, died at a local hospital. No charges were filed.
- July 7, 2016. Five law enforcement officials in Dallas, Texas are killed and seven others wounded when Micah Xavier Johnson, a 25-year-old Black war veteran, unleashed sniper fire during a peaceful Black Lives Matter rally. Johnson reportedly said he wanted to kill White police officers in retaliation for the police killings of Black men, including the killing of Alton Sterling in Baton Rouge, Louisiana and Philando Castile in suburban St. Paul, Minnesota days earlier. Johnson was eventually killed when a bomb attached to a police robot exploded where he was held out.

Policing and race in America is a cornerstone of political, economic, and social dynamics in regard to public policy and law enforcement behavior.

1

When disparate treatment occurs, based on race and ethnicity, claims to social equity may be diminished, along with perceived commitments to a just and fair society. The headlines are numerous, as is the anecdotal evidence. In this book, the objective is to explore policing and race in relationship to political challenges, economic realities, and social ramifications. This is done through the use of evidence-based research and established best practices as presented in twelve chapters written by accomplished scholars across various academic disciplines.

In my previous research (Ward 2002; Ward and Rivera 2014), I have argued that law enforcement racial profiling is systemic to the greater social mores regarding race and perceptions of criminal activity. In this book, I expand on that acknowledged understanding and ask the following questions: To what extent do racial disparities in police-community relations result from economic, political, and social inequities? And, to what extent is it the responsibility of government to address and eliminate such inequities?

The President's Task Force on 21st Century Policing, among other recommendations, stated that, "Building trust and nurturing legitimacy on both sides of the police/citizen divide is the fundamental principle underlying the nature of relations between law enforcement agencies and the communities they serve" (President's Task Force 2015). In relation to building that trust and legitimacy, the Final Report made the following observations.

- Law enforcement cannot build community trust if it is seen as an occupying force coming from outside to impose control on the community.
- Law enforcement culture should embrace a guardian—rather than a warrior mindset.
- Law enforcement agencies should also establish a culture of transparency which is critical to ensuring that decision-making is understood and in accord with stated policy.

From a social psychology perspective, studies (see Correll, Park, Judd and Wittenbrink 2007) found that participants in a laboratory experiment tended to shoot armed Blacks more frequently than armed Whites and that racial bias reflected the perception of threat—specifically threat associated with Black males. In addition to disparities in police use of force, racial profiling is another phenomenon often associated with policing and race. Racial profiling occurs when law enforcement officials stop individuals who are perceived to have a greater likelihood of being involved in certain kinds of criminal activity based on the individual's race or ethnicity. The practice may be defined as targeting members of specific racial and/or ethnic groups based on a belief that members of such groups are predisposed to committing certain types of crimes. This belief is often based on crude and generalized preconceptions on the part of law enforcement officials and even members of the greater community. From this perspective, law enforcement racial profiling is systemic and acquiesces from the broader societal ethos regarding race and criminal activity.

Epp, Maynard-Moody, and Haider-Markel (2017 and 2014) argue that the investigatory (pretextual) stop is at the heart of the problem regarding biased behavior in police interactions with African Americans. Using data from an original, scientific survey of drivers in the Kansas City metropolitan area, the authors show that racial disparities in police stops are concentrated in what they call the investigatory stop. According to the authors, officers not only disproportionately stop African Americans but question them intensively and perform more searches. Epp, Maynard-Moody, and Haider-Markel contend that the overwhelming majority of persons stopped in this manner are innocent. Yet, they experience psychological harm, and the experience erodes trust in and cooperation with law enforcement. The scientific results offered by Epp, Maynard-Moody, and Haider-Markel support long standing anecdotal evidence dating back to the 1990s, when the consequences of Driving While Black, and/or Driving While Latino, were first introduced into the public discourse and subsequent research (Ward 2002).

Regarding immigrant Latino populations, Armenta and Alvarez (2017) contend that research on local law enforcement should move away from an exclusive examination of public policies toward immigrants, to consider how the policing of immigrants actually occurs on the ground. For example, they argue that even policing practices that seem immigration-neutral are part of the *immigration control machinery*, in that the pretextual (investigative) stop encourages police officers to rely on their own implicit bias regarding who looks suspicious, putting officers disproportionately face to face with unauthorized Latino immigrants, as opposed to unauthorized non-Latino immigrants.

One often recommended political solution, or challenge, to reducing the incidence of racial profiling, and disparities in police use of force, has been to increase the number of African American police officers, as well as that of other racial and ethnic minorities. Yet, it has been shown (Ward and Rivera 2014; Wilkins and Williams 2008; Ward 2002) that simply increasing the number of Black police officers does not in and of itself reduce such disparities, as police officers (regardless of race and/or ethnicity) are more influenced by an organizational and law enforcement culture which sees African Americans, and African American men in particular, as being more prone to engage in certain types of criminal activity. This, in essence, represents a form of the aforementioned implicit bias as examined by social psychologists (see Rattan and Eberhardt 2010; Correll, Park, Judd, and Wittenbrink 2007). Thus, Kahn and Martin (2016) conclude that based on the scientific literature, effective intervention policies must address both actual police bias as well the perceptions of police bias, as not all perceived bias reflects actual bias, and actual bias can be enacted without its perception.

Regarding police-involved fatal shootings and Black suspects, research by Carrier et al. (2015), and based on content analysis of media reports between 2009 and 2012, showed that zero percent of unarmed Black suspects were shot and killed by Black police officers during that time period, compared to 66.7 percent who were shot and killed by White police officers, and thirty 33.3 percent who were shot and killed by Other (race) police officers. Such lends credence to the "inattentional blindness" scenario as postulated by Rattan and Eberhardt, and suggests that in spite of the presence of implicit and explicit bias in police stops, and the racial disparities in use of force, that Black police officers may be less inclined to perceive the unarmed Black suspect as posing a higher level of threat, compared to White police officers and Other (race) police officers. While quantitative studies have been done regarding how law enforcement policies and/or strategies may lessen the incidence of deadly force (Jennings and Rubado 2017), or how increasing the number of Black police officers may not influence the behavior of Black police officers until a critical mass is achieved (Nicholson-Crotty et al. 2017), neither of the studies controlled for the race or ethnicity of the officer and/or the race or ethnicity of the suspect, in police-involved shootings, as did the research by Carrier et al. (2015).

To what extent the results of these studies are reflected in actual law enforcement behavior is cause for concern. If indeed White officers see African American men as more threatening and thus fear for their own safety at a higher level than they would in similar encounters with White male suspects, such would to some degree explain the greater level of police violence and fatal shootings of unarmed African American men. As previously stated, Rattan and Eberhardt (2010) describe the phenomenon as the "inattentional blindness," and argue that people are naturally limited in what they perceive, and thus are limited in their judgment of others. In other words, individuals commonly make judgments or decisions about members of other ethnic or racial groups without seeing the whole picture. When *black-crime association* is connected to *inattentional blindness* such leads to explicit bias and implicit acceptance of stereotypes within the culture. Eberhardt asserts that this "influences how both ordinary citizens and police officers perceive and analyze the people and objects they encounter" (for quote, see Stichtenoth 2016).

Adherents to Critical Race Theory (CRT) would argue that the targeting of certain racial and ethnic groups, and the resulting police violence associated with it, is better explained by the racism engrained in the fabric and system of American society, including power structures based on White privilege and White supremacy, which perpetuate the marginalization of people of color. Thus, CRT adherents would reject a unidimensional approach to addressing the problems associated with policing and race and argue for multidimensionality, instead, due to the economic, judicial, social, and political power structures which sustain White supremacy and institutional racism (Delgado and Stefancic 2006).

Elaine Penderhughes (1989), in a broader discussion of race, suggests that disparities in societal perceptions may be understood through *power-assigning structures* that take the form of institutional racism, and affect the life opportunities, life-styles, and quality of life for both Whites and people of color. The author argues that in doing so, these *power-assigning structures* compound, exaggerate, and distort biological and behavioral differences and reinforce misconceptions, myths, and distortions on the part of both groups and one another. Similarly, Ward and Rivera (2014) contend that institutional racism makes for denials of the very reality of racism, or of a need to respond to others in a racially sensitive and culturally competent manner, whether it is intentional or unintentional.

In light of the problems caused by institutional racism, as well as implicit and explicit bias, studies (Jennings and Rubado 2017; Nicholson-Crotty et al. 2017) inquire as to whether or not specific law enforcement policies and increased minority representation may lower the incidence of racial disparities in police use of force, including deadly force. Nicholson-Crotty et al. (2017) found that a critical mass of Black officers is needed within a police department for Black officers to begin to show noticeable signs of explicit representation or turn from "blue" to "Black." Otherwise, unless there is a 40 percent or higher Black representation in the police department, Black officers continue to acquiesce toward the acceptable norms of the organization, including the exercise of implicit and explicit bias in their encounters with Black citizens. When it comes to the use of deadly force, Jennings and Rubado (2017) found that requiring officers to file a report when they point their guns at people, whether or not they fire, was the only policy associated with significantly lower rates of gun deaths. The authors leveraged a large-scale dataset of gun deaths by police officers in the United States, combined with agency-level policy data and community demographic data, to examine whether certain policies are associated with lower or higher rates of officer-involved gun deaths.

POLITICAL CHALLENGES

In my previous research (Ward 2002), I found that intervention policies caused a financial burden to the city of Houston, Texas in 1999 when a data collection program aimed at assessing the extent of racially motivated pretextual stops resulted in a reduction in the frequency of such stops, as officers feared they would be singled out for targeting people based on race. During the first two months of the program, 40,000 fewer tickets were written compared to the same time period the previous year. Such a drastic reduction in the number of traffic tickets written resulted in millions of dollars in lost revenue at a time when the city had already initiated spending cuts to balance revenue shortfalls. Furthermore, the Houston Police Officers Association contended that "traffic [pretextual] stops often identify fugitives with outstanding warrants or criminal charges, or those carrying illegal guns or drugs. Fewer stops mean fewer opportunities to get these people off the street" (p. 730). The International Association of Police Chiefs also claimed that pretextual stops result in more guns being taken off the street than any other tactic. And, the federal Drug Enforcement Administration estimated that 40 percent of all drug arrests were the outgrowth of traffic stops (Ward 2002).

Thus, it should be noted that the pretextual (or investigatory) stop is a practice endorsed by law enforcement organizations nationwide, as these organizations argue that the practice is legal (in most jurisdictions), and does not necessarily indicate the presence of racial profiling (see Davenport 2017; President's Task Force on 21st Century Policing 2015). However, the state of Washington outlawed pretextual stops in 1999, as did the state of New Mexico in 2008, along with fifteen additional states (including Texas) that ban racial profiling altogether, and pretextual stops to a lesser degree (May, Duke, and Gueco 2017; Ward and Rivera 2014, p. 111; NAACP Report 2014). Critics of the pretextual stop argue that it is a classic example of the ends justifying the means, as law enforcement officials have failed to qualify their argument by documenting how many stops generate arrests and provide probable cause for all stops made, regardless of whether an arrest was made or a citation issued (see Epp et al. 2017 and 2014; Blessett and Box 2016; Donohue and Barrett 2000; and Kocieniewski and Hanley 2000a, 2000b).

Part I in this book includes four chapters that address some of the political challenges related to policing and race in America.

In chapter 2, "What To Do When The Yelling Stops: How Black Lives Matter Can Have Lasting Impact," authors Bearfield, Maranto, and Kingsbury argue that the incentives of the political system, for Black Lives Matter and for its conservative opponents, tend to devalue Black (and other) lives, mobilizing constituencies rather than solving problems. Rather than invoking the social or political activist literature, the authors propose that to make

Black lives matter, reformers should instead demand transparency and make use of the innovation and/or administrative *reinvention literature*, suggesting that improved public organizations will result in improved public service, accomplished by recruiting and retaining better public servants and providing support for them to succeed. The authors argue that the intertwined problems of police violence toward African Americans (and in African American communities in general) should be seen less as matters of changing political values and improving representation than as matters of improving public sector performance.

In chapter 3, "Contemporary Police and Minorities in the United States: Causes, Theories, and Solutions," John Eterno and Christine Barrow contend that police performance management, sometimes called Compstat, zero tolerance, or broken windows, has changed the mindset of policing from working with communities to a war on crime. Using original data and combined with social science theory, the authors provide evidence of modern policing policy that leads to harmful and sometimes racist policing. Their data indicates that in the current performance management era, the rank and file and some managers *are reduced to number crunching automatons*. This they argue is in stark contrast to the ideal of community policing where officers are supposedly proactive problem-solvers, working closely with the neighborhoods they serve.

In chapter 4, "Leveraging the Intersection of Politics, Problem and Policy in Organizational and Social Change: An Historical Analysis of the Detroit, Los Angeles, and Atlanta Police Departments," Grandage, Aliperti, and Williams use historical case studies of the Detroit, Los Angeles, and Atlanta police departments to highlight the challenges of organizational change in the midst of racial and social unrest. Environmental conditions, which serve to promote change in response to societal influences, are explored with an emphasis on how an intersection of politics, policy, and problem can accelerate change.

In chapter 5, "Government Skepticism Trickling from Immigration to Matters of Health," Cruz Nichols, LeBron, and Pedraza focus on the politics of immigration and health, two issue areas marked by large-scale bureaucratic developments in the last fifty years. Using regression analysis, they find evidence that the Secure Communities program, the centerpiece of contemporary immigration enforcement between 2008 and 2014, is associated with mistrust in the government as a source of health information among Latinos, but not other racial/ethnic groups. For example, the authors contend that Latinos who live in communities where immigration enforcement is most intense express lower levels of trust in government, including access to health information. Therefore, a major spillover effect to expanding immigration enforcement is how individuals view the institutions charged with the provision of public goods.

Economic Realities

In regards to economic realities stemming from racial disparities in employment decisions, Pager and Quillian (2005) considered the relationship between employers' attitudes toward hiring ex-offenders and their actual hiring behavior. The authors used data from an experimental audit study of entry-level jobs and matched it with results from a telephone survey of the same employers. The objective was to measure the willingness of the employers to hire Black and White ex-offenders, based on employer self-reports and compared to actual hiring decisions. Results showed that employers who expressed a greater likelihood to hire ex-offenders in the survey were no more likely to hire an ex-offender in practice. However, whereas the survey results indicated no difference in the likelihood of hiring Black versus White ex-offenders, audit results show large differences by race.

Hence, if African Americans are disproportionately represented in the criminal justice system due to pretextual or investigative stops, implicit bias, and tougher sentencing guidelines, repercussions may have long-term economic consequences. Evidence suggests that racial disparities even exists in the sentencing of juvenile offenders. A study sponsored by a consortium of child advocacy and civil rights groups, titled "And Justice for Some," concluded that a Black youth offender is six times more likely to be jailed than a youth offender who is White, even if the two commit the same crime and have the same criminal backgrounds. Latino youths, according to the study, are three times more likely than White youths to do time (Office of Juvenile Delinquency 2000; also see Ward 2002). According to Myers (2002), the state of Minnesota disproportionately incarcerates more African American men than any other state, with Blacks twenty times more likely to be jailed than their percentage in the general population (also see Johnson 2001). The author argues that such a disparity may lead law enforcement and the general population to conclude that Blacks are more inclined to be criminals and should thus be apprehended at a greater rate than Whites. From a cost versus benefit perspective, Myers asks the question as to whether or not the cost of racial profiling outweighs the alleged greater benefit in terms of efficiency, if one accepts the premise that racial profiling (pretextual or investigatory stops) generates higher expected profits than random stops and searches. His contention is that such a premise is politically driven and not based in sound policy analysis, as "racial profiling in particular, is seen to proceed in a confrontational political environment with little appreciation for, or attention to, components of policy analysis" (p. 298). Furthermore, Blessett, and Box (2016) identified how the use of pretextual stops in Ferguson, Missouri (and other jurisdictions) posed economic inequities to African Americans because of the heavy reliance on the issuance and payment of citations to balance city budgets, causing the authors to refer to it as *sharecropper finance*. This practice was also highlighted in a federal government report (Department of Justice 2015, pp. 9–15; also see Berman et al. 2016). Knowles et al. (2001), using data from the Maryland State Patrol, found that non-race profiles in drug interdiction programs may actually lead to an increase in efficiency. The authors conclude that "Statistical discrimination, even if not due to prejudice, may be considered unfair because innocent drivers experience different probabilities of being searched depending on their race" (p. 207), and argue that implementing color-blind search behavior does not necessarily entail a cost in terms of efficiency in interdiction.

Thus, Part II of this book includes chapters addressing some of the economic realities of policing and race in America related to issues of poverty, incarceration, and joblessness.

In chapter 6, "What Have We Learned about Incarceration and Race? Lessons from Thirty Years of Research," Samuel L. Myers, Jr. reviews the stylized facts about incarceration rates from 1970 to the present and explores the variety of explanations for the growth of Black imprisonment. Two specific empirical tests are conducted. One is a test of the hypothesis that there is an efficiency justification for the racial differential in imprisonment. Using decades-old federal prison data, the author shows the existence of substantial discrimination in sentencing that cannot be attributable to racial differences in anticipated recidivism rates. A second test examines the hypothesis that the rise in racial disparities in incarceration is due to increases in arrests for drugs.

In chapter 7, "Should More Law Enforcement Be the Answer to Crime?" Roland Zullo uses US county data from 2002 to 2011 to examine three governmental functions and their relation to violent and property crimes. Results indicate a strong negative association between public services and crime, and that regions with high densities of minorities are especially sensitive to changes in public services. Of the three functions, education is the strongest and most consistent crime deterrent, followed by law enforcement and social welfare. The results imply that expanding educational opportunities is a more effective use of government spending in relation to a reduction in violent and property crimes.

In chapter 8, "Punishing Members of Disadvantaged Minority Groups for Calling 911," Friedman and Albo examine the experience of lower-class individuals who believe that they are being defrauded at a place of business—commonly a fast-food restaurant—and find themselves interacting with intransigent cashiers who refuse to make an adjustment or to refund the customer's payment. Friedman and Albo point to a pattern of news reports that describe these incidents and chronicle how the dissatisfied customer calls 911 and is then arrested or given a summons for making a nonemergency call to the 911 service. Referencing literature about the adverse experiences of lower-class members of disadvantaged minority groups with the criminal justice system, the authors assert that the arrests are due more to the personal characteristics of the accused (poor and uneducated) and less to do with the offense of having called 911.

Social Ramifications

Social ramifications of policing and race in America may stem, in part, from both political and economic inequities, as well as social and psychological phenomena. For example, Davis (1997) argues that unlike the mere inconvenience that non-minority *innocents* may experience when subjected to pretextual stops, minority *innocents* suffer additional secondary costs when stopped solely based on their race and/or ethnicity. Under these circumstances, Davis argues that minority *innocents* are subjected to *indignities, embarrassment, humiliation, and psychological and emotional damages that far outweigh the putative benefits of increasing apprehension of drug dealers*. Furthermore, the political challenges of delivering a more just and fair criminal justice system cannot escape the economic realities that people of color are often disadvantaged due to implicit bias, as well as income and educational inequalities, that are reinforced through structural and institutional racism.

Civil rights groups, including Black Lives Matter, may demand a greater level of social equality in the dispensing of criminal justice, and interactions between African Americans and members of law enforcement. Yet, proponents of a *law and order mentality* may disassociate from any notion that law enforcement is racially biased in the dispensing of justice, or in encounters with racial and ethnic minorities, and instead acquiesce to a belief that an individual's encounter with law enforcement should be judged solely on that individual's behavior, and respect for law enforcement, and not on a racial and/or ethnic basis.

Part III in this book includes chapters that address some of the social ramifications of policing and race in America including psychological trauma, police reforms, social change, and a multidisciplinary framework for the study of racialized police violence.

In chapter 9, "Check Your Bubble! Mindful Intersections of Trauma and Community Policing," Sharlene Graham Boltz offers a narrative of how human beings interpret language and behavior through their individual and cultural perspectives, including encounters with trauma. The cultural perspective she contends is informed by life experiences, childhood instruction, and inherent values. It creates a corporate interpretive bubble through which language and behavior are judged. The individual perspective is informed by experiences with family, friends, and community. It includes the expectations, values, and beliefs forged from those experiences. Boltz concludes that interpretive bubbles collide when law enforcement officers engage traumatized individuals under the guise of maintaining command and control compliance.

In chapter 10, "Assessing Racial and Ethnic Differences in the Consequences of Police Use of Force," Ellison and Steiner argue that exposure to police use of force may have negative consequences for recipients' subsequent behavior because it is similar to other forms of violence. According to the authors, these effects may also depend on whether individuals' viewed the use of force as legitimate, and their racial and ethnic background. Using data from the most recent Survey of Inmates in Local Jails (2002), the authors examine whether jail offending (rule violations) is more common among inmates who had force used during their arrest, and in particular, those who experienced force but did not resist arrest. They compare these effects among Blacks, Hispanics, and Whites.

In chapter 11, Dillon et al. in an exploration of policing and race dynamics on college campuses, present findings from focus group assessments conducted with African American male students enrolled at two institutions of higher learning in the state of Georgia, based on personal experiences and perceptions of campus law enforcement. The chapter explores potential technologies and presents a brief synopsis of an application that could serve as a catalyst that not only enhances public trust and public confidence, but also augments the safety of citizens and officers. The authors argue that with the assistance of technology and the necessities it provides, it is possible to develop effective technological systems to improve the partnership between students and campus law enforcement through coproduction.

In chapter 12, "Community Policing as a Solution: What is the Evidence?," Lauren Hamilton Edwards and Ian Klein seek to understand whether community policing, as a strategy for improving policing relationships with racial and ethnic minority communities, is warranted to the level of which the strategy is often advised. Edwards and Klein's is a systematic review of the research that specifically examines the outcomes of community policing, and ends with a discussion of the current best practices in New York City and Oakland, California.

In chapter 13, "Developing a Comparativist Ethics for the Evaluative Study of Racialized Police Violence," Rivera and Ward explore interdisciplinary treatments of race and police violence from historical, political, social, and institutional perspectives for the purpose of framing a more holistic understanding of police interactions with communities of color. This eclectic approach asks how are we to arrive at a cogent disciplinary standpoint suited to evaluative analysis? And, building on such an epistemic platform, how does the analyst specify an analytical perspective suited to morally-fraught issues, such as police racism and violence?

In chapter 14, "Reflections on Challenges, Realities and Ramifications," we return to my original questions posed at the outset of this book. That is, to what extent do racial disparities in police-community relations result in economic, political, and social inequities? And, to what extent is it the responsibility of government to address and eliminate such inequities?

REFERENCES

Armenta, Amada and Isabela Alvarez (2017) "Policing immigrants or policing immigration? Understanding local law enforcement participation in immigration control," in *Sociology Compass*, Vol. 11, No. 2. pp. 1–10.

Berman, Mark, Sari Horwitz, and Wesley Lowery (2016) "Justice Department sues city of Ferguson to force policing reform," *The Washington Post*, February 11.

Blessett, Brandi and Richard C. Box (2016) "Sharecropper Financing: Using the Justice System as a Public Revenue Source," in *Public Integrity*, Vol. 18. pp. 113–126.

Carrier, Joseph, Lamar Valentine, Charles E. Menifield, Lacy D. Pederson, and Byron Price, "Myth or Legend:Are Black suspects more likely to be shot and killed by white law enforcement officers?" Paper presented at the American Society for Public Administration Conference, Chicago, March, 2015, pp. 6–10.

Correll, Joshua, Chalres M. Judd, and Bernd Wittenbrink (2007) "The influence of stereotypes on decisions to shoot," *European Journal of Social Psychology*, Vol. 37. pp. 1102–1117.

Delgado, Richard and Jean Stefancic (2006) *Critical Race Theory: An Introduction.* New York: New York University Press.

Davis, Angela J. (1997) "Race, Cops, and Traffic Stops," *University of Miami Law Review*, Vol. 51, U. Miami L. Rev. 425.

Davenport, Vince E. (2017) "Investigative Police Stops—Necessary or Insidious? A Practitoner's Viewpoint," in *Public Administration Review,* Vol. 77, No. 2. pp. 179–180.

Department of Justice (2015) *Investigation of the Ferguson Police Department,* United States Department of Justice. March 4, pp. 9–15.

Donohue, Brian and Kathy Barrett (2000) "State Knew about Racial Profiling."*Star Ledger*, November 26, p. 1.

Epp, Charles, Steven Maynard-Moody, and Donald Haider-Market (2017) "Beyond Profiling: The Institutional Sources of Racial Disparities in Policing," in *Public Administration Review*, Vol. 77, No. 2. pp. 168–178.

Epp, Charles, Steven Maynard-Moody, and Donald Haider-Markel (2014) *Pulled Over: How Police Stops Define Race and Citizenship.* Chicago, University of Chicago Press.

Ho, Afred Tat-Kei and Wonhyuk Cho (2017) "Government Communication Effectiveness and Satisfaction with the Police: A Large-Scale Survey Study," in *Public Administration Review*, Vol. 77, No. 2. pp. 228–239.

Jennings, Jay T. and Meghan Rubado (2017) Preventing Deadly Force: The Relationship Between Police Agency Policies and Rates of Officer-Involved Gun Deaths," in *Public Administration Review*, Vol. 77, No. 2. pp. 217–226.

Johnson, T. (2001) "Racial Disparity Initiative," Minneapolis, MN: Council on Crime and Justice.

Kahn, Kimberly B., and Karen D. Martin (2016) "Policing and Race: Disparate Treatment, Perceptions, and Policy Responses," in *Social Issues and Policy Review*, retrieved on July 31, 2017 at http://onlinelibrary.wiley.com/doi/10.1111/sipr.12019/full

Kocieniewski, David, and Robert Hanley (2000a) "Racial Profiling Routine, New Jersey Finds." *New York Times*, November 28.

Kocieniewski, David, and Robert Hanley (2000b) "An Inside Story of Racial Bias and Denial, New Jersey Files Reveal Drama Behind Profiling." *New York Times*, December 3.

Knowles, John, Nicola Persico, and Petra Todd (2001) "Racial bias in motor vehicle searches: Theory and evidence," in *Journal of Political Economy*, Vol. 109, No. 1. pp. 203–229.

Myers, Samuel L. Jr., (2002) "Analysis of Racial Profiling as Policy Analysis," in *Journal of Policy Analysis and Management*, Vol. 21, No. 2.

Nicholson-Crotty, Jill, Sean Nicholson-Crotty, and Sergio Fernandez (2017) "Will More Black Cops Matter? Officer Race and Police Involved Homicides of Black Citizens," in *Public Administration Review*, Vol. 77, No. 2. pp. 206–216.

Penderhughes, Elaine (1989) *Understanding Race, ethnicity, and power: The key to efficacy in clinical practice.* New York: Free Press.

President's Task Force on 21st Century Policing (co-chairs Charles H. Ramsey and Laurie O. Robinson), *Final Report on 21st Century Policing.* Washington, DC: Office of Community Oriented Policing, 2015.

Rattan, Aneeta and Jennifer L. Eberhardt (2010) "The role of social meaning in inattentional blindness: When the gorillas in our midst *do not go* unseen," in *Journal of Experimental Social Psychology*, Vol. 46. pp. 1085–1088.

Smith, Mark (1999) "HPD Writing Fewer Traffic Tickets under New Data-Gathering Policy." *Houston Chronicle* (Star Edition), October 17, A1–4.

Stichtenoth, Keith (2016) "Alumna Shares insights into Race, Policing, and What We Don't See," University of Cincinnati Alumni Association. Retrieved on July 8, 2016 at https://www.uc.edu/stories/alumna-shares-insights?erid=1880386&trid=74c55c49-6632-47a-a9-6ae0e8ebc33c

Ward, James D. and Mario A. Rivera (2014) *Institutional Racism, Organizations and Public Policy.* New York: Peter Lang Publishing.

Ward, James D. (2002) "Race, Ethnicity and Law Enforcement Profiling: Implications for Public Policy," in *Public Administration Review*, Vol. 62, No. 6. pp. 726–735.

Wilkins, Vicky M., and Brian N. Williams (2008) "Black or Blue: Racial Profiling and Representative Bureaucracy," in *Public Administration Review*, Vol. 68, No. 4. pp. 654–664.

Part I

POLITICAL CHALLENGES

Chapter 1

What to Do When the Yelling Stops

How Black Lives Matter Can Have Lasting Impact

Domonic A. Bearfield, Robert Maranto, and Ian Kingsbury

GOING BEYOND SYMBOLIC POLITICS TO IMPROVE POLICING

Enabled by social media, a technology shock to the political system, Black Lives Matter activists have done more than ever before to bring the problem of police violence against people of color to the national agenda. There is no doubt that this has considerable value, and has struck a chord with African Americans and progressives generally. Yet it is not clear whether Black Lives Matter will actually save Black (or other) lives. History is replete with instances of social movements which made no headway in changing public perceptions, much less public policy. We argue that given the high stakes involved, Black Lives Matter can and should be different, and suggest a fundamentally new paradigm for how to make it so.

Quite simply, the intertwined problems of police violence toward African Americans and violence generally in African American communities should be seen less as matters of changing political values and improving representation than as matters of improving *public sector performance*. In the pages following, we discuss why disproportionate numbers of African Americans distrust law enforcement authorities and how this, and new technologies led to the Black Lives Matter movement, and to its opposition. Essentially, those on all sides have embraced symbolic politics approaches apt to build their political resources, but not fundamentally improve police performance and thus save Black (and other) lives. We argue instead for a *public management* approach. Police work, essentially, is public management undertaken by street level bureaucrats (Lipsky 1980; Wilson 1978). By studying more successful organizations and copying them, we can improve policing, saving

Black lives. The example of the New York Police Department (NYPD) is instructive.

Social Movements and Political Change

Social movements are held together by diverse motivations, including active antipathy toward perceived minority or majority out-groups (Kinder and Kam 2009; Haidt 2012), ideology, social or solidary motives, the charisma of the founder, and even the material interests of members who find paid employment working in movements. Chiefly, movements need causes, resources, and political entrepreneurs to organize potential groups, that is, those likely to be motivated, into active interests (Wilson 1995; Alinsky 1971; Kingdon 1995).

In certain respects, the information technology age has moved beyond such traditional paradigms, enabling organizers with cognitively accessible labels to mobilize large numbers of supporters rapidly, in mass protests garnering attention. Occupy Wall Street, and more recently, the Women's March on Washington immediately following the Trump inauguration, offer American examples. The protest movements of the Arab Spring, whose followers and members took far greater (and often fatal) risks, offer larger and perhaps more historically notable examples. Rapid, large-scale protest is now possible, but to what effect? In Russia, Iran, and many of the nations affected by the Arab Spring, authorities violently suppressed protests, and activists paid a significant economic and physical price for their dissent. While this degree of repression has not recently occurred in the United States, protests still often fail to achieve policy objectives. If protests quickly dissipate without further programmatic development or political action, or if worse still, large segments of the public perceive disruption without purpose and hence resent and quietly resist activists, then the efforts are unlikely to change public policy.

Though intensified by the disruptive impacts of information technology, in some respects these issues are not new. Dionne (1991) described the period immediately before the information technology era, portraying public alienation from modern politics and politicians as reflecting the tendency of political activists to play to their bases, seeking emotive responses to and support for messages and resources rather than building coalitions and actually solving problems faced by citizens. In some sense such concerns about the nature of interest groups date back to the 1950s literature on goal displacement, suggesting that organizations founded to achieve particular social missions may over time become more oriented toward the employment of members, as purposive incentives shift to materialistic ones (Merton 1957; Wilson 1995). This suggests the desirability to focus movements on, to use a business term, *deliverables*. If social movements merely organize conflict, but do not actually bring about improvements in social problems, then one might question their social utility.

A History of Racism

The need for improvement in administrative outcomes is perhaps nowhere more vital than in the case of Black Lives Matter. The term itself touched a nerve among African Americans in particular, since in so many ways in most of the American past, including the recent past, Black lives did not matter, as indeed a vast literature shows. Until relatively recently, African Americans were told where to live, meaning that they had to pay high prices for substandard housing (Massey and Denton 1993). African Americans were barred from White schools, forced to attend schools allocated a small fraction of the resources sent to White schools (Buck 2010; Tillerson-Brown 2016). Certification boards backed by public authorities forbade African Americans entry into most licensed occupations. Indeed many professions, with state support, developed licensing rules to protect White professionals and skilled workers from competition with African Americans (Williams 1983). When one considers a *true* history including the likes of the Tuskegee Experiment (a secret experiment by the US Public Health Service from 1932 to 1972, using *uninformed* African American males as subjects to study the course of untreated syphilis), it is not surprising that many African Americans believe such demonstrably *false* narratives as those proposing that the government invented AIDS or disseminated crack cocaine to perpetrate genocide against African Americans (Turner 1993). It also explains high levels of African American political unity (Dawson 1994; Kinder and Kam 2009).

Perhaps nowhere was discrimination more severe, however, than in the realm of law enforcement. As Thomas Hobbes posits, the first duties of any legitimate regime are to develop and maintain a monopoly on force, and to protect the lives and property of all citizens who follow the rules of the polity. Traditionally, and to a considerable degree even now, American police failed to protect the lives and property of African Americans. This was a particularly jarring inequity since police did typically protect the lives and property of Whites, and showed particular sensitivity toward the mission of protecting Whites from any discomfort arising from contact with Blacks in nonsubmissive roles. In the precivil rights South, in particular, as Myrdal (2008) details "[t]here are practically no curbs to the policeman's aggressiveness when he is dealing with Negroes whom he conceives as dangerous or as 'getting out of their place'" (p. 540). Similarly, in her award-winning *Ghettocide*, Jill Leovy (2015) notes that for matters of racial control the "Southern legal system of the 1930s hammered Black men for such petty crimes as stealing and vagrancy, yet was often lenient toward those who murdered other Blacks" (p. 6). To some degree this legacy continues in the relatively haphazard police efforts solving what are sadly relatively common Black on Black homicides, sometimes referred to by police with the chilling term NHI, "no human involved." (Ibid). Brookings Institution researchers Reeves and Holmes (2015) point out that if young Black males were a nation, they would have the highest recorded homicide rate, a matter of indifference to most public officials. Indeed the theme of the award-winning *Boyz in the Hood* pronounced that tragically, since police did not offer justice in cases of homicide in their neighborhoods, members of the community had to act on their own.[1] Even where police attempt to do their often difficult work, protecting all citizens including African Americans from crime while also eschewing police brutality, racial profiling can delegitimize policing. In their rigorous empirical examination of discretionary police traffic stops, Epp, Maynard-Moody, and Haider-Markel document how the disproportionate stopping of African Americans undermines law enforcement legitimacy in Black communities, ultimately reducing civilian cooperation in fighting crime (Epp, Maynard-Moody, and Haider-Markel 2014).

Not only did, and to a considerable degree does, the legal system look the other way at African Americans victimized by crime, law enforcement authorities may take part in that victimization. In cities like Baltimore (Baum 2010) and New York (Timoney 2010), it was until recently the norm for individual police officers to shoot African Americans in multiple incidents without suffering investigation, much less discipline or prosecution. While police did not record the numbers of their shootings until quite recently, we do know from a memoir of policing in New York City (Ibid) that in the 1960s and early 1970s, 90–100 (disproportionately Black) deaths at the hands of police annually were not unusual, typically with no officers disciplined. Naturally, this pervasive, institutional oppression affected how African Americans viewed police, despite calls by some African Americans and Whites to increase support for law enforcement in the wake of large increases in homicide and other crimes in majority African American areas in the 1960s and 1970s (Wilson 1975).

Like public service generally, policing is fundamentally political, with bureaucrats requiring regime support and in democracies, reasonably broad (if not necessarily majority) backing (Bayley and Stenning 2016). This suggests an important question: Did most White Americans support police oppression of African Americans? More positively, one might describe these interactions as public bureaucracies with challenging missions policing high crime areas, over time, developing heuristics which amounted to institutional racism. Notably, by the 1970s most police departments were integrated, often at highest levels. Analysts find limited evidence that this more than marginally changed either police behavior or community-police relations (Moskos 2008; Wilson 1975; Hong 2016; Carter 2014). More ominously, the profession may attract individuals with psychological tendencies to embrace authoritarianism, as indeed some police professionals suggest (Bratton and Knobler 1998). Clearly, through most of American history police oppression of African Americans had broad White support. In many and perhaps most places, the very missions of police departments failed to protect and even endangered African Americans (Myrdal 2008). Yet there is strong empirical evidence (Sniderman and Piazza 1993) that by the 1980s the vast majority of Whites found such police behavior unacceptable. Accordingly, the mission of Black Lives Matter should be less about changing White values as Martin Luther King sought to and did, or changing laws, as Thurgood Marshall sought to and did (Rosenberg 1991; Branch 1988), and more about making transparent the practices of nontransparent police bureaucracies, and changing those practices which need changing.

The Travails of Bureaucratic Reform of Policing

In short, we argue that to actually save Black lives, Black Lives Matter must tackle the difficult processes of facilitating change within public bureaucracies, and fostering greater levels of professionalism within those bureaucracies.[2] Of course, public bureaucracies are by their nature complex, nontransparent, and resistant to change. Organization insiders have the most knowledge of operations, and typically eschew change, as a long line of research indicates. Those working inside organizations feel emotionally invested in existing practices, and find change difficult (Kelman 2005). For street level bureaucrats like police (and teachers), who have strong cultures, autonomy, loyalty to fellow practitioners, and considerable social distance from clients, change is more difficult still, particularly should it require members to break ranks with their colleagues (Lipsky 1980; Wilson 1978). In short, in some sense the appellation Black Lives Matter is both strong and weak, strong because the privileged by and large agree that police should protect rather than target African Americans; weak because real change requires reform within strong, nontransparent policing bureaucracies apt and able to resist such reform. Political systems have considerable difficulty sustaining this kind of detailed, multilayered structural administrative reform. It is, as President Obama's statement opening the start of this essay implies, far easier to bring attention to a problem than to fix it. Our hope is that Black Lives Matter actually goes beyond bringing attention.

Black Lives Matter, and its Opponents, as Political Movements

In prior work, one of us demonstrated that policing, like education, is fundamentally *political*. We find considerable empirical evidence that police commissioners are terminated or retained based not on crime rates, nor police treatment of civilians, but rather due to scandals, and more importantly collegiality, that is, whether mayors and city council members *like* top cops (Maranto and Wolf 2013).[3] Indeed a researcher with the Police Executive Research Forum states that there is no larger research on why police commissioners are fired (phone interview, July 22, 2010), though those in the field assume that crime rates have no impact on job security. Smaller studies suggest that collegiality in fact trumps performance (Ranguet and Dodge 2001). Notably, reforming police in departments in ways leading to substantial improvements might tend to alienate police officers and their unions, leading to leaking and other actions undermining police commissioners (Maranto and Wolf 2013; Timoney 2010). Accordingly, police commissioners have little incentive to improve police performance regarding either crime fighting or police brutality toward civilians.

At the same time, Black Lives Matter is itself fundamentally a political movement, although one that is increasingly interested in administrative reform. Campaign Zero, an organization with close ties to the Black Lives Matter movement has started to track, research, and push for police reform. Reforms include ending the use of "broken windows" policing, encouraging police departments to examine their use of force policies, demilitarizing policing, increasing community oversight, promoting independent investigation and prosecution of police shootings, increased training, the end of for profit policing, examining police contracts to remove unfair protections of police officers, and adopting the use of body cameras.[4] Still, we believe that there is more to be done. In prior work (Bearfield, Maranto, and Wolf, 2016) we rank cities (and thus their police departments) based on composite measures of police professionalism, that is, levels of police shootings of civilians and homicide rates, since we argue that more professional police bureaucracies can minimize each. This is an argument which should appeal to activists, arguing that improving policing can save Black (and other) lives.

As Figure 1.1 reports, we find strong correlations between the numbers of reported Black Lives Matter protests (per 100,000 residents) and metropolitan area political ideology (.66) and Obama vote share (.62). More protests occur in more liberal metropolitan areas, and similarly, in those with larger Obama presidential victory margins. Yet we find no correlations (-.05) between the extent of Black Lives Matter protests and police professionalism, nor with the individual components of police professionalism, homicide rates, and per capita police killings of civilians. Black Lives Matter protests are no more likely to occur in cities in which police fail to protect and to serve. Indeed, Black Lives Matter activists called for the ouster of then NYPD Police Commissioner William Bratton (Jamieson 2016), whose city had unusually low

	metropop	demons~s	Obamam~n	profsc~e	ideology	dem~100k	povert~e	hom~100k	pol~100k
metropop	1.0000								
demonstrat~s	0.6900	1.0000							
Obamamargin	0.3988	0.6876	1.0000						
profscore	0.2028	0.0178	-0.1596	1.0000					
ideology	0.0462	-0.3710	-0.4721	0.2257	1.0000				
demosper100k	0.0802	0.7236	0.6246	-0.0461	-0.6591	1.0000			
povertyrate	0.1322	-0.1624	-0.1523	-0.4542	0.0133	-0.4270	1.0000		
homicid-100k	-0.0215	0.0018	0.1506	-0.7045	-0.2508	-0.0731	0.8368	1.0000	
polices~100k	-0.2255	-0.1522	0.0418	-0.8678	-0.1090	-0.1047	0.3954	0.4707	1.0000

Metropop = population of metro area, taken from Annual Estimates of the Resident Population: April 1,2010 to July 1,2014- United States-- Metropolitan and Micropolitan Statistical Area; and for Puerto Rico. *US Census Bureau*. Retrieved February 1, 2017 from https://factfinder.census.gov/faces/tableservices/jsf/pages/productview.xhtml?src=bkmk

Demonstrations = estimated number of demonstrations in that city based on number of unique events reported in the media, as reported by https://elephrame.com/textbook/. Elephrame is an archive of data and ideas taken from media reports of protests and relying on the help of community members to report such protests. It offers the best data source available given the decentralized nature of Black Lives Matter.

Obamamargin = Obama margin of victory in 2012. For example, if he won by 8 points it was recorded as +8. If he lost by 4 then it was recorded as -4; taken from Presidential Election Results. *NBC News*. Retrieved February 1, 2017 from http://elections.nbcnews.com/ns/politics/2012/all/president/#.WKDz6PkrLIU.

Profscore = Police Professionalism Score calculated from Bearfield et al. In Press.

Ideology= the policy preferences of the city. Data from page 38 of this document: http://www.ctausanovitch.com/Municipal_Representation_140502.pdf

Demosper100k = number of demonstrations per 100k residents, demonstrations/metropop.

Poverty rate = Metropolitan area poverty rate calculated from Poverty USA. *Poverty Map*. Retrieved from http://www.povertyusa.org/the-state-of-poverty/poverty-map-state/#

homicid~100k = homicides per 100k residents, from Bearfield et al. (In press).

polices~100k = policeshootings per 100k residents, from Bearfield et al. (In press).

Figure 1.1   Sources of Variables.

levels of homicide, and whose police killed 76% *fewer* civilians per capita than American police departments as a whole (Bearfield et al.).

If, perhaps, Black Lives Matter has not focused as much on solutions as a public management approach would dictate, the same can be said of police unions and police chiefs associations, their think tank based backers (Mac-Donald 2016), and the current occupant of the White House. To its credit, the Police Executive Research Forum (PERF), an organization representing police commissioners, issued a sensible report (2016) detailing ways to drastically reduce police shootings of civilians. Among other things, PERF proposed additional training to identify mental illness, to evaluate potentially violent situations more accurately, to deescalate confrontations when possible, to respond to nongun threats with nonlethal means, to discourage officers from using force simply because aggressive suspects were within twenty-one feet, and generally to embrace responses proportionate to the dangers presented. PERF also advocated policies prohibiting or strongly discouraging shooting at or from moving vehicles, as well as use of force against individuals who pose dangers only to themselves. Better and more consistent training of police dispatchers could also reduce police violence. Finally, PERF proposed documenting use of force incidents, making those reports transparent, and holding officers accountable for the inappropriate use of force. Unfortunately, in a rare display of solidarity both the Fraternal Order of Police (labor) and the International Association of Chiefs of Police (management) issued a joint statement denouncing the proposals (Jackman 2016). In short, policing organizations seemingly put police solidarity ahead of improving public service, and saving Black (and other) lives.

We need to make a final point. Due in part to the opposition of police departments, and the relative inattention of those outside the activist community, we still do not know the extent of police violence against civilians. As then-FBI Director James Comey (2015) lamented in the wake of the Ferguson unrest, his Bureau "didn't know whether the Ferguson police shot one person a week, one a year, or one a century." If Black lives actually mattered, this situation would be intolerable. Clearly, finding out how many Black (and other) lives are taken by police, and how this carnage varies by department, should be a key priority for Black Lives Matter and related groups. We find little evidence that it is. To some degree the knowledge void is being filled by journalists (Kindy, Kimberly, and Kelly 2015; Kimberly et al. 2015).

A Way Forward: Making Black Lives Matter

We argue that the incentives of the political system, for Black Lives Matter and for its conservative opponents, tend to devalue Black (and other) lives, mobilizing constituencies rather than solving problems. Accordingly, rather than invoking the activist literature, we propose that to make Black lives matter, reformers should make use of the administrative *reinvention* literature. This literature proposes that by improving public organizations we can improve public service, in part by recruiting and retaining better public servants and providing support for them to succeed. In the long run, such administrative success could restore public trust in government (Barzelay and Armajani 1992; Kelman 2005; Hatry 2006). For law enforcement, the actual proves the possible. Real world experience shows that police reform to save Black (and other) lives is in fact possible.[5]

As Bearfield et al. document, police departments in New York, El Paso, San Diego, Austin, and San Jose have exemplary records in keeping both homicides and police killings of civilians low. While Austin and San Jose have low poverty rates, the other three cities have both high poverty and high levels of police success, suggesting that they offer lessons for those wishing to make Black (and other) lives matter. Further, while El Paso makes considerable use of community policing and is reputed to have good community relations (Huff 2005), Austin reportedly does not (Jankowski 2016). Notably, scholars have not to our knowledge addressed police success in any of these cities, with the partial exception of New York. (This alone suggests that scholars give insufficient attention to public administration successes.) Accordingly, here we will treat NYPD. In the late 1960s and 1970s, NYPD presided over rapidly rising homicide rates, accompanied by large numbers of police shootings of civilians. (Regarding the latter, we have no idea if police killings of civilians increased or decreased in the 1960s and early 1970s— merely that rates were far higher than today.) Pressured by the American Civil Liberties Union and other outside organizations, NYPD gradually improved protocols for police use of force, trained officers in said protocols, and also began to improve recruitment of officers, recruiting nationally rather than merely locally to increase personnel quality. Over the long-term, police shootings of civilians declined, likely as a result of these reforms (Timoney 2010). Additional reforms pioneered by the first African American NYPD commissioner, Benjamin Ward, placed greater control of NYPD in the hands of the commissioner, enabling the top cop to replace precinct commanders, the key leaders in the system with those supportive of the commissioner's agenda. Notably, police, like other street level bureaucrats, traditionally had considerable autonomy owing to the nontransparency of their work (Lipsky 1980). Better reporting systems began to change this in the 1980s and 1990s. When William Bratton first took charge of NYPD in 1994 (he returned in 2014–2016), he made full use of these changes to professionalize NYPD, promoting leaders effective at reducing crime and not harming civilians, while retiring less professional leaders. Over time, these organizational changes seemingly led to a greater than 80% reduction in homicides[6] and near 90% reduction of police shootings of civilians (though the latter occurred over a longer time period). We estimate that reforming NYPD over the course of two decades saved 25,000 lives, disproportionately *Black* lives (Maranto and Wolf 2013). Strong empirical evidence shows that these declines in crime (and in police shootings of civilians) are unprecedented in scope, did not reflect demographic or economic changes in New York, and resulted from changed *behavior* on the part of police and possible offenders rather than increased incarceration. Incarceration actually declined during much of the period, and some evidence suggests that fewer crimes occurred since the probability of apprehension rose, leading would-be criminals to change behavior. The New York record in this regard is unique, and a very strong indication that policing matters (Zimring 2011; Kelling and Sousa 2001). In fact, our findings are in line with a 2016 report from Campaign Zero showing that New York City has fewer police related deaths than most major metropolitan police departments (McKesson, Sinyangwe, Elzie, and Packnett 2016).

Further, evidence suggests that NYPD did not become abusive to become effective. Former NYPD Commissioner Kelly (2015) argued that controversial and racially suspect "stop and frisk" tactics were key to the crime declines. Evidence calls this into question. In response to a court order, Mayor De Blasio and Police Commissioner Bratton substantially curtailed such stops in 2014. As even Heather Mac Donald (2016), a critic of both De Blasio and Black Lives Matter admits, after an initial spike in crime police changed tactics and kept crime low even after more than 80% declines in stop and frisk (Pearson and Balsamo 2016). Seemingly, effective professional policing is possible without racially suspect and often humiliating tactics.

Given these facts on the ground, why don't other police departments adopt similar personnel reforms to professionalize personnel? Why don't mayors and other political leaders push them to? Why aren't Black Lives Matter activists doing more to pressure police to reform along the lines successful in saving Black lives in New York? The steps to do so would seem apparent. Activists should pressure the FBI to rank cities based on their policing effectiveness, and the US House and Senate should hold hearings highlighting effective practices. The US Department of Justice should develop a watch list of ineffective police departments. Such moral sanctions would affect business investment decisions. Over the long-term they may impact city elections and thus drive police departments to improve practices in ways assuring that Black lives, and indeed all lives matter.

So why is no one interested in taking such steps? The answers lie within broader critiques of modern American political conflict, which focus more on mobilizing constituencies than addressing public problems. Also, even when parties are interested in engagement, gaining access to the proper decision makers can be challenging. And finally, one depressing conclusion may be that for politicians, police departments, and activists, scoring political points matter—Black lives don't.

NOTES

1. Interestingly, this is also one of the themes of a memoir from another marginalized subculture, *Hillbilly Elegy*.

2. As Mehta and Teles (2014) point out, professions are delineated by a well-developed knowledge base, serious quality control regarding the knowledge, skills and abilities of those entering the profession (not everyone can be a police officer), common standards of practice, and a moral code expressing the profession's commitment to social good.

3. In this and additional work we find evidence that regarding school superintendents, student learning has little or nothing to do with one's job security. See: Maranto, Robert, Julie Trivitt, Malachi Nichols and Angela Watson. "School superintendents have no contractual obligation to improve learning." Washington: Brookings Institution, 2016.

4. Additional information can be found on the Campaign Zero website. https://www.joincampaignzero.org/solutions/

5. Arguably, an early example of the professionalism literature is offered by Kaufman (1960). Among the lessons applicable to police regard the importance of careful selection, recruitment, indoctrination, and promotion to keep an organization strong. See also George Kelling and William Sousa, *"Do Police Matter?"* Manhattan Institute Civic Report 22 at http://www.manhattan-institute.org/pdf/cr_22.pdf

6. We largely ignore other crime statistics since they are subject to considerable manipulation on the part of police (Bratton, 2010).

REFERENCES

Alinsky, Saul. 1971. *Rules for Radicals.* New York: Vintage Books.

Barzelay, Michael and Babak J. Armajani. 1992. *Breaking through Bureaucracy.* Berkeley: University of California.

Baum, Howell. 2010. *Brown in Baltimore.* Ithaca: Cornell University Press.

Bayley, David and Phillip Stemming. 2016. *Governing the Police.* New Brunswick: Transaction Publishers.

Bearfield, Domonic, Robert Maranto and Patrick Wolf. *Can Police Professionalism reduce crime and police brutality?" Paper presented at the Mini-Conference on Policing and Race, January 29-February 30, 2016.* Cincinnati, Ohio.

Branch, Taylor. 1988. *Parting the Waters.* New York: Simon and Schuster.

Brandl, John. 1998. *Money and Good Intentions are not Enough.* Washington: Brookings Institution.

Bratton, William and Peter Knobler. 1998. *The Turnaround.* New York: Random House.

Bratton, William. "Crime by the Numbers," *New York Times,* February 17, 2010.

Buck, Stuart. 2010. *Acting White.* New Haven: Yale University Press.

Carter, Stephen. "Laws Puts Us All in Same Danger as Eric Garner," *Bloomberg LP.* December 4, 2014.

Comey, James. "Hard Truths: Law Enforcement and Race" (speech, Washington, February 12, 2015, FBI, at https://www.fbi.gov/news/speeches/hard-truths-law-enforcement-and-race

Dawson, Michael. 1994. *Behind the Mule.* Princeton: Princeton University Press.

Dionne Jr, E.J. 1991. *Why Americans Hate Politics*. New York: Simon and Schuster.

Epp, Charles, Seven Maynard-Moody and Donald Haider-Markel. 2014. *Pulled Over: How Police Stops Define Race and Citizenship*. Chicago: University of Chicago Press.

Haidt, Jonathan. 2012. *The Righteous Mind*. New York: Pantheon.

Hatry, Harry. 2006. *Performance Measurement: Getting Results*. Washington: The Urban Institute Press.

Hobbes, Thomas. 2010. *Leviathan-* Revised edition edited by Ian Shapiro. New Haven: Yale University Press.

Hong, Sounman. 2016. "Representative Bureaucracy, Organizational Integrity, and Citizen Coproduction: Does an Increase in Police Ethnic Representativeness Reduce Crime?"*Journal of Policy Analysis and Management* 35(1): 11–33.

Huff, Dan. "A Q&A with Richard Wiles, El Paso chief of police," *El Paso Inc.*, April 9, 2005.

Jackman, Tom. "Protocol for reducing police shootings draws backlash from unions, chiefs group," *Washington Post,* March 31, 2016.

Jamieson, Amber. "New York City protesters demand police commissioner Bratton be fired," *The Guardian*, August 1, 2016.

Jankowski, Phillip. "Study: Austin police don't dedicate enough time to community policing," *My Statesman,* August 17, 2016.

Kaufman, Herbert. 1960. *The Forest Ranger*. Baltimore: John Hopkins University Press.

Kelling, George and William Sousa. *"Do Police Matter?"* Manhattan Institute Civic Report 22 at http://www.manhattan-institute.org/pdf/cr_22.pdf. 2001, No. 22.

Kelly, Ray. 2015. *Vigilance*. New York: Hatchette Books.

Kelman, Steven. 2005. *Unleashing Change*. Washington: Brookings Institution.

Kinder, Donald and Cindy Kam. 2009. *Us Against Them*. Chicago: University of Chicago Press.

Kindy, Kimberly, Marc Fisher, Julie Tate, and Jennifer Jenkins, "A Year of Reckoning: Police Fatally Shoot Nearly 1,000,"*Washington Post*, December 24, 2015.

Kindy, Kimberly and Kimbrielle Kelly, "Thousands Dead, Few Prosecuted," *Washington Post*, April 11, 2015.

Kingdon, John. 1995. *Agendas, Alternatives, and Public Politics*. New York: Harper Collins.

Leovy, Jill. 2015. *A True Story of Murder in America*. New York: Penguin Random House.

Lipsky, Michael. 1980. *Street Level Bureaucracy*. New York: Russell Sage Foundation.

MacDonald, Heather. 2016. *The War on Cops*. New York: Encounter Books.

Madhani, Aamer. "Cities find police staffing is no easy proposition," *USA Today*, September 22, 2016.

Maranto, Robert and Patrick Wolf. 2013. "Cops, Teachers, and the Art of the Impossible: Explaining the Lack of Diffusion of Innovations That Make Impossible Jobs Possible." *Public Administration Review* 73(2): 230–240.

Maranto, Robert, Julie Trivitt, Malachi Nichols and Angela Watson. 2016 "School superintendents have no contractual obligation to improve learning," Washington: Brookings Institution.

Massey, Douglas and Nancy Denton. 1993. *American Apartheid*. Cambridge: Harvard University Press.

McClain, Dani. "What does Black Lives Matter Want? Its Demands Are Clearer than Ever," *The Nation*, August 1, 2016.

McKesson, DeRay, Samuel Sinyangwe, Johnetta Elzie and Brittany Packnett, "Police Use of Force Policy Analysis," *Campaign Zero* (2016)

Mehta, Jal and Steven Teles. "Professionalism 2.0: The Case for Plural Professionalism," pp. 109–34 in Frederick M. Hess and Michael Q. McShane edited *Teacher Quality 2.0: Toward a New Era in Education Reform* (Cambridge: Harvard Education Press, 2014).

Merton, Robert. 1957. *Social Theory and Social Structure*. Glencoe, IL: Free Press.

Moskos, Peter. 2008. *Cop in the Hood*. Princeton: Princeton University Press.

Myrdal, Gunner. 2008. *An American Dilemma*. New Brunswick: Transaction Publishers.

Pearson, Jake and Michael Balsamo. "NYC officials aim to loosen arrest policy," *Arkansas Democrat Gazette*, March 7, 2016.

Police Executive Research Forum, *Guiding Principles on Use of Force*. Washington: Police Executives Research Forum, March 2016, at http://www.policeforum.org/assets/30%20guiding%20principles.pdf

Ranguet, Fred and Mary C. Dodge. 2001. "The Problems of Police Chiefs: An Examination of the Issues in Tenure and Turnover." *Police Quarterly* 4: 268–288.

Reeves, Richard and Sarah Holmes. 2015. *Guns and Race: The Different Worlds of Black and White Americans*. Brookings Institution Social Mobility Memos, December 15, at http://www.brookings.edu/blogs/social-mobility-memos/posts/2015/12/15-guns-race-different-worlds-reeves

Rosenberg, Gerald. 1991. *The Hollow Hope*. Chicago: University of Chicago Press, 1991.

Sniderman, Paul and Thomas Piazza. 1993. *The Scar of Race*. Cambridge, MA: Harvard University Press.

Tillerson-Brown, Amy. "Struggles for Educational Equity in Prince Edward County, VA: Resistance, Southern Manifesto Ideologies, and School Choice." *Journal of School Choice* 10(4): 446–461.

Timoney, John. 2010. *Beat Cop to Top Cop: A Tale of Three Cities*. Philadelphia: University of Pennsylvania Press.

Turner, Patricia. 1993. *I Heard It Through the Grapevine: Rumor in African-American Culture*. pp. 446–461. Berkeley: University of California Press.

Vance, J.D. 2016. *Hillbilly Elegy*. New York: Harper Press.

Vogel, Kenneth and Sarah Wheaton, "Major donors consider funding Black Lives Matter," *Politico*, November 13, 2015.

Warwick, Donald. 1975. *A Theory of Public Bureaucracy*. Cambridge: Harvard University Press.

Williams, Walter. 1983. *The State Against Blacks*. New York: McGraw-Hill.

Wilson, James. 1995. *Political Organizations*. Princeton: Princeton University Press.

Wilson, James. 1975. *Thinking About Crime*. New York: Basic Books.

Wilson, James. 1978. *Varieties of Police Behavior*. Cambridge: Harvard University Press.

Wilson, James. 1989. *Bureaucracy*. New York: Basic Books.

Wilson, William. "The other side of Black Lives Matter," *Brookings Institution Social Mobility Memos*, December 14, 2015.

Zimring, Frederick. 2011. *The City that Became Safe*. New York: Oxford University Press.

Chapter 2

Contemporary Police and Minorities in the United States

Causes, Theories, and Solutions

John A. Eterno and Christine S. Barrow

Race relations between police and minorities in the United States are generally lukewarm and, at times, volatile. Police leadership, directly or indirectly, with intent or without, may be at least partially responsible for the racist behaviors observed in lower ranking officers. Aggressive stop and frisk, driving while Black, and racial profiling are examples of common euphemisms for racist policing. Racist policing means actions whereby police abuse their authority or conduct illegal activity based primarily on race. When such activities are regularly practiced by entire departments our research suggests that it is often due to a management strategy focused almost exclusively on crime control. Police performance management, sometimes called Compstat, zero tolerance, or broken windows, has changed the mindset of policing from working with communities to a war on crime. Using specific data collected by the authors combined with social science theory, this chapter will show evidence indicating that modern policing policy leads to harmful and sometimes racist policing. Our data substantiates that in the current performance management era, the rank and file and some managers are reduced to numbers crunching automatons. This is in stark contrast to the ideal of the community policing era where officers are supposed to be proactive, problem solvers who work closely with the neighborhoods they are supposed to serve. Contrary to the in vogue overly aggressive policing doctrine, we suggest police work with communities. Indeed, our suggested strategy will have the twofold effect of helping protect due process rights and concurrently enhancing crime fighting efforts. Reducing crime occurs by: allowing intelligence to be transferred to police from currently disenfranchised communities; adding support for police on the front lines from communities; police collecting, recording, and acting on more accurate information (rather than hiding information from superiors); and officers becoming proactive, problem solvers rather than bean counting bureaucrats.

Current events demonstrate the importance of these insights into concerns with modern policing. The election of Donald Trump as president with campaign promises to build a wall along the Mexican border, deport immigrants, ban Muslims from traveling to the United States, and expand stop and frisk nationwide, could seriously damage relations among police and minorities. One example of this can be seen in New York City. Police leaders developed a policy of spying on Muslim communities without objective cause other than "to stop terrorism." These actions were taken by officers in New York City's Demographics' Unit. Spying on Muslims without any suspicion was certainly questionable if not illegal. The department has admitted to these surreptitious behaviors (even doing these activities in other states without notifying proper authority such as the Federal Bureau of Investigation or the governor) and stated publicly that no terrorists were caught even after many years of spying and surveillance (Levitt, 2017). Other events show that these are not localized policies but have emerged nationwide. There are a substantial number of American police departments who are or have been involved in civil suits or investigated for racist practices. Many of these are under court monitoring and/or consent decrees to ameliorate racist practices. Some of these departments are large agencies: New Jersey State Troopers, New York City Police Department, Los Angeles Police Department, Baltimore City Police, Pittsburgh Police, Maryland State Police, New Orleans Police to name a few. These are not departments who are practicing under the former Jim Crow laws of the Deep South but modern and often well-respected police agencies. In fact, the New York City Police Department (NYPD) has a federal monitor due to a civil suit in the court case *Floyd v. City of New York* (2013). Importantly, the NYPD is considered a role model for other agencies (Bayley, 1994). Thus, even this leading agency has significant and troublesome issues with minority communities. This chapter reviews some of the key reasons why racist policing exists in modern police agencies. We will review some key issues such as the police culture, the common police performance management system, and various fallacies related to policies such as "stop and frisk."

Stop and frisk is an important tactic used by many police agencies. It is based on the United States Supreme Court case *Terry v. Ohio* (1969). This case gives police officers the power to forcibly stop, question and sometimes frisk and search suspects. Officers must have, however, a level of proof known as reasonable suspicion. This is a level below probable cause, needed to legally arrest someone (being about 50 percent sure someone violated the law), but above mere suspicion (a hunch). Forcibly stopping a suspect can be an excellent tool for officers if used properly. Ill-advisedly, NYPD, as we will see, abused this power and is now under a consent decree ordered by the federal courts for unconstitutional and racist policing.

RACISM IN THE UNITED STATES

Understanding racial/ethnic tensions is especially important in a heterogeneous country such as the United States. Recent statistics from the United States Census Bureau indicate that as of July 2016, Whites who are not Hispanic make up 61.6 percent of the United States. Hispanics make up 17.6 percent; Blacks 12.2 percent, Asian 5.6 percent, American Indian/Alaskan Native 9 percent and two or more races 2.6 percent (US Census Bureau, 2016) (numbers may not add to 100 due to rounding). Thus, the United States is a diverse nation whose population constantly changes over time due to immigration, birth and death rates, and other factors.

Throughout the history of the United States there have been various painful episodes with respect to race relations. From the founding of the country, slavery was an issue. Eventually, a Civil War had to be fought to end that horrid practice. Even that was not enough to stop racist behaviors, however, as Jim Crow laws spread throughout the South and discrimination against Blacks and other minorities was rampant. The handling of Native Americans is also a stain on the American soul. Further, one of the most egregious handling of minorities was Executive Order 9066. President Franklin Delano Roosevelt, shortly after the bombing of Pearl Harbor during a period of wartime hysteria, ordered the internment of Japanese Americans mostly on the West Coast. It was not until 1998 that President Ronald Reagan apologized for the country and ordered some reparations (Cho, 2005; History Channel, n.d.). Fear, not reason, clearly drove this misguided policy similar to spying of Muslims in New York.

The due process revolution of the 1950s and 1960s led to some semblance of racial equality (and other equalities especially related to the 14th Amendment and the Bill of Rights). During this period the United States Supreme Court began to chip away at various practices by police and other institutions that clearly violated basic rights. For example, *Brown v. Board of Education, Miranda v. Arizona* and *Mapp v. Ohio* were key United States Supreme Court cases providing and protecting basic rights. Additionally, the Civil Rights Act of 1964, outlawing discrimination based on race, color, religion, sex, or national origin helped usher in a new era of efforts by the federal government to stem discrimination. Indeed, the Equal Employment Opportunity Commission was formed and enforces these and other laws, acts, and orders. Unfortunately, despite all this, discrimination still exists—although usually not as overtly. Evidence for this is extensive. An example of this is the fairly extensive list of police agencies formerly or currently under some type of scrutiny from the courts or other federal agencies for fostering racist policies and/or practices.

Democracy, Policing, and Racism

In a democracy, police must follow the law while they enforce the law. If there are no boundaries on police power, the work of searching, stopping, arresting, and so forth becomes a simplistic exercise in abuse of power. Placing limitations on police power is the hallmark of a healthy free society. However, this makes law enforcement challenging at best. This is the ultimate conundrum for police in democratic societies; it is essentially left to them to properly balance crime fighting with due process rights of citizens.

The contemporary police agency in the United States generally has fairly strict entry requirements including a character background check, a medical, a psychological, a physical, and a written examination. On average, law enforcement training academies (excluding field training) are about 840 hours or 21 weeks long but vary across the nation (Reaves, 2016). Many agencies now have civilian complaint review, strong internal affairs units, and some level of street supervision. Some agencies are now adding educational and/or military experience requirements to become an officer. Professional organizations such as the International Association of Chiefs of Police now offer model policies and best practices. There is also an accreditation movement which seeks to standardize and professionalize agencies as well as improve law enforcement practices (Committee on Accreditation of Law Enforcement Agencies (CALEA)). Most states (all except five) have decertification (Goldman & Puro, 2001) so that officers who engage in illegal or grossly unethical acts cannot get employment in another agency in that state. Even with these and other checks on police behavior, evidence of racism among police is still observed. Given the prevalence of consent decrees and the like, we cannot say racist policing is rare.

Policing in the United States is fundamentally a local matter. That is, states (or local subdivisions) decide minimum selection, performance, and conduct standards for police. Police management also develops and implements policy and as indicated above essentially polices itself in this regard. Law enforcement officers enforce law, at least theoretically, under the guide of the social contract. This means that local community standards and culture should influence officers. Officers work with a mandate that is ultimately from the people who are being policed. While the law gives the police the formal power to enforce the rules of society, it is the people who allow this. The people willingly, for the most part, follow the guidelines set under the rule of law. Police then enforce those laws with the consent of the governed. This is how democratic policing should work. The police should not be an army of occupation. There usually is no need to browbeat a willing public; rather, the police work with the majority of the public to fight crime and terrorism. At times, however, this can go astray such as in the Deep South under Jim Crow. Under Jim Crow laws, the police enforced a code of conduct established by the White majority. This was a clear abuse of power and a violation of even the loosest reading of the Constitution of the United States—especially, but not exclusively, the 14th amendment's equal protection and due process clauses (passed after the Civil War specifically to prevent discrimination). Thus, police in democratic society should generally work with the consent of the governed under what is known as the social contract (Eterno, 2003; Eterno & Silverman, 2012).

The concept that the police and the public agree and that the laws are essentially a reflection of a common accepted set of values is referred to as the consensus view of law and government. Other social scientists argue that the government tries to control people through the police. The police, rather than working under the social contract, are part of the elite trying to keep those not part of the elite in their "place." This is called the conflict viewpoint. In essence, conflict theorists suggest that the police are a tool of the ruling class usually described as Whites, wealthy and/or male. Certainly the South under Jim Crow was an example of this. Consensus theorists argue, however, that Jim Crow laws were dysfunctional and will ultimately die out since they are not allowing society to function properly. While there is no clear answer to the consensus versus conflict theory debate, we make the assumption that we live in a democracy and that constitutional law and the principles of the social contract are critically important to policing a free society. Conflict theorists often argue for a radical solution to inequality. However, we point out that one of the characteristics of Dr. Martin Luther King Jr. that makes him stand out is his call for nonviolent change of racist laws. Democracy is supposed to protect all people's rights and he understood this. Change can be made through the democratic process including voting and the courts. As Winston Churchill stated in a speech to the House of Commons, "No one pretends that democracy is perfect or all-wise. Indeed it has been said that democracy is the worst form of Government except for all those other forms that have been tried from time to time." So while there are serious issues in our society, it is the democratic process that best deals with those problems. This, we think, agrees with the spirit of Dr. Martin Luther King, Jr. and is the best approach to act on issues of policing and racism in the United States.

Another way to understand policing and racism in democratic society is through the work of Herbert Packer. Packer (1966) talks of two models of the criminal justice process. He calls one the crime control model which he likens to an assembly line. Officers make arrests and suspects are processed quickly through the criminal justice system. In this way crime is minimized as suspects are "rounded up," convicted, and jailed in a rapid and efficient process. In such a model suspects are generally assumed to be guilty as they pass quickly through the system. Packer (1966) terms a second model, and nearly opposite, due process. He likens this to an obstacle course. In this model obstacles such as *Miranda warnings*, or probable cause for searches or reasonable suspicion for stops restrict officers from simply interrogating suspects, making arrests, or forcible stops at will. In this model the main concern is for citizen's rights and the assumption is that individuals need to be protected from the abuse of government power. Crime control and due process represent opposing viewpoints. It is finding the proper balance that represents a great challenge to our police and our society. Because there is a trade-off between the crime control and due process, the fundamental difficulty in democratic society is where to draw the line.

Generally, as threats become greater more power is given to police. For example, in the United States the writ of habeas corpus has only been suspended three times in its history: the Civil War, the Japanese attack on Pearl Harbor, and the terrorist attack on 9/11. The executive branch (i.e., law enforcement) is given tremendous powers during these turbulent times. However, as threats subside, police power recedes. Thus, the greater the threat, the more power we grant to police. We assume, for the purposes of this chapter, that the war on terror has few boundaries and is not likely to totally subside; therefore, police will have expanded powers for the foreseeable future.

The Police Culture and Other Influences on Police Behavior

Social scientists have also identified four well-known influences on police behavior: the law, the police culture, the community, and the police bureaucracy (or agency policies) (Eterno, 2003). The police culture emphasizes the importance of the group, the influence of peers—other officers (Crank, 1995; Drummond, 1976; Fielding, 1989; Manning, 1987; Reiss, 1971; Stoddard, 1968; Westley, 1970). It is sometimes called the informal code to distinguish it from formal rules. In general, this informal code stresses the need for officers to maintain respect, to band together, and to not trust the legal system.

Police also, unlike many occupations, have great discretion. They do not enforce every single law with equal vigor but use their discretion to determine those laws and people who will receive the greatest sanctions—summons and/or arrest. There are many reasons for this discretion such as the legislature may not want every law enforced vigorously, other duties may be more important, sympathy with a violator, trading no enforcement for information, the arrest may harm the status of the person, and much more. Also, unlike most other jobs, police do not have supervisors standing over them while they are patrolling the streets. They are generally left on their own. Of course, this gets complicated as there are many pressures on officers from management, community members, politicians, the media, other officers, and more. Officers must sort through this mix of pressures and decide the best course of action—sometimes at odds with various persons in power.

Many citizens see officers as very powerful figures but the truth is not so clear-cut. Officers are at the bottom of the government hierarchy and are the most visible part of government. Incorrect decisions can lead to severe consequences (sometimes justifiable, sometimes not). Officers can be arrested and convicted for actions they thought were correct. The government they work for may not indemnify them (e.g., paying legal fees, supplying a legal team) as well. Not only can this be devastating in a criminal case but, if sued civilly, officers can lose everything they own. This is not to mention civilian complaints, violations of rules, and other checks on their behaviors.

Explanations for police behavior are, of course, widespread. James Q. Wilson (1977) in his seminal work *Varieties of Police Behavior* divides police agencies into three basic categories. He terms them watchman, legalistic, and service. The watchman style essentially answers radio runs and keeps an eye on things—making sure nothing gets out of hand. Officers in this style are reactive in nature. The legalistic style is far more active and officers will respond to incidents being sure to write a summons or make an arrest—following the law more closely. Service style departments take all calls seriously but are less likely to respond with formal actions such as arrest. The type of agency an officer works for will influence his/her actions. Legalistic agencies, in particular, will often demand formal responses from officers such as arrests, forcible stops, and summonses. We will discuss some of the pitfalls of this style when we talk about the newest rage in policing termed performance management. We will contrast this with a different style of policing that some departments still practice called community policing.

All three have advantages and disadvantages that require police policymakers to carefully understand the costs and benefits of choosing a particular style. Having this understanding is a prerequisite for police leaders to properly navigate the choppy waters of this era. At times, police leaders and policy experts, unfortunately, adopt a "tough on crime" stance or simply follow other agencies (especially NYPD) without fully evaluating the ramifications of their actions beforehand. It is only after a crisis occurs that they begin their evaluation or, even worse, just stubbornly stay a course with little or no evidence to support that path. A good example of this, to be discussed later in this chapter, is NYPD's overly aggressive stop and frisk program in the first decade of the twenty-first century.

The legalistic style has become, by far, the most popular among police departments. Its diaspora began with the New York City Police Department's so-called success story. In 1994, newly elected Mayor Rudolph Giuliani brought in police commissioner, William Bratton. Bratton and his team, most notably Jack Maple, developed the Compstat performance management system. It focused on reducing index crime in New York City. There were centralized meetings at police headquarters where commanders of precincts were interrogated on crime in their areas. Commanders were held strictly accountable for what occurred on their watch. Computerized crime mapping, accountability, and bringing all parties into one room helped make Compstat a great success. As crime decreased precipitously and awards mounted for the new system, numerous agencies emulated the NYPD method.

This revolution in policing is well-documented. A recent survey by the Police Executive Research Forum (PERF) indicates that Compstat is now ubiquitous. In 2011, the survey was sent to 326 of PERF's member agencies with 166 responding. The survey indicated that 79 percent of the agencies utilized Compstat. Further, over half (52 percent) indicated that they began using Compstat between 2006 and 2010 (Bureau of Justice Assistance, Police Executive Research Forum, 2013). In addition, the sheer number of agencies now using computers for crime analysis, crime mapping, and hotspot identification indicate the widespread adoption of NYPD Compstat-like performance management systems. In the United States, a nationwide study of police agencies in 2007 showed that 100 percent of the agencies serving populations of 250,000 or more were using computers for crime analysis and crime mapping. Further, 80 percent of those same agencies are also using computers for hotspot identification (Reaves, 2010). Additionally, as we will discuss, over time the system morphed into a numbers game as commanders were pushed to make their numbers look good at any cost (Eterno, Verma, & Silverman, 2016; Eterno & Silverman, 2012). Other studies also suggest the diaspora of the basic philosophy of NYPD (Lerman & Weaver, 2014; Stuart, Armenta, & Osborne, 2015; Stuart, 2015).

While performance management is very important, social scientists have also identified the negative impact of the police culture as critical to understanding police behavior. Euphemisms such as the "blue wall of silence" or "testilying" certainly suggest that the police culture is able to defy organizational guidelines, community norms, and legal constraints. In fact, the police culture may promote violating the law and other guidelines. There is a persuasive argument that such practices are widespread and endemic to the policing profession. Stoddard (1968: 201–213), for example, writes, "illegal practices of police personnel are socially prescribed and patterned through the informal 'code' rather than being a function of individual aberration or personal inadequacies of the policeman himself."

Many authors have further suggested that certain aspects related to the police culture are especially powerful in predicting police behavior. In particular, one aspect known as the "attitude test" has been studied extensively and found to have a strong influence on police behavior (see, for example, Brown, 1981; Riksheim & Chermak, 1993; Black, 1970; Bayley, 1986; Lundman, 1994; Sykes & Clark, 1975; Westley, 1970; Worden & Shepard, 1996). The attitude test is based on the idea that the police culture demands that officers maintain respect. If a suspect does not show respect for an officer (failing the attitude test), the chances increase that the officer will take some sort of action, appropriate or not, against the individual. This could include, for example, an illegal search.

Another important influence on police behavior is the community in which the officers' work. Researchers have suggested that the socioeconomic status of a community, in particular, will have a significant impact on officers' legal behavior (Brooks, 1993; Riksheim & Chermak, 1993). Many researchers predict officers to be illegal more frequently in poor neighborhoods. Conflict theorists, in particular, have espoused this point of view (e.g., Lynch & Groves, 1989). Some studies have supported this conclusion. Brooks (1993: 154), for example, states, "It is generally supported in the literature that individuals in the lower socioeconomic strata receive harsher treatment by the police." Skolnick (1966: 215–226) too feels that the impact of, "searching first and asking questions later will be felt most strongly in ghetto areas." Some experts, then, suggest that those who live in poor neighborhoods are more likely to be the target of illegal police conduct.

However, police agencies claim that they enforce the law impartially and fairly regardless of the neighborhood. For example, the New York City Police Department *Police Student's Guide* (1997, Police Science: 3–6) states, "Protect the lives and property of our fellow citizens and impartially enforce the law." Efforts aimed at community policing are, in fact, completely contradictory to the claims of the aforementioned researchers. For example, the New York City Police Department *Community Policing Guidebook* states,

> The philosophy of Community Policing is based on the concept that only by joining in partnership with the citizens of New York can we achieve our common goal of reducing crime and random violence. It is a cooperative effort involving all affected participants from neighborhood, government, social, civic, business, educational and religious groups. The community will be afforded legitimate opportunities to help decide how their neighborhoods are policed. Such citizen involvement is not just encouraged, but is essential because of the vast amount of information that citizens possess which the police can use to prevent and solve crime.

Complicating matters, more recent research suggests that officers are not acting illegally simply based on the wealth of a neighborhood (Eterno, 2008; Fyfe, Klinger, & Flavin, 1997). Are police officers more likely to conduct illegal activities, such as unlawful searches, in poor neighborhoods? While there is evidence in the empirical literature to suggest that illegal activity does occur, this point of view is heatedly contested by police officials and more recent research.

Another influence on police behavior suggested by social scientists is the police bureaucracy. There are essentially two views of the bureaucracy. One is that it is very influential and compels officers to follow the law and guidelines. Police administrators see the organization and themselves as highly successful in influencing officers to properly and, what is more important, to legally do their job. They suggest this is accomplished through management strategies, policies, and so on, regardless of what academics say (see especially Bratton, 1996). Formal written rules and regulations of police departments certainly indicate that police organizations are, at a minimum, attempting to follow the rule of law.

Despite the content of written rules, formal rules, and policies are not necessarily the preferred behaviors that an organization wants from its officers. This is a second way of seeing the organizational rules; they are written but often seen as obstructions to be overcome rather than followed. Reuss-Ianni (1983: 116–117) feels that, "Street cops view bureaucratic controls as further confusing and compounding the difficulties they experience performing their job, rather than assisting them in dealing with the ambiguities and uncertainties." Brown (1981) feels that administrators are more inclined to tolerate abuses of the law more than other officer misconduct. As Bayley and Bittner (1984: 109–113) write, "Supervisors indicate—sometimes subtly, sometimes directly—what they prefer by way of action." In fact, if illegal or racist behavior is to be encouraged, this cannot be written for fear of lawsuits and/ or other forms of retaliation. If some sort of illegal behavior is wanted, say an illegal search and seizure, supervisors are more likely to hint (e.g., a wink and/or a nod) that they want such behavior rather than write a formal policy about conducting an illegal search. Other than written policy, management has at its disposal numerous tools to influence officer behavior such as verbal statements to officers. For example, supervisors may state they need more arrests and tolerate whatever conduct must be done to produce them.

The appearance given by police organizations, then, is that the agency wants supervisors to reinforce written rules and regulations. Yet, this is not necessarily the case. As Rubinstein (1973: 401) writes, "If they [supervisors] oblige their men to adhere to all of the legal rules, they will only reduce the number of vice arrests that are being made and cause their captains, divisional inspectors, and the chief inspector to demand increases . . . which will be accompanied with threats of transfer."

While there are certainly questions about officers following the law, whether officers are racist is quite mixed in the research. For example,

Mastrofski, Worden, and Snipes, (1995) point out in their study based on ride-alongs in Richmond, Virginia that legal variables such as evidence strength, offense seriousness, and the victim's preference show positive effects on the probability of arrest; extralegal variables such as race, gender, wealth, and personal reputation have inconsistent findings. Also, Riksheim and Chermak (1993) in summarizing the scientific literature on arrest decisions point out that some variables remain unresolved (education, experience of officer, officer race, and attitude). Essentially, the research is mixed in this area. Nevertheless, the extent of departments under court monitoring or other federal scrutiny indicates that while overt Jim Crow type racism is far less common, we suggest a more covert type of racism may be lurking. Our research and experience suggests that a hidden racism, usually unconsciously supported by a strong crime control, performance management ethos, is occurring. While often not purposeful, it is very powerful due especially but not exclusively to departments adopting an unhealthy and strong top-down legalistic style of policing combined with bureaucratic, cultural, and neighborhood contexts. Compstat, stop and frisk, and spying on Muslims by the New York City Police Department are excellent examples of this.

In sum, based on our research and understanding of the vast literature in this area, we suggest that most police are exceedingly professional. However, the performance management system, including, but not limited to, an extreme focus on numbers (rather than communities and people) is problematic. This unhealthy focus on crime numbers (rather than due process) combined with other factors, especially but not exclusively, the police culture has led to unwanted, unforeseen, and unhealthy consequences including racist policing.

Police Performance Management

One well-known management system developed by the New York City Police Department is the process previously introduced called Compstat (compare statistics). Compstat attempts to control police behavior by focusing, to a great extent, on the power of higher-ranking officers and, in particular, the Commanding Officer (C.O.) of a precinct. Compstat meetings are held regularly (usually twice a week) in which high-ranking officers hold the C.O. of a precinct strictly accountable for everything that occurs in the precinct, including especially, but not exclusively, crime statistics. There are both positive and negative aspects to this management system (Eterno & Silverman, 2012).

On the positive side Compstat allows for more accountability; brings together various department units that, in the past, failed to communicate regularly; helps focus department resources; and encourages innovative thinking that can quickly be transmitted to the entire department (Silverman, 2001).The Compstat process has received numerous accolades from police administrators and academicians alike. Its success has been considered tantamount to an upheaval in policing administration. As discussed, numerous police agencies are attempting to replicate the process in their jurisdictions (Eterno, Verma, & Silverman, 2016). Compstat's four-part mantra became the rallying cry for police throughout the democratic world: accurate and timely intelligence, effective tactics, rapid deployment, and relentless follow-up.

On the negative side, the way the NYPD operationalizes Compstat has led to a numbers crunching, overcentralized bureaucracy that fails to recognize local community needs; bosses that put enormous pressures on officers to write summonses, make arrests, conduct forcible stops so the numbers can be reflected at Compstat meetings; manipulation of crime reports to make the numbers of crimes look better than they actually are; and a department obsessed with its image rather than its mission (Eterno & Silverman, 2012; Eterno, Verman, & Silverman, 2016).

From 2002 through 2012, the negative aspects of Compstat were emphasized. Initially healthy, the agency morphed into a top-down bureaucracy with powerful quotas enforced by supervisors. These unchecked aggressive policing policies focused almost exclusively on crime control combined with other factors such as a strong police culture eventually led to racist policing by the NYPD (*Floyd v. City of New York,* 2013).

Methods and Analysis

In this short chapter, we present some of our research that supports our theme—that police performance management has a deleterious effect leading to aggressive and, at times, racist policing. While this is only a snippet of the multilayered research we have conducted in this area, it gives the reader a good understanding of the basis for our conclusions.

We present two tables that were also presented in *Floyd v. City of New York* (2013). In this case, the NYPD was found liable for unconstitutional and racist policing. We point out that in the precursor to the *Floyd* case, *Daniels v. City of New York,* both sides amicably settled. It was only after the NYPD began its unremittent focus on numbers of arrests, summonses, and forcible stops after 2002 that questions once again surfaced about police legal behavior with respect to stops. In 2002, for example, there were approximately 100,000 stops by police. Crime had decreased by over 60 percent. Within the span of nine years the NYPD was doing nearly three-quarters of a million documented forcible stops. These stops were of mostly of minorities and the vast majority—over 85 percent led to no action by police. Importantly, very few guns were taken off the streets by this tactic even though the police commissioner constantly stated this was one of the main reasons for the stop policy. Crime too was not markedly decreasing as it had in the past. Therefore, the aggressive tactic came into question. We note that the police department continued to actively endorse the policy and put pressure on officers even after being faced with the facts that the policy was not effective. The facts were that stops were getting very few guns off the streets. Indeed, only 0.2 percent of stops resulted in guns being removed from suspects (NYCLU, 2017).

We conducted two large-scale surveys—one in 2008 and the other in 2010. Both surveys showed nearly the exact same results using different samples. The first survey was conducted on retired captains and above using information supplied by the Captain's Endowment Association. The second survey (we present two tables from this survey only for the sake of brevity) uses an NYPD retiree database open to all retired NYPD officers. Both surveys were completely anonymous and voluntary. Anonymity is suggested for surveys that ask sensitive questions and is more likely to lead to valid responses. The sample sizes were 491 for the 2008 survey and 1,962 for the 2010 survey. The 2010 survey, presented in this chapter, was sent via email to potential respondents. We had a return rate of 48.2 percent which is good for a contemporary email survey (Sheehan, 2001). The results of both surveys are very similar with totally different samples suggesting our findings accurately portray what was happening on NYPD at the time.

The following data analyses (which are cited in the *Floyd* case) show that while pressures to conduct forcible stops increased, simultaneously the pressures to obey the law decreased (see Tables 2.1 and 2.2). This unfortunate, yet powerful, combination ushered in an era of racist policing. Officers were focused on conducting stops in fear of being denied vacation time, losing good assignments; being place on punishment posts, and/or having supervisors harass them. Officers began stopping anyone, even without the requisite legal requirement (reasonable suspicion—see *Terry v. Ohio*, 1968). These

Table 2.1　2012 Survey Findings

		Year of retirement			
		before 1995	*1995 until 2001*	*2002 until 2012*	*Total*
stop pressure	low	297	127	205	629
		57.8%	36.7%	24.4%	37.0%
	medium	170	153	341	664
		33.1%	44.2%	40.5%	39.0%
	high	47	66	295	408
		9.1%	19.1%	35.1%	24.0%
Total		514	346	841	1701
		100.0%	100.0%	100.0%	100.0%

Gamma = .461. p<.000.
Kendall's tau b =.302. p<.000.

Table 2.2   2012 Survey Findings

		Year of retirement			
		before 1995	1995 until 2001	2002 until 2012	Total
obey constitutional rights pressure	low	109	63	187	359
		20.7%	17.2%	22.1%	20.6%
	medium	183	132	357	672
		34.7%	36.0%	42.2%	38.6%
	high	235	172	302	709
		44.6%	46.9%	35.7%	40.7%
Total		527	367	846	1740
		100.0%	100.0%	100.0%	100.0%

Gamma = -.106. p<.002.
Kendall's tau b = -.067. p< .000.

forcible stops fell predominantly on minorities as the department claimed they were needed to reduce crime.

The department tried to justify its aggressive stop and frisk program. It suggested it was responsible for the huge crime drop and getting guns off the streets. With respect to the crime drop, what the department did not say was that crime was already down in 2002, when the super-aggressive tactic began, 60 percent. Importantly, the 60 percent drop was accomplished with comparatively few forcible stops (about 100,000). From 2002 to 2011, the number of forcible stops grew exponentially to a peak of nearly 700,000 in 2011. The department saw little benefit from these wild increases. They also claimed that this tactic was getting guns off the streets. However, in reality very few guns were being removed due to forcible stops (less than 0.2 percent of stops led to a gun) and other tactics such as gun buy-back programs, detectives enhancing arrests by interrogating suspects about guns, and working with federal authorities to stop gun-running from other states into New York City. Eventually, with numerous innocent mostly minorities being stopped (over 85 percent of stops were of completely innocent people including high-school students simply leaving school), the New York Civil Liberties Union and the Center for Constitutional Rights had enough. They sued the city again (*Floyd's* precursor case is *Daniels v. City of New York*) and won. NYPD is currently under court monitoring for its racist policing.

The performance management system and pressures by management are largely responsible for this (Eterno, Barrow, & Silverman, 2016). The rank and file is, by and large, exceedingly professional. However, when coerced by management to produce numbers to be reflected at Compstat meetings without regard to consequences or the communities, the result is predictable and horrible. Professional and highly trained officers were reduced to automatons—getting the numbers for their bosses at any cost.

New York City is only the tip of the iceberg. Most departments followed NYPD's lead during this period attracted by the huge crime decline. We will not go into detail about the crime report manipulations that occurred during this period as well but suffice it to say that the scope of the crime decline is questionable (Eterno, Verma, & Silverman, 2016). Many other police departments found themselves in similar situations as the NYPD (Eterno & Silverman, 2012). Such aggressive policing tactics without being balanced by legal guidelines and supervisory controls was largely responsible for these behaviors.

We point out, however, that it is also likely that the police culture (especially the attitude effect—the need to maintain respect in the field) also influenced these behaviors by police. The attitude effect, which is part of the police culture is well known to social scientists. Research has generally confirmed its impact (Worden & Shepard, 1995; Lundman, 1994). However, there is some research that indicates that while the effect exists, it does not overpower legal restrictions (Klinger, 1994). The attitude effect essentially means that officers are highly influenced by the demeanor of the person they are dealing with. If that person is contrite and respectful, the officer is more likely to be lenient. If the person is disrespectful or hostile, the officer is more likely to use his/her legal authority and arrest or summons the individual. This effect ultimately comes from the police culture, which, in part, comes from the dangerousness of the work environment—officers have to stick together to survive. Just like any culture the police culture has its own language, norms, and belief systems. It can have positive effects such as officers backing each other up but also negative consequences such as "testilying" (when officers lie to put someone in jail) and the so-called blue wall of silence (officers do not rat each other out). The attitude effect combined with pressures (or lack thereof) from Compstat has deleterious consequences especially with minority youth in poor neighborhoods who have their own set of pressures from their peers and neighborhoods.

Impact of Overly Aggressive Police Policies in Neighborhoods

The pressures placed on officers to write summonses, make arrests, and conduct forcible stops have been discussed in this chapter. As previously mentioned, researchers have suggested that the socioeconomic status of a community will have a significant impact on officers' legal behavior. Current research consistently points to the impact these unchecked aggressive policies have on minority communities.

The number of forcible police stops grew significantly from 2002 to 2011. The forcible stops that fell on predominantly minority communities left a negative impact particularly on youth. In regard to police stops, youth in New York City are disproportionally targeted as compared to other age groups. The statistics confirm that many of the city's youth experience being stopped by the police, not once or twice but multiple times. In a recent VERA institute of Justice report, 44 percent of youth respondents reported having been stopped nine or more times (Fratello, Rengifo, & Tyrone, 2013).

There were several justifications for these stops including getting guns off of the streets, but the fact that there is very little crime detected during such a high number of stops suggests that a recalibration of the volume of stops and a rethinking of reasons for them may be in order. Table 2.1 on the pressures of stop and frisk suggests that there is less pressure on officers to obey the law. The impact of officers stopping citizens with little regard to obeying the law was reflected in a recent study of young men and women who lived in a Brooklyn precinct with a high rate of police stops (Barrow & Jones-Brown, 2014).

Having been stopped multiple times and not informed of any wrongdoing, young men and women developed tactics to avoid police attention. Residents were able to identify what factors attracted police attention. For example, they avoided locations where police officers frequented such as public housing projects and refrained from wearing attire the police associated with criminal behavior. As a result these individuals are forced to modify their behavior, to avoid police harassment (Barrow & Jones-Brown, 2014).

This mentality is evident in multiple studies on policing. In an investigation on policing in urban communities, Brunson and Miller (2006) learned some young men attempted to reduce their chances of coming under suspicion by avoiding certain areas and certain people altogether. Additional studies pointed out the conflicted feelings of making attempts to avoid police stops. Gau and Brunson (2015) also learned that youth in urban areas felt vulnerable if they were by themselves when stopped by the police. As a result to shield themselves from this vulnerability they opted to spend more time with friends and family and avoided going out in public alone. This strategy, ironically invited even more scrutiny and unlawful stops from police, as officers seemed unable to distinguish these self-help behaviors from gang activity (Gau & Brunson, 2015).

Although law enforcement officials would argue that these stops are justified in efforts to lower crime and deter criminal activity, the result is often an increased distrust in the police as a legitimate institution. A blanket approach that treats all young minority males as (potential) criminals can have the effect of making enemies out of them, irrespective of their level of criminal involvement. The battle lines are drawn, and police end up on one side and minority youth on the other (Gau & Brunson, 2015). Perspectives on procedural justice have been used to explain neighborhood reactions to police experiences. Procedural justice perspectives argue that the legitimacy of police is linked to public judgments about the fairness of the processes through which the police make decisions and exercise authority (Sunshine & Tyler, 2003). Having to modify one's behavior to cope with negative police attention has implications for police policy.

What law enforcement officials fail to understand is that when law-abiding citizens are wrongfully accused of criminal activity, they will not seek police assistance for protection from criminal activity. Procedural injustice by police can help perpetuate crime problems. The young minority males in particular often expressed disillusionment and disaffection. In neighborhoods plagued by persistent actual and threatened violence, residents are greatly in need of personal protection. When the police are seen as uncaring, unpredictable and themselves an intermittent source of intimidation and violence, people turn to other sources of safety. In addition, evidence is revealed that compromised legitimacy can encourage young males to engage in certain self-protective behaviors that can, in turn, increase their risk of becoming the targets of police scrutiny (Gau & Brunson, 2015).

An additional consequence of aggressive police procedures is the lack of willingness to obey the police. Antrobus et al. (2015) found trust in the police to use procedural justice strongly predicted an individual's feelings of obligation to obey police. Lastly, community norms that the police are legitimate lead people to feel a greater duty to obey the police (Dai et al., 2011).

There has been support for the argument that views about police legitimacy influence public satisfaction with police: people who view police as more legitimate are more likely to be satisfied with police service's (Hinds & Murphy, 2007). Research has also found that procedural justice factors have strong impacts on the willingness of citizens to cooperate with and/or support for the police (Dai et al., 2011).

Recommendations

Realizing the fallout of aggressive policing policies combined with a comprehensive knowledge of current scientific evidence on police behavior helps identify possible solutions for alleviating these issues. The first suggestion can help ensure officer safety as well as citizen safety. Many studies suggest that in urban communities young males, particularly minority males, feel harassed, belittled, and disrespected by the police (Brunson & Miller, 2006; Jones-Brown, 2000; Mastroski et al., 2002, Barrow & Jones-Brown, 2014).

First, during interactions with the police, citizen disrespectful behavior may be a response provoked by police demeanor. An attitude of hostility, an angry tone, or unnecessary remarks by the interacting officer could be viewed by the citizen as an indicator of disapproval of his/her social identities, lack of police professionalism and legitimacy, and poor relationship with the police (Dai et al., 2011). However, the findings about the effects of police demeanor and consideration of citizen voice also suggest the pivotal role of police behavior in reducing citizen noncompliance and disrespect. Indeed, respectful policing with citizen participation in police decision-making is an effective strategy to promote citizen cooperation during interactions.

Experimental trials have shown that people's attitudes toward police and intolerance of certain types of crime can be improved when police make a deliberate effort to be respectful and neutral in the manner in which they engage citizens, to treat those persons with dignity, and, in the case of a police-initiated encounter, to fully explain the reasons for the stop (Antrobus et al., 2015).

As important as this is, the attitude of the suspect is also critical to police response. The police culture must be taken into account. The well-known "attitude effect" or the demeanor of the suspect is just as critical. For example, not listening to officer's commands will likely lead to more aggressive responses from the officer. Thus, training programs for officers on their demeanor on the one hand, combined with education programs at local schools and community's addressing citizens' responses to police stop encounters could prove invaluable.

The next suggestion places emphasis on police obligation to obey the law. If protecting constitutional rights during police stops is a priority, then the number of unwarranted police stops of law-abiding citizens must be limited to legal intrusions when necessary—not merely to make quotas or to appease supervisors. Police, to the extent possible, need to be more efficient and effective. In addition to obeying the law and not looking for other sources of safety, citizens who believe police use procedural justice when police exercise their authority are more likely to view police as legitimate. In turn, citizens will be more satisfied with police services. If residents are satisfied with police service, they are more willing to call the police and notify them of actual criminal wrongdoing; citizens will not look to other forms of protection such as firearm usage or protection by their peers. Citizens who see something will rarely say anything if they feel victimized by the police (Eterno, Barrow, & Silverman, 2017).

Basic crime detection intelligence will slip through the cracks as officers alienate minority youth. But, the fact that there is very little crime detected during such a high number of stops suggests that a recalibration of the volume of stops and a rethinking of reasons for them may be in order.

The next suggestion deals with limiting negative contact with the police. Repeated police contact for no wrongdoing limits police legitimacy. In a recent study on the role of neighborhood organizations in Brooklyn, New York, the Brownsville Recreation Center (BRC) has worked with various agencies to address the needs of youth residing in urban communities. The research suggests that informal interactions between youth and police can help build trust and understanding. Because so many BRC participants expressed unfavorable police interactions, perhaps facilitating some leisure activities for youth and police at the center would help change perceptions for both police and participants (Barrow, 2012).

Positive contacts could be cultivated through community policing programs (e.g., school liaison officers), whereas negative contacts could be reduced by avoiding overly aggressive enforcement and by treating young people with respect, dignity, and fairness (Chow, 2011).

At the same time, if police officers learn more meaningful tactics to approach urban youth, this could reduce the group wide suspicion that appears to exist in these communities.

Police and minority communities will continue to experience levels of distrust and apathy as long as needless and inefficient aggressive policing policies remain in practice. The residents in these communities subjected to police stops also seek protection from criminal activity, however not at the cost of their autonomy. When citizens have to change their behaviors and lifestyles to avoid the possibility of unconstitutional stops, it lowers willingness to work with the police. Crime can be lowered in these communities if residents and police are willing to work together. Thus, community partnerships between police and minority communities will be very effective.

The performance management system in vogue must temper its top-down style placing less pressure on officers to write summonses, make arrests, and conduct forcible stops. Rather, the focus needs to be on partnerships with the community, team leadership, and problem-solving activities by police. Leaders who inspire officers are far more effective than those who use fear as the main motivator. Activity, in terms of policing, must move beyond mere counts of summonses, arrests, and stops. Rather, reducing neighborhood fear, proactive yet targeted and effective policing, getting information and intelligence from a willing community, using discretion effectively and, overall, an insistence of working with neighborhoods rather than acting as an 'army of occupation' are necessary and recommended. It must become a balance between crime control and due process in an attempt to strengthen the social contract.

Politicking in a democracy is complicated but it is meant to be that way by design. Officers' powers are checked and balanced with the ultimate power in the hands of the people. If performance management must be used it must *not* be top-down, focused exclusively on crime control, and disrespectful of both community members and lower ranking officers. Therefore, other measures of success must be developed such as intelligence tips from the public, neighborhood contacts, level of fear in a neighborhood, citizen satisfaction, and so forth. It is suggested that police of all ranks need to be respectful of their own (a team approach would help); this must be combined with police making a concerted effort not to browbeat the public. This is not an easy approach nor is it meant to me. Democratic policing is, simply put, a difficult task.

REFERENCES

Antrobus, Emma, Ben Bradford, Kristina Murphy, and Elise Sargeant. (2015). "Community Norms, Procedural Justice, and the Public's Perceptions of Police Legitimacy." *Journal of Contemporary Criminal Justice.* 31(2): 151–170.

Barrow, Christine S. (2012). Understanding the Role of Parochial Control in a Disadvantaged Brooklyn Community. Doctoral Dissertation. Rutgers University.

Barrow, Christine S. and Delores D. Jones-Brown. (2014). "Unreasonable Suspicion: Youth and Policing in New York City." In *The New York City Police Department: The Impact of Its Policies and Practices.* Boca Raton, FL: CRC Press.

Bayley, David H. (1986). "The Tactical Choices of Police Patrol Officers."*Journal of Criminal Justice* 14: 329–348.

Bayley, David H., and Egon Bittner. (1984)." ¢Learning the Skills of Policing." In Dunham and Alpert (1993): 106–129.

Bayles, D.H. (1994). *Police for the Future.* New York, NY: Oxford University Press.

Black, Donald. (1970). "Production of Crime Rates." *American Sociological Review* 35: 735–748.

Bratton, William J. (1996). "Great Expectations: How Higher Expectations for Police Departments Can Lead to a Decrease in Crime." Unpublished paper.

Brooks, Laure Weber. (1993). "Police Discretionary Behavior: A Study of Style." In Dunham and Alpert (1993): 140–164.

Brown, Michael K. (1981). *Working the Street.* New York: Russell Sage Foundation.

Brunson, Rod K., and Jody Miller. (2006). "Young Black Men and Urban Policing in the United States." *British Journal of Criminology* 46(4):1–28.

Bureau of Justice Assistance, Police Executive Research Forum. (2013). "Compstat: Its origins, evolution, and future in law enforcement agencies." Retrieved November 13, from http://policeforum.org/library/compstat/Compstat.pdf

Cho D. H. (2005). Executive Order 9066. *Encyclopedia of Racism in the United States.* (pp. 217–218). Westport, CT: Greenwood Publishing.

Chow, H.P. (2011). "Adolescent attitudes towards police in a Western Canadian city." *Policing: An International Journal of Police Strategies & Management,* 34(4): 638–653.

Churchill, Winston. Speech to the House of Commons, 11 November 1947.

Crank, John P. (1995). "Understanding Police Culture." Unpublished paper presented at the Annual Meeting of the Academy of Criminal Justice Sciences, March 7–11, Boston.

Dai, Mengyan, James Frank, Ivan Sun. (2011). "Procedural justice during police-citizen encounters: The effects of process-based policing on citizen compliance and demeanor." *Journal of Criminal Justice.* 39: 159–168.

Drummond, Douglas S. (1976). *Police Culture*. Beverly Hills, CA: Sage.

Eterno, J. (2003). *Policing within the Law: A Case Study of the New York City Police Department*. Westport, CT: Praeger.

Eterno, J. A. (2003). *Policing within the Law: A Case Study of the New York City Police Department*. Westport, CT: Praeger.

Eterno, J.A., & Silverman, E. B. (2012). *The Crime Numbers Game: Management by Manipulation*. Boca Raton, FL: CRC Press.

Eterno, J. A., Verma, A., & Silverman, E. B. (2016). "Police Manipulations of Crime Reporting: Insiders' Revelations." *Justice Quarterly*. 33(5): 811–835. doi:10.1080 /07418825.2014.980838.

Eterno, John A. (2008). "The Influence of Neighborhood Wealth on Police Decisions to Invoke the Law: An Empirical Assessment of Conflict Theory." *Professional Issues in Criminal Justice*. 3(3).

Eterno, John A., Barrow, Christine S., Silverman, Eli B., (2017). "Forcible Stops: Police and Citizens Speak Out." *Public Administration Review, 77*(2): 181–192.

Fielding, Nigel G. (1989). "Police Culture and Police Practice." In Mollie Weatheritt, ed. (1989). *Police Research: Some Future Prospects*. Brookfield, VT: Gower.

Fratello, Jennifer, Andres F. Rengifo, and Jennifer Trone. (2013). *Coming of Age with Stop and Frisk: Experiences, Self-Perceptions, and Public Safety Implications*. NewYork: Vera Institute of Justice, Center on Youth Justice.

Fyfe, James J., David A. Klinger, and Jeanne M. Flavin. (1997). "Differential Police Treatment of Male-on-Female Spousal Violence." *Criminology* 35(3): 455–473.

Gau, Jacinta M. and Rod. K. Brunson. (2015). "Procedural Injustice, Lost Legitimacy, and Self- Help: Young Males' Adaptations to Perceived Unfairness in Urban Policing Tactics." *Journal of Contemporary Criminal Justice* 31(2): 132–150.

Goldman, Roger, and Puro, Steven. (2001). "Revocation of Police Officer Certification: A Viable Remedy For Police Officer Misconduct." *Saint Louis University Law Journal* 45: 541–579.

Hinds, Lyn and Kristina Murphy. (2007). "Public Satisfaction With Police: Using Procedural Justice to Improve." *The Australian and New Zealand Journal of Criminology* 40(1): 27–42.

History Channel. FDR Signs Executive Order 9066. Retrieved November 21, 2016 from http://www.history.com/this-day-in-history/fdr-signs-executive-order-9066

Jones-Brown, Delores. (2000). "Debunking the Myth of Officer Friendly: How African American Males Experience Community Policing." *Journal of Contemporary Criminal Justice* 16(2): 209–229.

Klinger, David A. (1994). "Demeanor or Crime? Why 'Hostile' Citizens Are More Likely to Be Arrested." *Criminology* 32(3) (August): 475–493.

Lermam, A. & Weaver, V. (2014). *Arresting Citizenship: The Democratic Consequences of Crime Control*. Chicago: University of Chicago Press.

Levitt, Leonard. (2017). NYPD Confidential. http://nypdconfidential.com/

Lundman, Richard J. (1994). "Demeanor or Crime? The Midwest City Police-Citizen Encounters Study." *Criminology* 32(4): 631–653.

Lynch, Michael J., and W. Byron Groves. (1989). *A Primer in Radical Criminology*. New York: Harrow and Heston.

Manning, Peter K. (1987). "The Police Occupational Culture in Anglo-American Societies." Draft, March 3, 1987. Intended for William G. Bailey ed. (1989) *Encyclopedia of Police Science*. Dallas: Garland.

Matrofski, Stephen D., Robert E. Worden, and Jeffrey B. Snipes. (1995). "Law Enforcement in a Time of Community Policing." *Criminology* 33(4): 539–563.

Mastroski, Stephen D., Michael D. Reisig, and John D. McCluskey. (2002). "Police Disrespect toward the Public: An Encounter-Based Analysis." Criminology 40(3): 515–551.

NYCLU (New York Civil Liberties Union). (2017). Stop and Frisk Facts. Retrieved July 11, 2017 from https://www.nyclu.org/en/stop-and-frisk-facts

New York City Police Department. "Police Student Guide."

New York City Police Department. "Community Policing Guidebook."

Packer, Herbert. (1966). "The Courts, the Police, and the Rest of Us." *Journal of Criminal Law and Criminology* 57: 238–240.

Reaves, B. A. (2010, December). Local Police Departments 2007. Bureau of justice statistics, Table 22. http://bjs.ojp.usdoj.gov/content/pub/pdf/lpd07.pdf

Reaves, B. A. (2016, July). *State and Local Law Enforcement Academies, 2013* (USA, Bureau of Justice Statistics, Office of Justice Programs). Retrieved November 18, 2016, from https://www.bjs.gov/content/pub/pdf/slleta13.pdf

Reiss, Albert J, Jr. (1971). T*he Police and the Public*. New Haven, CT: Yale University Press: 156, 160–163, 170–171. Reprinted in Lundman (1980); 253–259.

Reuss-Ianni, Elizabeth. (1983). *Two Cultures of Policing*. New Brunswick, NJ: Transaction Books.

Riksheim, Eric C., and Steven M. Chermak. (1993). "Causes of Police Behavior Revisited." *Journal of Criminal Justice* 21(4): 353–382.

Rubinstein, Jonathan. (1973). *City Police*. New York: Ballantine Books.

Sheehan, K. B. (2001). "E-mail survey response rates: A review." *Journal of Computer-Mediated Communication*, 6. doi:10.1111/j.1083—6101.2001.tb00117.x

Silverman, E. B. (2001). *NYPD Battles Crime: Innovative Strategies* in Policing. Boston: Northeastern University Press.

Skolnick, Jerome. (1966). *Justice without Trial: Law Enforcement in Democratic Society*. New York: John Wiley and Sons.

Stoddard, Ellwyn R. (1968). "The Informal 'Code' of Police Deviancy: A Group Approach to Blue-Coat Crime." *Journal of Criminal Law, Criminology and Police Science* 59: 201–213. Reprinted in Lundman (1980): 226–253.

Stuart, F. (2015). *Down, Out and Under Arrest: Policing and Everyday Life in Skid Row*. Chicago: University of Chicago Press.

Stuart, F., Armenta, A., & Osborne, M. (2015). "Legal Control of Marginal Groups." *Annual Review of Law and Social Science*. 11: 235–254.

Sunshine, J., & Tyler, T.R. (2003). "The role of procedural justice and legitimacy in shaping public support for policing." *Law and Society Review*. 37(3): 513–547.

Sykes, Richard E., and John P. Clark. (1975). "A Theory of Deference Exchange in Police-Civilian Encounters." *American Journal of Sociology* 81: 587–595. Reprinted in Lundman (1980): 91–105.

United States Census Bureau. (2016). Retrieved November 8, 2016 from https://www.census.gov/quickfacts/table/PST045215/00

Westley, William A. (1970). *Violence and the Police: A Sociological Study of Law, Custom, and Morality*. Cambridge, MA: MIT Press.

Wilson, James Q. (1977). *Varieties of Police Behavior*. Cambridge, MA: Harvard University Press.

Worden, Robert E., and Robin L Shepard. (1996). "Demeanor, Crime, and Police Behavior: A Reexamination of the Police Services Study Data." *Criminology* 34(1): 83–105.

Chapter 3

Leveraging the Intersection of Politics, Problem, and Policy in Organizational and Social Change

An Historical Analysis of the Detroit, Los Angeles, and Atlanta Police Departments

Andrew J. Grandage, Britt S. Aliperti,
and Brian N. Williams

Recent events across the nation suggest that relationships between the police and the public in a number of jurisdictions may be at a crossroads. Numerous police involved shootings serve as visible reminders of the precarious state of police-community relations across the United States, especially in the context of police-minority community relations. These occurrences impact public trust and confidence and have helped to create a jaded view of local law enforcement's primary mission, which is to serve and protect the community. As a consequence, the President's Task Force on 21st Century Policing identified building trust and legitimacy as the first pillar of six reform efforts deemed critical to improve current policing practices (The President's Task Force on 21st Century Policing 2015).

Local police departments, like all public organizations, operate within an open-system environment and seek to manage and function based upon their past, present, and future. Identifying primary features of these systems and how they evolve in response to each other is essential in analyzing organizational change. To realize their purposes in a democratic society, police departments must adapt and be responsive to social imperatives (Burns and Stalker 1961; Katz and Kahn 1966). Occasionally, police departments make significant transformations, revealing important considerations for the study of organizational change. They represent a relatively underexplored topic within this literature, with more needed attention and scholarly collaboration between criminal justice and organizational theorists. We use historical case studies of the Detroit, Los Angeles, and Atlanta police departments to highlight the challenges of organizational change in the midst of racial and societal unrest. Environmental conditions, which serve to promote change in response to societal influences, are explored with an emphasis on how an intersection of politics, policy, and problem can accelerate change (Kingdon 1995). The lessons learned from these cases offer important implications for effective leadership, administration, and management both within police departments as well as across the communities they serve.

The organization of this chapter is as follows. First, we discuss building trust and enhancing police legitimacy by placing it in an historical context with a focus on representative bureaucracy. The literature review then begins by introducing perspectives on organizational change advanced by scholars in criminal justice and organizational theory. We then proceed to describe the open-system environment police departments operate in, the web of politics they are embedded within, and the implications for organizational transformation during times of societal unrest across the communities they serve. Next, we explain the selection of our cases and methodology. The historical case studies are presented with the following organizing themes: race, space, and belonging during the civil rights movement; a subsequent convergence of politics, policy, and problem which offered the potential for accelerated change in establishing representative police forces; factors which served as driving and restraining forces to this end; and an assessment of how modern day police-community relations were shaped by these developments. We conclude by outlining implications for political and judicial control of police departments, organizational change, the reconciliation of democratic and administrative imperatives, self-governance, and highlight future challenges along these lines.

BUILDING TRUST AND ENHANCING POLICE LEGITIMACY

The challenge of building community trust between law enforcement and communities and enhancing the legitimacy of policing is not a new phenomenon (Kerner Commission 1968). Since the inception and adoption of Western policing, in general, and police practices in the United States, in particular, law enforcement has been charged with engaging the public in order to fulfill its mission to serve and protect. In 1829, Sir Robert Peel noted, "The police are the public and the public are the police: the police being the only members of the public who are paid to give full time attention to duties which are incumbent on every citizen in the interests of community welfare and existence" (Reith 1948).

Current events highlight the challenge of bringing the theory of the Peelian Principle into contemporary practice. The historical baggage of past policies and practices of yesterday have had a shadowing effect that negatively impacts contemporary police-citizen collaboration (Williams 1998; Williams, Kang, and Johnson 2016).

Prior to receiving public funds and the subsequent transition to a professional occupation, early police practices utilized citizen volunteers and citizen-based watch groups to ensure public safety and public order (Websdale 2001; Archbold 2013). These informal citizen-based watch groups and patrols evolved into more formal types of patrols in the creation of centralized law enforcement agencies. One historical, citizen-based construction that sought to ensure the enforcement of laws was the Southern slave patrols (Berlin 1976; Reichel 1998). These patrols operated prior to and after the end of the Civil War. This police practice created divisions in communities of the newly emerging free American society (Archbold 2013). These divisions have had a negative rippling effect across time and have increased the sense of distrust that some within the African American community have with law enforcement today (Websdale 2001).

The intersection of belonging, place, and race has been one of challenge in American society, in general, and within American policing in particular (Bass 2001; Bonner 2014: Boyles 2015; Anderson 2012; Anderson 2015). A discussion of these issues requires an emphasis on representative bureaucracy, a term first coined by J. Donald Kingsley in 1944. Representative bureaucracy is concerned with how the demographic characteristics or features of bureaucrats affect the distribution of outputs to clients who mirror or share these demographic features. Two forms of representation have been distinguished by the literature: passive and active. Passive representation is concerned with whether the bureaucracy has the same demographic features—such as race, religion, sex, income, or class—as the population it serves whereas active representation addresses how representation influences policy making and implementation (Mosher 1968, 1982; Pitkin 1967).

Recent studies have pointed to prospective benefits of a representative bureaucracy within police departments from the perspective of street level bureaucrats (Close and Mason 2006; Close and Mason 2007; Bradbury and Kellough 2010). Moreover, empirical analysis has suggested that the inauguration of a Black mayor leads to mostly indistinguishable urban policies with one exception: the hiring of more Black police officers (Hopkins and McCabe 2012). The antecedent conditions of active representation and their driving and restraining forces serve as an initial set of components to understanding the past, present, and future of community policing relationships and its prospects for positive change. Investigation is needed to understand how external social and political factors influence police administration in this regard. New theoretical frameworks are especially intriguing given the need for accelerated change coupled with the continued efforts to provide more scholarly collaboration among criminal justice and organizational theorists (Hassel, Zhao, and Maguire 2003; Willis, Mastrofski, and Weisburd 2007; Zhao et al. 2001; Cordner 2017; Nicholson-Crotty and O'Toole 2004; Bradbury and Kellough 2010).

LITERATURE REVIEW

The study of organizational change within police departments is character- ized by its emphasis on the evolution from mechanical bureaucratic structures which placed a premium on technical efficiency to flexible and adaptive structures more suitable for responding to community needs (Zhao 1996; Thurman, Zhao, and Giacomazi 2001). Kelling and Moore (1988) describe three eras of policing: political, professional, and community. They provide seven indicators of change to help mark the end of one era and the beginning of the next: authorization, function, theoretical framework, organizational design, environment, operational strategies, and outcomes. From the per- spective of the criminal justice literature, these structural changes symbol- ize a professionalization of the field and a gradual adoption of community policing practices. However, from the perspective of organizational theorists, such changes may be interpreted as part of larger trends during the twentieth century, representing a broader reform movement, organic systems, contin- gency theory, and growing skepticism of centralized bureaucratic structures (Rainey 2014; Ostrom 1974). An objective of organizational theorists ought to be identifying the essential elements to be considered in the theoretical framework needed to help explain why these organizations change not in the aggregate, but within their social environments.

Open Systems, Web of Politics, and Organizational Transformation

Local police departments, like all public organizations, operate within an open system (Katz and Kahn 1966). Police departments, as organic organiza- tions, respond to social, economic, and technological imperatives (Burns and Stalker 1961). As public entities, they must adapt to environmental variations in order to carry out responsibilities under the auspices and influence of other governmental authorities while delivering important services and crucial functions. When police functions are discharged in an inappropriate, biased, or unprofessional manner, they create problems for citizens, ranging from small irritations or frustrations to life-threatening interactions (Kerner Com- mission 1968; President's Task Force on 21st Century Policing 2015). As such, police departments operate within and are influenced by what has been described as a web of politics (Aberbach and Rockman 2000). Our depiction of this web is provided in Figure 3.1. Notice that police departments reside in an organizational universe where social, political, judicial, and administrative imperatives influence police operations. However, the social will is only institutionalized in these operations to the extent that it is intermediated properly through the other pathways. Thus, for social will to be properly reflected in police operations, it likely involves a conjunction of conditions along these lines to facilitate change.

To focus the subject matter, we distinguish between what we will refer to as incremental and accelerated change throughout the essay. In the former, a relatively narrow set of policy alternatives are considered which differ only slightly in degree from the status quo or previous policy decision. Attention is focused on the branch of several issues and not necessarily the root of one in particular. This allows for the correction of error through successive limited comparisons and reduces conflict under conditions of annularity and pluralism (Lindblom 1959; Wildavsky 1964). In an environment of accelerated change, policy options and choices represent priorities aimed at institutional reform and differ in substantial ways from previous policy. Conflicts in the present can be viewed as necessary transaction costs to achieve long-term goals, particularly when a policy issue rises to the agenda that has political support and a workable policy solution (Kingdon 1995). If we assume an incremental environment, change could easily result from a disjunction of conjunctions which a power structure sits upon, consistent with certain

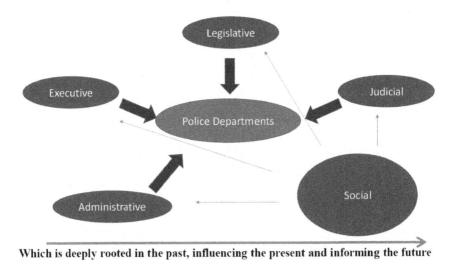

Which is deeply rooted in the past, influencing the present and informing the future

Figure 3.1   Police Departments Operate with an Open System.

theories of causality in the social sciences (Marini and Singer 1988). It is these interdependencies, among social, political, legal, and administrative imperatives, which warrants review.

Embedded within this web of politics are numerous ecological and environmental dimensions. Rainey (2014) has identified seven dimensions of an organization's environment including technological, legal, political, economic, demographic, ecological, and cultural conditions. These conditions, in theory, serve to make and shape the organization, both in terms of policy and practice. Consequently, it is imperative for leaders and managers of public organizations to understand and appreciate the needed steps for effective organizational transformation and successful implementation of organizational change in response to environmental or ecological conditions that shape policy and practice.

Organizational change is a reality within the open-system environment that local law enforcement and other public sector institutions and organizations exist. Greiner (1967) identified seven phases of successful organizational change. These phases included the pressure and arousal phase, the intervention and reorientation phase, the diagnosis and recognition phase, the invention and commitment phase, the experimentation and search phase, and the reinforcement and acceptance phase. Greiner's pattern for successful organizational change has points in common with Kotter's (1995) eight steps for successful organizational transformation. Kotter identified the following as crucial elements of successful organizational transformation: establishing a sense of urgency; forming a powerful guiding coalition; creating a vision; communicating that vision; empowering others to act on the vision; creating short-term winds; consolidating improvements that can produce further change; and institutionalizing the new approach.

The combination of Greiner and Kotter's approaches suggest certain determinants of successful implementation of change within public sector organizations. These determinants have been encapsulated and articulated by Rainey (2014) and require managerial leaders to: (1) ensure the need; (2) provide a plan; (3) build internal support to overcome resistance; (4) ensure top management support and commitment; (5) build external support; and (6) provide resources to institutionalize the change and pursue comprehensive change. Rainey and Rainey (1986) have provided a roadmap that highlights the three general conditions for successful change within a federal agency. These conditions include: (1) a durable power center committed to successful change due to an internal change agent and strong, stable leadership by public sector careerists; (2) a political window of opportunity that provides the appropriate timing for collective action and support; and (3) a comprehensive, clear, and long-term change strategy that utilizes group processes to develop and implement major structural reform. These conditions are crucial to successful large-scale planned change, particularly the resistance to these change efforts received based upon the perceptions of their costs, threatening nature, and doing something new and different.

The roadmap that Rainey and Rainey (1986) have provided highlights the path to successful change from a federal agency perspective, but what about the needed conditions that face local public organizations like police departments during times of social unrest? What lessons can history teach us? These are pertinent and salient questions when considering the often-repeated expression that all politics is local.

CASE SELECTION AND METHODOLOGY

The premise of this chapter is that organizational change within police departments cannot be properly understood apart from an historical analysis of their social and political environments. Accordingly, we conducted case studies of the Detroit, Los Angeles, and Atlanta police departments to reveal connections between their social environments, political institutions, and administrative structures. This type of analysis exposes the limitations of federal policies, such as the Civil Rights Act of 1964 and Voter Rights Act of 1965, in bringing about policy changes at the local level. First, Title VII of the Civil Rights Act of 1964, which prohibited discriminatory employment practices, did not apply to state and local governments until 1972. The Voter Rights Act transferred power to local constituencies in mayoral elections; however, even if a mayor campaigned on police reform, electoral institutions could still be insufficient. This is because if the powers of the mayor are weak in general, but particularly as it relates to personnel policies of the police department, issues of political control become easily exposed. Moreover, affirmative action cases had yet to set precedent for programs aimed at remedying historical imbalances in the civil service system (Kellough 2006). In summary, there was potential for the social will to be reflected in police operations through incremental changes to the status quo, given these political and legal developments. A factor, which could serve to accelerate this change, is the rise of a strong mayor focused on police reform who implements proactive policies to that end.

Detroit, Los Angeles, and Atlanta each elected their first Black mayors in 1973, with police reform front and center on the policy agenda. The mayors of Detroit and Los Angeles, Coleman Young and Tom Bradley, respectively, both held office until 1993. Atlanta would form a durable power center over this same period. Maynard Jackson served as mayor of Atlanta until meeting his term limits in 1982. His policies would be continued by his successor, Andrew Young, who held office until meeting his term limits in 1990.

Jackson then held office again until 1994. Thus, selecting these cities allows us to observe how these departments evolved over a common two-decade period with these social, political, and legislative conditions aligned. Variations among the cities allow for comparisons of differing environmental conditions and their relation to organizational change. For example, in Detroit and Atlanta the powers of the mayor are strong whereas in Los Angeles they are weak. Los Angeles has a more diverse community than Atlanta and Detroit in terms of Hispanic and Asian populations. Atlanta and Detroit both realized Black majorities whereas Los Angeles did not. Also along the lines of demographics, Detroit's workforce and economic base have plummeted over these decades whereas Atlanta and Los Angeles have experienced notable growth. Black police chiefs were promptly appointed following the 1973 mayoral elections in Atlanta and Detroit whereas in Los Angeles this was not the case. Atlanta and Detroit also implemented affirmative action plans earlier than Los Angeles.

Figure 3.2 shows how the composition of the forces evolved over the study period.[1] More precisely, it provides representation ratios for Black officers, with the numerator as the percentage of the Black officers within a force and the denominator as the percentage of Black citizens within a population. A ratio greater than one indicates overrepresentation whereas a ratio less than one indicates underrepresentation. The figures associated with the preintervention period are the compositions of the forces at the time of 1973 mayoral elections. All forces substantially increased the representation of Black officers during the study period. Detroit's representation of Black

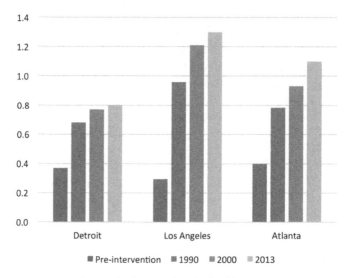

Figure 3.2   Representation Ratios by City for Black Officers.

officers doubled from 0.4 to 0.8. Los Angeles had the most dramatic increase, rising from 0.3 to 1.3. Atlanta, whose first Black police officers were hired just twenty-five years prior in 1948, rose from 0.4 to 1.1. Figure 3.3 provides the percentage of the Black population by decade to show the relative share and growing presence of minorities in each city. Detroit and Atlanta's Black citizens began to form a majority leading up to the 1973 elections whereas in Los Angeles the percentage was only 20% at this time. Figure 3.4 shows the representation of the forces along other dimensions as of 2013. In Atlanta and Los Angeles, Black and White populations are represented equally. This is not the case in Detroit where Whites make up less than a tenth of the

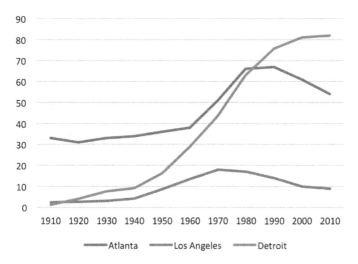

Figure 3.3   Percentage of Black Population by City.

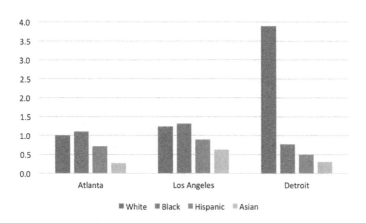

Figure 3.4   Representation Ratios by City, 2013.

population, but account for a third of the force. In each city, both groups have better representation than Hispanic and Asian populations. The departments have made strides considering their circumstances, but can learn from their past in managing their present and future in becoming more diverse on these and other dimensions.

We now explain the social, political, and legal developments, which led to the establishment of more representative police forces in each city.

DETROIT

Detroit's booming industrial base and destination as a major migration city left key questions unresolved relating to societal integration (Capeci and Wilkerson 1990; Bates 2012). Issues surrounding race, space, and belonging characterized the city. How would a scarce amount of land be allocated among competing claims of White and Black citizens? Would the White workers accept Blacks as their equals in the booming factories?

Detroit's Black residents were treated as second-class citizens, segregated into crammed living spaces, which often housed multiple families as Whites consistently protested the construction of Black housing (Detroit Historical Society, N.D.). The construction of the Sojourner Truth Housing project in 1942, which was a Black housing project embedded in a Polish neighborhood, serves as a visible reminder of these tensions. The Michigan National Guard was needed to keep an armed crowd of over 1,000 White protestors from attacking Black families attempting to move into their new homes. Just a year later, when Packard Motor Company placed Whites and Blacks side by side in assembly lines, a hate strike took place where roughly 25,000 White workers walked off their jobs. This was significant because Detroit was assuming responsibility for a significant amount of wartime production—the walk-off symbolized a prioritization of race over country in a time of war. These local racial tensions and their connection to wartime production caught the attention of the national media. In 1942, *Life Magazine* published "Detroit is Dynamite," a critical article on Detroit. It asserted that Detroit could destroy either Hitler or the United States and that rioting was a likelihood in the city's near future.

As predicted, Detroit experienced an historical race riot in June of 1943. The event began at Bell Isle, a public park, and soon spread to the city's streets. The Detroit Police Department (DPD) had the situation under control later in the evening; however, rumors on both sides of the conflict regarding actions of the others escalated tensions. DPD could not contain the violence and 6,000 federal troops were required to restore order. The riot would claim thirty-four lives, twenty-five of which were Black, seventeen of whom were killed by police—however, the police did not kill a White citizen (Detroit Historical Society, N.D). Police-minority relations were poor leading up to the riots; however, this served to make conditions worse: "In the period between 1943 and 1953, police brutality became a symbol of everything that was wrong with Detroit" (Hawkins and Thomas 1991, p. 83). The Black community in Detroit pressed for clarification in the use of firearms by the police in apprehending suspects. A decade after the riots, DPD was only 2% Black as its percentage of Black residents approached 20% (Hawkins and Thomas 1991).

Mayor Jerome Cavanagh, who served from 1962 to 1970, selected police commissioners who were considered sensitive to the civil rights movement throughout his tenure, but this was not considered effective at changing the behavior of police at the street level (Fine 2007). Detroit's racial tensions erupted again in 1967. Whereas the 1943 riots symbolized tensions between Black and White citizens in the context of a "melting pot," the 1967 riots represented dissatisfaction with governance—continuing inequalities, lagging civil rights, and an oppressive local police force (Capeci and Wilkerson 1990). The events began following the raid of an after-hours club in a predominately Black neighborhood and the subsequent arrests of eighty-two Black patrons. A crowd of residents gathered, angered as they witnessed the patrons being loaded into police wagons. As the wagons left, looting began and the situation escalated to a riot. The initial policy regarding the use of deadly force was unclear at the time the riots broke out. However, neither the mayor nor the police commissioner explicitly forbid the use of weapons and ordered the police to exercise discretion regarding the extent of force necessary in each incident (Rhine 1968). Once again, federal troops would be deployed to restore order in the City. The riot claimed forty-three lives, thirty-three of which were Black, many again at the hands of the DPD (Rhine 1968).

The 1969 mayoral election would then serve as a referendum on police representation and reform. The election featured the Sheriff of Wayne County, Roman Gribbs, and a moderate Black candidate who was active in the civil rights movement, Richard Austin. Gribbs campaigned on a fight against crime in the streets, proposing that small units be assigned to specific problem areas. Gribbs won the election in what was one of the closest mayoral elections the City had experienced (Thompson 2004). Gribbs then implemented a controversial program under the acronym STRESS (Stop the Robberies Enjoy Safe Streets). This was considered a policy priority due to 21,000 reported street robberies in 1970, with sixty-nine of them resulting in murder (Darden and Thomas 2013). The program consisted of disguising armed and ready policeman as robbery prone citizens. In the program's first nine months, 1,400 arrests were made and reported robberies fell by 4%; however, the initiative received mixed support from the community as thirteen Black citizens were killed by the STRESS unit (Darden and Thomas 2013). Thousands of the

City's residents—black and white—gathered in peaceful protest following the death of two teenage youth apprehended in the program.

Police reform would be front and center once again in the 1973 mayoral election. Coleman Young, a Black candidate who prioritized police reform, defeated the incumbent mayor and former sheriff, Roman Gribbs. When he entered office in 1974, only 17% of DPD was Black whereas Blacks represented 46% of the city's population (Love 1981). Upon his election, Young promptly disbanded the STRESS unit established by his predecessor and implemented major personnel reforms within the DPD (Love 1981; Hawkins and Thomas 1991). The first stage consisted of aggressive outreach efforts to increase diversity by taking visits to Black communities, establishing recruiting offices in the inner cities, and trying to change the narrative by asking for help from the community. Mayor Young then altered entrance and promotional exams to reflect less of a cultural bias, enforced residency requirements for officers, appointed a Black police chief and established a new Board of Commissioners for the police department. These policies would be met with resistance as White officers perceived them to be a form of "reverse discrimination" (Love 1981). Subsequent Supreme Court rulings, which will be discussed in more detail in a later section, would provide precedent for the implementation of affirmative action policies. By 1987, the force was 47% Black and would reach 61% by 1998 (Hawkins and Thomas 1991).

In summary, Coleman Young leveraged the intersection of politics, policy, and problem in driving accelerated change to form a representative police force; most specifically, by leveraging his powers as strong mayor to restructure personnel policies. We now turn to an assessment of police-community relations in Detroit at the conclusion of Coleman Young's tenure as mayor in 1994 and major developments thereafter. At the conclusion of Young's tenure, allegations of corruption within the city government and DPD began to emerge. Coleman Young's first appointed Black Chief of Police, William Hart, was a close ally of Young's. In 1992, Hart was convicted of embezzlement after stealing more than two million dollars from the city over a period of several years. The funds were intended to be used for undercover drug operations. Leading up to the trial, Young was quick to claim that the investigation was an effort on behalf of federal prosecutors to harass Black officials. Despite the conviction and hard evidence on Hart, Young stood by his Chief. Thus, while strides were undoubtedly made in establishing a representative police force, corruption at the highest level of the DPD served to discount the trust that the lower ranks were trying to establish on the street, which still left much to be desired in the way of improvements.

These needed improvements were manifest in two consent decrees signed by the DPD, the City of Detroit, and the Department of Justice. The investigation leading to the decree was initiated at the request of the City. The first decree concerned the use of force, arrest, and witness detention. The second addressed the conditions of confinement in holding facilities. The US Attorney for the Eastern District of Michigan and the Assistant Attorney General for Civil Rights at the Department of Justice praised city leaders for reaching the resolution in a collaborative manner, stating that it represented a significant step in reducing civil rights abuses within DPD (United States Department of Justice 2003). Major provisions of the consent decree consisted of the following: revisions to use of force policy and training, with an emphasis on de-escalation techniques; supervisory review of probable cause for arrests; prohibiting the detention of an individual without probable cause and improvements in procedures for the investigation of officer misconduct. In August of 2014, a joint motion was filed to terminate the decree after the courts found that the city was in substantial compliance with the consent judgment, the original concerns underlying the case no longer existed, and that the reforms were institutionalized. Assistant Police Chief James White spoke to the impact the decree had on the organizational culture of DPD:

> We don't look at this process as the end of a journey. This isn't a new concept for us. We're happy to end the governmental oversight, but the reforms we have engaged in over the past 13 years are no longer new to us. They are embedded in our police. They are how we believe now. ... and we will be truly an example for other forces across the country (Baldas 2016).

DPD has made other strides in representation during the twenty-first century along the lines of gender and sexual orientation. Detroit's first female Chief of Police, Ella Bully Cummings, led the department through the consent decree, from 2003 to 2008. In 2013, Detroit established a lesbian, bisexual, gay and transgender (LBGT) liaison unit to bridge the gap and improve a traditionally challenging relationship with this community. The executive director of Equality Michigan, a Detroit based LBGT group, Stephanie White, stated in an interview with the Detroit News, "Our lives were not taken seriously. Crimes against our community were not taken seriously ...We're 25 years later and here we stand in partnership with Chief (James) Craig" (Williams 2017). To commemorate the establishment of the unit, the pride flag flew for the month of June. Chief James Craig commented, "Although today's flag raising is a small gesture, it says a lot for our community. Detroit has got your back" (Williams 2017).

LOS ANGELES

We begin our review of the Los Angeles Police Department (LAPD) with a focus on corrupt practices and racial tensions in the first half of the twentieth century. Mayor Frank Shaw was the first mayor to be recalled from a major city in 1938. Ostensibly, this recall symbolized a reform movement, being dubbed the Los Angeles Urban Reform Revival by Shaw's successor, Fletcher Brown. However, the extent of corruption, which occurred in the City, has been subject to debate, with specific objections raised toward the notion of machine politics supporting corrupt practices (Viehe 1980). "Shaw was not a machine politician in the usual sense of the word, since the Los Angeles machine existed in appearance, not in fact … . In fact, the machine had such little control over its members that they did not necessarily support the same candidates" (Viehe 1980, 290–291). The City wanted a clean and efficient government with little interference from partisan politics and this was reflected in weak powers upon the mayor in general, but particularly in regard to political control over the police department (Wilson 1998; Cannon 1999; Escobar 2003). This was evident in Section 202 of the City's charter which effectively ruled out external accountability by stipulating that police misconduct would be investigated internally by boards comprised of fellow officers and that the chief could only lower the disciplinary recommendation, not increase it (Escobar 2003).

The effort to reduce the perceived of level corruption in the city did little, if anything, to increase the level of trust between LAPD and its minority citizens. Whereas in Detroit and Atlanta, police-community relations in the first half of the twentieth century primarily dealt with conflicts between the established White community and disenfranchised Blacks, in Los Angeles, relations were also unacceptable to Latino residents. The lack of trust LAPD failed to build with its Latino community is perhaps best symbolized by the Zoot Suit Riots (Del Castillo 2000; Pagan 2003). The police and press consistently portrayed Mexican youths as "pachucho hoodlums and baby gangsters," fueling the belief that Latino's were incapable of living within a White and civilized democratic society (Del Castillo 2000; Pagan 2003). Zoot suits, cultural attire worn by Latino Youth, were long jackets with baggy pants. During the rationing of World War II, White Americans began to resent the seemingly excessive use of cloth. Conflict escalated after a set of altercations between stationed military personnel and Zoot suiters in the summer of 1943. Within days, roughly 200 stationed US military personnel bussed themselves to East Los Angeles, which was the center of the Mexican-American community. They then proceeded to attack any Mexican-Americans they encountered. After the riots, the local media was heavily criticized for their role in stereotyping Mexican-Americans. The police would face criticism as well for their accommodative and unapologetic role in the riots (Del Castillo 2000; Pagan 2003).

Relations between the LAPD and its minority communities would not improve during the next couple decades under the tenure of Chief William H.

Parker, who prioritized professionalization and departmental independence over community relations and accountability (Escobar 2003). Police brutality would be exposed again in 1951 following "Bloody Christmas," when officers beat seven young men in their custody. The event held significance as it revealed how LAPD would deal with public criticism in the coming decades: asserting a tenet of police professionalism to be independent of political control, acting on that tenet with the support of the City's charter which prevented external review of police misconduct, and portraying activists and victims of police brutality as communists, hoodlums, radicals, or whatever happened to fit the narrative at the time (Escobar 2003).

The lingering impact of these oppressive institutional practices was manifest in the Watts Riots of 1965. What began as a simple traffic stop quickly escalated into a larger scene as a crowd gathered to witness the arrest of a drunk driver in the predominately Black neighborhood of Watts. Violence broke out as witnesses began throwing objects at police due to questionable tactics in apprehending the suspect and his mother who arrived at the scene. After a night of turmoil, Chief Parker relayed to the media that he could not provide any idea of how the situation could be brought under control. Accordingly, the National Guard, California Highway Patrol, and the LAPD formed 16,000 members of what Chief Parker referred to as the "attacking force" (Hinton 2016). This attacking force took the persona of an overseas military occupation, going as far as posting signs threatening to shoot citizens, for example, "Turn left or get shot." Citizens responded by attempting to drive out the occupation. Curfews were put in place, giving LAPD the authority to apprehend any citizen in what became a warzone after several days of chaos. The riot would last several days and claimed thirty-four lives—many of which were lost due to the use of deadly force by LAPD.

Similar to Detroit, the 1969 mayoral election in Los Angeles would serve as a referendum on police reform, but fell short. It pitted the incumbent Sam Yorty against Tom Bradley, a former LAPD officer who was the first Black City Council member in Los Angeles. Although Bradley held a substantial lead in months leading up to the election, Yorty won in part by portraying Bradley as a radical and Black militant (Holli 1999). Bradley would then unseat Yorty in the 1973 election, capturing 57% of the vote when only 15% of the population was Black. When Bradley entered office, only 5% of LAPD officers were Black (Cannon 1999). However, Bradley did not possess the powers of a strong mayor, limiting his reach into influencing personnel policies of the LAPD (Wilson 1998; Cannon 1999). The true impetus for a representative police force would then not come from the Mayor's Office or leadership within LAPD, but from a discrimination lawsuit filed against LAPD leading to a consent decree. A female sergeant, Fanchon Blake, filed a civil suit on the grounds that LAPD's hiring and promotion practices discriminated against women and minorities (Lasley 2012). After several years of litigation, the consent decree was agreed to in 1981. The most significant of the requirements were that 20% of sworn officers be female and that the percentages of minority officers represent the community. These were significant changes at the time, given that only 2% of the force was female. Moreover, minorities identified in the decree (Black, Hispanic, and Asian) only comprised 18% of the force, but made up 31% of the population (Lasley 2012).

Relations between LAPD and its minority citizens were further compromised under the leadership of Chief Daryl Gates. Chief Gates earned a national reputation in some circles of law enforcement for innovative police practices, such as Special Weapons and Tactics (SWAT) teams and the Emergency Command Control Communications System (ECCCS). However, the same cannot be said of building a trust in the community. Gates made national headlines for controversial statements. In 1982, he commented that chokeholds likely did more harm to Blacks than "normal people" because their arteries did not open as quickly. In a Senate hearing in 1990, he stated that casual drug users "ought to be taken out and shot," labeling it treason. Perhaps more controversial than his statements were some of the policies he implemented.

In response to gang related crimes, LAPD established a special unit, Total Resources Against Street Hoodlums, carrying the insensitive acronym of TRASH. Local activists called for the abolition of the unit. LAPD renamed the unit CRASH, substituting the word Community for Total. One initiative of the CRASH program was "Operation Hammer," where Gates expanded gang-sweeps in areas of South Central and East Los Angeles under what could be considered conditions of a military occupation. For example, at its peak in 1988, LAPD apprehended 1,453 people in a single weekend (Klein 1997). An investigative study by the *Los Angeles Times* found that out of more than 300 reported cases of brutality from 1980 to 1991, less than fifty were considered for prosecution (Freed 1991). In summary, key improvements in police-community relations did not accrue in Los Angeles following the election of Tom Bradley due in large part to the lack of political control the mayor held over LAPD and its entrenched bureaucracy. It would take another intersection of policy, problem, and politics for major progress.

In March of 1991, a videotape of four LAPD officers beating a Black man, Rodney King, at a traffic stop was released. These horrifying images were quickly disseminated in national media outlets. With these horrific acts caught on video, many Los Angeles residents believed justice would finally be served to what had come to be perceived as an occupation army. Mayor Bradley and Chief Gates had clashed previously on Gates' controversial comments and policies, but all Bradley could do was ask for Gates' resignation as a weak mayor in this circumstance. Roughly a year later, the four officers were acquitted of charges. As soon as the verdict broke, rioting began. The riots lasted almost a week and claimed sixty-three lives and an unprecedented amount of property damage. Federal troops would be deployed to Los Angeles once again to bring an end to the riots. Following the riots, the Christopher Commission was formed by Mayor Bradley to conduct a comprehensive assessment of LAPD's operations. The main findings of the Commission consisted of the following: a significant amount of officers used excessive force; officers ignored written guidelines of LAPD on the use of deadly force; a management failure to analyze and act on data available to the Department which clearly pointed to issues of excessive force; a need to hold accountable those who stay silent and that many officers were repeat offenders and should have been dismissed. The findings of the Christopher Commission served as a call for reform; however, the LAPD's CRASH unit was exposed for poor practices again in the Rampart scandal just a few years later. The offenses were extensive, with activities ranging from LAPD officers selling stolen drugs, assisting in a bank robbery, and police brutalities. Absent control over the bureaucracy, where would the change come from?

Following the Rampart corruption scandal, the Department of Justice notified the City of Los Angeles that it would be filing a civil suit against LAPD due to a pattern of excessive force, false arrests, and unreasonable searches and seizures. The Department of Justice threatened to sue for complete control of LAPD if the city did not agree to the decree. LAPD was freed of the federal oversight in 2013. Progress made under the decree is evident in commentary provided by the mayor as well as the American Civil Liberties Union. Mayor Antonio Villaraigosa stated immediately after the decree was lifted, "In these last 12 years the Los Angeles Police Department did not just comply with the consent decree, they took it to heart. They used it as a guide to change their culture" (Rubin 2013). Hector Villagra, Executive Director of ACLU of Southern California stated that the consent decree "accomplished its purpose by and large" and that the force was no longer "your father's Los Angeles Police Department" and commended leaders within the city for their role in facilitating change (American Civil Liberties Union of Southern California 2013).

Indeed, the makeup of the force now better reflects its community along the lines of minority representation for rank and file employees as indicated in Figures 3.1 and 3.3. Additionally, following the resignation of Chief Gates, LAPD had its first Black police chief appointed, Willie Williams, who was succeeded by another Black officer, Bernard Parker. However, at the executive level similar strides have not been made along other dimensions. LAPD has yet to have its first Hispanic chief, despite a Hispanic population that accounts for nearly half of the City's total population. Moreover, the first female to become a Commander was not until 1997. LAPD has named female

Deputy Chiefs, but has also yet to appoint a female police chief. These tides could shift as LAPD recently appointed its first Latino female commander in 2015.

ATLANTA

The modern Ku Klux Klan made the city of Atlanta its headquarters as far back as 1915 (Jackson 1967). The Klan dominated the labor unions of the Atlanta Police Department (APD) for the first half of the twentieth century (APD N.D.). In 1948, APD hired its first eight Black police officers. These initial hires were politically motivated as Mayor William Hartsfield sought votes from a newly mobilized Black electorate of 10,000 strong (Myrnick-Harris 2006). Chief Herbert T. Jenkins, who served as Chief from 1947 to 1972, had joined the Klan in 1931—a practice that was all but mandatory within the organization at the time (Jackson 1967). Jenkins publicly stated that he had "no plans for upgrading Negro Patrolmen" (Bayor 1996, p. 179). Moreover, various restrictions were placed on the officers that reinforced their second-class status. For example, Black officers were not permitted to arrest White citizens until 1962. Institutional mechanisms continued to suppress and undermine Black officers. Thus, APD would be in many respects the same organization it had been in previous years during the 1950s.

The backdrop of Auburn Avenue provided an active and engaged community with a common political resolve. In fact, the "unofficial Mayor" of Auburn Avenue, John Wesley Dodds, helped to secure the political promise made by Mayor Hartsfield in hiring the first Black police officers (New Georgia Encyclopedia N.D.). As the Black population of Atlanta increased, community leaders became increasingly politically active over issues of representation. This activism was reflected in collaborations between historically Black colleges, civic-minded organizations, and churches. The 1962 mayoral election offered a potential step forward for the community, as Hartsfield, who had served as mayor since 1942, would not seek reelection. The election pitted staunch segregationist, Lestor Maddox, against Ivan Allen Jr., who supported the civil rights movement. Allen Jr. defeated Maddox by capturing the Black and liberal vote. On his first day in office, Allen Jr. ordered that all "White" and "colored" signs be removed from City Hall and authorized Black police officers to arrest White citizens (New Georgia Encyclopedia N.D). Moreover, Allen Jr. was the only Southern elected official to show support for the proposed public accommodations section of the Civil Rights Act. This local election was key for the City of Atlanta considering the degree of institutional racism in the state of Georgia. The defeated mayoral candidate, Lester Maddox, capitalized on racial tensions following the Civil Rights Act in 1964, and won the 1966 Gubernatorial election after receiving support from the Ku Klux Klan (Short 1999). One can only imagine the degenerative policies Maddox would put in place had he been elected mayor.

Allen Jr. helped facilitate incremental changes during his administration by authorizing the arrest of White citizens by Black officers, assigning Black officers to regular patrols, and desegregating the force (APD N.D.). By 1969, the force was 20% Black; however, more than half of the City's population was Black at this time and this level of representation would hold until the 1973 election (Bayor 1996; Dulaney 1996). In this way, a White dominated police force with minimal integration and little upward mobility for minorities remained the cultural norm within APD. Moreover, police brutality was still a concern and would be front and center in the 1973 mayoral election. Between 1973 and 1974, police killed twenty-three blacks—a figure Black residents believed would decrease with better representation in APD (Jones 1978). This led to the backing of a Black candidate, Maynard Jackson, who ran on a platform of being proactive in his approach to increasing representation within the ranks of APD and other issues of police reform. Jackson's landslide victory in 1973—in which he secured nearly 60% of the vote—gave him the political mandate to act as a strong executive in executing his policy priorities.

Shortly after coming into office, and despite having the cooperation of the city personnel board to pursue this directive, Jackson quickly realized he had little support from the entrenched White leadership of APD. In 1973, when the city personnel board made a recommendation that two-thirds of all new hired officers be Black until the racial imbalance was eliminated, Police Chief Inman publicly declared he would resist any such policies (Headly 1998). Understanding that Inman would be uncooperative moving forward, Jackson formulated a plan to aggressively restructure the APD. Through a modification to the city charter, Jackson organized a Public Safety Bureau to which the APD would be subordinate to—appointing his longtime ally Reginald Eaves as its first Public Safety Commissioner (Jones 1978). In this manner, Jackson circumvented the power of Chief Inman, allowing him and Eaves full discretion of hiring practices for the department. This effectively relegated Inman to little more than a figurehead. Eaves was concerned with increasing Black representation on every administrative level of the department, making the percentage of sergeants, lieutenants, captains, and majors more accurately reflect the diverse population they served. Under Jackson's approval, Eaves demoted more than one hundred White supervisory personnel and handpicked their replacements, thirty of which were African American (Dulaney 1996).

Change under Jackson serves as an example of the inherent difficulties in this transformational process for public organizations. The policies Eaves implemented engendered feelings of "reverse discrimination," increased animosity among White stakeholders internally, and drove public criticism. The media in Atlanta fueled much of the civic outcry surrounding Eaves and the use of racial quotas in hiring (Dulaney 1996). The department now had a host of reverse discrimination lawsuits in addition to the backlog of suits filed by Black officers prior to Jackson's election. The lawsuits grew so great in number that a freeze on hiring and promotion was put in effect from 1976 to 1982. Police operations suffered as a result, response times increased, and the cost of overtime exceeded $25,000 per week by 1978 (Bayor 1996). These conflicting pressures—both internally and externally—to either maintain the status quo or radically change the makeup of the Atlanta Police Department, contributed to the complexity of the change process.

Despite these conflicting pressures, the convergence of social, political, and legal factors provided a unique window of opportunity for Jackson to capitalize on in reforming the police department. In the decade following 1975, the Atlanta Police Department experienced a substantial increase in Black officers, resulting in the city leading the nation in Black representation with 47.2% of its ranks being African American (Lewis 1989). Change was not limited to within the APD. Under Jackson and the city's first affirmative action officer, the percentage of Black public professionals in general increased from 19.2% in 1973 to 42.2% only five years later (Tuck 2001).

The progress made by Jackson would require continuation under another mayor as he faced term limits in 1981. At the urging of Coretta Scott King for him to run for office, Andrew Young began his mayoral campaign. He won the office and continued the APD's transformation and by extension the transformation of the city in general. The city overwhelmingly approved of Young's policies geared toward active representation, reelecting him to a second term in 1985 with an incredible 81% of the vote. By embracing Young and his continued stance on inclusion and representative bureaucracy, the citizens likewise embraced Atlanta's motto of "The City too Busy to Hate." At the conclusion of Maynard Jackson and Andrew Young's twenty-year tenure, Beverly Harvard was appointed as Chief of Police, making her the first Black female to hold that position in a major US city. What was once a culture of exclusion and disorderly service became one heralded for its inclusion and community policing (Kasdon 2006).

However, despite the significant transformation APD made in the latter half of the twentieth century, it is certainly not perfect. Like all police departments, it faces complex challenges and at times fails to meet the expectations of the communities in which it serves. Periodically, situations arise which shed light on the precarious nature of police-minority community relations. These can provide opportunities for organizations to reexamine policies or practices that do not align with a commitment to community-based policing. Three such examples in APD concern the discovery of corruption, the establishment of an aggressive drug fighting squadron, and relations with the LBGT community. In 1996, a major corruption scandal was discovered internally within APD. The scandal involved police officers extorting money from drug-dealers in exchange for protection. Chief Harvard was alerted of the actions of the corrupt practices and promptly notified authorities. Accordingly, APD swiftly established a Corruption Unit in 1996 to prevent further indiscretions.

In response to the city's growing drug problem and related violence, the APD established a drug fighting squadron known as the Red Dog unit—getting its name from the acronym *Running Every Drug Dealer Out of Georgia*. By utilizing aggressive tactics including the use of informants, undercover officers, and large-scale paramilitary style drug seizures and arrests, this unit helped to increase the number of drug indictments in Atlanta by 137% from 1985 to 1989 (United States Department of Justice 1991). However, the aggressive nature of the Red Dogs, and the culture surrounding the unit led many within minority communities to question the "all out" tactics they employed. In 2009, these concerns came to a head when a gay bar was targeted and raided by the unit following reports of public sex acts and overt drug activity routinely occurring in the club. During the raid, patrons reported being taunted, insulted with homophobic slurs, and forced to lie face-down on a floor covered with broken glass for hours without explanation from officers. No illegal activity among the patrons was discovered as a result of this raid, and the manner in which the Red Dog unit and the APD conducted the investigation outraged many in the LBGT community. As a result, a gay-rights group, Lambda Legal, filed a series of federal lawsuits against the APD, which ultimately cost the city millions. In 2011, Mayor Kasim Reed decided to disband the divisive unit and an LBGT liaison unit was established. APD has continued its efforts to establish trust with the LBGT community.

Like all organizations, the present and future for the ADP are informed by its past. With this in mind, the department has been innovative in securing a force that is not only racially representative, but likewise in areas of gender, ethnicity, and sexual orientation. The Department continually looks forward by implementing innovative personnel policies. As such, the department is now heralded as a national leader in community policing; specifically, areas of partnerships, collaboration, outreach, hiring reform, and long-term recruiting efforts grounded in active representation (Kasdon 2006). APD also makes active efforts to attract Latino officers for the growing Latin-American population. These efforts range from mass media advertising in Spanish-language media outlets to fliers in local Latino restaurants.

IMPLICATIONS

American history is filled with trials and tribulations, as well as accomplishments and triumphs. The case studies of the Detroit, Los Angeles, and Atlanta police departments serve as microcosms of American history. Institutional racism requires institutional reform. The evolution of these organizations offer lessons that local police departments can learn from, providing both contemporary and future implications of how to leverage organizational and social change at the delta of politics, policy, and problems.

To focus the subject matter, we distinguished between incremental and accelerated change. In an environment of accelerated change, policy options and choices represent priorities aimed at institutional reform. We showed that institutional reform within police departments could be facilitated by a convergence of social, political, and legal conditions. The mayoral elections of 1973 in Detroit, Los Angeles, and Atlanta represented an historic alignment of these conditions. Each of these mayors faced unique challenges in their local, social, and political environments, revealing lessons learned along the lines of political and judicial control, organizational change, the reconciliation of democratic and administrative imperatives, and self-governance.

The conditions under and the extent to which administrative activities should be subject to political control has been a central theme of American political and administrative theory since its formative years (Wilson 1887; Goodnow 1900). The evolution of the LAPD highlights the perils of asserting a tenet of police professionalism to be independent from political control and acting on that tenet through the support of a city charter in an undemocratic manner. The intervention by Maynard Jackson in modifying Atlanta's charter represents the ability of a strong mayor to realize political control over an entrenched bureaucracy. The initiation of the consent decree on behalf of the City of Detroit shows that when the powers of a strong mayor do not necessarily prevail over an entrenched bureaucracy, judicial control can be an effective supplement to political control to realize more active representation. Finally, that the Department of Justice was prepared to seize control over LAPD if the city did not agree to the most recent consent decree signals a failure to self-govern.

Internal resistance to organizational transformation illustrates the difficulty of the change process. Actions taken by leaders to overcome it represent transformational leadership. The legal environment when these mayors took office required proactive personnel policies for accelerated change. The ruling in *Griggs v. Duke Power Company* (1971) established disparate impact, allowing for the modification of testing procedures, which disproportionately screened out Black applicants. The extension of Title VII in 1972 to state and local governments prohibited discriminatory employment practices.

Although these represented important developments and supported positive incremental change, they did not set precedent for preferential hiring which was needed to reform these institutions. Accordingly, the strong mayors of Detroit and Atlanta implemented affirmative action programs without precedent yet firmly established in the courts and soon found themselves with a host of "reverse discrimination" lawsuits. The ruling in *United Steelworkers of America v. Weber* (1979) allowed for voluntary affirmative action plans by a private employer. However, it was not settled that this would guide the statutory review of affirmative action undertaken by a public employer until 1987 (Kellough 2006). In this sense, Mayor Coleman Young of Detroit and Mayor Maynard Jackson of Atlanta could be commended for being proactive and leveraging the intersection of politics, policy, and problem to reform institutions when provided this window of opportunity and political runway. Of course, the same cannot be said of Los Angeles, where hiring reforms were realized through an internal lawsuit, which led to a consent decree.

The premise of this chapter is that organizational change within police departments cannot be properly understood apart from an historical analysis of their social and political environments. It is at this point that we feel confident in stating that an organizational or departmental centric focus misses the relevant unit of analysis, unnecessarily shrinks the scope of debate, and, more generally, lacks descriptive validity. We have connected institutional reform to several factors which are external to police departments. These linkages demonstrate that change is an intersection of social, political, legal, and managerial imperatives and not a one-way street. To be clear, this is not to discount the efforts of internal change agents, just to offer a different framework that places a premium on the external environment. Moreover, a focus on change within a department may emphasize bureaucratic innovation at the expense of social innovation, potentially confusing means for ends. For example, LAPD has been lauded for several technical innovations, such as the SWAT team, ECCCS and data-driven techniques. However, these are means to a larger democratic end: justice for all. To praise LAPD, or other departments for that matter, for these technical innovations while they fail to achieve their democratic purposes amounts to a triumph of technique over purpose (Sayre 1948).

CONCLUSION

Local police departments operate within an open-system environment and seek to manage and function based upon their past, present, and future. Identifying primary features of these systems and how they evolve in response to each other is essential in analyzing organizational change. Occasionally, police departments make significant transformations, revealing important considerations for the study of organizational change. To focus the subject matter, we distinguished between incremental and accelerated change. Our cases were selected to understand how the intersection of politics, policy, and problem facilitated accelerated change in reforming institutions in the face of racial and societal unrest. Political control, most specifically discretion over personnel policies, was argued to be a necessary condition for institutional reform. This allowed for a window of opportunity for leaders to act on a political mandate in the face of bureaucratic and legal resistance. Where local political control was insufficient, federal judicial control served as an effective supplement. The case studies demonstrate that organizational change for police departments cannot be understood apart from an historical analysis of their social, political, and legal environments. These findings align with various studies on representative bureaucracy and the reduction of the unequal treatment of minority constituents. The lessons learned from these cases offer important implications for effective leadership, administration, and management; both within police departments as well as across the communities they serve, as new challenges unfold for police departments along other lines of diversity. These cases, in the context of police policies and practices, show that it is possible for public organizations to transform from a position of *"power over"* to a platform of shared power or *"power with"* (Follett 1918). At the intersection of politics, policy, and problems, organizational and social change is possible given these conditions.

NOTE

1. These figures are calculated using Census data for population composition. For officer representation relating to the "pre-intervention" period, see references within each case study (Love, 1981; Cannon, 1999; Bayor, 1996; Dulaney, 1996). Figures for 1990 and 2000 come from a report issued in 2002 from the justice department, "Police Departments in Large Cities, 1990—2000." This data can be found at https://www.bjs.gov/content/pub/pdf/pdlc00.pdf. Data for officer representation from 2013 was sourced from a 2015 special report issued by *Governing*, "Diversity on the Force: Where Police Don't Mirror Communities." *Governing*'s data is itself sourced from Law Enforcement Management and Administrative Statistics, which is a survey conducted by the Bureau of Justice Statistics.

REFERENCES

Aberbach, Joel D., and Bert A. Rockman. *In the Web of Politics: Three Decades of the US Federal Executive*. Brookings Institution Press, 2001.

American Civil Liberties Union of Southern California. 2013. "ACLU/SC's Statement on the end of the LAPD's Consent Decree." Accessed July 11, 2017: https://www.aclusocal.org/en/news/acluscs-statement-end-lapds-consent-decree

Anderson, Elijah. "The white space." *Sociology of Race and Ethnicity* 1, no. 1 (2015): 10–21.

Archbold, Carol A. *Policing: A text/reader*. Thousand Oaks, CA: Sage Publishers.

Atlanta Police Department. N.D. History of the APD. Accessed April 15, 2015: http://www.atlantapd.org/about-apd/apd-history.

Baldas, Tresa. 2016. "Detroit police finally rid of federal oversight." *Detroit Free Press,* March 31. Accessed July 10, 2017: http://www.freep.com/story/news/local/michigan/detroit/2016/03/31/detroit-police-finally-rid-federal-oversight/82491776/

Bass, Sandra. "Policing space, policing race: Social control imperatives and police discretionary decisions." *Social Justice* 28, no. 1 83 (2001): 156–176.

Bates, Beth Tompkins. *The Making of Black Detroit in the Age of Henry Ford*. University of North Carolina Press, 2012.

Bayor, Ronald H. *Race and the Shaping of Twentieth-Century Atlanta*. University of North Carolina Press, 2000.

Berlin, Ira. *Slaves Without Masters: The Free Negro in the Antebellum South*. Pantheon, 1975.

Bonner, Kideste Mariam Wilder. "Race, space, and being policed: A qualitative analysis of residents' experiences with southern patrols." *Race and Justice* 4, no. 2 (2014): 124–151.

Boyles, Andrea S. *Race, Place, and Suburban Policing: Too Close for Comfort*. Universtiy of California Press, 2015.

Bradbury, Mark, and J. Edward Kellough. "Representative bureaucracy: Assessing the evidence on active representation." *The American Review of Public Administration* 41, no. 2 (2011): 157–167.

Burns, Tom E., and George Macpherson Stalker. *The Management of Innovation*. (1961). New York, NY: Oxford University Press.

Cannon, Lou. *Official Negligence: How Rodney King and the Riots Changed Los Angeles and the LAPD*. Basic Books, 1999.

Capeci, Dominic J., and Martha Wilkerson. "The Detroit rioters of 1943: A reinterpretation." *The Michigan Historical Review* (1990): 49–72.

Close, Billy R., and Patrick L. Mason. "After the traffic stops: Officer characteristics and enforcement actions." *Topics in Economic Analysis & Policy* 6, no. 1 (2006). pp. 1–41.

Close, Billy R., and Patrick Leon Mason. "Searching for efficient enforcement: Officer characteristics and racially biased policing." *Review of Law & Economics* 3, no. 2 (2007): 263–321.

Cordner, G. "Police culture: Individual and organizational differences in police officer perspectives." *Policing: An International Journal of Police Strategies & Management* 40, no. 1 (2017):11–25.

Darden, Joe T., and Richard W. Thomas. *Detroit: Race Riots, Racial Conflicts, and Efforts to Bridge the Racial Divide*. MSU Press, 2013.

Del Castillo, Richard Griswold. "The Los Angeles" zoot suit riots" revisited: Mexican and Latin American perspectives." *Mexican Studies/Estudios Mexicanos* 16, no. 2 (2000): 367–391.

Detroit Historical Society. N.D. "The Race Riot of 1943." Accessed July 10, 2017. https://detroithistorical.org/learn/encyclopedia-of-detroit/race-riot-1943

Dulaney, W. Marvin. *Black police in America.* Bloomington, Indiana: Indiana University Press, 1996.

Escobar, Edward J. "Bloody Christmas and the irony of police professionalism: The Los Angeles Police Department, Mexican Americans, and police reform in the 1950s." *Pacific Historical Review* 72, no. 2 (2003): 171–199.

Fine, Sidney. *Violence in the Model City: The Cavanagh Administration, Race Relations, and the Detroit Riot of 1967.* East Lansing, Michigan: Michigan State University Press, 2007.

Follett, Mary Parker. *The New State: Group Organization the Solution of Popular Government.* University Park, PA: Penn State Press, 1918.

Freed, David. 1991. "Police Brutality Claims Are Rarely Prosecuted." *Los Angeles Times,* June 7. Accessed July 10, 2017: http://articles.latimes.com/1991-07-07/news/mn-3054_1_police-brutality

Goodnow, Frank. *Politics and Administration.* New York, NY: The Macmillan Company.

Greiner, Larry E. *Patterns of Organization Change.* Brighton Watertown, MA: Harvard Business Review, 1967.

Hassell, Kimberly D., Jihong "Solomon" Zhao, and Edward R. Maguire. "Structural arrangements in large municipal police organizations: Revisiting Wilson's theory of local political culture." *Policing: An International Journal of Police Strategies & Management* 26, no. 2 (2003): 231–250.

Hawkins, Homer, and Richard Thomas. 1991. "White policing of black populations: A history of race and social control in America." In *Out of Order? Policing Black People,* edited by E. Cashmore and E. McLaughlin: Routledge, 1991.

Headley, Bernard D. *The Atlanta Youth Murders and the Politics of Race.* Carbondale, IL: SIU Press, 1998.

Hinton, Elizabeth. *From the War on Poverty to the War on Crime.* Cambridge, MA: Harvard University Press, 2016.

Holli, Melvin G. *The American Mayor: The Best and the Worst Big-City Leaders.* University Park, PA: Penn State Press, 1999.

Hopkins, Daniel J., and Katherine T. McCabe. "After it's too late: estimating the policy impacts of black mayoralties in US Cities." *American Politics Research* 40, no. 4 (2012): 665–700.

Jackson, Kenneth T. *The Ku Klux Klan in the City, 1915—1930.* Vol. 123. Lanham, MD: Rowman & Littlefield, 1967.

Jones, Mack H. "Black political empowerment in Atlanta: Myth and reality." *The ANNALS of the American Academy of Political and Social Science* 439, no. 1 (1978): 90–117.

Kasdon. Alexa. 2006. "Increasing Diversity in Police Departments: Strategies and Tools for Human Rights Commissions and Others." Presented at Kennedy School of Government's Executive Session on Human Rights Commissions and Criminal Justice John F. Kennedy School of Government, Harvard University.

Katz, Daniel, and Robert Kahn. "Open systems theory." *Readings on Organization Theory: Open-Systems Approaches* (1971): 13–32.

Kellough, J. Edward. *Understanding Affirmative Action: Politics, Discrimination, and the Search for Justice.* Washington, DC: Georgetown University Press, 2006.

Kingdon, John W. "The policy window, and joining the streams." *Agendas, Alternatives, and Public Policies* (1995): 172–189.

Klein, Malcolm W. *The American Street Gang: Its Nature, Prevalence, and Control.* Oxford University Press, 1997.

Kotter, John P. "Leading change: Why transformation efforts fail." Harvard Business Review, Volume March-April 1995, (1995): 59–67.

Lasley, James. 2012. *Los Angeles Police Department Meltdown: The Fall of the Professional-Reform Model of Policing.* Boca Raton, Florida: CRC Press.

Lewis, William G. "Toward representative bureaucracy: Blacks in city police organizations, 1975—1985." *Public Administration Review* (1989), 49: 257–268.

Lindblom, Charles E. *The Science of "Muddling Through."* Volume 12, No. 2. *Public administration review* (1959): 12(2), 79–88.

Love, Nancy. "Detroit Police Officers' Association v. Young: The Operational Needs Justification for Affirmative Action in the Context of Public Employment." *Black Law Journal* 7 (1981): 200.

Marini, Margaret Mooney, and Burton Singer. "Causality in the social sciences." *Sociological methodology* 18 (1988): 347–409.

Mosher, Frederick C. *Democracy and the public service.* New York, NY: Oxford University Press, 1968.

Mosher, Frederick C. *Democracy and the public service.* New York, NY: Oxford University Press, 1982.

Myrnick-Harris, Clarissa. 2006. "Atlanta in the Civil Rights Movement: Part Two." *Perspectives on History,* Accessed April 15, 2015. https://www.historians.org/annual-meeting/past-meetings/supplement-to-the-121st-annual-meeting/atlanta-in-the-civil-rights-movement-part-two

New Georgia Encyclopedia. 2005. "John Wesley Dodds." Accessed July 15, 2017: http://www.georgiaencyclopedia.org/articles/history-archaeology/john-wesley-dobbs-1882-1961

New Georgia Encyclopedia. 2004. "Ivan Allen Jr."Accessed July15, 2017: http://www.georgiaencyclopedia.org/articles/government-politics/ivan-allen-jr-1911-2003

Nicholson-Crotty, Sean, and Laurence J. O'Toole Jr. "Public management and organizational performance: The case of law enforcement agencies." *Journal of Public Administration Research and Theory* 14, no. 1 (2004): 1–18.

Ostrom, Vincent. *The Intellectual Crisis in American Public Administration:* Tuscaloosa, Alabama: University of Alabama Press, 1974.

Pagán, Eduardo Obregón. *Murder at the Sleepy Lagoon: Zoot Suits, Race, and Riot in Wartime LA.* Chapel Hill, North Carolina: University of North Carolina Press, 2003.

Pitkin, Hanna Fenichel. *The Concept of Representation.* University of California Press, 1967.

Rainey, Glenn W., and Hal G. Rainey. "Breaching the hierarchical imperative: The modularization of the social security claims process." *Bureaucratic and Governmental Reform* (1986): 171–96.

Rainey, Hal G. *Understanding and Managing Public Organizations.* Hoboken, New Jersey: John Wiley &Sons, 2014.

Reichel, Philip L. "Southern slave patrols as a transitional police type." *American Journal of Police* 7 (1988): 51.

Reith, Charles. *A short history of the British police.* New York, NY: Oxford University Press, 1948.

Rhine, Barbara. "Kill or Be Killed: Use of Deadly Force in the Riot Situation." *California Law Review* 56 (1968): 829.

Rubin, Joel. 2013. "Federal judge lifts LAPD consent decree." *Los Angeles Times,* May 16. Accessed July 10, 2017: http://articles.latimes.com/2013/may/16/local/la-me-lapd-consent-decree-20130517

Sayre, Wallace S. "The triumph of techniques over purpose." (1948): 134–137.

Short, Bob. *Everything is Pickrick: The Life of Lester Maddox.* Macon, Georgia: Mercer University Press, 1999.

Steven Tuck. *Beyond Atlanta: The Struggle for Racial Equality in Georgia, 1940—1980.* Athens, GA: University of Georgia Press, 2001.

Stivers, Camilla. *Gender images in public administration: Legitimacy and the administrative state.* Thousand Oaks, California: Sage Publications, 2002.

The Kerner Commission. Report of the National Advisory Commission on Civil Disorders. 1968.

The President's Task Force on 21st Century Policing. Final Report, 2015. The United States Department of Justice. 2015.

Thompson, Heather Ann. *Whose Detroit?: Politics, labor, and race in a modern American city.* Ithaca, New York: Cornell University Press, 2004.

Thurman, Quint, Jihong Zhao, and Andrew L. Giacomazzi. *Community policing in a community era: An introduction and exploration.* Los Angeles, CA: Roxbury Publishing Company, 2001.

United States Department of Justice. 2003. "Justice Department Files Consent Decrees Concluding Investigation of Detroit Police Department." Accessed July 10, 2017. https://www.justice.gov/archive/opa/pr/2003/June/03_crt_352.htm

United States Department of Justice. GGD-91—40. The War on Drugs. 1991.

Viehe, Fred W. "The Recall of Mayor Frank L. Shaw: A Revision." *California History* 59, no. 4 (1980): 290–305.

Websdale, Neil. *Policing the Poor: From Slave Plantation to Public Housing.* Lebanon, New Hampshire: Upne, 2001.

Wildavsky, Aaron B. *Politics of the Budgetary Process.* Boston, MA: Little Brown (1964).

Williams, B.N., Kang, S.C. and Johnson, J. (Co)-Contamination as the Dark Side of Co-Production: Public value failures in co-production processes. *Public Management Review* 18, no. 5 (2016):692–717.

Williams, Brian N. *Citizen Perspectives on Community Policing: A Case Study in Athens, Georgia.* Albany, NY: SUNY Press, 1998.

Williams, Candice. 2017. "Craig to LBGT community: 'Detroit has got your back,'" *The Detroit News*, June 6th.

Willis, James J., Stephen D. Mastrofski, and David Weisburd. "Making sense of COMPSTAT: A theory-based analysis of organizational change in three police departments." *Law & Society Review* 41, no. 1 (2007): 147–188.

Wilson, James Q. 1998. "The Closing of the American City." *New Republic,* May 1998.

Wilson, Woodrow. "The study of administration." *Political Science Quarterly* 2, no. 2 (1887): 197–222.

Zhao, J., Lovrich, N.P. and Robinson, T.H. "Community policing: is it changing the basic functions of policing?: Findings from a longitudinal study of 200+ municipal police agencies." *Journal of Criminal Justice* 29, no. 5 (2001):365–377.

Zhao, Jihong. *Why Police Organizations Change: A Study of Community-Oriented Policing*. Washington, DC: Police Executive Research Forum, 1996.

Chapter 4

Policy Feedback

Government Skepticism Trickling from Immigration to Matters of Health

Vanessa Cruz Nichols, Alana M. W. LeBrón, and Francisco I. Pedraza

How might the dynamics of one bureaucracy shape one's future engagement and communications with the government outside that bureaucracy? Since 2008, the United States has deployed two major bureaucratic expansions. Although designed to curb costs and improve access to and quality of health care, the largest health care policy initiative in half a century, the Patient Protection and Affordable Care Act of 2010 (ACA) is projected to cost over $1 trillion through 2025 (Congressional Budget Office 2015). Also costly to individuals, families, and communities, the American criminal justice system is increasingly central to strategies to identify, detain, and "remove all removable aliens" living in the United States (US Department of Homeland Security 2003). Spending on immigration enforcement reached $17.9 billion in 2012 (in 2012 dollars), surpassing the total combined expenditures for all other federal law enforcement operations (Meissner et al. 2013). Increased funding supports operations like the Secure Communities program (SComm), a program that exemplifies the broader shift toward interior immigration enforcement strategies that rely on collaborations between local police and immigration enforcement agencies, as well as an emphasis on identifying and removing noncitizens classified as high-priority criminals (Meissner et al. 2013).

The growing US Latino population is an important stakeholder in immigration and health care bureaucratic expansions. The ACA was introduced at a point when the US faced the largest number of uninsured Americans in history—18 percent in 2010 (Kaiser Family Foundation 2013). As one in three of the nonelderly uninsured, Latinos represent a disproportionate share of premium-lowering healthy persons in the population (Kaiser Family Foundation 2013), and a 96 percent majority of deportations from the US since 2010 (Transactional Records Access Clearinghouse (TRAC) 2014). Latinos are policy targets deeply implicated in, and simultaneously valued and marginalized by, the major US health care and immigration policy innovations of the twenty-first century.

While he was conducting Latino-targeted ACA outreach initiatives to bolster health insurance enrollment, then-President Obama addressed growing criticism from Latinos over deportations. A major concern that Latino community leaders underscore is the fear that personal information required to enroll in health insurance programs through new governmental health insurance marketplaces could be shared with immigration officials, exposing the unauthorized status of enrollees or undocumented household members (Easley 2014). In a March 2014 interview on the Spanish language cable network Univision, former President Obama reassured Latinos that immigration officials could not use personal information that consumers provide when signing up for health insurance through the online marketplace. As evidence, he cited executive policy issued through the US Bureau of Immigration and Customs Enforcement (2013) (ICE). However, one observer remarked: "[Latino families] hear [the president's] assurance, but because of the level of deportations that have happened, there's a lot of families that don't know whether they can trust that assurance" (Easley 2014).

This anecdote captures the ways in which salient considerations about one arm of government can influence judgments about another arm of government. It suggests that Latinos drew lessons from immigration enforcement experiences, which informed their trust in government-sponsored efforts to court potential health insurance enrollees. We ask whether exposure to state powers engaged in expulsions undermines trust in welfare state efforts to communicate with citizens? How widespread is distrust of governmental outreach with respect to matters of health? To what extent is distrust concentrated among a specific group and driven by a specific aspect of interactions with the state?

Answers to these questions may reveal how policy implementation in one domain affects implementation in another. The scope of this paper does not involve the prevalence of those who became insured through the health insurance marketplaces that emerged under the ACA. Instead, we examine the extent to which an immigration enforcement program with the broadest territorial coverage in US history, SComm, compromises trust in government communication. We contend that the state's deployment of the power of expulsion conveys lessons about the trustworthiness of the government. Because such lessons vary by *where* and for *whom* the deployment of threat is concentrated, distinct cognitive associations about state trustworthiness vary across different groups and locations.

Below we discuss the literature on trust in government, and how policy teaches ordinary people lessons that feed back into politics. Next, we introduce hypotheses that link immigration enforcement to trust in government communications. Then, we analyze data from the 2011 Health Information National Trends Survey (HINTS), to compare individual-level trust in health information from the government among a national sample of Latinos, Blacks, Asians, and Whites. We find that Latinos living in locales with greater immigration enforcement report less trust in health information from the government. However, the judgments of non-Latinos are unrelated to immigration enforcement. We discuss the implications for immigration and health care policy, as well as for political engagement, political equality, and efficiency in governance.

POLICY FEEDBACK AND
DOMAIN-SPECIFIC TRUST IN GOVERNMENT

There is growing appreciation in mass politics research that as policy reconfigures who gets what, this reconfiguration impacts the political system and future outputs from the system (Mettler and Soss 2004; Pierson 1993). That is, public investments in some citizens, but not others, redistributes money and time, thus changing the constituent pressures that influence politicians as they craft future policy (Campbell 2002; Mettler 2005). Policy also feeds back into policy processes by shifting "patterns of social understandings" (Pierson 2004, 36). As Schneider and Ingram (1993, 340) explain, "[p]olicy teaches lessons about the type of groups people belong to, what they deserve from the government, and what is expected of them." What Soss (1999, 363) terms the "educative effects" of policy can be positive, as seen with GI Bill benefits that teach veterans they are worthy citizens whose civic contributions are appreciated (Mettler 2005). They can also be negative, such as lessons from welfare participation restrictions that create more reticent citizens (Schneider and Ingram 1993; Soss 1999).

The logic of policy feedback processes inspires research on the individual attitudinal and behavioral consequences of contact with the law enforcement arms of the state. For instance, Weaver and Lerman (2010) find that the severity of encounters with the criminal justice system reduces trust in government. Similarly, Rocha, Knoll, and Wrinkle (2015) find evidence that deportations are linked to lower levels of trust in government, particularly among Latinos. These studies on individual-level trust in government complement and corroborate two key insights from previous policy feedback research: (1) a person's experiences with a particular policy or agency of the state can "spill over" to define their general views of government; and (2) a negative experience with the state lowers political participation among lower-income citizens. These two policy feedback insights are critical because they suggest, as Schattschneider (1960) originally argued and Schlozman et al. (2012) later echoed, that policy can reinforce inequalities by removing some voices from the public chorus that guides policymaking and holds elected officials accountable.

We extend these insights about trust in government by heeding the call of Levi and Stoker (2000, 499) "to think of political trust as domain-specific— one trusts a given political actor with respect to some problems, policies or activities but not others." A domain-specific analysis of individual-level trust in government is an important addition to the literature because scholars increasingly agree that trust is defined in such terms at this level. Trust is a relational, contingent, and domain-specific judgment about the trustworthiness of another (Braithwaite and Levi 1998; Levi and Stoker 2000). For this reason, we are motivated to ask whether, in the minds of the general public, immigration enforcement renders the government less trustworthy in seemingly unrelated outreach efforts, like when it dispenses health information to the public. Our analysis complements the findings reported in existing studies on "general" trust by drawing out more specific implications for governance associated with a loss in trust for a particular facet of government.

The policy feedback approach does acknowledge the importance of the "relational" and "contingent" components of trust in government, but it does so using slightly different language. Whereas Braithwaite and Levi (1998) emphasize that vulnerability to harm from state behavior is a premise on which citizen trust may be betrayed, the policy feedback framework theorizes that people are both vulnerable to harm and susceptible to social promotion, contingent on public policy. For mass publics, the consequence of public policy is that it constructs and positions social groups in distinct relations to the state, both in terms of their political power, as well as whether they are viewed favorably or unfavorably in society (Campbell 2003; Schneider and Ingram 1993). The relational and contingent aspects of trust in government are therefore addressed in the policy feedback framework by underscoring that feedback processes (as it pertains to mass publics) are about *whom* among the broader public is exposed to *which* public policy, *how* that exposure occurs, and with *what* consequence to attitudes and behavior.

A crucial point in the policy feedback approach is that policy lessons are internalized by members of the target population. Internalizing policy lessons means that cognitive associations crafted in the process of forming judgments are called to mind when forming subsequent evaluations, thus generating a cumulative assessment about the person or institution in question. Negative or positive cognitive associations about the government can facilitate aversion or attraction to the government. While Hardin (1998) and Levi and Stoker (2000) rely on people's knowledge and experience with the government and bureaucracies to assess government trustworthiness, policy feedback scholars refer to this as "educative effects."

Here, we apply these insights to the overlap between immigration and health care policy domains. Endogenous to the social construction of immigrant and criminal stereotypes are welfare stereotypes that are rooted in social insurance programs with citizenship-based restrictions (i.e., Temporary Assistance for Needy Families, State Children's Health Insurance Program, and ACA-subsidized health insurance coverage) (Fox 2012; Jacobson 2008). Welfare program restrictions mirror the exclusionary design found in policies like e-Verify that requires checking the immigration status of employees, and are reinforced by immigration enforcement programs like SComm that aim to identify and detain undocumented immigrants who are in a local jail. Because undocumented status cannot be identified by race or other ascriptive trait, the charge for bureaucrats to be vigilant of undocumented immigrants raises the specter of racial profiling, a strategy whereby bureaucrats use racial and ethnic stereotypes as heuristics to orient their scrutiny (Golash-Boza 2012). From the perspective of persons who are most likely to be profiled, such policies and bureaucratic practices compromise the trustworthiness of the state and create aversive mental associations that are more amenable for forming judgments about other points of contact with the state.

Because 96 percent of US deportations involve immigrants from Latin American countries, and because a majority of Latinos believe their group absorbs the brunt of restrictive immigration policies (Manzano 2011; Merolla et al. 2012), we anticipate that the government as an attitude object is aversive in the minds of Latinos, particularly Latino immigrants. What bridges this aversion specifically to health policy is public policy stipulating immigration-based exclusion to various welfare state programs.[1] By contrast, and serving as comparison groups, we expect that the cognitive bridges that non-Latinos hold between the state as immigration law enforcer and provider of health information are not aversive. Because the source of mistrust is domain specific, we should not see that immigration enforcement structures trust in nongovernmental sources of health information or those associated with a potential "paper" trail with the government (Fox 2012).

We hypothesize that judgments about the government's enforcement arms condition judgments about the government as a welfare state. Specifically, we hypothesize that local levels of increased immigration enforcement will be associated with (1) reduced trust in government as a source of health information for Latinos, and (2) will be unrelated to trust in government as a source of health information for Whites, Blacks, and Asians. To further test our theoretical claim, we also hypothesize that (3) among Latinos, local levels of immigration enforcement are unrelated to trust in sources of health information that protect one's privacy.

DATA, DESIGN, AND METHODS

We evaluate the hypotheses outlined above using the 2011 Health Information National Trends Survey (HINTS), which is administered by the National Cancer Institute and provides individual-level data on the health status, behaviors, and health communication among a nationally representative sample of US adults. This paper analyzes data from Cycle 1 of the HINTS 4 data collection process, which included queries about trust in different sources of health information. Cycle 1 (n=3,959) was conducted from October 2011 through February 2012. The stratified sample of households in the HINTS dataset was selected without cluster sampling. The strata included those in a low minority, high minority, or Central Appalachia strata. We use person-level weights for the full sample and the jackknife method to reflect the features of the sample design. Thus, we do not expect there to be a correlation with the counties and our outcomes of interest because the HINTS sample is not based on a clustered sample.[2]

Surveys with sizeable subsamples of racial and ethnic minority groups are rare; HINTS allows us to extend Rocha et al. (2015) and Weaver and Lerman (2010) with analyses that include 461 Latino respondents, 2,431 White respondents, 576 non-Latino Black respondents, 168 Asian respondents, and 323 individuals from other ethnic/racial groups.[3] HINTS administers the survey in English and Spanish, a feature that is critical to inferences to the broader Latino population. The premise of our research design and analysis is that Latinos, Blacks, Whites, and Asians occupy structurally distinct locations in the US racial hierarchy (Masuoka and Junn 2014). If disparate relations exist between the state and social groups, then different judgments about the state should form across groups. Specifically, if trust as a relational experience with the state is structured by different experiences with coercive arms of the state, then the internalization of policy lessons as depicted in models of policy feedback should produce different relationships between immigration enforcement and trust in government as a source of health information. We would know that our theoretical expectations are wrong if we find that among Blacks, Asians, or Whites, distrust in health information from the government also declines with greater immigration enforcement. To test whether Latinos are skeptical generally, we also assess the relationship between immigration enforcement levels and Latinos evaluations of other sources of health information.

We gauge domain-specific *trust in government* with the following measure: "In general, how much do you trust information about health or medical topics from governmental health agencies?" Although the four available responses range from "a lot" to "not at all," modeling the responses as an ordinal outcome, and specifically the Brant test of parallel regression assumption, shows that a single equation does not adequately capture the relationship between immigration enforcement and trust in the government as a source of health information. In the proceeding analyses we use logistic regression to model an indicator that collapses the responses into a dichotomous outcome, coded 1 if the respondent trusts government health information "a lot" or "some," and 0 otherwise. This strategy also addresses micronumerosity challenges, as the number of racial/ethnic minorities in the data limit the power of statistical analysis to detect relationships that are discernable from the null. The unweighted distribution of our domain-specific indicator of trust in government agencies as a source of health information is 73 percent among Latinos, 72 percent among Whites, 76 percent among Blacks, and 82 percent among Asians. Given the dichotomous nature of our main outcome variable, we use logit model estimations in our analyses. Aside from trust in health information from government agencies, HINTS respondents were queried about trust in health information obtained from sources from the Internet, charity organizations, physicians, family members, religious leaders, radio, magazines, and television. These outcomes of interest were coded in the same dichotomous nature as trust in government agencies.

One key advantage of HINTS is that it includes a measure of self-reported anxiety. Psychological mechanisms like fear and anxiety are key causal links between social context and behavioral response (Beckjord et al. 2008; Marcus et al. 2000; Pantoja and Segura 2003). Fear more often spurs cautious thought processing and careful consideration of one's behavioral strategies (Brader 2006; Marcus et al. 2000), whereas anxiety and anger tend to motivate individual or collective action when encountering the stressor (Marcus et al. 2000; Lerner and Keltner 2001). We rely on measures of worry and anxiety as proxies of perceived threat, thus facilitating the link between the deportation climate in one's county and different governmental agencies (or points of contact with the state).[4] A second advantage of HINTS is that it includes indicators of whether an individual has health insurance, and whether that insurance is provided through an employer or through a public agency (i.e., Medicaid or Medicare). People whose health care needs are covered by Medicaid or Medicare may draw on that experience, and the bureaucratic experiences associated with it, to assess the trustworthiness of health information from the government. By accounting for health insurance status and its source, we parse judgments that are formulated through participation in these government health care-related programs from assessments that health information from the government is worthy of trust (Campbell 2003; Moynihan and Herd 2010).

The HINTS includes measures of demographic characteristics relevant to perceptions of trustworthy sources of information, including gender, nativity, socioeconomic status, relationship status, and language proficiency (Clayman et al. 2010; Manierre 2015; Nguyen and Bellamy 2006; Zarcadoolas et al. 2005). For summary statistics of these important demographic variables and additional individual-level characteristics, refer to Table 4.1. Age is a continuous variable (range: 18 to 99 years). Gender (female=1), nativity (US-born=1), and marital status (married=1) are dichotomous indicators. We measure English language proficiency using respondents' self-reported comfort with speaking English, recoded to range ordinally from 0 to 1, with 0 representing feeling "completely comfortable" and 1 representing feeling "not at all" comfortable speaking English, leaving middle categories that are assigned equidistant values in between. Level of education was recorded from 0 to 1, with 1 representing postgraduate education and 0 representing less than eight years of schooling, assigning equidistant values in between to five additional education categories.

Measuring Immigration Enforcement

We need a measure of immigration enforcement that corresponds to the county an individual lives in. We meet this need using three metrics drawn from archival data collected between 2008 and 2011 by Immigration and Customs Enforcement (ICE) regarding SComm program enforcement practices: the count of fingerprint submissions that local officials send to ICE, the number of individuals whose fingerprints match federal lists of persons subject to further scrutiny, and the number of individuals removed or deported.[5] We combine these indicators into a composite score calculated as:

$$\text{Immigration Enforcement} = 1 + \left[\frac{\text{Low Priority Removals}}{\text{Total Removals}} * \log\left(\frac{\text{Matches / Submits}}{\text{PercentForeignBorn}} \right) \right]$$

where submissions, matches, and removals are cumulative counts tallied since the date of SComm activation in a county. The county-level distribution of this measure across the United States is shown in Figure 4.1, along with the distribution of exposure to SComm immigration enforcement among HINTS respondents.

The first component measures the proportion of "low-priority" removals to total removals, an indicator proposed by Pedroza (2013) to capture the degree of discretion in deportation powers exercised by federal authorities. Sorting counties along a range from universal enforcement to focused enforcement on "high-priority" removals, we tap the intensity with which an aversive policy lesson is conveyed to a broader public. A higher ratio indicates greater cause to perceive trust in government as breached, which we anticipate will be the understanding for Latinos but not for other groups. Elsewhere, Rocha

Table 4.1 Summary Statistics

	Total Sample (n=4,151)			Latino (n=461)			White (n=2,843)			Black (n=657)			Asian (n=190)		
	N	*Mean*	*SD*	*N*	*Mean*	*SD*	*N*	*Mean*	*SD*	*N*	*Mean*	*SD*	*N*	*Mean*	*SD*
Immigration enforcement	2565	0.14	0.4		0.18	0.36		0.15	0.42		0.04	0.4		0.18	0.31
Age in years	3891	53.95	16.55		48.28	15.96		55.16	16.54		52.85	15.68		47.37	14.96
Self-rated worry	3863	0.19	0.3		0.21	0.32		0.17	0.28		0.24	0.34		0.18	0.3
Education	3874	0.62	0.28		0.51	0.31		0.66	0.26		0.56	0.27		0.73	0.27
English proficiency	3804	0.05	0.17		0.21	0.31		0.01	0.07		0.04	0.13		0.24	0.29
Dichotomous Variables	*N*	*Percent*		*N*	*Percent*		*N*	*Percent*		*N*	*Percent*		*N*	*Percent*	
Married	3,848	52.3		452	53.5		2,798	57.4		647	30.3		188	64.9	
Medicare/ Medicaid	3,856	14.8		444	25.0		2,776	10.6		636	27.4		189	10.1	
Employer health insurance	3,928	75.8		454	56.6		2,827	81.1		651	60.7		190	81.1	
Trust government health info	3,776	72.1		433	73.2		2,737	71.4		607	76.6		180	81.1	
US-born	3,912	86.3		461	55.1		2841	91.6		654	89.1		190	24.7	
Female	3,856	59.8		445	60.5		2,789	58.2		631	67.5		185	55.7	

Sources. 2011 Health Information National Trends Survey, n=4,151; immigration enforcement metrics from Department of Homeland Security, Bureau of Immigration and Customs Enforcement Secure Communities interoperability reports (2008–2011), www.ice.gov.

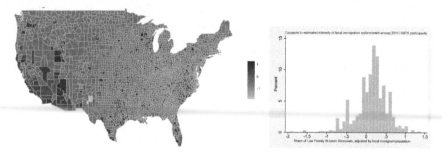

Figure 4.1   Secure Communities Enforcement 2011, Exposure among HINTS 4, Cycle 1 Participants. *Source.* Authors' constructed measure using Secure Communities metrics available at www.ice.gov, and a Department of Homeland Security formula to detect "anomalous jurisdictions."

et al. (2015) argue and find that deporting people who are classified as "low-priority," in particular, reduces general trust in the government.[6]

The second component of the enforcement measure taps the degree of local police contribution to SComm, operationalized here with a formula that the Department of Homeland Security uses to monitor and "detect anomalous jurisdictions" (Department of Homeland Security 2011, 2). The Department of Homeland Security uses the "foreign-born arrestee comparison" to identify "jurisdictions where aliens appear to constitute a significantly greater fraction of the arrested population than they do of the general population." We use this comparison to weight the scope of implementation of our first component. This strategy allows our measure to distinguish counties with greater numbers of immigrants, as well as the general level of local police enforcement. Our composite measure accounts for whether enforcement is applied in a targeted or universal fashion, as well as the degree to which an individual is more or less likely to be ensnared by local police in the first place. From the perspective of policy feedback, this composite measure taps the intensity with which a policy lesson is conveyed to policy targets. Specifically, our measure represents the degree to which trust is breached, and therefore, at least for Latinos, undermines trustworthiness in other points of contact with the state.

Statistical Model

In order to approximate the relational and contingent aspects of trust in government, we invoke a comparative relational analysis in our evaluation of the proposed hypotheses. Thus, we conduct split-sample analyses by race/ethnicity. The premise of the approach, explicated elsewhere by Masuoka and Junn (2014), is that Latinos, Blacks, Whites, and Asians occupy structurally distinct locations in the US racial hierarchy. If disparate relations exist between the state and social groups, then judgments formed by members within each group are more appropriately analyzed separately from one another. The comparative relational analyses comport with the conceptual definition of trust as relational, as well as the policy feedback notion that policy lessons are internalized by policy targets. For our purpose, we would know that our theoretical expectations are wrong if we find that distrust in government health information among Blacks, Asians, or Whites is also patterned by immigration enforcement. To address the question of whether these patterns vary by nativity, in separate models, we interact immigration enforcement with nativity.

RESULTS

To what extent does local exposure to immigration enforcement pattern trust in government health information outreach?[7] As seen in Table 4.2, results of the logit estimation indicate that immigration enforcement is, in fact, significantly associated with distrust in health information from the government, but

Table 4.2 Logistic Regression Estimates of Trust in Government as a Source of Health Information

	Latinos	Whites	Blacks	Asians
Immigration enforcement	-1.60**	0.02	-0.20	1.07
	(0.74)	(0.20)	(0.83)	(0.97)
US-born	-0.10	0.76	1.43	1.75
	(0.47)	(0.61)	(1.47)	(1.75)
Female	-0.57	0.17	0.58	0.40
	(0.45)	(0.18)	(0.58)	(0.86)
Self-rated worry	0.72	-0.04	0.02	0.56
	(0.76)	(0.36)	(0.80)	(1.89)
Education	0.99	1.08**	-0.81	-0.43
	(0.72)	(0.37)	(1.14)	(1.91)
Low English language comfort	0.18	0.83	-0.94	1.60
	(0.85)	(1.73)	(2.13)	(2.43)
Age in years	-0.01	-0.01	-0.02	-0.04
	(0.01)	(0.01)	(0.01)	(0.06)
Married	-0.47	-0.03	1.15*	1.30
	(0.44)	(0.21)	(0.57)	(1.16)
Medicare/Medicaid insurance	0.19	0.27	-0.82	0.70
	(0.48)	(0.26)	(0.79)	(1.54)
Constant	2.03*	-0.28	1.28	1.52
	(1.05)	(0.97)	(2.07)	(4.17)
N	312	1,322	356	112

Source. Health Information National Trends Survey, 2011Standard errors in parentheses.
*$p < .10$, **$p < .05$.

only among Latinos, as predicted by Hypotheses 1 and 2. The immigration enforcement logit coefficient (-1.60) for Latinos in Table 4.2 is significant (p-value = .0185; one-tailed test). By contrast, model estimates for non-Latinos are not distinguishable from zero, suggesting no statistically discernable relationship between immigration enforcement and trust in government as a source of health information among Blacks, Whites, and Asians. If we had observed meaningful or uniform differences across these various groups, this would undermine our interpretation that immigration enforcement specifically structures judgments of the government's trustworthiness in health domains among members of the enforcement-targeted group. However, given the large standard errors associated with our model in Table 4.3, we cannot say the negative effect observed among Latinos is substantially different for this particular group in the split-sample analyses.

We illustrate the substantive impact of immigration enforcement intensity on trust in health information from the government in Figure 4.2, which traces a series of predicted probabilities with 95 percent confidence intervals based upon the results of Table 4.2. For Latinos, across the full range of our composite immigration enforcement measure, from lower to higher levels, the predicted probability of trusting health information from the government decreases with increasing immigration enforcement. The magnitude of the reduction in trust in government health agencies is 60 percent as we move from low levels of immigration enforcement to higher levels. By contrast, the effect appears to be quite flat for Whites and Blacks. For Asians, the lower starting point of trust in government appears to be indistinguishable from zero. This suggests that policy lessons rooted in immigration enforcement are not internalized uniformly across members of different racial and ethnic communities.[8] How highly correlated is trust in government with other sources of information?

Immigration Enforcement and Other Sources of Health Information

Although we have shown disparate enforcement-to-trust relationships across racial and ethnic groups, one might reasonably ask whether the link is unique to governmental sources of information. Next, we test whether Latinos are generally more mistrusting of any source of information in response to immigration enforcement (Hypothesis 3). If Latinos are skeptical of any source of information, then we have no reason to believe respondents are making a specific connection between the government agencies enforcing deportation policies and the government agencies distributing health information.

As shown in our logit estimates in Table 4.3,[9] we find that those sources of information with the perceived potential to expose personal information to

Table 4.3 Split-Sample Logistic Regression Estimates of Trust in Other Source of Health Information Such as the Internet, Charities, Physicians, Family Members, Religious Leaders, Radio, Magazine, and Television

	Internet	Charities	Physicians	Family	Religious leaders	Radio	Magazines	Television
Among Latino respondents								
Immigration enforcement	-1.04*	-1.21**	-0.83	-0.41	-0.69	-1.05	-0.61	-1.00
	(0.62)	(0.50)	(0.63)	(1.06)	(0.60)	(0.92)	(1.16)	(0.75)
Constant	0.43	2.07*	4.13**	0.90	2.55**	1.61	-0.17	1.22
	(1.08)	(1.13)	(1.91)	(1.50)	(1.22)	(1.34)	(1.40)	(1.24)
N	306	309	319	311	309	305	309	308
Among White respondents								
Immigration enforcement	-0.23	-0.22	-0.37	-0.10	-0.12	-0.24	-0.12	-0.17
	(0.20)	(0.19)	(0.36)	(0.16)	(0.20)	(0.25)	(0.26)	(0.20)
Constant	0.10	-1.23*	-0.66	1.98***	0.63	-1.32**	0.09	-1.05*
	(1.22)	(0.63)	(4.15)	(0.64)	(0.97)	(0.64)	(0.89)	(0.61)
N	1,323	1,324	1,359	1,341	1,334	1,319	1,333	1,330
Among Black respondents								
Immigration enforcement	-0.43	0.33	-1.45**	0.72	0.52	0.53	-0.75	-1.04**
	(0.83)	(0.58)	(0.71)	(0.61)	(0.78)	(0.96)	(0.51)	(0.51)
Constant	1.40	4.03***	5.90***	0.83	2.98*	1.06	-0.57	0.73
	(1.81)	(1.02)	(0.93)	(1.64)	(1.62)	(1.45)	(1.35)	(1.33)
N	351	352	338	357	357	353	353	355
Among Asian respondents								
Immigration enforcement	1.20	-0.66	1.34	-0.72	0.20	-1.12	-0.63	-0.43
	(1.26)	(1.31)	(5.11)	(1.40)	(1.96)	(1.68)	(1.19)	(1.24)
Constant	4.86	-2.34	6.13	-1.16	0.12	-0.03	-1.17	1.36
	(3.04)	(1.90)	(8.70)	(2.78)	(4.69)	(2.12)	(2.12)	(3.99)
N	110	112	115	113	112	110	112	112

Source. Health Information National Trends Survey, 2011.
Standard errors in parentheses. Analyses include control items for nativity, gender, worry, education, low English language comfort, age, marital status, and Medicare/Medicaid insurance.
* p < .10, ** p < .05, *** p < .01.

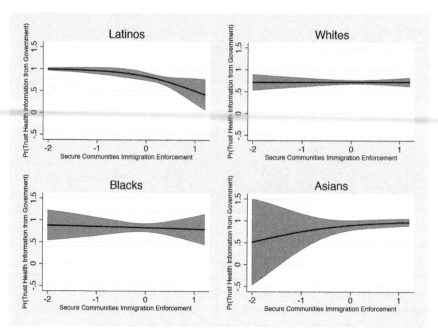

Figure 4.2   Predicted Probability of Immigration Enforcement on Trust in Government as a Source of Health Information by Race and Ethnicity. *Source.* Health Information National Trends Survey, 2011; ICE Secure Communities.

government bureaucrats and governmental databases, such as the Internet and charities, were correlated with the spillover effects of immigration enforcement and the extent to which people found them trustworthy. While predicting trust in the Internet as a source of health information, the immigration enforcement variable is marginally associated with lower levels of trust for Latinos (p-value = .05; one-tailed test). For charity sources of health information, the immigration enforcement variable also predicts lower levels of Latino trust (p-value = .01; one-tailed test). Thus, we did not find that Latinos were growing more skeptical in an unsophisticated manner. As seen in the remainder of the table, we do not find other racial groups experiencing similar patterns of distrust in the Internet or charities.[10]

To explain the skepticism Latinos are exhibiting toward the Internet, Hoffman et al. (1996) finds this outlet represents a two-way form of communication, one that often requires personal information be shared. According to Ha and Jung Lee (2011), consumers increasingly turn to online resources for their health information. Skepticism surrounding charity organizations is not unfounded, and falls in line with previous scholarship regarding a concern for privacy of information. Historically, immigration authorities have worked closely with charity organizers during times of crises, gaining access to the personal information supplied on relief applications by Mexicans and Mexican Americans (Fox 2012). Furthermore, recall that one concern that critics of interior immigration enforcement operations voiced to President Obama during his ACA outreach to Latinos is that sharing private information would expose Latino families to risk of deportation. Perhaps the underlying mechanism is a concern about sharing private information with any source. Unlike the protections for personal information that are assumed in personal relationships with family members, and unlike the confidentiality afforded in patient-physician relationships, engaging with the state and charities is difficult to do anonymously.

DISCUSSION

Recent studies show that trust in government declines as a function of exposure to law enforcement (Rocha et al. 2015; Weaver and Lerman 2010). We extend these findings by evaluating domain-specific trust in government, and by comparing the link between immigration enforcement and trust in government-provided health information across different racial and ethnic groups. The evidence is striking: Latinos who live in counties where immigration enforcement is the most intense, at least as implemented through the SComm program, are less likely to trust health information from government agencies. By contrast, Blacks, Asians, and Whites do not appear to judge health information from the government on the basis of immigration enforcement. In general, we did not find that Latino skepticism about sources of health information is universal or structured in an unsophisticated manner. The policy lessons that immigration enforcement conveys to Latinos primarily shape attitudes toward government health agencies.

Schneider and Ingram (1993, 340) explain that "[p]olicy teaches lessons about the type of groups people belong to, what they deserve from government, and what is expected of them." People internalize messages from their experience with the government and its institutions (Soss 1999). With negative experiences with the carceral state, we can understandably expect there to be greater skepticism toward the government (Weaver and Lerman 2010). In this paper, the carceral state is represented by higher levels of SComm immigration enforcement by local law enforcement authorities at the county level. We demonstrate that these interactions are not restricted to the policy's target population or targeted policy scope. This finding is in line with Soss (1999), who explains that welfare participation provides the most direct connection to a government institution for many people. These institutional experiences then shape how people view the government as a whole. These results remained robust while accounting for Medicaid and Medicare participation, which serves to hold constant another potential form of experience with the government (Schneider and Ingram 1993; Soss 1999; Campbell 2003). We find that local immigration law enforcement, as represented by the institutional implementation of SComm at the county level, provides a powerful and substantively negative governmental experience for Latinos. Subsequently, these experiences determine the level of skepticism Latinos hold toward the government when interfacing with other aspects of the state—largely depicting the source in question as a threat (Herring et al. 2013, 1062).

Assessments of the trustworthiness of the government as a source of health information have enormous implications for public service outreach efforts that the government spearheads. For example, if agencies like the Centers for Disease Control and Prevention (CDC) are associated with the government in the minds of Latinos, then health outreach initiatives that the CDC directs about seasonable flu vaccinations, cancer screenings, and disease outbreak warnings may be viewed with skepticism by Latinos, thus stymieing their salubrious impact.

Our findings with respect to declining trust in charities suggest that the reticence to trust health information from the government may be linked specifically to the requirement to provide personal identifying information. Skepticism about sharing personal information with any entity, including the government and charities, might reinforce distrust in other sources that require personal details. In general, immigrants might worry about any questions or status inquiries that may create a paper trail that could trace back to themselves or their families. Thus, the findings here have implications for governance and policy feedback effects that extend beyond narrow policy scopes.

During the Great Depression, relief workers and charity organizers shared with immigration authorities the personal information supplied on relief applications by Mexicans and Mexican Americans (Fox 2012). Bureaucratic practices that link social service use, ethnicity, and immigration status continue to find policy expression today. One notable effort to codify the cooperation between local public bureaucrats and federal immigration authorities is California's 1994 Proposition 187. The initiative aimed to restrict undocumented immigrants from using public services, including schooling. The measure mandated that public workers identify and report to officials any person who they suspected of being undocumented. Thus, it is easy to see how immigrants might harbor generalized worries about any questions or status inquiries their paper trail at these charities might provoke for themselves or their families. These findings have implications for governance and the extent to which communication flows easily, with policy feedback effects that extend beyond narrow policy scopes.

What mattered to Latinos in our opening anecdote was whether they could trust the specific assurances that then-President Obama was giving about immigration policy not being connected to health care policy. Concerns among Latinos about immigration enforcement are sufficiently acute to forego enrollment in health insurance (Fix and Passel 1999; Watson 2014), and in some cases, avoid health care providers (Beniflah et al. 2013; Hacker et al. 2011; Toomey et al. 2014; White et al. 2014). What mattered to the administration was that the distrust of government that is partially rooted in immigration enforcement does not undermine how the government performs its job to deliver health services. The administration's concern was sufficiently acute so as to stress on the www.healthcare.gov website, as well as through a formal statement of "agency policy" for ICE (2013), that "Your information will never be used for enforcement purposes when you apply to health care.gov or a state marketplace." The results here suggest that the previous administration was well aware of the skepticism surrounding questions of citizenship status in one's household and those seeking health information.

Although we did not examine ACA enrollment patterns, our analysis does comport with the challenge facing policy makers in implementing the ACA that was suggested by the anecdote in the introduction. The success of the ACA in increasing coverage and reducing health care costs depended on: (1) mandatory enrollment; and, (2) enrollment among younger, premium-lowering populations. To the extent that immigration enforcement breached trust in government in the domain of health provision, the level of participation in ACA-mandated enrollment would be lower than expected among Latinos, reducing expected cost savings anticipated from enrolling a youthful demographic. Our conclusion is that Latinos are navigating a sense of *exclusion* from one domain (i.e., immigration) as they engage in another domain where they are *sought* after (i.e., health care matters).

The Latino-targeted ACA outreach effort was initially anemic. Only after criticisms about a poorly translated Spanish-language version of the health care.gov website and low signup rates among Latinos in the first open enrollment periods, did a focused and better financed Latino outreach effort appear. Nevertheless, available evidence indicates that the ACA has reduced the number of uninsured Americans (Levitt 2014; Sanger-Katz 2014). However, if the ACA had been implemented in a policy environment with less interior immigration enforcement, it might have extended health insurance coverage to a greater extent and sooner than it did, particularly among Latinos. It seems reasonable that less interior immigration enforcement, particularly during the initial ACA rollout, would have meant incurring fewer costs in the efforts to customize Latino outreach.

These findings should be understood in the context of some limitations. The HINTS data does not provide country of origin measures. Thus, we are not able to parcel out associations with country of origin or political ideology in our models. Country of origin differences might be particularly relevant, as immigrants may draw on experiences with their home government to inform their view of US government. Furthermore, some immigrants might have access to more resources that are contingent on immigration status, and might be more trusting of the United States as a result.

CONCLUSION

If the question about who gets what is the quintessential definition of politics, then public forms of health communication are subject to political dynamics. The policy-driven attitudes that we observe about trust in disparate sources of health information tap into some of the less obvious political dynamics that are catalyzed by immigration enforcement. The authority and power of policies need not be contained to the substantive domains that legislators intended to target. Spillover effects in one policy domain to another imply that the interpretation we accord to policies can inform the meaning we imbue in other areas of life that are associated with that policy.

What it means to be an equal citizen in America is not simply a matter of whether you have citizenship or not. Some rules render citizenship less than equal (e.g., felony, age restrictions). This matters to Latinos in their day-to-day life for at least two reasons. First, the focus of immigration enforcement efforts was once concentrated at the border, particularly between the United States and Mexico. Now, enforcement-oriented immigration policies are equally preoccupied with the interior. Second, a key strategy of the new immigration enforcement era is cross-jurisdiction coordination. To the extent that immigration enforcement implicates a broader social group than policy designers intended, our investigation documents the way public policies can shape politics beyond the problems they are designed to solve. In this case, it is the welfare arm of the state that has become entangled with the coercive arm of the state.

NOTES

1. Historical and contemporary accounts of immigration enforcement policy trace negative stereotypes of Latinos to immigration and welfare state policy (Chavez 2013; Jacobson 2008; Ngai 2004). Most notably, the concept of "illegal alien" defines immigrants as criminals and is conflated with Latino identity (Ngai 2004).

2. More details on the sample methodology of HINTS 4 Cycle 1 are available at http://hints.cancer.gov/instrument.aspx

3. The non-Hispanic "other" category consists of people who identify as non-Latino (NL) Hawaiian, NL Pacific Islander, NL Alaskan Native, NL Native–American, and/or NL mixed with multiple aforementioned races.

4. We measure "self-rated worry" using an item in the HINTs that asked respondents: "Over the past 2 weeks, how often have you experienced feeling nervous, anxious, or on edge?" We recoded the variable to range from 0 to 1 for four response options: "nearly everyday," "more than half the days," "several days," and "never."

5. Archival data are available at www.ice.gov. As part of SComm, local authorities submit information about all individuals in their custody to federal authorities through IDENT/IAFIS, "a data conduit connecting the FBI's Integrated Automatic Fingerprint Identification System (IAFIS) with DHS US-VISIT's Automated Biometric Identification System (IDENT)." The SComm program uses this "interoperability tool" to identify people for further scrutiny under immigration law.

6. The intent of SComm was to prioritize undocumented immigrants who were categorized as Level 1 (L1), which includes those charged with felonies like homicide, sexual assault, and kidnapping. ICE records show that many jurisdictions report majority low-priority removals, classified as Level 2 (L2) and Level 3 (L3) immigrants to indicate minor offenses like non-violent drug misdemeanors and traffic violations. In November 2014, President Obama acknowledged the incongruence between SComm's mission and implementation, and announced a renewed focus on the removal of noncitizens classified as L1 offenders. SComm's name is now the Priority Enforcement Program.

7. Bivariate analyses of trust in government health information by race and ethnicity indicate that the least trusting groups of government health information outreach are Latinos and Whites, with a one percentage point difference between them. The most trusting groups are Blacks and especially Asians.

8. We then examined whether these patterns vary by nativity. Although Latino immigrants are the most common profile of deportees, we find that their US-born counterparts respond similarly to immigration enforcement. The lack of differences based on nativity suggests that the lessons associated with immigration enforcement are internalized similarly by Latinos. Results available upon request.

9. We then examined whether these patterns vary by nativity. Although Latino immigrants are the most common profile of deportees, we find that their US-born counterparts respond similarly to immigration enforcement. The lack of differences based on nativity suggests that the lessons associated with immigration enforcement are internalized similarly by Latinos. Results available upon request.

10. It is worth noting Black respondents reported lower levels of predicted likelihood to trust their physicians and television outlets as sources of health information as immigration enforcement increased in their counties.

REFERENCES

Beckjord, Ellen Burke, Lila J. Finney Rutten, Neeraj K. Arora, Richard P. Moser, and Bradford W Hesse. 2008. "Information Processing and Negative Affect: Evidence from the 2003 Health Information National Trends Survey." *Health Psychology* 27(2):249–57.

Beniflah, Jacob D., Wendalyn K. Little, Harold K. Simon, and Jesse Sturm. 2013. "Effects of Immigration Enforcement Legislation on Hispanic Pediatric Patient Visits to the Pediatric Emergency Department." *Clinical Pediatrics* 52(12):1122–26.

Brader, Ted. 2006. *Campaigning For Hearts and Minds How Emotional Appeals in Political Ads Work.* Chicago: University of Chicago.

Braithwaite, Valerie, and Margaret Levi, eds. 1998. *Trust and Governance.* New York: Russell Sage Foundation.

Campbell, Andrea Louise. 2002. "Self-Interest, Social Security, and the Distinctive Participation Patterns of Senior Citizens." *The American Political Science Review* 96(3):565–74.

Campbell, Andrea Louise. 2003. *How Policies Make Citizens: Senior Political Activism and the American Welfare State.* Princeton, NJ: Princeton University Press.

Chavez, Leo R. 2013. *The Latino Threat.* Redwood City, CA: Stanford University Press.

Clayman, Marla L., Jennifer A. Manganello, Kasisomayajula Viswanath, Bradford W. Hesse, and Neeraj K. Arora. 2010. "Providing Health Messages to Hispanics/Latinos: Understanding the Importance of Language, Trust in Health Information Sources, and Media Use." *Journal of Health Communication* 15(supp3):252–63.

Congressional Budget Office. 2015. "Updated Budget Projections: 2015 to 2025." Congress of the United States. https://www.cbo.gov/sites/default/files/cbofiles/attachments/49973-Updated_Budget_Projections.pdf

Easley, Jonathan. 2014. "Obama to Hispanics: We Won't Deport Relatives Because You Enroll in ObamaCare." *The Hill*, March 18. Accessed March 5, 2015. www.thehill.com/policy/healthcare/ 201076-obama-makes-o-care-pitch-to-hispanics-the

Fix, Michael E., and Jeffery S. Passel. 1999. "Trends in Noncitizens' and Citizen's Use of Public Benefits Following Welfare Reform: 1994—1997." *Urban Institute.* http://www.urban.org/research/publication/trends-noncitizens-and-citizens-use-public-benefits-following-welfare-reform

Fox, Cybelle. 2012. *Three Words of Relief: Race, Immigration and the American Welfare State from the Progressive Era to the New Deal.* Princeton, NJ: Princeton University Press.

Golash-Boza, Tanya Maria. 2012. *Immigration Nation: Raids, Detentions, and Deportation in Post-9/11 America.* Boulder, CO: Paradigm Publishers.

Ha, Sejin, and Yun Jung Lee. 2011. "Determinants of Consumer-Driven Healthcare: Self-Confidence in Information Search, Health Literacy, and Trust in Information Sources." *International Journal of Pharmaceutical and Healthcare Marketing* 5(1):8–24.

Hacker, Karen, Jocelyn Chu, Carolyn Leung, Robert Marra, Alex Pirie, Mohamed Brahimi, Margaret English, Joshua Beckmann, Dolores Acevedo-Garcia, and Robert P. Marlin. 2011. "The Impact of Immigration and Customs Enforcement on Immigrant Health: Perceptions of Immigrants in Everett, Massachusetts, USA." *Social Science & Medicine* 73(4):586–94.

Hardin, Russell. 1998. *Trust in Government.* In *Trust and Governance.* Edited by Valerie Braithwaite and Margaret Levi. New York: Russell Sage Foundation, 9–27.

Herring, David R., Katherine R. White, Linsa N. Jabeen, Michelle Hinojos, Gabriela Terrazas, Stephanie M. Reyes, Jennifer H. Taylor, and Stephen L. Crites Jr. 2013. "On the Automatic Activation of Attitudes: A Quarter Century of Evaluative Priming Research." *Psychological Bulletin* 139(5):1062–89.

Hoffman, Donna L., William D. Kalsbeek, and Thomas P. Novak. 1996. "Internet and Web Use in the U.S." *Communications of the ACM* 39(12):36–46.

Jacobson, Robin. 2008. *The New Nativism: Proposition 187 and the Debate over Immigration.* Minneapolis: University of Minnesota Press.

Kaiser Family Foundation. 2013. "Medicaid and the Uninsured: Health Coverage for the Hispanic Population Today and Under the Affordable Care Act, publication #8432." Kaiser Commission on Key Facts, The Henry J. Kaiser Family Foundation. https://kaiserfamilyfoundation.files.wordpress.com/2013/ 04/84321. pdf (accessed August 5, 2015).

Lerner, Jennifer S., and Dacher Keltner. 2001. "Fear, Anger, and Risk." *Journal of Personality and Social Psychology* 81(1):146–159.

Levi, Margaret, and Laura Stoker. 2000. "Political Trust and Trustworthiness." *Annual Review of Political Science* 3(1):475–507.

Levitt, Larry. 2014. "How Well Is the Affordable Care Act Working?" *The JAMA Forum.* http://newsatjama.jama.com/2014/07/09/jama-forum-how-well-is-the-affordable-care-act-working/ (accessed: October 25, 2015).

Manierre, Matthew J. 2015. "Gaps in Knowledge: Tracking and Explaining Gender Differences in Health Information Seeking." *Social Science & Medicine* 128:151–58.

Manzano, Sylvia. 2011. "One Year After SB1070: Why Immigration Will Not Go Away." *Latino Decisions*, May 9. http://www.latinodecisions.com/blog/2011/05/09/ one-year-after-sb1070-why-immigration-will-not-go-away/ Accessed: June 5, 2015.

Marcus, George E., W. Russell Neuman, and Michael MacKuen. 2000. *Affective Intelligence and Political Judgment.* Chicago: University of Chicago Press.

Masuoka, Natalie, and Jane Junn. 2014. *The Politics of Belonging.* Chicago: University of Chicago.

Meissner, Doris, Donald M. Kerwin, Muzaffar Chishti, and Claire Bergeron. 2013. "Immigration Enforcement in the United States: The Rise of a Formidable Machinery." Migration Policy Institute Technical Report.

Merolla, Jennifer L., Adrian D. Pantoja, Ivy A.M. Cargile, and Juana Mora. 2012. "From Coverage to Action: The Immigration Debate and Its Effects on Participation." *Political Research Quarterly* 66(2):322–35.

Mettler, Suzanne. 2005. *Soldiers to Citizens.* New York: Oxford University Press.

Mettler, Suzanne, and Joe Soss. 2004. "The Consequences of Public Policy for Democratization Citizenship: Bridging Policy Studies and Mass Politics." *Perspectives on Politics* 2(1):55–73.

Moynihan, Donald, and Pamela Herd. 2010. "Red Tape and Democracy: How Rules Affect Citizenship Rights." *The American Review of Public Administration* 40(6):654–70.

Ngai, Mae M. 2004. *Impossible Subjects: Illegal Aliens and the Making of Modern America.* Princeton, NJ: Princeton University Press.

Nguyen, Giang T., and Scarlett L. Bellamy. 2006. "Cancer Information Seeking Preferences and Experiences: Disparities Between Asian Americans and Whites in the Health Information National Trends Survey (HINTS)." *Journal of Health Communication* 11(S1):173–80.

Pantoja, Adrian, and Gary M. Segura. 2003. "Fear and Loathing in California: Contextual Threat and Political Sophistication among Latino Voters." *Political Behavior* 25(3):265–86.

Pedroza, Juan Manuel. 2013. "Removal Roulette: Secure Communities and Immigration Enforcement in the United States." In *Outside Justice: Immigration and the Criminalizing Impact of Changing Policy and Practice*, edited by David C. Brotherton, Daniel L. Stageman, and Shirley P. Leyro. New York: Springer, 45–65.

Pierson, Paul. 1993. "When Effects Become Causes: Policy Feedback and Policy Changes." *World Politics* 45(4):595–628.

Pierson, Paul. 2004. *Politics in Time*. Princeton, NJ: Princeton University Press.

Rocha, Rene R., Benjamin R. Knoll, and Robert D. Wrinkle. 2015. "Immigration Enforcement and the Redistribution of Political Trust." *The Journal of Politics* 77(4):901–13.

Sanger-Katz, Margot. 2014. "How well is the Affordable Care Act Working?" *The New York Times*, October 26. Accessed: October 25, 2015. http://www.nytimes.com/interactive/2014/10/27/us/is-the-affordable-care-act-working.html?_r=0#/

Schattschneider, E. E. 1960. *The Semisovereign People: A Realist's View of Democracy in America*. Hinsdale, IL: Dryden Press.

Schlozman, Kay Lehman, Sidney Verba, and Henry E. Brady. 2012. *The Unheavenly Chorus*. Princeton, NJ: Princeton University Press.

Schneider, Anne, and Helen Ingram. 1993. "Social Construction of Target Populations." *American Political Science Review* 87(2):334–47.

Soss, Joe. 1999. "Lessons of Welfare: Policy Design, Political Learning, and Political Action." *The American Political Science Review* 93(2):363–80.

Toomey, Russell B., A.J. Umana-Taylor, David R. Williams, Elizabeth Harvey Mendoza, Laudan B. Jahromi, and Kimberly A. Updegraff. 2014. "Impact of Arizona's SB 1070 Immigration Law on Utilization of Health Care and Public Assistance among Mexican-Origin Adolescent Mothers and Their Mother Figures." *American Journal of Public Health* 104(S1):S28–S34.

TRAC (Transactional Records Access Clearinghouse). 2014. "ICE Deportations: Gender, Age, and Country of Citizenship." *Transactional Records Access Clearinghouse*, Available online: http://trac.syr.edu/immigration/ reports/350/. Accessed: June 13, 2015.

US Bureau of Immigration and Customs Enforcement. 2013. "Clarification of Existing Practices Related to Certain Health Care Information." Office of the Director, Department of Homeland Security. http://www.ice.gov/doclib/ero-outreach/pdf/ice-aca-memo.pdf.Accessed August 5, 2015.

US Department of Homeland Security. 2003. "Endgame: Office of Detention and Removal Strategic Plan, 2003—2012, Detention and Removal Strategy for a Secure Homeland." Bureau of Immigration and Customs Enforcement, Office of Detention and Removal. http://aclum.org/endgame.Accessed on August 4, 2015.

US Department of Homeland Security. 2011. "Secure Communities: Statistical Monitoring." Technical report, Department of Homeland Security.

Watson, Tara. 2014. "Inside the Refrigerator: Immigration Enforcement and Chilling Effects in Medicaid Participation." *American Economic Journal: Economic Policy* 6(3): 313–38.

Weaver, Vesla M., and Amy E. Lerman. 2010. "Political Consequences of the Carceral State." *American Political Science Review* 104(4): 817–33.

White, Joseph. 2013. "Cost Control after the ACA." *Public Administration Review* 73(S1):S24–S33.

White, Kari, Valerie A. Yeager, Nir Menachemi, and Isabel C. Scarinci. 2014. "Impact of Alabama's Immigration Law on Access to Health Care Among Latina Immigrants and Children: Implications for National Reform." *American Journal of Public Health* 104(3):397–405.

Zarcadoolas, Christina, Andrew Pleasant, and David S Greer. 2005. "Understanding Health Literacy: An Expanded Model." *Health Promotion International* 20(2):195–203.

Part II

ECONOMIC REALITIES

Chapter 5

What Have We Learned about Incarceration and Race?

Lessons from Thirty Years of Research

Samuel L. Myers, Jr.

America's prisons disproportionately house African American males. Incarceration has become almost a norm for the experience of many Blacks. One common explanation for the high concentration of Black males in prisons and jails is the rise of drug use and drug sales—particularly of low-priced crack cocaine—in the 1980s. This explanation proffered by Fryer et al. (2013) and in the popular media undermines an alternative causal explanation for the rise of Black incarceration explored in a series of coauthored books and articles over the past thirty years by Myers that argue that there are clear labor market equilibrating effects of Black male incarceration and that explicit discrimination in the criminal justice system explains some if not most of the racial disparity in incarceration (Darity and Myers 1998a; Darity and Myers 2000, 283; Darity, Myers, Sabol and Carson 1994; Myers and Sabol 1987a; 1987b). The discrimination comes in the form of discrimination in stops and frisks, in arrests, in bail setting and release while pending trial, in conviction rates and guilty pleas, in sentence lengths and ultimately in time served. The main distinction between the conventional wisdom—that Blacks disproportionately sell and use drugs and therefore are disproportionately arrested and convicted—and the alternative view that racial disparities in incarceration serves a functional purpose in labor markets is a distinction between behavioral explanations for the rise in incarceration versus structural explanations.

This chapter reviews the stylized facts about Black incarceration rates from 1970 to the present and explores the variety of explanations for the growth in Black imprisonment. Two specific empirical tests are conducted in this review. One is a test of the hypothesis that there is an efficiency justification for the racial differential in imprisonment. Using decades-old federal prison data, I show the existence of substantial racial discrimination in sentencing that cannot be attributable to racial differences in anticipated recidivism rates.

A second test examines the hypothesis that the rise in racial disparities in incarceration is due to increases in arrests for drugs. Surprisingly and quite contrary to popular opinion, I find that increased arrests for drugs had a larger impact on White arrests than on Black arrests.

The chapter then summarizes some of the consequences of the huge racial disparity in incarceration and suggests implications for future research.

STYLIZED FACTS ABOUT BLACK INCARCERATION RATES, 1970S TO PRESENT

Incarceration rates in the United States are the second highest in the world.[1] Figure 5.1 shows that incarceration in the United States is higher than it is in Cuba, Russia, Thailand and many smaller countries like Panama. Only the tiny island nation of Seychelles has a higher incarceration rate. There is a distinct racial dimension to this high rate of incarceration. Black incarceration rates are six to seven times that of Whites (Pew Research Center 2013). It has not always been so. Prior to emancipation, prisons in America were largely White. Racial disparities in imprisonment date to postreconstruction years, but, nonetheless, were a part of a relatively sparse use of imprisonment in the United States. There were less than 200,000 persons housed in federal and state prisons in 1970. Incredibly, incarceration rose from 200,000 in the 1970s to more than 1.5 million in 2010.[2] Table 5.1 shows the dramatic increase in

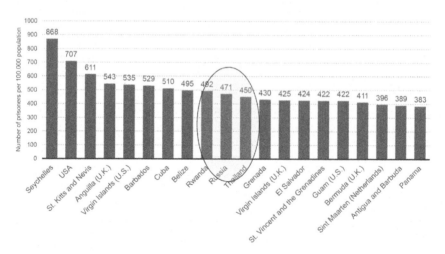

Figure 5.1 Countries with Largest Number of Prisoners per 100,000 of the National Population, as of June 2014. *Source.* ICPS. Countries with the largest number of prisoners per 100,000 of the national population, as of June 2014. https://www.statista.com/statistics/262962/countries-with-the-ost-prisoners-per-100-000-inhabitants/ (accessed June 25, 2014).

imprisonment from 1980 to 2000. The number more than doubled in the decade between 1980 and 1990; it more the quadrupled between 1980 and 2000. What is also apparent, though, is that the Black share of those imprisoned first rose from 45.7 percent to 47 percent and then actually dropped to 46.2 percent during this period. By 2010, the Black share had dropped once again to 37.9 percent. As Figure 5.2 reveals, the drop in the Black share of those incarcerated is associated with the rise in the White incarcerations after 2000, which I will show later to be attributable to White drug arrests.

Sharp increases 1970s–1990s; Rise in White incarcerations in 2000s

There is no dispute, however, that incarceration rose dramatically during the 1970s to the 1990s. The 1990s saw Black numbers increasing above White

Table 5.1   Prisoners under State and Federal Jurisdiction: 1974, 1980, 1990, 2000, and 2010

	Total Number	Percent Black
1974	229,721	47.0%
1980	328,695	45.7%
1990	774,375	47.0%
2000	1,321,200	46.2%
2010	1,550,600	37.9%

Source. US Department of Justice, Office of Justice Programs, Bureau of Justice Statistics.

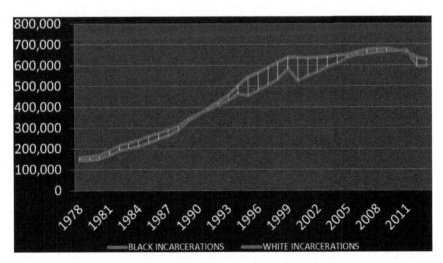

Figure 5.2   Total Incarcerations, Blacks and Whites, 1978–2013. *Source.* United States Department of Justice. Office of Justice Programs. Bureau of Justice Statistics. National Prisoner Statistics, 1978–2013. ICPSR35608-v1. Ann Arbor, MI: Inter-university. Consortium for Political and Social Research [distributor], 2015–01–09. http://doi.org/10.3886/ICPSR35608.v1.

numbers of those incarcerated until the 2000s when Black numbers peaked and White numbers continued to rise. Before entertaining a model to explain these changes, we consider the long list of possible explanations offered in the literature for the substantive growth in incarceration during the period.

Catalogue of Explanations

The array of social and economic explanations for the growth in imprisonment in America can be divided into those that offer structural explanations and those that offer behavioral explanations. The structural explanations look at labor market distortions, the role of poor schools and the use of suspensions as pipelines to first the juvenile justice system and then to the adult criminal justice system. The structural explanations examine the role of segregated housing, discrimination in real estate and credit markets that can produce segregated islands of isolation and discrimination within the criminal justice system.

Behavioral explanations explore the role of drug sales and drug use, the rise of theft and larceny as rational alternatives to legal labor market pursuits and the pathology of thrill-seeking and antiauthoritarianism suggesting that criminal participation is a form of social dysfunction.

Myers and Sabol 1987b have explored empirically the Rusche and Kircheimer structural thesis that prisons act as labor market equilibrating devices. When there is superfluous labor, prisons drain off unwanted workers. When there are labor market shortages, prisons release workers into the labor pool to keep wages from rising. This hypothesis suggests a positive relationship between unemployment rates and incarceration rates, something evident in Figure 5.3, which plots unemployment rates against incarceration rates over the period from 1960s to the late 1990s. Although there is clearly a positive and statistically significant trend line, there are glaring deviations from the trend in the early 1990s.

Conventional behavioral explanations posit that high unemployment produces high incentives to engage in criminal activities and that high rates of criminal involvement produce high arrests rates and high incarceration rates. The difficulty of testing this hypothesis, however, is that crime rates are unobserved, imperfectly captured by offenses reported to police, and very possibly endogenous to police and law enforcement activities. Many of the major studies adopting the Becker rational choice model as a starting point use the FBI's Uniform Crime Reports and arrest data failing to account for the underreporting of crimes and/or the inaccuracy of measuring criminal activities by arrest rates (for more on the underreporting problem, see Myers, (1980)).

Conventional behavioral explanations for racial disparities in incarceration look more explicitly at alleged offender decisions that result in higher rates of traffic stops, arrests and failure to post bail, guilty pleas, longer sentences and

Figure 5.3 Unemployment versus Incarceration. *Source.* Unemployment Rates—United States Bureau of the Census, Historical Statistics of the United States, Colonial Times to 1970, and the Economic Report of the President, Feb. 1998. Incarceration Rates and Crime Index Rates—Bureau of Justice Statistics Bulletin and Prisoners in 1993 (Darity and Myers 2000, Table 9.1 Unemployment Versus Incarceration, page 283).

lower probabilities of probation or parole. The point of these models is to establish whether the racial disparity is "efficient" or rationally based on the desire to minimize social costs or maximize arrests or convictions of guilty offenders.

In the case of traffic stops, Mason has provided a thorough critique of the existing models that putatively show that it is offender behavior (e.g., drug carrying) that explains the racial differences in stops (Mason 2007). Similar critiques can be leveled against the behavioral models that predict racial differences in arrests and convictions. The central limitation of the empirical tests of these models, however, is that the available information—until recently—largely has been limited to characteristics of the offender and the offense, excluding critically important information on the arresting officer, prosecutor or judge.

Nevertheless, it is possible to use indirect methods to differentiate between the structural and behavioral explanations for the racial disparities in incarceration and to test the efficiency hypothesis.

The (in) Efficiency of Racial Disparities in Incarceration

In a largely overlooked treatise produced at the invitation of Alfred Blumstein, then the president of the American Society of Criminology, I argued against the prevailing wisdom among mainstream criminologists that the observed racial disparity in incarceration was due to racial disparities in criminal involvement (Myers 1993). The alternative hypothesis, I argued, that the disparity was due to discrimination in sentencing, had not been properly tested. The correct test is to estimate separately equations for time served for Blacks and Whites and then to compute "equal treatment" values of the sentences served for Blacks. If there is no difference between the actual time served and the equal treatment values, then there is no discrimination. The results using federal prison data showed that there are statistically significant and legally meaningful disparities in sentences served that cannot be explained by observed characteristics of offenders or characteristics of the crimes or offenses. In short, there is discrimination in sentencing.[3]

One can take this model one step further and ask this question: what would recidivism of Blacks be had they faced equal-treatment (and thus shorter) sentences? The mechanism for this change in sentencing is release on parole. Persons who are released sooner serve shorter sentences than those who are not released on parole, all other things being equal. Assuming that there is a deterrent effect of longer prison sentences, the model suggests that releasing Blacks sooner may result in additional crime in a bias-free sentencing world. This is the efficiency argument, although it is an entirely empirical issue of just how much additional crime is likely to occur by ridding the parole release mechanism of racial discrimination. The results are compelling: the coefficients of the sentencing variable are small and statistically insignificant; the effect of eliminating disparities in parole release results in one extra recidivist for every 222 releases.

Are racial disparities in incarceration due to racial disparities in drug arrests?

A second claim worth investigating is the claim that racial disparities in incarceration are due to racial disparities in drug arrests. Blacks are more likely to be arrested than Whites and are also much more likely to be incarcerated as Figures 5.4 and 5.5 show. But to establish a causal link between the black-white disparity in arrests and the black-white disparity in incarceration requires a bit more legwork.

In the appendix, I detail a model that estimates the impacts of drug arrests on incarceration rates. This is done separately for Blacks and Whites for the years 1980 to 2012.[4] A separate model estimates the effects of differences in drug arrest rates on differences in incarceration. Independent variables include: unemployment rates (by race, gender, age-group and year); arrest rates by race by type; offence rates by type, overall arrest rates, overall unemployment rates and overall drug incarceration rates. Alternative specifications include lagged and current values of these variables and determinants of incarceration rates. The main finding of the model estimation is that there are larger impacts of lagged White drug arrests on White incarceration rates than lagged Black drug arrests on Black incarceration rates. This finding is robust across alternative model specifications and counters the conclusion that the

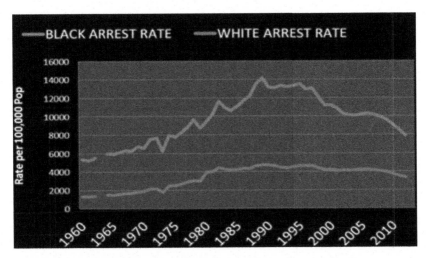

Figure 5.4   Black-White Differences in Arrests Rates, 1960–2013. *Source.* US Department of Justice, Federal Bureau of Investigation, Uniform Crime Reporting Statistics; ICPSR Inter-university Consortium for Political and Social Research. Uniform Crime Reporting Program [United States]: Arrests by Age, Sex, and Race for Police Agencies in Metropolitan Statistical Areas, 1960–1997 http://www.icpsr.umich.edu/icpsrweb/NACJD/studies/2538?paging.startRow=1&fundingAgency=United+SState+Department+of+Justice.+Office+of+Justice+Programs.+Bureau+of+Justice+Statistics&keyword%5B0%5D=drug+abuse&fundingAgency%5B1%5D=United+States+Department+of+Justice.+Federal+BureaB+of+Investigation; Bureau of Justice Statistics, Arrest Data Analysis Tool http://www.bjs.gov/index.cfm?ty=datool&surl=/arrests/index.cfm#

cause of the racial gap in incarcerations is the racial gap in drug arrests. *Figure 5.6* reports the coefficients on the lagged drug arrest rates in the estimates of the ln-incarceration rates. The interpretation of these coefficients is the percentage change in incarceration rates due to a change in drug arrest rates. The effects are larger for Whites than for Blacks, consistent with the finding that racial disparities in drug arrests alone are not the causal factor explaining the racial gap in incarceration.

One can argue about whether other factors, such as the persistent racial disparity in arrests for virtually all crimes, contribute more directly to the long-term pattern of imprisonment of Blacks in America. What is not in dispute is the dire consequences for the heavy representation of Black males in America's prisons and jails.

Dire Consequences

The list of unintended consequences of disproportionate imprisonment of Blacks is enormous. The most widely cited consequence is political

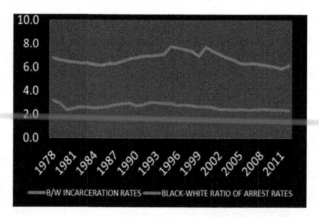

Figure 5.5   Disparity in Incarcerations Greater than in the Disparity in Arrests. *Source.*
United States Census Bureau, Population Estimates https://www.census.gov/popest/data/
national/asrh/pre-1980/PE-11.html. ICPSR Inter-university Consortium for Political and
Social Research. Uniform Crime Reporting Program [United States]: Arrests by Age, Sex,
and Race for Police Agencies in Metropolitan Statistical Areas, 1960–1997 http://www.
icpsr.umich.edu/icpsrweb/NACJD/studies/2538?paging.startRow=1&fundingAgencf=Un
ited+States+Department+of+Justice.+Office+of+Justice+Programs.+Bureau+of+Justice+
StStatisti&keyword%5B0%5D=drug+abuse&fundingAgency%5B1%5D=United+States+
DepartmDep+of+Justice.+Federal+Bureau+of+Investigation. Bureau of Justice Statistics,
Arrest Data Analysis Tool http://www.bjs.gov/index.cfm?ty=datool&surl=/arrests/index.
cfm#; United States Department of Justice. Office of Justice Programs. Bureau of Justice
Statistics. National Prisoner Statistics, 1978-2013. ICPSR35608-v1. Ann Arbor, MI: Inter-
university Consortium for Political and Social Research [distributor], 2015-01-09. http://
doi.org/10.3886/ICPSR35608.v1.

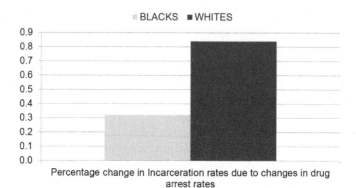

Figure 5.6   Effects of Drug Arrests on Incarceration Rates. *Source.* Author's calculations
from Appendix 1, Tables 2 and 3.

disenfranchisement. As of 2014, felons could not vote in Alabama, Arizona,
Delaware, Florida, Iowa, Kentucky, Mississippi, Nevada, Tennessee, Virginia
or Wyoming. There are labor market consequences as well. Convicted felons

in most states are prohibited from holding a host of occupational licenses and thus cannot hold particular jobs. In Texas, for example, convicted felons cannot be employed in work with children (childcare, education), with the elderly (home care) and cannot hold licenses as locksmiths, barbers, electricians or pharmacists. In Minnesota, convicted felons cannot be employed as mortgage originators, insurance agents, nursing or home care assistants, audiologists, physical therapists, dentists or veterinarians.

Darity and Myers (1998b) have argued, moreover, that another unintended consequence of disproportionate incarceration is destabilization of Black families through the reduction of the supply of marriageable Black males. The increase in the share of Black families headed by females lies behind the widening racial gap in family incomes in the decades between 1980 and 2000 (Darity, Myers and Chung 1998).

Implications for the Future

What have we learned over the past thirty years about the relationship between race and incarceration? If anything, we should have learned that it was not until *White* incarceration rates soared, notably due to increased drug arrests, that economists paid much attention to the unsustainable expansion of imprisonment as a policy solution to problems of crime. Indeed, the long-term drop in crime rates that accompanied the expansion of imprisonment has often been cited as a compelling *rationale* for increased punishment via incarceration.

Still unresolved after thirty years is the explicit role that labor market disequilibrium plays in structurally promoting changes in incarceration. The weak findings about the relationship between unemployment and imprisonment in the past thirty years may well be due to the fact that the cyclical fluctuation in economic activities relevant to the pre1990s no longer prevails. The mapping of the relationship between unemployment rates and incarceration rates during the 1990s shows significant deviations from the long-term trend.

Now that millions of inmates have completed their sentences and are returning to their communities, there is a crisis of what to do about these persons who have languished in prisons often for decades. The policy proposals offered include: Increased training and expansion of jobs for returning ex-offenders; social services and counseling to promote reintegration into communities; subsidies for hiring ex-offenders; investment in family support services; training for entrepreneurship opportunities; promotion of small business ownership; apprentices for skilled trades (e.g., electricians, plumbers, painters); and rethinking licensing restrictions. The main problem with these policy proposals is that there are other claimants for precisely these same investments: returning veterans; graduations of welfare-to-work programs; displaced blue color workers in manufacturing industries; and recent high school graduates and other youth entering the labor market. There appears to be little political support for the very investments that could remedy the problems that ex-offenders will face when they reenter the labor market. There seems to be even less political support for investments that could remedy the problems that **Black** ex-offenders face. In short, over the past thirty years we have created a new class of unwantedness among Black males that leaves us worse off than we were when we initiated the dramatic expansion of imprisonment as an apparent *solution* to the problem of unwantedness and superfluous Black labor.

NOTES

1. See, Institute for Criminal Policy Research, World Prison Brief, http://www.prison-studies.org/highest-to-lowest/prison_population_rate?field_region_taxonomy_tid=All

2. US Department of Justice, Office of Justice Programs, Bureau of Justice Statistics, "Prisoners in 2010" US Department of Justice, Office of Justice Programs, Bureau of Justice Statistics, "Prison and Prisoners in the United States, 1990" US Department of Justice, Office of Justice Programs, Bureau of Justice Statistics, "Prisoners in State and Federal Institutions on December 31 1982" US Department of Justice, Office of Justice Programs, Bureau of Justice Statistics, "Prisoners in State and Federal Institutions on December 31 1980."

3. The methodology for estimating the portion of the sentencing disparity that is unexplained—the amount due to discrimination—assumes that the model is correctly specified, that important observables are not omitted, and that relevant independent variables included in the model are not themselves tainted by discrimination. Omitted variables and model misspecification might bias the discrimination measure upward. Inclusion of variables that are tainted by discrimination might bias the discrimination measure downward.

4. This technique is known as an intertemporal decomposition and expands upon the conventional Blinder-Oaxaca decomposition (Darity and Myers 1998a). The main purpose of this type of decomposition is to measure the impacts of explained factors—such as drug arrests—on racial disparities in the dependent variable, in this instance, incarceration rates. One can also use this methodology to measure intertemporal discrimination, but if discrimination biases the independent variables then the resulting decomposition will underestimate the amount of discrimination or unexplained disparity in the dependent variable.

REFERENCES

Center for the Study of Social Policy. 2012. *Results-Based Public Policy Strategies for Promoting Workforce Strategies for Reintegrating Ex-Offenders.* https://

www.cssp.org/policy/papers/Promoting-Workforce-Strategies-for-Reintegrating-Ex-Offenders.pdf

Darity, William A., and Samuel L. Myers, Jr. (2000). "The Impact of Labor Market Prospects on Incarceration Rates." In *Prosperity for All? The Economic Boom and African Americans: The Economics Boom and African Americans*, edited by Robert Cherry and William M. Rodgers, III, 279–307. New York: NY: Russell Sage Foundation.

Darity, William A., and Samuel L. Myers, Jr. 1998a. *Persistent Disparity: Race & Economic Inequality in the U.S. Since 1945*. Northampton, MA: Edward Elgar Publishing.

Darity, William A., and Samuel L. Myers, Jr. 1998b. *The Unintended Impacts of Sentencing Guidelines on Family Structure*. Report to the National Institute of Justice, November 18.

Darity, William A., Samuel L. Myers, Jr., and Chanjin Chung. 1998. "Racial Earnings Disparities and Family Structure." *Southern Economic Journal* 65(1): 20–41.

Darity, William, Samuel L. Myers Jr., William J. Sabol, and Emmett Carson. 1994. *The Black Underclass: Critical Essays on Race and Unwantedness*. New York: Garland Press.

Epp, Charles R., Steven Maynard-Moody, and Donald Haider-Markel. 2017. "Beyond Profiling: The Institutional Sources of Racial Disparities in Policing." *Public Administration Review* 77(2): 168–178.

Epp, Charles R., Steven Maynard-Moody, and Donald P. Haider-Markel. 2014. *Pulled Over: How Police Stops Define Race and Citizenship*. Chicago: University of Chicago Press.

Fryer, Roland G., Paul S. Heaton, Steven D. Levitt, and Kevin M. Murphy. 2013. "Measuring Crack Cocaine and its Impact." *Economic Inquiry* 51(3): 1651–1681.

Mason, Patrick L. 2007. "Driving While Black: Do Police Pass the Test?" *Swedish Economic Policy Review* 14: 79–113. Retrieved from http://www.sweden.gov.se/sb/d/9983/a/97618

Myers, Jr., Samuel L. 1993. "Racial Disparities in Sentencing: Can Sentencing Reforms Reduce Discrimination in Punishment?" *University of Colorado Law Review* 64(3): 781–808.

Myers, Jr., Samuel L., and William J. Sabol, 1987a. "Business Cycles and Racial Disparities in Punishment." *Contemporary Policy Issues* 5(4): 46–58.

Myers, Jr., Samuel L., and William J. Sabol, 1987b. "Unemployment and Racial Differences in Imprisonment." *The Review of Black Political Economy* 16(1–2): 189–209.

Myers, Jr., Samuel L. 1980. "Why Are Crime Rates Underreported? What is the Crime Rate? Does It 'Really' Matter?" *Social Science Quarterly* 61(1): 23–43.

Pew Research Center. 2013. "Chapter 3: Demographics & Economic Data by Race." In *King's Dream Remains and Elusive Goal; Many Americans See Racial Disparities*. http://www.pewsocialtrends.org/2013/08/22/chapter-3-demographic-economic-data-by-race/#incarceration

Chapter 6

Should More Law Enforcement be the Answer to Crime?

Roland Zullo

Controversy over police use of force in minority neighborhoods like Ferguson, Missouri, raise questions regarding the proper allocation of public resources for dealing with crime. Persons residing in racially and ethnically diverse communities endure an above average risk of violent and property crime (Hipp 2007; Shaw and McKay 1942), which in turn impairs social achievement (Sampson and Sharkey 2008). The usual and logical political response to crime is to expand law enforcement. Shifting resources to policing, however, typically means fewer resources for other public services, some of which may deter crime by addressing root causes of criminal behavior. Our primitive understanding of the relationship between public services and crime prevents us from appreciating these potential trade-offs.

To make progress, I examine three categories of governmental services and their association with violent and property crime: law enforcement, social welfare, and education. Law enforcement refers to activities for investigating crime and prosecuting offenders, which largely consists of police and courts. Social welfare refers to social service and public health agencies that assist populations in dealing with depravation. Education refers to publicly provided training, including grade schools, colleges, and vocational schools.

The research extends an emergent literature that associates economic institutions with crime (Lee 2008; Peterson et al. 2000; Wo 2014). A contribution is made by looking beyond the effects of private establishments and law enforcement to examine the crime-deterring role of other public functions. A second contribution is made by testing for a differential effect of public services on crime across regions with high proportions of minorities. Results suggest that public services deter violent and property crime, especially in areas with large numbers of minorities. Further, the best investment in public resources is not in policing, but in education.

THREE CRIME THEORIES AND PUBLIC SERVICE

Shaw and McKay (1929) connected crime to habitat by observing that offenders disproportionately resided in economically disadvantaged Chicago neighborhoods. From this, Shaw and McKay conclude that crime is caused by the "social disorganization" that accompanies residential instability. Approaching social disorganization from the opposite direction, Sampson, Raudenbush, and Earls (1997) report that subjective measures of collective efficacy, defined as cohesion among neighbors and a willingness to take action for a neighborhood goal, is negatively associated with violence. Social disorganization or collective efficacy (SD-CF) theories predict that crime is higher in communities that lack the capacity to control antisocial behavior, and both ideas have robust empirical support in the literature (Pratt and Cullen 2005).

Given that public services are resources that are often shaped by the communities in which they are embedded, it can be hypothesized that public services of all types, but especially those locally governed, would augment the informal network that suppresses crime. However, SD-CF theories say nothing about the relative effect of enforcement, social welfare, and education strategies toward crime. Service type and content is less important than the extent that a particular service is responsive to the community, and whether the service mission addresses disorganization or enhances collective efficacy. A police unit that is sensitive to the culture and character of a community, one that responds to community needs should reduce crime, whereas a police unit perceived as hostile force might facilitate disorganization or impair collective efficacy.

Becker's (1968) rational choice model, the second theoretical model, is often invoked by scholars testing the deterrent effect of law enforcement. Consistent with the cost-benefit template of economics, governments reduce crime by raising the probability of conviction or severity of punishment (Ehrlich 1975; Levitt 1995; Loftin and McDowall 1982; Marvell and Moody 1994). The theorized effect applies to opportunity costs as well (Ehrlich, 1996); governments could establish social benefits with eligibility contingent on a clean criminal record, thus incentivizing law-abiding behavior.

While the rational choice model plausibly applies to positive incentives created by government, tests are scarce. In a rare evaluation, Sabates and Feinstein (2008) examine the effect of education subsidies in the United Kingdom that target poor sixteen to eighteen year old males, and report a modest, conditional decline on area burglary rates. More common is for research to treat the private labor market as a proxy for opportunity costs, based on the hypothesis that citizens will refrain from crime when employment prospects are abundant (Freeman 1996; Gould et al. 2002; Raphael and

Winter-Ebmer 2001). Another approach is to treat crime as a function of education achievement, assuming that higher educated persons commit fewer crimes because they suffer greater opportunity cost of arrest and incarceration (Lochner 2004; Lochner and Moretti 2004). Broadly this research suggests a potential crime-reducing role for government by creating ladders of opportunity, but the mainstay application concerns punishment.

A third body of thought, strain theory, originates with Merton's (1938) seminal observation that "[a]bberant conduct ... may be viewed as a symptom of disassociation between culturally defined aspirations and socially structured means" (p. 674). Messner and Rosenfeld (2001) extend Merton's conceptualization of anomie to postulate that the comparably high US crime rate is caused by a culture that prioritizes wealth attainment, paired with the impotence of noneconomic institutions in creating legitimate pathways for reaching wealth norms. Strain theory does not presuppose a contemporary capitalistic context; by beginning with socially defined success, the theory can apply to any social situation. In general form, individuals commit crime when they fail to achieve positively valued social goals or cannot escape from undesirable (or negatively valued) situations due to structural or societal barriers (Agnew 1992).

In a competitive, capitalistic context strain theory should be most relevant to social welfare and education strategies for crime reduction. The provision of essential forms of welfare support is expected to alleviate crime-inducing stressors; educational opportunities should enable citizens to achieve aspirational goals. A law enforcement response, in contrast, is a reaction to crime symptoms rather than underlying causes. Strain theory would therefore predict that the social welfare and education functions of government would be more effective than law enforcement at reducing crime.

Data and Measures

I conduct a multilevel population study with crime regressed on demographics, institutional structure, and economic condition. County is the unit of analysis, with crime statistics from the Uniform Crime Reports (ICPSR). Offense counts for four violent crimes: murder, rape, robbery, and aggravated assault; and four property crimes: arson, motor vehicle theft, larceny, and burglary are analyzed. Crime data for US counties over the 2001 to 2011 period yields about 33,300 observations. The use of lagged variables and missing values (comprising 1.6 percent of all possible county-year combinations; all attributed to nonreporting by local enforcement jurisdictions; ICPSR) results in a sample of 30,056 final observations from 2002 to 2011, inclusive.

Socioeconomic controls are required that capture economic conditions (Allen 1996). Three variables measure county economic hardship:

unemployment, poverty rate, and median income. Poverty and median income are from the US Census Small Areas Estimates. County unemployment data are from the Bureau of Labor Statistics, Local Area Unemployment Statistics.

Variables for economic *conditions* need to be distinguished from *structure*. Where conditions measure hardship, structure refers to the configuration of employers and nonmarket institutions. Several private institutional variables were derived from the Census, County Business Patterns (CBP). Following Lee (2008), I construct measures for private institutions that have been found to be positively or negatively associated with crime (Roncek and Maier 1991). To control for access to alcohol, the number of drinking establishments and alcohol retail outlets are combined (Alcohol). To control for the presence of firms that specialize in predatory lending made under stressful conditions, the number of pawn shops, check cashing operations, and firms providing consumer loans are combined into a variable (Cash). The number of religious establishments (Church) and civic organizations (Civic), both expected to reduce crime, are included. Counts for these variables are standardized on a per capita basis.

The CPB establishment data lacks information on public institutions. For this I turn to Quarterly Census of Employment and Wages (QCEW) data. The QCEW provides employment counts by industry, allowing for the creation of employment ratios for private industries and public services. Four ratios are developed to capture the extent and form of public services: (1) employment in the public sector to total employment (Public Jobs), (2) employment in police and other law enforcement positions to total (Police; North American Industry Classified System [NAICS] 922), (3) employment in public education to total (School; NAICS 611), and (4) employment in both health or social services to total employment (Welfare; NAICS 621 and NAICS 624). The variables Police, School, and Welfare are subsets of Public Jobs, and are the proxies for the three government strategies: law enforcement, social welfare, and education.

Simultaneity bias is an issue with the deployment of public resources for policing (Marvell and Moody 1996), and the same might be said for governments that adopt a social welfare or education response to crime. To more accurately estimate the effect of these public allocations on crime, the four public service variables are lagged one year. The variables are also centered to aid in the interpretation of interaction coefficients.

Two additional structure measures are developed from the QCEW. First is a ratio of manufacturing jobs in the county. Manufacturing is negatively associated with rural crime (Lee 2008), and the inclusion in the models extends the test nationwide. The second measure is a version of the Herfindahl index constructed using three-digit NAICS groups that assesses the county concentration of private industry employment. Low values of the Herfindahl index indicate a high degree of employment diversity within the county, whereas high values indicate greater homogeneity. Thus, if all employment in a county is in the same three-digit NAICS category, the Herfindahl index would equal one.

County demographic measures are from the US Census, and they include the proportion of residents in two age brackets, 15 to 24 years and 25 to 34 years. Ethnicity is the proportion of persons claiming Hispanic origin and race is the proportion claiming solely African American heritage. Ethnicity and race are centered. A final control is population density. Variable definitions and descriptive statistics are presented in Table 6.1.

Methods

Following Osgood (2000), crime counts were analyzed using negative binomial, multilevel regression, with an exposure adjustment for county population. The equation is:

$$Y_{ijt} = \beta_0 + \beta_1\left(R_{ijt-1}\right) + \beta_2\left(G_{ijt-1}\right) + \beta_3\left(D_{ijt}\right) + \beta_4\left(G_{ijt-1} \times D_{ijt}\right) + \beta_5\left(C_{ijt}\right)$$

$$+ \beta_6\left(\text{Time} - \text{Trend}\right) + \alpha_i + \alpha_i\left(\text{Time} - \text{Trend}\right) + \gamma WR_{jt} + \mu_{ijt},$$

Where Y_{ijt} is the crime count in county i, state j and year t; and β are the estimated coefficients for the sample intercept, crime rate (violent or property) in the previous year (R_{ijt-1}), governmental structure (G_{ijt}), demographics (D_{ijt}), their interaction ($G_{ijt-1} \times D_{ijt}$), economic conditions, private institutional structure and other controls (C_{ijt}), and a linear time trend. The α_i terms are random error components for county intercepts and α_i (Time-Trend) are random error components for county slopes. The γWR_{jt} component is a spatial lagged function, where W is a $n \times n$ matrix of spatial weights comprised of the inverse distance between the population centers of the states, R_{jt} is the state violent or property crime rate in each j state in year t, and γ is an estimated autoregressive parameter. The W value is one whenever a county is located within a state, thus county crime is controlled by the crime rate in its respective state. The term μ_{ijt} is the unexplained sample error.

Our approach is a latent growth curve model (Rabe-Hesketh and Skrondal 2008) featuring temporally and spatially lagged variables for county crime rate. The lagged crime rate component means that the remaining right hand variables are predicting the year-over-year change in crime. A spatial lagged component adjusts for interdependence between units based on proximity (Anselin 1988). In this study, county crime is adjusted by crime rates in the fifty states, with the strongest association for the state in which the county

Table 6.1   Variables, Definitions, and Descriptive Statistics

Variable	Definition	Mean (s.d.)
Dependent Crime Variables		
Violent Crime	Reported violent crime counts (murder, rape, robbery, and assault) per county per year.	440.923 (2069.236)
Violent Crime Rate	Violent crime per capita (lagged control)	0.003 (0.003)
Murder	Murders per county per year.	5.195 (27.827)
Rape	Rapes per county per year.	28.852 (88.528)
Robbery	Robberies per county per year.	134.774 (816.893)
Assault	Aggravated assaults per county per year.	272.103 (1172.610)
Property Crime	Reported property crime counts (arson, vehicle theft, larceny, and burglary) per county per year.	3193.557 (11178.650)
Property Crime Rate	Property crime per capita (lagged control)	0.024 (0.016)
Burglary	Burglaries per county per year.	701.826 (2385.894)
Larceny	Larcenies per county per year.	2129.429 (6998.886)
Vehicle Theft	Vehicle thefts per county per year.	340.653 (1924.345)
Arson	Arsons per county per year.	21.648 (99.407)
Economic Structure Variables		
Public Jobs	Ratio of employment in public sector to total employment.	0.234 (0.099)
Police	Ratio of employment in public sector for NAICS 922 to total employment.	0.016 (0.026)
School	Ratio of employment in public sector for NAICS 611 to total employment.	0.111 (0.050)
Welfare	Ratio of employment in public sector for NAICS 621 and NAICS 624 to total employment.	0.005 (0.009)
Manufacturing	Ratio of employment in manufacturing to total employment.	0.172 (0.127)
Herfindahl Index	Employment concentration by NAICS three-digit industry.	0.059 (0.042)
Church	Religious organizations per capita	0.001 (0.000)
Civic	Civic organizations per capita	0.000 (0.000)
Alcohol	Alcohol drinking and packaged retail establishments per capita.	0.000 (0.000)
Cash	Pawn shops, check cashing, and consumer loan establishments per capita.	0.000 (0.000)
Demographic Variables		
Age 15–24	Ratio of persons age 15 to 24	0.135 (0.036)
Age 25–34	Ratio of persons age 25 to 34	0.115 (0.021)
Hispanic Origin	Ratio of persons of Hispanic origin	0.075 (0.125)
African American	Ratio of persons that are African–American	0.089 (0.143)

Pop Density (1,000)	Persons per square mile / 1,000	0.263 (1.739)
Economic Conditions Variables		
Unemployment Rate	Unemployment rate per county.	0.065 (0.028)
Poverty Pate	Rate of population in poverty, all ages.	0.151 (0.060)
Household Income (1,000)	Median household income / 1,000.	41.024 (10.873)

is located and decreasing thereafter based on the distance from state population centers. County random error components for intercepts control for unobserved stable county traits, while error components for county slopes adjust for unobserved factors affecting crime trends. The latter are critical for adjusting for change in county policy to address crime, such as an increase in law enforcement expenditures.

Results

I begin with models that predict violent and property crime as general categories. Table 6.2 presents the results for violent crime.

The first model includes demographic controls for race, age, and ethnicity along with population density. The constant, which indicates an average year-over-year change given the controls, indicates a decline in violent crime incidents over the decade. The rate of that decline, measured by the year trend variable, suggests a slight (yet not statistically significant) deceleration in the decline.

Reflecting the longstanding problem of male youth crime (Freeman 1996), the decline in violent crime was not as rapid in counties with high proportions of persons aged 15 to 24 and 25 to 34. Similarly, violent crime rates did not drop as fast in counties with higher proportions of Hispanics and African Americans. A 1 standard deviation increase in the proportion of Hispanics equates with 0.074 times more incidents. A 1 standard deviation increase in the proportion of African Americans equates with 0.290 times more incidents.

The second model introduces the variables for economic conditions and structure. Of the three economic conditions: unemployment, poverty, and median income, only unemployment breaches conventional levels of statistical significance, and the predicted effect is substantively modest. A 1 standard deviation gain in the unemployment rate raises the predicted rate of violent crime incidents by 0.011.

The economic structure variables exhibit comparatively greater predictive power. A 1 standard deviation gain in private institutions dealing with

Table 6.2 Violent Crime and Public Service, US Counties, 2002—2011

	(1)	(2)	(3)
Violent Crime Rate (t-1)	58.389***(8.672)	59.388***(8.756)	59.375***(8.737)
Unemployment		0.403*(0.173)	0.411* (0.173)
Poverty		-0.115 (0.173)	-0.086 (0.173)
Household Income (1,000)		-0.002 (0.001)	-0.002* (0.001)
Church		-56.598* (22.1849)	-58.127** (22.156)
Civic		123.805* (61.550)	108.904 (61.411)
Alcohol		28.691 (35.354)	25.903 (35.094)
Cash		336.484*** (60.100)	320.191*** (59.771)
Manufacturing		-0.160*(0.081)	-0.166* (0.081)
Herfindahl Index		-0.754** (0.218)	-0.744** (0.218)
Public Jobs (t-1)		-0.776*** (0.126)	-0.254 (0.189)
Police (t-1)			-0.743* (0.369)
School (t-1)			-1.313*** (0.280)
Welfare (t-1)			-0.387 (0.802)
Population Density	0.013(0.007)	0.009 (0.005)	0.007 (0.004)
Age 15–24	1.715*** (0.281)	1.595*** (0.276)	1.817*** (0.284)
Age 25–34	3.597*** (0.448)	3.281*** (0.440)	3.233*** (0.450)
Hispanic Origin	0.571*** (0.095)	0.538*** (0.092)	0.533*** (0.092)
African-American	1.778*** (0.127)	1.757*** (0.130)	1.731*** (0.130)
Year Trend	0.002 (0.001)	0.003(0.002)	0.004 (0.002)
Constant	-7.701*** (0.081)	-7.545*** (0.105)	-7.567*** (0.105)
Random Components			
County	0.253 (0.021)	0.225(0.020)	0.220 (0.020)
Year trend	0.002 (0.000)	0.002(0.000)	0.002 (0.000)
-LL	140701.64	140609.59	140590.83
AIC	281527.3	281363.2	281331.7
N (groups)		30,056	

All regressions include spatial component γWR_{jt}. Asterisk * is statistical significance at 0.05, ** statistical significance at 0.01, *** statistical significance at 0.001. Robust standard errors in (parentheses).

predatory cash exchanges (pawn shops, check cashing, and consumer loans) is associated with 0.048 times more violent crime incidents. Unexpectedly, a 1 standard deviation increase in the density of civic organizations is associated with 0.019 times more violent crime. Church density appears to lower the number of violent crimes; 1 standard deviation yields 0.027 times fewer crimes. Alcohol outlet density is not a statistically significant predictor of crime.[1]

Three economic structure measures derived from the QCEW display relatively strong predictive power. A 1 standard deviation increase in the ratio of manufacturing jobs is associated with 0.020 times fewer violent crime incidents. A 1 standard deviation gain in the Herfindahl Index is associated with 0.031 times fewer crimes. Thus, the extent that an economy is based on the same industry appears to have a salutary effect on violent crime rates. Finally, a 1 deviation gain in the ratio of public sector jobs equates with 0.074 times fewer violent crimes.

The third model disaggregates the public sector job ratio by introducing variables for the ratio of enforcement jobs (Police), the ratio of public education jobs (School), and the ratio of county jobs providing social and health services (Welfare). With the inclusion of these ratios, the public jobs ratio represents employment in any remaining government function (e.g., parks, streets, sewerage, and so forth). The Akaike Information Criterion (AIC) statistics indicates that the public sector breakout improved the model fit.

Of the four ratios, School has the largest estimated effect, especially when standardized by variation. A 1 standard deviation increase in the ratio of public school personnel (s.d. = 0.050) is predicted to reduce violent crime by a multiple of 0.063. By comparison, a 1 deviation increase in the public jobs ratio (our catchall for various public services) is predicted to reduce crime by a multiple of 0.025. Law enforcement is ranked third, with a 1 deviation gain reducing crime by a multiple of 0.019. Finally, a standard deviation gain in the social welfare ratio equates with 0.003 times fewer crimes. Only the School and Police coefficients, however, are statistically significant at α = 0.05 levels.

Table 6.3 presents identical models for property crime.

The first model with demographics and population density displays patterns that are similar to the violent crime results in Table 6.2. A major difference is that the variable for the proportion of Hispanic residents is statistically insignificant. Another difference is that the coefficient for year trend is positive and statistically significant. And so while year-over-year property crime declined over the decade, the rate of decline diminished over time.

Both age categories are positive and statistically significant. A 1 standard deviation gain in the proportion of persons aged 15 to 24 and 25 to 34 increases the property crime rate by a factor of 0.094 and 0.061, respectively.

Table 6.3 Property Crime and Public Service, US Counties, 2002–2011

	(1)	(2)	(3)
Property Crime Rate (t-1)	9.811*** (1.726)	10.028*** (1.720)	9.997*** (1.714)
Unemployment		0.738*** (0.144)	0.741*** (0.144)
Poverty		-0.026 (0.137)	-0.005 (0.137)
Household Income (1,000)		0.001 (0.001)	0.001 (0.001)
Church		-90.561*** (21.201)	-91.145*** (21.088)
Civic		54.439 (50.839)	47.890 (50.601)
Alcohol		27.685 (25.872)	27.958 (25.816)
Cash		285.039*** (50.579)	276.975*** (50.119)
Manufacturing		-0.112 (0.072)	-0.121 (0.072)
Herfindahl Index		-1.200*** (0.214)	-1.192*** (0.216)
Public Jobs (t-1)		-1.190*** (0.123)	-0.772*** (0.164)
Police (t-1)			-0.748* (0.303)
School (t-1)			-1.039*** (0.240)
Welfare (t-1)			0.037 (0.794)
Population Density	0.010 (0.008)	0.001 (0.004)	-0.000 (0.004)
Age 15–24	2.494*** (0.295)	2.397*** (0.282)	2.561*** (0.287)
Age 25–34	2.848*** (0.455)	2.138*** (0.426)	2.135*** (0.433)
Hispanic Origin	0.033 (0.105)	0.039 (0.092)	0.043 (0.093)
African–American	0.700*** (0.118)	0.744*** (0.114)	0.731*** (0.114)
Year Trend	0.008*** (0.002)	0.006* (0.002)	0.006** (0.002)
Constant	-5.668*** (0.095)	-5.541*** (0.106)	-5.567*** (0.106)
Random Components			
County	0.294 (0.033)	0.230 (0.029)	0.226 (0.029)
Year trend	0.002 (0.000)	0.002 (0.000)	0.002 (0.000)
-LL	203292.16	203086.08	203069.74
AIC	406708.3	406316.2	406289.5
N (groups)		30,056 (3,085)	

All regressions include spatial component γWR_{it}. Asterisk * is statistical significance at 0.05, ** statistical significance at 0.01, *** statistical significance at 0.001. Robust standard errors in (parentheses).

A deviation gain in the ratio of African Americans is associated with 0.105 times more property crime.

As with violent crime, Model 2 shows that the unemployment rate is the only significant predictor of property crime among the economic condition measures. One standard deviation gain in unemployment is associated with 0.021 times more property crime. The predictive strength of unemployment, compared with poverty and household income, suggests mechanisms connected to the labor market.

Of the private institutions, religious organization density appears to reduce property crime, with a 1 standard deviation change resulting in a decline of 0.043. The density of predatory loan outlets is associated with increased property crime; a 1 standard deviation gain yielding a multiple of 0.041. Alcohol outlets and civic organizations do not appear to affect property crime rates. The ratio of manufacturing jobs in the county is negatively associated with crime, but statistically insignificant. As with the violent crime equations, the Herfindahl Index is negatively associated with property crime; a standard deviation increase reduces crime by 0.050. The most substantive structural factor tested is the ratio of public sector jobs, where a 1 standard deviation gain reduces property crime by an estimated factor of 0.111.

The final model tests the public service categories. A 1 standard deviation gain in ratios for Public Jobs, School, Police, and Welfare yield the following multiples: 0.074, 0.050, 0.019, and 0.000, respectively. All but the coefficient for Welfare is statistically significant. Coupled with the results for violent crime, the results suggest that resources toward public education, or perhaps other nondescript public services, might be more effective at deterring crime than expanding law enforcement.

Further support for this inference can be drawn from Table 6.4, which presents the four violent crimes and four property crimes regressed on Public Jobs, Police, School, and Welfare. The coefficient estimates are based on the same model three of Tables 6.2 and 6.3; full output was suppressed to conserve space.

School, the public education measure, is the only governmental function that is negatively associated and statistically significant across all crime categories. Police, the measure of the relative size of law enforcement, is negatively associated with all crime categories, and has comparably large point estimates for murder, burglary, vehicle theft, and arson. School displays larger point estimates for the more common crimes of rape, robbery, assault, and larceny. The breakout further suggests that public health and welfare functions are effective at deterring rape and vehicle theft. The most general measure of public services, Public Jobs, yields negative and statistically significant coefficients for rape, robbery, burglary, larceny, and vehicle theft.

Table 6.4 Violent and Property Crime Components and Public Service, US Counties 2002–2011

	Violent Crime				Property Crime			
	Murder	Rape	Robbery	Assault	Burglary	Larceny	Vehicle Theft	Arson
Public Jobs (t-1)	-0.248	-1.002***	-1.875***	-0.015	-0.437**	-0.898***	-0.807***	-0.294
	(0.241)	(0.240)	(0.280)	(0.197)	(0.156)	(0.170)	(0.209)	(0.249)
	[0.024]	[0.095]	[0.170]	[0.001]	[0.042]	[0.085]	[0.077]	[0.029]
Police (t-1)	-1.522**	-0.208	-1.426*	-0.547	-0.925**	-0.529	-1.482***	-1.818**
	(0.496)	(0.462)	(0.603)	(0.385)	(0.326)	(0.325)	(0.422)	(0.602)
	[0.039]	[0.005]	[0.037]	[0.014]	[0.024]	[0.014]	[0.038]	[0.046]
School (t-1)	-1.352**	-1.001**	-2.235***	-1.224***	-0.639**	-1.128***	-1.040**	-1.407**
	(0.391)	(0.382)	(0.433)	(0.297)	(0.232)	(0.257)	(0.299)	(0.429)
	[0.065]	[0.049]	[0.105]	[0.059]	[0.031]	[0.055]	[0.051]	[0.068]
Welfare (t-1)	-0.827	-2.745*	-1.870	-0.011	0.601	0.048	-2.408*	-0.157
	(1.722)	(1.173)	(1.101)	(0.876)	(0.733)	(0.859)	(1.125)	(1.600)
	[0.006]	[0.021]	[0.014]	[0.000]	[-1.005]	[-1.000]	[0.018]	[0.001]

All regressions include the full list of predictor variables in Tables 7.2 and 7.3, and spatial component γWR_{jt}. Asterisk * is statistical significance at 0.05, ** statistical significance at 0.01, *** statistical significance at 0.001. Robust standard errors in (parentheses). The predicted multiplicative decreased effect based on a one standard deviation increase is in [brackets].

Table 6.5 displays the coefficients for the interaction terms between race and ethnicity and public jobs. The intent is to explore whether the crime response to the size of the public sector varies with the racial and ethnic composition of the region.

The number of statistically significant interaction coefficients, all in the same direction, indicates that regions with minority populations disproportionately benefit from an economy where a large share of employment is in the public sector.

Implications and Limitations

Prior research has concentrated on economic conditions as the cause of crime, examining factors such as unemployment (Freeman 1996; Raphael and Winter-Ebmer 2001), local wages (Grogger 1998; Gould et al. 2002), or the relative ability of persons to access education (Lochner 2004; Lochner and Moretti 2004; Sabates and Feinstein 2008). Associating crime with economic opportunity explicitly treats crime as a choice made by persons that lack attractive alternatives. A parallel line of inquiry has investigated the relationship between crime and economic structure, emphasizing the proximity of private for-profit and nonprofit institutions (Lee 2008; Wo 2014). Few within this stream have examined the crime-deterring effect of public services beyond policing. An exception is Peterson, Krivo, and Harris (2000), who find evidence that violent crime is lower when poor communities have recreation centers.

Our research combines these literature streams by including economic conditions and economic structure variables in the models, and overall it appears that structure better predicts violent and property crime. Two previously untested structure variables display a strong and consistent negative association with crime: the Herfindahl Index and the ratio of public sector jobs in the economy. Corroborating earlier work, the density of religious establishments is negatively associated with crime, and the presence of predatory loan establishments is positively associated with crime. Other tested structure variables proved to be less reliable predictors.

The strong association between the regional size of the public workforce and crime suggests an important crime-deterring role for nonmarket, politically derived goods and services. Similarly, the consistently strong findings for the Herfindahl Index imply a crime-deterring value from large, stable industries. Both results challenge the philosophy calling for minimal government and antimonopolized private sectors.

Regions with higher proportions of racial and ethnic minorities are especially sensitive to the size of the public sector. There are at least two possible explanations. Jobs in the public sector are generally more stable, and often

Table 6.5 Interactions between Public Jobs and Demographics across Violent and Property Crimes, US Counties, 2002–2011

	Violent Crime				Property Crime			
	Murder	Rape	Robbery	Assault	Burglary	Larceny	Vehicle Theft	Arson
Hispanic Origin	-2.931**	-1.629	-3.249**	-0.220	-1.066	-0.026	-2.606*	-3.268**
	(1.093)	(1.022)	(1.147)	(0.888)	(0.884)	(0.944)	(1.012)	(1.187)
African–American	-4.462***	-0.800	-3.153**	-0.557	-0.902	0.814	-2.085*	-1.336
	(0.842)	(0.790)	(0.924)	(0.635)	(0.624)	(0.726)	(0.980)	(1.278)

All regressions include the full list of predictor variables in Tables 7.2 and 7.3, and spatial component γWR_{jt}. Asterisk * is statistical significance at 0.05, ** statistical significance at 0.01, *** statistical significance at 0.001. Robust standard errors in (parentheses).

provide more generous benefits than in the private sector. Public jobs might offer the security and gainful employment necessary for families to succeed, particularly those in struggling urban areas (Wilson 1996). Alternatively, our ratio measures may capture the strength of regional public services, and through the direct provision of education, law enforcement, social welfare, and others, communities are able to reduce crime. Identifying the causal mechanism will be left for future research.

Disaggregating the public job ratio into law enforcement, social welfare and health service, and education expands the tested range of public functions. Of these, education most consistently correlates with lower crime. All others display a selective association with crime. Law enforcement correlated with lower rates of murder, robbery, burglary, vehicle theft, and arson; social welfare and health service with less rape and vehicle theft; general public services with less rape, robbery, burglary, larceny, and vehicle theft. A major implication is that an augmentation of law enforcement to deal with crime might not be an optimal use of public resources. Rather, the findings imply that shifting resources toward law enforcement might exacerbate crime if it entails a reallocation away from other public functions. Creating educational opportunity appears to be the most promising path.

The findings offer something for all three theoretical frameworks. The body of thought typically favored by sociologists, social disorganization, or collective efficacy, can find value in the relationship between economic structure and crime. The consistent negative association between crime and religious organizations is consistent with the position that safe congregations build social cohesion. Findings for the Herfindahl Index conform to the idea that a shared cultural experience improves collective efficacy. The body of thought typically embraced by economists, rational choice, is supported insofar that higher levels of law enforcement do appear to deter certain crimes. Moreover, the findings for education suggest that opportunity costs are a factor.

Strain theory is supported on several levels. The positive association between unemployment and crime, paired with the absence of a statistical effect for poverty and median household income, imply that the absence of job opportunities and not relative depravation is a cause. The inconsistent, yet negative association between the ratio of manufacturing jobs and crime hints at the potential effects of blue-collar job loss. The solid relationship between public education and crime, and the selective effect of social welfare and health services on crime, suggest that providing opportunity and dealing with social stressors resolves crime-inducing anomie.

This study has limitations. As with any population analysis, what is assessed is the relationship between aggregate population measures, and unsuitable for drawing inferences about individual behavior. The analysis is also limited by the time frame. I look at the first decade of the twenty-first century, so any inference beyond that era is speculative. On the plus side, this research relied on publicly available data, and employed analytical methods that are robust for nonrandom forms of measurement error.

NOTE

1. I caution against reading too much into this finding. The measure captures liquor stores and drinking establishments only. Many states allow other points of access to alcohol, such as restaurants, grocery stores, convenience stores, and drug stores, which were not included.

REFERENCES

Agnew, Robert. 1992. Foundation for a General Strain Theory of Crime and Delinquency. *Criminology*, 30 (1): 47–87.

Allen, Ralph C. 1996. Socioeconomic Conditions and Property Crime: A Comprehensive Review and Test of the Professional Literature. *American Journal of Economics and Sociology*, 55(3): 293–308.

Anselin, Luc.1988. *Spatial Econometrics: Methods and Models*. Dordrecht, NL: Kluwer Academic Publishers.

Becker, Gary S. 1968. Crime and Punishment: An Economic Approach. *Journal of Political Economy*, 76(2): 169–217.

Ehrlich, Isaac. 1975. The Deterrent Effect of Capital Punishment: A Question of Life and Death. *American Economic Review*, 65(3): 397–417.

Ehrlich, Isaac. 1996. Crime, Punishment, and the Market for Offenses. *The Journal of Economic Perspectives*, 10(1): 43–67.

Freeman, Richard B. 1996. Why Do So Many Young American Men Commit Crimes and What Might We Do About It? *Journal of Economic Perspectives*, 10(1): 25–42.

Grogger, Jeff. 1998. Market Wages and Youth Crime. *Journal of Labor and Economics,* 16(4): 756–91.

Gould, Eric D., Bruce A. Weinberg and David B. Mustard. 2002. Crime Rates and Local Labor Market Opportunities in the United States: 1979–1997. *The Review of Economics and Statistics,* 84(1): 45–61.

Hipp, John R. 2007. Income Inequality, Race, and Place: Does the Distribution of Race and Class Within Neighborhoods Affect Crime Rates? *Criminology*, 45(3): 665–97.

ICPSR. Uniform Crime Reporting Program Data [United States]: County-Level Detailed Arrest and Offense Data, various years *United States Department of Justice; Federal Bureau of Investigation. Available at the* Inter-university Consortium for Political and Social Research, Ann Arbor, MI.www.icpsr.umich.edu

Lee, Matthew R. 2008. Civic Community in the Hinterland: Toward a Theory of Rural Social Structure and Violence. *Criminology*, 46(2): 447–78.

Levitt, Steven D. 1994.The Effect of Prison Population Size on Crime Rates: Evidence from Prison Overcrowding Litigation. *NBER* working paper 5119.

Lochner, Lance. 2004. Education, Work and Crime: A Human Capital Approach. *International Economic Review*, 45(3): 881–43.

Lochner, Lance and Enrico Moretti. 2004. The Effect of Education on Crime: Evidence from Prison Inmates, Arrests, and Self-Reports. *American Economic Review*, 94(1): 155–89.

Loftin, Colin and David McDowall. 1982. The Police, Crime, and Economic Theory: An Assessment. *American Sociological Review*, 47(3): 393–401.

Marvell, Thomas B. and Carlisle E Moody. 1994. Prison Population Growth and Crime Reduction. *Journal of Quantitative Criminology*, 10(2):109–40.

Marvell, Thomas B. and Carlisle E Moody. 1996. Specification Problems, Police Levels and Crime Rates. *Criminology*, 34(4): 609–46.

Merton, Robert K. 1938. Social Structure and Anomie. *American Sociological Review*, 3(5): 672–82.

Messner, Steven F. and Richard Rosenfeld. 2001. *Crime and the American Dream, Third Edition*. Belmont, CA: Wadsworth/Thompson Learning.

Osgood, D. Wayne. 2000. Poisson-Based Regression Analysis of Aggregate Crime Rates. *Journal of Quantitative Criminology*, 16(1): 21–43.

Peterson, Ruth D, Lauren J. Krivo and Mark A. Harris. 2000. Disadvantage and Neighborhood Crime: Do Local Institutions Matter? *Journal of Research in Crime and Delinquency*, 37(1): 31–63.

Pratt, Travis C. and Francis T. Cullen. 2005. Assessing Macro-level Predictors and Theories of Crime: A Meta-Analysis. *Crime and Justice: A Review of Research*, 32: 373–450.

Rabe-Hesketh, Sophia, and Skrondal, Anders.2008. *Multilevel and Longitudinal Modeling using Stata*. College Station, TX: Stata Press Publication.

Raphael, Steven and Rudolph Winter-Ebmer. 2001. Identifying the Effect of Unemployment on Crime. *Journal of Law and Economics*, 44(1): 259–83.

Roncek, Dennis W. and Pamela A. Maier. 1991. Bars, Blocks, and Crimes Revisited: Linking the Theory of Routine Activities to the Empiricism of 'Hot Spots.' *Criminology*, 29: 725–53.

Sabates, Ricardo and Leon Feinstein. 2008. Effects of Government Initiatives on Youth Crime. *Oxford Economic Papers*, 60(3): 462–83.

Sampson, Robert J, Stephen W. Raudenbush and Felton Earls. 1997. Neighborhoods and Violent Crime: A Multilevel Study of Collective Efficacy. *Science,* 15(277): 918–24.

Sampson, Robert J. and Patrick Sharkey. 2008. Neighborhood Selection and the Reproduction of Concentrated Racial Inequality. *Demography,* 45: 1–29.

Shaw, Clifford R. and Henry D. McKay. 1929. *Delinquency Areas*. Chicago, IL: University of Chicago Press.

Shaw, Clifford and Henry D. McKay. 1942. *Juvenile Delinquency and Urban Areas*. Chicago: University of Chicago Press.

Wilson, William J. 1996. *When Work Disappears: The World of the New Urban Poor*. New York: Alfred A. Knopf.

Wo, James C. 2014. Community Context of Crime: A Longitudinal Examination of the Effects of Local Institutions on Neighborhood Crime. *Crime & Delinquency*, (forthcoming to print).

Chapter 7

Punishing Members of Disadvantaged Minority Groups for Calling 911

Barry D. Friedman and Maria J. Albo

On occasion, a news organization will publish a report about a person who believes that he has been defrauded by a business and complains to 911. A common theme of such articles is that a customer placed a food order at a restaurant, paid for it, and was then served something other than what he ordered. The employees do not satisfy the customer, the customer calls 911 to report the alleged fraud, and, when police officers arrive, they arrest the customer for reporting a nonemergency situation on the emergency telephone line.

The authors explore such a sequence of events. The customer sincerely believes that she is a victim of fraud. She believes that the police department has a role in refereeing the dispute. We suppose that the customer is acting in good faith. On the other hand, the police department has concern about 911 lines being tied up for what it regards as nonemergency situations. The news organizations report these matters when a customer is arrested. The customer is subjected to ridicule.

What is right and what is wrong about these incidents? Our purpose is to evaluate the actions of those who are involved.

911 SYSTEMS

The Logic of 911 Systems

The designation of 911 as the common telephone number for accessing local governments' emergency services was a breakthrough in the protection of public safety. The 911 number is easier to remember than a ten-digit number. O'Looney wrote that Emergency 911 services quickly proved to be cost-effective when the start-up costs "are distributed over the course of 10 to 15 years." The implementation of a 911 system usually causes emergency-response units to receive more calls. O'Looney (1997, 1, 11, 12) observes, "Many [911] calls will not be true emergencies; nevertheless, they will be calls for citizens who need help of some kind."

The perceptions of what factors constitute an actual emergency may differ between the government and citizens and even among citizens. On what basis does one evaluate a particular situation and decide whether it is an actual emergency that emergency-services officials will recognize to be a justified reason to call 911?

Problems with 911 Systems

Just as 911 systems are apt to stimulate more reports of emergencies, so their very existence also invites calls about nonemergencies. Sparrow et al. (1990, 105) wrote, "Most 911 calls don't concern crimes. The ones that do don't usually reach the police in time to allow immediate apprehension of criminals." When a person calls 911, expenses begin to mount.

If the caller is reporting an actual emergency, emergency-management officials will be philosophical about the costs. However, if there is no emergency, emergency-management officials will find the costs to be regrettable, and may even decide to hold somebody accountable for the waste of time and effort of trained responders whose capabilities would be more effectively directed elsewhere. Said Leon and Sands (1975, 3), "[A] false alarm can help kill a person as effectively as shooting him."

Some problems involve *intentional misuse*. Presumably, callers who make crank calls to 911 do so with a malevolent purpose. Some 911 systems have reported that people have called to get weather reports and telephone number look-up service.

Some problems involve *unintentional misuse*. Presumably, some non-emergency calls to 911 are made by people who have no actual intention to misuse the system. Sampson reported in 2004 that wireless-phone technology was causing 911 calls to be made unbeknownst to the phones' owners. She wrote: "The National Emergency Number Association reports that phantom wireless calls account for between 25 and 70 percent of all 911 calls in some U.S. communities" (Sampson 2004, 2, 3).

Another category of 911 calls involves people who are reporting a matter that is properly a concern of the police department but is not an actual emergency. The problem might be that "the caller's car was broken into the previous night, or the caller has been involved in a noninjury vehicle accident" (Sampson 2004, 5). Most officials will say that a caller reporting such a matter should not call 911 but, instead, should call the ten-digit telephone number of the appropriate office. However, while the public *has* been trained through public-service announcements (PSAs) and other public-information devices to call 911, it has *not* been trained to look up ten-digit telephone numbers.

STRATEGIES FOR MANAGING PROBLEMS

Insofar as the prominent problem of 911 systems is nonemergency calls, the first action to be taken in managing the problem is to clearly define the circumstances that justify a call to 911. For example, the authorities might establish the principle that a call is justified when the caller is reporting an imminent and significant threat to life, health, and/or property.

A reduction in nonemergency calls may be accomplished through *public education*. O'Looney (1997, 11, 12) said that a local government needs to initiate a program of public education about how to use the 911 system at the system's inception. Sampson reported that Wakefield, Massachusetts, authorities "send information packets to first-time 911 abusers" (Sampson 2004, 21).

Another option is to handle 911 calls with a *differentiated response*. Rather than setting out to crack down on callers to 911 systems, it may be fairer and more effective to find an economical way to direct calls to the person or office where the inquiries properly belong. Mazerolle et al. (2005, ii, 5) reported the creation by some local governments in the mid-1990s of 311 nonemergency number systems to alleviate the problem of nonemergency calls to 911.

As a last resort, *penalties* may be necessary. Because some callers will deliberately misuse the 911 system, it is hard to envision a government that will allow all offenders to perpetrate the offense with impunity. Many governments have outlawed abuse of the system, making false or harassing 911 calls "a prosecutable offense, punishable with a fine or jail time." For less severe cases, more appropriate responses may be civil sanctions.

BECOMING THE ACCUSED BY CALLING 911

Latreasa L. Goodman, 27, visited a McDonald's restaurant and asked and paid for an order of ten Chicken McNuggets. A riveting drama ensued. The restaurant had actually run out of Chicken McNuggets. The cashier offered to substitute a McDouble cheeseburger. Goodman declined to accept the substitution and asked for a refund. The cashier refused to refund Goodman's money, because "all sales are final." Goodman reportedly exclaimed, "I don't want a McDouble and a small fry." Convinced that she had been defrauded, she called 911, stating, "This is an emergency." When the police response was not as quick as she wanted, she called 911 two more times and was told that a police officer was on the way. The officer who arrived served Goodman with a notice to appear in court, the charge being misuse of the 911 system (Greenlee 2009).

Our thesis is that unschooled individuals who call 911 because of an unsatisfactory, albeit trivial, business transaction are acting properly in accordance with the admonition, "Don't take the law into your own hands." Emergency-management authorities sometimes explain the decision to cite or arrest the complainant by saying that the complainant is within her rights to complain to the police, but that she should have called the ten-digit telephone number of the police department or sheriff's office rather than 911. This explanation is arguably contrary to a common community-outreach slogan of police departments: If you're concerned about something, don't hesitate to contact us.

Undoubtedly, government authorities are sending conflicting messages to the public. Unsophisticated people are particularly at risk of being misled, and then of watching their rights be trampled on. As Pinson (2012, 40) wrote, "[T]he fact that less than half of all victimizations are reported to police raise the question of whether our justice system can operate effectively without this important piece of the puzzle." In the long run, citizens will not get fairness when they are made to feel fearful about calling the police for assistance.

We decided to explore the question of whether the arrest of callers to 911 under the aforementioned circumstances is consistent with the widely held belief that government officials in general, and law enforcement officials in particular, are very sensitive to the demands and desires of members of the upper class (who fall into the category of property owners, business people, etc.) and—with regard to lower-class individuals—primed more to keep a lid on them rather than to protect their interests. Thus, while people have been arrested for calling 911 for an unsatisfactory transaction at a McDonald's drive-through window, we suspect that police cars would arrive at the same McDonald's restaurant with their rotating red lights flashing and their sirens blaring if its management called 911 to report $20 having been stolen from a cash register.

We speculated that evidence can be gathered to demonstrate that uneducated, generally inattentive individuals pay a price for their low level of sophistication when, unable to distinguish strategically among various possibilities of addressing institutional unfairness, they call 911 and are prevailed over by power holders for the second time that afternoon.

Latreasa Goodman received a great deal of press for her call to 911. However, she is certainly not the only person to use the 911 system to report problems with a restaurant order. A Google search revealed a number of similar instances in which the caller believed that a call to 911 was warranted based on problems with the restaurant's failure to fulfill an order than had been paid for. In addition, in each case the caller attempted to resolve the issue with the store employee or management prior to placing the 911 call. Therefore, the call to 911 is a last resort and, we believe, a legitimate request for police intervention.

A Google search using the terms "people arrested for calling 911" yielded numerous results. Some of the results represented obvious misuse of the 911 system (based on Sampson's definition) including a call from 64-year-old Fleurette French in Florida who called to report "loneliness" and Crystal Spruill of North Carolina who called 911 twice because her boyfriend would not give her beer. However, when the search included the term "fast food," the results included cases that do not easily fall within the parameters of "misuse" as these case studies will demonstrate. In addition to consulting news articles found on the web, we also examined YouTube videos containing audio recordings of selected calls. The video-streaming service featured an entire playlist dedicated to "911 fast food calls."

EXPERIENCE OF DEMOGRAPHIC GROUPS WITH CRIMINAL JUSTICE

The Purpose of Law Enforcement

Thomas Hobbes described life in the absence of government as "nasty, brutish, and short" (Hobbes 1651/2009, 179). Therefore, the classical liberal theorists proposed that the populace should agree to the creation of a democratic system with a limited government, so that this government would protect the people from threats to their health and safety. A major instrumentality of such a government, write Sparrow et al. (1990, ix), is the law enforcement system.

However, no classical liberal theorist would imagine that any such government would operate without flaws. For illegitimate reasons, winners and losers would emerge. One of the threats to safety from which the White majority would demand protection was the population of nonWhites in the United States. Robbin Shipp and Nick Chiles (2014, 49, 50) review the history:

Law enforcement in the [United States] has always been the enemy of Black people.

To a large extent, law enforcement in the [United States], particularly in the American South, was *created* as a means to monitor, control, and punish Black people.

… [T]he relationship between the police and African Americans, even 150 years after Emancipation, is characterized by fear and loathing, abuse and death[.]

"There is no point in telling Blacks to observe the law," U.S. Senator Robert F. Kennedy said in 1965. "It has almost always been used against them." (Shusta et al. 2008, 171)

Reiman and Leighton (2010, 99) have described how American legislatures make laws that criminalize the kinds of activities that members of disadvantaged groups are more likely to do, classifying many of them as felonies, while being relatively noninterventionist about the kinds of activities that affluent people are likely to do. They write: "All the mechanisms by which the criminal justice system comes down more frequently and more harshly on the poor criminal than on the well-off criminal take place *after most of the dangerous acts of the well-to-do have been excluded from the definition of crime itself.*"

The pattern of brutality against nonwhites is offset by the generally respectful treatment by police departments of White individuals, which reflects the majority's concern about suffering by White people. Boyles (2015, 7) makes the stark point that police will "work to contain or remove racial minorities where they threaten to disrupt nearby White comfort—when Blacks are within close proximity to predominantly White locations or black-white overlap occurs in certain places." Walker et al. (2012, 42) write that this concern is reflected in "[the] pattern of more media emphasis on White, female missing persons. . . .Todd Boyd notes that the media's decision to focus on White women and not women of color may be 'an unconscious decision about who matters and who doesn't.'" White, middle- and upper-class individuals receive more compassionate, flexible treatment from the police as a routine. Based on a study of 3,475 delinquent boys in Philadelphia, Terence Thornberry "found that among boys arrested *for equally serious offenses* and who had *similar prior offense records*, police were more likely to refer the lower-class youths than the more affluent ones to juvenile court. The police were more likely to deal with the wealthier youngsters informally, for example, by holding them in the station house until their parents came rather than instituting formal procedures." The poor boys "were more likely to be institutionalized" in situations in which the affluent youths would receive probation (Reiman and Leighton 2010, 118).

THE SYSTEM'S NEED FOR A SUPPLY
OF ALLEGED OFFENDERS

The criminal-justice system could hardly justify its use of a budget and its employment of personnel if an ongoing supply of alleged offenders were not arrested, tried, and imprisoned. If the supply were refreshed on an ongoing basis with affluent, White individuals, the deafening outcry would threaten the support for that system. For law enforcement officials, the choice of whom to arrest and confine is automatic. Shipp and Chiles (2014, 14, 15) write:

> [T]he cold efficiency of the prison-industrial complex . . . requires a steady supply of bodies—suspects, defendants, inmates, ex–cons on probation—to sustain itself. In certain neighborhoods in certain cities of this nation, it seems nearly impossible for a Black boy to make it to manhood without being sucked into the system. In Washington, D. C., an estimated three out of four young Black men—and nearly all of those from the poorest neighborhoods—can expect to serve time in prison. In some of our major cities, as many as 80 percent of young Black males have criminal records.

Therefore, the logical place for police officers to position themselves is some location at which a lot of poor Blacks spend their time.

POLICE OFFICERS' TRAINING AND INSTINCT TO PROTECT THEMSELVES

The training that police officers undergo, the instructions that they receive from superiors, the culture that they develop, and their instinct to protect themselves result in sometimes rash decisions to stop and frisk a suspect, draw a weapon, and arrest and handcuff a suspect. For example, reports Groeneveld (2005, 36), the 1991 Christopher Commission stated that law enforcement personnel develop a "siege mentality," thus separating themselves from the communities that they police. By "rewarding officers for the number of calls they handle and arrests they make," police administrations ensure that there will be arrests rather than constructive interventions to resolve problems conclusively on the spot.

Police officers face more conspicuous threats to their safety than workers in most other fields. "Police officers frequently encounter aggressive, belligerent, and angry citizens (offenders, victims, bystanders), and the very mission of the police, as forces of order and social control, necessarily generates at least some friction with a segment of the populace" (Weitzer and Tuch 2006, 46). The intuition that police officers use to protect themselves suggests to them that certain categories of individuals pose the most dangerous threats to the officers' safety. Groeneveld (2005, 36, 62, 63) says that the creation in the officers' minds of such categories relies on "such superficial and ambiguous indicators as appearance, stereotypes, ingrained organizational biases, and the like." He adds that they may have little alternative: Patrol officers must develop "crude but sometimes effective strategies to gain compliance."

INSTITUTIONAL RACISM

Those who study the incidence of racist acts perpetrated by law enforcement and propose how to address the problem tend to evaluate racist inclinations of officers as individuals. "British criminologist Tony Jefferson . . . concludes that, '[a]ll the major British and North American studies, from the early post-war period on, agree that negative, stereotypical, prejudiced, and hostile attitudes to Blacks are rife amongst police officers'" (Weitzer and Tuch 2006, 80). However, some analysts of the tension between the police and minority groups suggest a focus on "institutional racism." Way and Patten (2013, 4) write: "While individual personalities have been shown to affect police behavior to some degree . . ., institutional choices made by police and city leaders and professional expectations of officers constrain some behaviors and incentivize others."

Ward and Rivera (2014, 50) explain: "[I]nstitutional racism is defined as a complex of embedded, systemic practices that disadvantage racial and ethnic minority groups, and, in consequence, needs to be assessed indirectly as well—for instance, in analyses of historically patterned discrimination and of the unintended, but still discernible, adverse impact of public policies and programs." Law enforcement agencies are not unique among government institutions in the existence of institutional racism, but the institutional racism of police departments tends to inflict damage on minority communities more persistently and destructively.

While the institutional racism such as existed under the direction of Birmingham, Alabama public-safety commissioner Bull Connor, from the 1930s to the 1960s would be conspicuous, other manifestations of institutional racism are more subtle and difficult to recognize. Ward and Rivera (2014, 69) write:

> [R]acism and discrimination need not be conscious or intentional to be felt, and to be operative, in organizations and programs of all kinds. . . .
>
> Racism, along with ethnic, gender, and other forms of bias, is insidious because it is so often hidden among institutional practices—which are aggregations of individual attitudes, behaviors, and actions, but, in their totality, more than that besides, more than the sum of these parts. Individual, group-mediated, and institutional forms of racism and bias may reinforce one another, but they are nonetheless distinct.

Banks (2009, 80) refers to the subtle aspect of institutional racism as "petit apartheid." Mark Halstead has explained institutional racism as being "the way that institutional arrangements and the distribution of resources in our society serve to reinforce the advantages of the White society" (Rivera and

Ward 2010, 81, 82). Those who manage many public institutions understand that there is an expectation that they will operate their agencies to perpetuate White advantage; "Institutional racism would then account for the lack of salutary diversity and equity outcomes in public sector organizations" (Ward and Rivera 2014, 2).

DISCRETION

Insofar as legislatures, when they enact laws, cannot foresee and describe every circumstance that will arise when the laws are administered, employees of the executive branch inevitably possess discretion that allows them to "fill in the details" of the laws as they enforce them. Law enforcement agencies and their officials have this authority. "The level of discretion increases as one moves down the hierarchy within a police force. . . .This means that patrol officers use discretion in nearly every situation that occurs, including situations that require use of coercive force." (Terry and Grant 2004, 162)

The implications of an individual police officer's discretion are wide-ranging and consequential. One discretionary decision involves whether to stop an individual and how to conduct the "contact." A police officer will tend to make a decision to stop an individual when the officer believes that there is a greater-than-average chance that there will be a basis to cite or arrest the target. The officer's demeanor will make an impression on the person who is stopped.

A growing body of research indicates that citizen attitudes are heavily influenced by how they feel officers treat them in an encounter. . . . It is not *what* the police do, but *how* they do it. This research is based on the concept of procedural justice, which holds that in any situation levels of satisfaction are mainly determined not by the outcome of encounters with the police but by the process, or what happens in encounters. Being stopped by the police and given a traffic ticket is an outcome. The process involves whether the officers is courteous and respectful.

Research supports the procedural justice perspective. Wesley G. Skogan found that people who had been stopped by the police had more favorable attitudes if they felt they were *treated fairly*, if the officer(s) *explained the situation* to them, were *polite*, and *paid attention* to what they had to say in their own behalf. Procedural justice research in other areas of life (for example, employment) consistently finds that people are most satisfied if they feel they had a chance to tell their side of the story. Skogan found important racial and ethnic differences in citizen participation, however. African Americans and Spanish-speaking Hispanics, for example, were "far less likely to report that police had explained why they had been stopped." Less than half of the African Americans and Hispanics thought the police treated them politely, and both groups thought they were treated unfairly. (Walker et al. 2012, 138)

The contact will conclude with the officer's discretionary decision to clear, warn, issue a citation to, or arrest the individual. An arrest significantly escalates the intensity of the contact.

In 1978, Van Maanen explored the thought process of a police officer who confronts what appears to be disruptive conduct. The situation compels the officer to size up the offender in terms of whether the conduct is deliberate or inadvertent and what his motivation is. If the officer views the offender "as culpable and blameworthy for his affronting action, . . . he will be dealt with by police in ways they feel appropriate." Once the police officer has placed the offender in that category, what happens next will not be favorable for the offender. The police officer will, in order to justify his punitive measures, classify the offender's behavior as "disorderly conduct," "assaulting a police officer," "the use of loud and abusive language in the presence of women and children," "disturbing the peace," or "resisting arrest." The next step is for the police officer to make the offender regret what he has done (Van Maanen 1978, 229, 231–33).

The result is a sorting process conducted by the police officer. If the offender is a member of one of these "outsider" groups, the officer is likely to be more inclined to make an arrest and transport the offender to the police station to be booked and held in the lockup. At that point, the offender's case may be referred to a prosecuting attorney. Another sorting process ensues.

[T]he position in the social structure has a lot to do with one's ability to manage the *consequences* of primary deviance. A teenager who is picked up for vandalism or joy-riding will be treated differently depending on how this behavior is perceived by the relevant authorities and what kind of resources the teen's family has at its disposal to influence social reactions to primary deviance.

According to labeling theory, lower-class individuals with limited resources are more likely to be treated as "criminals" deserving of punishment, whereas children from middle-class families are more likely to be offered second chances or therapeutic treatment options. In other words, *social class affects the ability to resist the criminal label.* This is important because once the label sticks, it will have major consequences on such life chances as educational and job opportunities, on friendships and other interpersonal associations, and even on your identity—the way you regard yourself as a member of the society. According to this theory, the association between social class and crime (secondary deviance) is real but socially constructed (Savolainen 2010, 547).

POLICE OFFICERS' ATTITUDES ABOUT, AND PROFILING OF, PEOPLE OF COLOR

As police officers attempt to identify people who are most likely to have committed a crime or who pose a threat to the officers' safety, it is entirely possible that—though they may have no desire to inflict damage on members of minority groups—they will subconsciously focus their attention disproportionately often on such individuals. A number of psychological studies have demonstrated that the appearance of a person of color will be linked in officers' minds with sinister motivations. Lane et al. (2007, 430, 439) explain:

> Several laboratories created controlled environments analogous to the police officers' situation. In one such study, Black and White men appeared one at a time on a computer screen, holding either a gun or a harmless object (e.g., a soda can). . . . If the target held a gun, participants were instructed to press one key to shoot; if it was a harmless object, they were told to press another key for don't shoot.

> The data revealed systematic racial bias in shooting, with faster and more accurate responses to unarmed White targets and armed Black targets compared with armed White targets and unarmed Black targets. Neither participants' endorsement of racial stereotypes nor their reports of feelings toward Blacks predicted shooter bias. Knowledge of cultural stereotypes, however, did predict shooter bias: Those with greater awareness of the stereotype of African Americans as hostile were more likely to mistakenly shoot unarmed Black suspects and not shoot armed White suspects. . . . Simple exposure to the stereotype that Blacks are hostile, even without endorsement of that stereotype, may be sufficient to create bias that alters split-second decisions and does so without conscious awareness.

Many researchers have concluded that police officers harbor stereotypes about people of color that suggest that such individuals are prone to criminal deviance and violence. Boyles (2015, 5) describes "differential policing," which "presumes [that] Blacks, particularly young men, are inherently deviant, and thus, suspicious and criminal in nature." Stereotypes may be based on people's experiences—perhaps, at some point, a police officer may have come into contact with some people of color who appeared to be of questionable character—and subsequently the officer makes spontaneous decisions about the behavior of others who look and act in a similar way. As Patterson explains, the officials may characterize such minority males as threats to future public safety who need to be dealt with forcefully (2010, 117, 128).

An active manifestation of stereotyping involves a patrol officer's calculation that a member of a minority group is present in a location at which the individual would not ordinarily be expected to be (Walker et al. 2012, 164). Boyles (2015, 100) says that "race and place are inseparable; their effects are intertwined." The formula of "race in the wrong place" leads to innumerable contacts between police and members of minority groups who are drawn into a whirlpool because they are in the wrong place at the wrong time. Boyles (2015, 7) explains:

> It is somewhere between "hoods" (neighborhoods) and "hoodies" (appearance) that Blacks, especially young men, come to be suspected of wrongdoing. As such, police scrutiny and aggression are not based solely on place *or* race, but they occur at the intersection of the two. Consequently, race, place, and policing cannot be understood as separate from one another. They must be recognized as overlapping forces that produce a set of often unavoidable circumstances for Blacks. Blacks, especially young men, by virtue of where they are and what they look like, can fall prey to criminal biases when found within predominately Black communities, and perhaps even more so, when found within predominantly White ones.

HOW POOR MEMBERS OF MINORITY GROUPS BECOME "CRIMINALS"

Any number of *societal conditions lead to "disproportionate minority contact."* Poor members of the community start out with flimsy connections to the police and other agencies and institutions, Pinson explains. "Disadvantaged communities are typically characterized as being least likely to develop and maintain relationships with external agencies. These communities are least able to secure needed police protection and public services." It is no mystery that people in these communities refrain from contacting law enforcement agencies (Pinson 2012, 11, 17).

Members of minority groups are caught in a vortex involving being disliked by the majority and, largely as a result, being all but trapped in a state of economic disadvantage. When society refuses to offer a hand up to impoverished individuals, they tend to experience the vicious cycle that poverty feeds. Reiman and Leighton (2010, 95) state: "We are long past the day when we could believe that poverty was caused by forces outside human control. . . . [P]overty exists in a wealthy society like ours *because we allow it to exist.*"

American mythology suggests that this is the land of opportunity for all, and that anyone can work his way out of the lower class. But the pathway out of the lower class is obstructed by society's intention to maintain a lower class. The race/poverty combination creates a powerful centrifugal force (Reitzel 2011, 163). Young members of minority groups are drawn into the vortex systematically. As an example, Nellis (2011, 14) describes what minority neighborhoods provide to youths:

> When one segment of the youth population is provided with substantially worse educational opportunities [and] lives in low-income and sometimes violent neighborhoods with unsafe parks and limited after-school options, its youth are already at a significant disadvantage to youth who receive high-quality education [and] live in communities with ample guardianship and safe outdoor spaces with wholesome after-school activities. There can be no denial that the differences between these groups fall on racial lines.

The result of these societal conditions is explained by social disorganization theory, according to Dawson–Edwards (2011, 236), who writes: "Socially disorganized communities are characterized by their inability to develop a consensus regarding their values, norms, roles or hierarchical structure. . . . [H]igh incarceration rates should be viewed as a contributing factor of community disorganization." Walker et al. (2012, 99) describe the result of the vortex as a large gap between the quality of life of the most affluent class and the poorest class, a large economic gap between White Americans and racial minorities and the growth of a very poor class—an essentially permanent underclass—in the past thirty years.

The salt in the wound is delivered by a law enforcement system that reserves its suspicion and contempt for those who are poor and are unlikely to advance (Way and Patten 2013, 16, 116). Walker et al. (2012, 182) summarize: "[T]he injustices suffered by racial and ethnic minorities at the hands of the police are a result of both discrimination against ethnic and racial minorities and the disproportionate representation of minorities among the poor."

Government institutions often carry out *policies and procedures that make poor, minority-group members criminals.* Neitz quotes Stephen Wexler, who wrote that living in poverty "creates an abrasive interface with society; poor people are always bumping into sharp legal things" (Neitz 2013, 143). Neitz also observes that while constitutional and statutory provisions very specifically outlaw oppression of women, Black people, and certain others, there is no such protection for people who suffer from poverty.

Coleman (2011, 22) says that there is little impedance in the circuit between a police contact with a young member of a minority group and his placement in a jail cell. " [D]isproportionality can . . . occur in adult jails and lockups as minority youth are more likely to be placed there versus being issued a citation for a court referral or immediately released in the field to a parent or guardian."

Law enforcement officers especially target people of color who are accused of assaulting White victims (McNamara 2004, 10, 11).

Nothing gets better for poor members of minority groups after they have been stopped. Decisions about whom to prosecute, what charges to make, whom to convict, and what kind of penalty should be imposed do disproportionate damage to poor, uneducated people. Reiman and Leighton's findings are troubling.

For the same criminal behavior, the poor are more likely to be arrested; if arrested, they are more likely to be charged; if charged, more likely to be convicted; if convicted, more likely to be sentenced to prison; and if sentenced, more likely to be given longer prison terms than members of the middle and upper classes. In order words, the image of the criminal population one sees in our nation's jails and prisons is distorted by the shape of the criminal justice system itself. It is the face of evil reflected in a carnival mirror, but it is no laughing matter.

[Bill] McCarthy found that, in metropolitan areas, for similar suspected crimes, unemployed people were more likely to be arrested than employed people.(Reiman and Leighton 2010, 111, 118)

Walker et al. (2012, 98) summarize the situation simply: "[B]eing African American makes you more likely to be falsely convicted of a serious crime and sentenced to many years in prison." Shipp and Chiles (2014, 19) have drawn the same conclusion: "[T]he prisons are reserved for a different (darker) population."

There is extensive concern that jails and penitentiaries are modern-day *debtors' prisons*. It would be difficult to construct a persuasive argument that maintains that the vast majority of jail and prison inmates in the United States would be there if they were not impoverished. "Our prisons are indeed, as Ronald Goldfarb has called them, the 'national poorhouse'" (Reiman and Leighton 2010, 99, 122). Poor people's inability to afford legal counsel places them at a distinct disadvantage (Nellis 2011, 8).

Many poor suspects sit in jail on account of their inability to afford bail. Alec Karakatsanis conducted a twenty-month-long tour of municipal courts across the United States. He found that American prisons by and large amount to "debtors' prisons." Many poor people sit in local jails because they can't afford bail (Karakatsanis 2015, 791).

EFFECTS ON BLACKS OF DISPROPORTIONATE MINORITY CONTACT

Disproportionate minority contact has inflicted *systemic harm on poor, minority communities*. "[I]n the United States, penal policy has been a powerful instrument in the reproduction of persistent and gross social inequalities" (Savolainen 2010, 560–61).

The frequency of contacts between the police and members of poor, minority communities imposes on these communities a level of stress and misery not known to the affluent majority population. Family life is disrupted when some members of the family are incarcerated, and community life is disrupted when some key individuals are removed for periods of time while they are the subject of criminal-justice processes.

The final injury to the community is the disfranchisement of not only prison inmates but also those who have paid their debt to society by serving out their prison terms but are deprived by state laws of the right to vote (Dawson–Edwards 2011, 248–49, 250). The exclusion from participation in politics, including elections, of so many members of poor, minority communities is a facet of the vicious cycle that ensure that poor members of minority communities will remain poor year after year and generation after generation.

Disproportionate minority contact causes Black people to develop *adverse attitudes about the police*. Those who have been victims of crimes often report that they have two reasons to feel aggrieved. The first reason is the crime itself. The second reason is their exclusion from the criminal-justice process as the crime is investigated and, if a suspect is identified, as decisions are made about whether to arrest and prosecute the suspect (Erez and Roberts 2010, 600).

It is not only the case that criminals are drawn primarily from the lower class. It is also the case that *victims* are likely to have lower-class status. Therefore, it may very well be that the word has spread through poor neighborhoods that a victim of crime may find himself in a difficult struggle to obtain justice. Wilson–Davis (2014) has confirmed that many citizens believe that they cannot get the attention of the criminal justice system when they have a problem.

We speculate, therefore, that a member of the lower class who believes that he is the victim of a crime might become particularly frantic about involving the police at the earliest possible moment and persisting in trying to get police attention to his feeling of loss. He might very well call 911, even if others would not agree that the incident is worthy of being classified as an emergency.

Countless researchers have conducted studies to explore the attitudes toward the police ("ATP") in poor, minority communities, and the results have been consistent. People of color believe that police departments and officers deliberately target them for stops, arrest, and imprisonment, and generally distrust the entire criminal justice system. Reitzel (2011, 170) has explained:

Each shooting of an unarmed African American man and each case where an African American perceives a police stop (frisk or search) as targeting them for no other apparent reason except for the color of their skin can undermine the legitimacy of the police and can further erode relations and any potential gains that might have been made. . . .

At the same time that members of poor, minority communities believe that they are targeted for stops and arrests, they also complain that police departments do not protect these communities from crimes that occur, leaving them feeling vulnerable and more resentful.

The result of beliefs that law enforcement officials are hostile to members of minority groups is hostility toward law enforcement. "When police have an almost arbitrary power of arrest over the majority of the populace, police and their moral perspective become an occupying force at odds with the community," says Moskos (2008, 181, 182). "This is why those most in need of police services—those most victimized by drugs and violent crime—are most likely to be antipolice. Our drug laws [are especially responsible for] creat[ing] this paradox."

This hostility and distrust by members of poor, minority communities toward the police exert a spiraling effect, manifested in instability and damage to the communities. One form that the hostility and distrust take is reluctance to assist police officers who are trying to intervene in or investigate a crime (Nellis 2011, 7).

Cooper (2004, 120) reports that members of these poor, minority communities have given up on being helped by police officers when these residents have been the victims of crimes:

> The unwritten rule in minority communities is that you should not report your victimization because the police, politicians, or prosecutors to whom you will make the report will not take action. [Ronald] Weich and [Carlos] Angulo write: "[T]he perception that the criminal justice system is not on their side leads many Black and Hispanic Americans . . . [not] to report criminal activity." Worse, minorities know all too well that a trip to the police station to report police brutality often means that you may be wrongly arrested for disorderly conduct in the lobby of the police station—that is how you are punished for daring to question the police. In other cases, you are harmed physically.

This reluctance to cooperate also reduces the residents' willingness to participate in trials of suspects and other processes of the system, as Peffley and Hurwitz (2010, 15, 16) describe: "It is likely that perceptions of injustice among African Americans have even served to worsen crime problems. At a minimum, we know that Blacks are significantly less likely to testify in court, provide information to the police, or even report crimes against them, largely because of a pervasive distrust of the system."

Only reform of police procedures will create a cooperative arrangement between the police and members of poor, minority communities that will remedy the results of distrust (Williams and Close 2010, 74).

STORIES OF BAIT-AND-SWITCH VICTIMS

In Jacksonville, Florida, Reginald Peterson sought assistance from 911 when the sandwiches he ordered were not made correctly. After attempting to resolve the situation with the store employees, Peterson became irate and left the store to call 911, prompting the employees to lock the door.

The YouTube audio, featuring Peterson calling 911 three times, was labeled "Dumbass calls 911 over sandwich" (Jacksonville, Florida, 911 System, 2009). On the audio recording, Peterson states, "I paid over $12 for two sandwiches and they were not made the way I wanted them. The woman (employee) did not tell me they would have to be made over. Now they have locked the door on me and with my sandwiches inside of the store. I want to get what I paid for." Peterson is heard apologizing to the 911 caller for raising his voice and acknowledged that he was upset about his order before requesting police intervention. Peterson then called 911 again to complain that officers had not yet arrived on the scene. Peterson repeatedly said that he simply wanted his sandwiches or his money. Officers attempted to explain the proper use of 911 to Peterson. He was ultimately arrested and charged with misuse of the 911 system.

Lorenzo Riggins of Albany, Georgia, called 911 to complain that he had received only seven of the eight sandwiches he ordered at McDonald's. According to the report, Riggins attempted to resolve the issue with the employee before calling 911 to request police assistance with his mistreatment. Riggins was ultimately arrested on a misdemeanor charge of "misuse of 911" which was dismissed after he spent a night in jail.

The news report quoted Riggins as claiming, "I called the police thinking everything was cool. I didn't know I was misusing 911. I want to be treated like a person with respect." Riggins was further upset because he never got the chance to explain his side of the story to police. Emergency officials stated that the Riggins arrest was warranted because those types of calls take dispatchers away from true emergencies (WALB 2013).

In Boynton Beach, Florida, Jean Fortune was unhappy with the cashier's handling of his order—specifically the fact that the restaurant had run out of lemonade. According to Fortune, the cashier should have informed him, when Fortune placed his order, that the restaurant did not have lemonade. Fortune did not want a substitute beverage.

The 911 operator informed Fortune, "You cannot call 911 because you are unhappy with your order. I know you do not seriously believe the police can make Burger King give you your food faster. Customer service is not a reason to call 911. 911 is if you are dying [or having a] life or death emergency" (Boynton Beach, Florida 911 System). After Fortune continued to express his displeasure with the service, the 911 operator advised him to move his car while he waited for the police. The operator attempted to reason with Fortune, stating, "Have you given them any money? Have they given you any food? Then you can drive away." He was eventually arrested and charged with misuse of the 911 system.

Raibin Raof Osman of Aloha, Oregon, became upset when he had to return to McDonald's after using the drive-through lane and then realizing that his juice was not included with the order. The McDonald's employee refused to replace the missing items and laughed at the customer's poor English. Osman, claiming that he "didn't know what other number to use," called 911 for police assistance. In this particular case, the dispatcher did not attempt to explain the proper use of 911, though police officers claim that they arrested Osman only after attempting to counsel him on proper use of 911. His family claimed that this was an innocent mistake that escalated (KPTV 2012).

While researching these cases, we noticed that there were certain similarities. First, in each case the caller had attempted to resolve the issue with the restaurant staff and resorted to 911 only as the situation escalated. It would seem that this use of 911, while misguided, does not specifically fall into the misuse categories as it is reasonable to request police assistance when a situation requiring mediation arises. As noted earlier, this is encouraged by many community-service outreach programs. Second, each of the victims was criminally charged with "misuse of the 911 system." As stated earlier, this classification is rather broad and the definition of what constitutes an emergency may differ in different communities. In reference to these particular cases, alternative sanctions may have been more appropriate than criminal charges as it seems (based on the recorded calls) that each of the victims believed that his situation warranted a call to police. Finally, each of these individuals arrested falls within a disadvantaged socioeconomic group and, therefore, was more likely to face arrest.

CONCLUSION

Significantly, in each of the highlighted cases, the victims attempted to resolve the issue directly with the restaurant management or staff prior to requesting police assistance. In addition, in each instance either police or the

911 operators themselves attempted to explain proper use of 911 to the victims prior to their arrests. We believe that punishing the victims, who believed that they were pursuing a legitimate means of resolving their disputes, only further degrades the relationships between police and these minority groups. *In future disputes, where police intervention may be warranted and necessary, not only will the victims hesitate to use 911 but other members of their community may be influenced as well (based on knowledge of the victims' experience). As these stories spread throughout communities, it becomes the prominent message counteracting any community-outreach efforts to engage citizens with the police.*

Social media have intensified this effect by allowing these stories to reach thousands of people and remain archived for future use. Before the Internet, stories such as these might have been forgotten with time but sites like YouTube make the whole incident available for view at any time. For example, the video featuring Reginald Peterson was uploaded in 2009 and had 99,234 views as of January 2016. Moreover, social media encourage viewers to mock the victims with insulting video titles like "Dumbass Calls 911 over Sandwich." The comment section featured hateful, racist comments causing further embarrassment to the victims.

The impact of the choice to arrest individuals who call 911 is twofold. We question whether an arrest is an appropriate course of action in these cases in which the victims were attempting to resolve their disputes in a legitimate manner (by involving the police). These instances do not represent "deliberate misuse" but rather a lapse in judgment and more importantly an opportunity to educate not only the victim but her community as well. O'Looney (1997) advocated the use of educational programs to combat potential misuse of the 911 system and communities such as Wakefield, Massachusetts, have programs in place to educate first-time 911 abusers rather than subjecting them to criminal charges (Sampson 2004, 21).

Abusing public services is unacceptable and should come with a penalty. However, the penalties should be appropriate to the "crime." *By arresting individuals for calling 911, police are sending the wrong message to the members of the community who need them the most. More importantly, they are missing a unique opportunity to communicate the proper use of 911 and improve relations in the communities they serve.*

REFERENCES

Banks, Cyndi. 2009. *Criminal Justice Ethics: Theory and Practice.* 2nd ed. Los Angeles: SAGE Publications, Inc.

Boyles, Andrea S. 2015. *Race, Place, and Suburban Policing: Too Close for Comfort.* Oakland, CA: University of California Press.

Boynton Beach, Fla., 911 System. 2009. "Burger King 911 call because of no lemonade." Retrieved from http://www.youtube.com/watch?v=m_VdaFLB2l4

Coleman, AndreaR. 2011. "Disproportionate Minority Contact (DMC): A Historical and Contemporary Perspective." In *Disproportionate Minority Contact: Current Issues and Policies*, ed. Nicolle Parsons–Pollard. Durham, NC: Carolina Academic Press.

Cooper, Christopher. 2004. "Prosecuting Police Officers for Police Brutality: From a Minority Perspective." In *Policing and Minority Communities: Bridging the Gap*, ed. Delores D. Jones–Brown and Karen J. Terry. Upper Saddle River, NJ: Pearson Prentice Hall.

DawsonEdwards, Cherie. 2011. "Politics, Policy and DMC Communities: The Impact of Community Political Disempowerment on DMC." In *Disproportionate Minority Contact: Current Issues and Policies*, ed. Nicolle Parsons–Pollard. Durham, NC: Carolina Academic Press.

Erez, Edna, and Julian V. Roberts. 2010. "Victim Participation in the Criminal Justice Process: Normative Dilemmas and Practical Responses." In *International Handbook of Criminology*, ed. Shlomo Giora Shoham, Paul Knepper, and Martin Kett. Boca Raton, FL: CRC Press, 599–618.

Greenlee, Will. 2009. "Fort Pierce woman calls 911 three times when McNuggets run out." Retrived on November 1, 2017 at archive.tcpalm.com/news/fort-pierce-woman-calls-911-three-times-when-mcnuggets-run-out-ep-400013080-347597021.html/.

Groeneveld, Richard F. 2005. *Arrest Discretion of Police Officers: The Impact of Varying Organizational Structures.* New York: LFB Scholarly Publishing, LLC.

Hobbes, Thomas. 1651/2009. *Leviathan: The Matter, Forme, & Power of Common Wealth Ecclesiastical and Civil.* Auckland, New Zealand: The Floating Press.

Jacksonville, Fla., 911 System.2009.Dumbass calls 911 over a Sandwich [title given by anonymous YouTube subscriber]. Retrieved from http://www.youtube.com/watch?v=BqQ5nrHBvzc

KPTV (Portland, Ore., television). 2012. "Family Calls 911 over Missing Orange Juice at McDonalds." Retrieved from http://www.youtube.com/watch?v=_Smzv2Zhc6E

Karakatsanis, Alec. 2015. "It Is Time to End Poverty Jailing." *Public Administration Review* 75 (November/December):791–792.

Lane, Kristin A., Jerry Kang, and Mahzarin Banaji. 2007. "Implicit Social Cognition and Law." *Annual Review of Law and Social Science* 3 (December):427–451.

Leon, George, and Leo G. Sands.1975. *Dial 911: Modern Emergency Communications Networks.* Rochelle Park, NJ: Hayden Book Company, Inc.

McNamara, Robert P. 2004. "Revering Some, Reviling Others." In *Policing and Minority Communities: Bridging the Gap*, ed. Delores D. Jones–Brown and Karen J. Terry. Upper Saddle River, NJ: Pearson Prentice Hall.

Mazerolle, Lorraine, Dennis Rogan, James Frank, Christina Famega, and John E. Eck. 2005. "Managing Calls to the Police With 911/311 Systems." Washington, DC: National Institute of Justice, Office of Justice Programs, US Department of Justice. February.

Moskos, Peter. 2008. *Cop in the Hood: My Year Policing Baltimore's Eastern District*. Princeton, NJ: Princeton University Press.

Neitz, Michele Benedetto. 2013. "Socioeconomic Bias in the Judiciary." *Cleveland State Law Review* 61, no. 1 (January):137–165.

Nellis, Ashley. 2011. "Policies and Practices That Contribute to Racial and Ethnic Disparity in Juvenile Justice." In *Disproportionate Minority Contact: Current Issues and Policies*, ed. Nicolle Parsons–Pollard. Durham, NC: Carolina Academic Press.

O'Looney, John. 1997. *Emergency 911 Services: A Guide for Georgia Local Governments*. Athens, GA: University of Georgia Carl Vinson Institute of Government.

Patterson, E. Britt. 2010. "Race, Drugs, and Juvenile Processing." In *Racial Divide: Racial and Ethnic Bias in the Criminal Justice System*, ed. Michael J. Lynch, E. Britt Patterson, and Kristina K. Childs. Boulder, CO: Lynne Rienner Publishers.

Peffley, Mark, and Jon Hurwitz. 2010. *Justice in America: The Separate Realities of Blacks and Whites*. New York: Cambridge University Press.

Pinson, Tonisia M. 2012. *A Study of Neighborhood Level Effects on the Likelihood of Reporting to the Police*. M.S (criminal justice) thesis, Georgia State University.

Reiman, Jeffrey, and Paul Leighton. 2010. *The Rich Get Richer and the Poor Get Prison: Ideology, Class, and Criminal Justice*. 9th ed. Boston: Allyn & Bacon.

Reitzel, John David. 2011. "Race, Crime and Policing: The Impact of Law Enforcement on Persistent Race-Differentiated Arrest Rates." In *Disproportionate Minority Contact: Current Issues and Policies*, ed. Nicolle Parsons–Pollard. Durham, NC: Carolina Academic Press.

Rivera, Mario A., and James D. Ward. 2010. "Institutional Racism, Diversity and Public Administration." In *Diversity and Public Administration: Theory, Issues, and Perspectives*, 2nd ed. Mitchell F. Rice. New York: M.E. Sharpe, Inc.

Sampson, Rana. 2004. *Misuse and Abuse of 911*. Washington, DC: Office of Community Oriented Policing Services, U.S. Department of Justice. August.

Savolainen, Jukka. 2010. "Class, Inequality, and the Etiology of Crime." In *International Handbook of Criminology*, ed. Shlomo Giora Shoham, Paul Knepper, and Martin Kett. Boca Raton, FL: CRC Press, 541–566.

Shipp, Robbin, and Nick Chiles. 2014. *Justice While Black: Helping African-American Families Navigate and Survive the Criminal Justice System*. Chicago: Bolden, 2014.

Shusta, Robert M., Deena R. Levine, Herbert Z. Wong, Aaron T. Olson, and Philip R. Harris. 2008. *Multicultural Law Enforcement: Strategies for Peacekeeping in a Diverse Society*.4th ed. Upper Saddle River, NJ: Pearson Prentice Hall.

Sparrow, Malcolm K., Mark H. Moore, and David M. Kennedy. 1990. *Beyond 911: A New Era for Policing*. New York: Basic Books.

Terry, Karen J., and Heath B. Grant. 2004. "The Roads Not Taken: Improving the Use of Civilian Complaint Review Boards and Implementation of the Recommendations from Investigative Commissions." In *Policing and Minority Communities: Bridging the Gap*, ed. Delores D. Jones–Brown and Karen J. Terry. Upper Saddle River, NJ: Pearson Prentice Hall.

Van Maanen, John. 1978. "The Asshole." In *Policing: A View from the Streets*, ed. Peter K. Manning and John Van Maanen. New York: Random House, 221–238.

Barry D. Friedman and Maria J. Albo

WALB (Albany, Ga., television). 2013. "Man Arrested after calling 911 to report wrong sandwich order!." Retrieved from http://www.youtube.com/watch?v=g7cAeqcBfpk

Walker, Samuel, Cassia Spohn, and Miriam Delone. 2012. *The Color of Justice: Race, Ethnicity, and Crime in America*. Belmont, CA: Wadsworth, Cengage Learning.

Ward, James D., and Mario A. Rivera. 2014. *Institutional Racism, Organizations & Public Policy*. New York: Peter Lang Publishing, Inc.

Way, Lori Beth, and Ryan Patten. 2013. *Hunting for "Dirtbags": Why Cops Over-Police the Poor and Racial Minorities*. Boston: Northeastern University Press.

Weitzer, Ronald, and Steven A. Tuch. 2006. *Race and Policing in America: Conflict and Reform*. New York: Cambridge University Press.

Williams, Brian N., and Billy R. Close. 2010. "Perceptions of Bias-Based Policing: Implications for Police Policy and Practice." In *Racial Divide: Racial and Ethnic Bias in the Criminal Justice System*, ed. Michael J. Lynch, E. Britt Patterson, and Kristina K. Childs. Boulder, CO: Lynne Reinner Publishers.

Wilson–Davis, Tosha. 2014. "Expanding the Role of Public Administration: The Open-Door Policy in Criminal Justice." *PA Times*, July 15.

Part III

SOCIAL RAMIFICATIONS

Chapter 8

Check Your Bubble!

Mindful Intersections of Trauma and Community Policing

Sharlene Graham Boltz

Human beings interpret language and behavior through their individual and corporate cultural perspective. The cultural perspective is informed by life experience, childhood instruction and inherent values. The individual cultural perspective creates an interpretative bubble through which language and behavior is judged. The interpretative bubble is informed by our experiences with our family, friends and community and the expectations, values and beliefs. The individual interpretative bubble is space within which we work, create our families and engage with others, so long as their interpretative bubble bears considerable resemblance to our own. However, when our interpretative bubbles interact with the interpretative bubble which is informed by a trauma experience, the collision is often painful, and sometimes, fatal.

This chapter will address the interpretative bubbles created by human experience in two key areas: trauma and community policing. The interpretative bubbles humans create, which are defined and regulated by race, gender and class, are greatly impacted by experiences with trauma. Those interpretative bubbles collide when law enforcement officers engage traumatized individuals under the guise of maintaining command control and compliance. While it is true that maintaining the safety of the public is a stated goal of law enforcement, recent events involving violence, death, public protest and scrutiny of policing decisions, demand mindful reflection upon the intersectional reality of historical trauma and policing objectives. This chapter begins with a hypothetical fact pattern to provide a framework for consideration of the intersection of interpretative bubbles, policing objectives and human experiences with historical traumas. The hypothetical does not seek to define all encounters between the public and law enforcement but rather to illustrate the intersection of issues which challenge the goals of community policing where historical trauma is present. The chapter concludes with the consideration of several mindful and trauma-informed approaches to engage decision-making processes which occur when interpretative bubbles collide on the street.

THE SCENARIO: THE EVENT HORIZON WHEN INTERPRETATIVE BUBBLES COLLIDE

Five adolescent males have gathered outside of a local arcade. The boys are laughing loudly, joking and jostling one another. A police officer drives by the group and stops. The officer exits his cruiser and approaches. The officer tells the boys, "Settle down and move along!" with an authoritative tone. The boys frown at the officer, posture their disgust and with mumbling and grumbling, express their annoyance. All, but one, slowly moves away from the arcade entrance. The officer looks at the noncompliant adolescent and raises his voice. The officer shouts, "You heard me. Move!" The one boy is frozen and does not respond. His affect is flat. The officer grabs the boy by the arm, pushes the boy forward and bends the boy, face first, over the hood of the cruiser. The boy blinks, as if awakening from a trance. The officer presses the boy hard against the car and begins to perform a "pat down" search of the boy's pants pockets, front and back, sliding his hand along the inside and outside of the boy's legs. The boy jerks to stand up and yells, "Oh Hell No!" The officer pushes the boy with force against the car hood, and handcuffs the boy. The boy begins to shake, as tears stream from his eyes, he yells, "No! No! No! I won't let you! Not again! Stop! Stop!" Another officer arrives at the scene. The boy is twisting, jerking, trying to stand erect. The boy is arrested and charged with disorderly conduct and resisting arrest. The boy is visibly angry and through his tears can only say, "No! No!"

One interpretative bubble suggests that this event presents an undisciplined youth, who refused to comply and resisted arrest. Just comply and submit. And yet, there is another interpretative bubble which is informed by a historical trauma.

The boys at the arcade are classmates enjoying an in-service day off from school. As the boys are leaving the arcade and exchanging farewells before going home, a police car pulls up. The officer exits the vehicle and approaches the group. "Settle down and move along!" the officer yells. The group give a "stink eye" to the officer and slowly move away from the arcade. All, with the exception of one, comply with the officer's directive. However, the one boy, previously in a state of calm while he and his friends stood outside of the arcade, is startled by the arrival of the police officer. But, this boy stands frozen in his tracks. This boy has heard a sound, a voice, with a familiar inflection and vibrato from his past. A voice he heard several times before as a nine-year-old. This voice was the voice of his uncle. In an instant, the mind of this now fifteen-year-old is pulled back into time to the day his mother left him and his younger brother in the care of his uncle. His uncle yelled at him to "Move Along!" pushing the boy forward into his uncle's bedroom. His uncle, a tall, muscular man, pushed the boy face down on the bed and held him there, undeterred by the boy's protest, as he pulled down the boy's pants. He tried to yell, but his uncle said that he would kill his little brother if he uttered a sound. His uncle rubbed his legs. . . . All he could remember is the fear. The panic which consumed him when he heard the sound of the zipper on his uncle's pants. The pain. . . so much pain. The tears and muffled words as his uncle pressed the boy's face deeper into the bed. His mind racing with so many questions. "Why?!What is going on? Why is he doing this to me? What did I do? What is happening? The pain. The pain from behind. Stop! Stop! Stop! Someday I will be bigger. Someday, I will be strong enough to stop you." The boy, now fifteen, has the ability to yell at his uncle and shouts, "Oh Hell No!" "No! No! No!" "I won't let you! Stop! Stop!" The adolescent is thinking, "I am older now. I can fight back!" The adolescent awakes from his flashback as he hears the sound of handcuffs on his wrists. He is angry. He cries. Trying to understand what just happened. All he can say is, "No! No!"

This adolescent boy is the victim of a child rape. At this moment, it matters not whether this rape was discovered or the uncle was held to account. The adolescent has transitioned from calm, to startle, to alarm, to fear, to terror within the interpretative bubble of his stored memory, triggered by the sound of the officer's voice. He relives the experience in his memory. He feels the trauma associated with this memory as a present sensation. And, he has rehearsed an alternative ending. An ending where he fights against his uncle to prevent the rape. An ending where he is in charge of his own body. And yet, when he awakens from the flashback, the child finds himself in handcuffs, heading to jail, his life in ruins as a consequence of an historical trauma which he was powerless to control. This is the interpretative bubble of the adolescent boy who was a victim of rape, an experience of a sexual assault that neither his friends nor the officer were aware, but shared by one in six boys before the age of eighteen in the United States.[1]

When Interpretative Bubbles Collide

The scenario presents two interpretative bubbles formed by the cultural experiences of the officer and the adolescent. Culture, for the purpose of this piece is defined as the sum of customary beliefs, social forms and material traits of an ethnic, social or religious group.[2] The term incorporates attitudes, values, goals, practices and everyday life experiences, including trauma. In this scenario, the police officer brings to the interaction with the adolescents, an interpretative bubble perspective which is informed by his/her cultural experience. The officer, while driving past the arcade and observing the boys, determines that the group must disperse to avoid trouble. Upon exiting the cruiser, the police officer operates from the perspective of command control in order to establish authority and gain compliance or control the situation. The question raised is whether the expectation for obedience is informed by the actuality of a perceived threat or a missed interpretation of behavioral cues observed through the interpretative bubble of police or personal culture or the stress and developing vicarious trauma experienced by prolonged exposure to "the worst of the worst." Expectations informed by the latter interpretative bubble do not provide the space for evaluation of physical symptoms of trauma exhibited by the adolescent's behavior.

The interpretative bubble of the police officer is not formed as a consequence of police training. Recent investigative reports published by the United States Department of Justice as a consequence of violent interactions and allegations of excessive force by law enforcement officers in Cleveland, Ohio and Ferguson, Missouri, reveal that officers receive inadequate training on the issues of mental health within the communities they serve. Indeed, the December 2015 report entitled, "Stress On the Street (SOS): Race, Policing, Health, and Increasing Trust Not Trauma," published by Human Impact Partners, echoes the concern of inadequate mental health training and recognizes the need to address vicarious trauma within the ranks of law enforcement.[3] The officer's expectation that his commands will be obeyed without exception is itself an interpretative bubble informed by his life experience as a law enforcement officer, his culture, his childhood and the inadequate comprehension of the impact of trauma on the human mind. If the officer has no experience or understanding about the lasting impact of trauma on the human brain, manifestations of that trauma are subject to misinterpretation. For the adolescent, the flashback is a manifestation of a severe traumatic experience which is informing his interpretation of the actions taken by the officer. The child's visible manifestations of behavior such as "freezing," flat affect, lack of focus, verbal statements, tears and escalation from a state of calm to agitation, demands attention, comprehension and de-escalation, in lieu of arrest.

The Brain on Trauma

An understanding of brain functionality, from resting or calm states to terror associated with prior experiences of extreme fear or unanticipated trauma, is necessary for an informed response to trauma by law enforcement. In the human brain, "the prefrontal cortex is the most evolved region" that controls our "highest order of cognitive abilities."[4] Located in the frontal region of the brain,

The prefrontal cortex (PFC) intelligently regulates our thoughts, actions and emotions through extensive connections with other brain regions…: the ability to keep in mind an event that has just occurred, or bring to mind information from long-term storage, and use this representational knowledge to regulate behavior, thought and emotion.[5] (Goldman-Rakic 1996)

When a person experiences an emotional or traumatic event, the brain begins to release stress hormones from the amygdala, located in the middle regions of the brain.[6] As the intensity of the emotional or traumatic experience escalates from calm to arousal, arousal to alarm, alarm to fear and fear to terror, the release of stress hormones from the amygdala increases and causes the prefrontal cortex to shut down. Although the brain is able to absorb or record sights, sounds, smells and other physical sensations, stress hormones from the amygdala cause the older, reptilian regions of the brain to take control. Those older parts, such as the hippocampus, rely on imbedded patterns of behavior, historical in nature, to operate in the presence of a perceived danger or threat. It is at this point that the freeze, fight or flight response is common.

The scenario illustrates the transformations occurring to the adolescent's brain, once startled, quickly progressed to arousal, to alarm, to fear, to terror, as the memory of the rape resurfaces. The child is held hostage by the memory. As the research by Arnsten and others have shown, the prefrontal cortex is disabled and other behaviors manifest.[7] (Arnsten, 2009) The child behaves in a manner symptomatic of dissociation or tonic immobility, including freezing in place, facial expressions or affect which is flat, verbalizations and visual responses which seem disconnected from the present. Dissociation or dissociative behavior is an act of self-protection from overwhelming sensations or emotions associated with the unanticipated trauma.[8] (Chu 1990) Tonic Immobility is induced by conditions of fear and physical restriction or the perception of the inability to escape.[9] (Humphreys et al. 2010) It appears as pronounced verbal immobility, trembling and muscular rigidity, sensations of cold, numbness or insensitivity to intense or painful stimulation.[10] (Martin et al. 2011) However, whereas the child is exhibiting behaviors which merit further inquiry by the officer prior to arrest, a deeper question is whether the officer also exhibits symptoms of prior traumatization in the escalation of his actions toward the child.

Manifestations of post-traumatic experiences in the form of flashbacks are not novel. Since World War II, the post-traumatic experiences of soldiers returning from the battlefield have been documented with urgency, given the increasing prevalence of suicide by returning military personnel and veterans.[11] (Grossman 2008) Depression, flashbacks, paralyzing fear and panic, as well as other manifestations of post-traumatic stress have been documented. Lt. Col. Dave Grossman, in his books, *On Combat*, recounts stories of veterans who are serving as law enforcement after military service and the post-traumatic states experienced by the officers.[12] Documented situations where the law enforcement officer and veteran experiences a flashback or exhibits other symptoms of reexperiencing a traumatic event in a critical incident situation are particularly concerning.[13] Risk of serious injury to the officer himself or the citizen in the path of an officer caught in the throes of a post-traumatic memory is high when the decision-making mechanism in the prefrontal cortex are compromised. However, is it possible that an officer who has not been directly impacted by a traumatic event, can nevertheless be vicariously impacted by trauma, and therefore manifest forms of post-traumatic effects similar to that of the adolescent? Such vicarious trauma could cause a transformation of emotional brain functionality as the officer experiences alarm, intense fear, feelings of helplessness or horror and terror through the direct or indirect experiencing, witnessing or being confronted by events involving actual or threatened death or serious injury to self or others.[14] The Diagnostic and Statistical Manual of Mental Disorders, Fifth Edition (DSM-5) recognizes the potential for post-traumatic symptoms to develop vicariously as a consequence to "repeated or extreme exposure to aversive details of traumatic event(s).[15] Whereas the DSM-5 indicates the primacy of trauma directly experienced or witnessed, as predictive of more serious symptoms of post-traumatic stress disorder (PTSD), "a growing body of research indicates that indirect exposure, such as learning about homicide; physical or sexual assault or traumatic death in combat, disaster, or terrorism occurring to a loved one can precipitate PTSD symptoms"[16] (Friedman et al. 2011).

The awareness of indirect or vicarious trauma experiences, and symptomatic PTSD, as a risk factor for first responders, reinforces the concern for the behavior and decision-making demonstrated by the police officer in the scenario presented, as well as, officers on the street who may be at risk of developing PTSD as a consequence of prolonged exposure to aversive details of traumatic events. Law enforcement officers experience fear, severe stress, even terror, in certain situations where the risk of serious bodily harm or death is a possibility. Accordingly, it is not illogical to argue that officers in such an emotional state would experience the same release of stress hormones which reduced functionality of the prefrontal cortex as the adolescent, triggered by the sound of the officer's voice. The Stress on the Street report confirms the increasing level of stress and symptoms of PTSD which manifest among officers in Ohio and the potential impact on decision-making during encounters with the public.[17] Thus, it is imperative that attention be given to the risk of unreasonable escalations of police responses to interpreted behaviors when post-traumatic symptoms from other historical trauma experiences are present.

The Historical Trauma of Societal Oppression

The scenario presented in this piece primarily seeks to address the extent to which the experience of direct trauma and post-traumatic stress symptomology can influence the interpretative bubbles of both the police officer and an adolescent who is a victim of rape. However, new research informs us that there exists a type of post-traumatic stress which is the consequence of other historical traumas experienced vicariously by historically oppressed persons.[18] (Rocha-Rego et al. 2012) Specifically, community concerns and perceptions of fairness informed by the history of oppression experienced by Black and brown people at the hands of law enforcement and others, as well as, actions taken by law enforcement officers that did not always represent the highest of ethics as it related to Black and brown people in this country, contribute to the interpretative bubble for the individual and the community at large.[19] The origins of law enforcement from a posse that recovered runaway slaves, to officers who were secret members of organizations such as the Ku Klux Klan during the Civil Rights Movement, to officers who themselves have committed atrocities on Black and brown men, women and children ranging from kidnapping, abuse, rape, assault and murder with impunity, create a cultural context for historical trauma which is passed down from generation to generation.[20] These vicarious traumatic experiences of a group form the interpretative context for both the community and the police officer as part of their daily encounters.

While law enforcement, generally, may bristle at the notion of being viewed as potential perpetrators of violence and abuse, officers must bear the responsibility of the knowledge of historical abuses which form the interpretative context of individuals who share characteristics of those who were previously subjected to abuse. Indeed, it may be unfair to bear the burden of being seen through the lens of the worse members of your group, and yet the reality is that Black and brown people who dwell in the inner city are often viewed through the lens of the worst members of their group as well. The suspicion of all Black and brown boys being "up to no good," is an interpretative bubble which is influenced by limited experience with the group as a whole. This is where the problem resides. Reports stemming from investigations of police departments in Baltimore, Chicago, Cincinnati, Cleveland, Ferguson and New Orleans, reveal that a police culture informed by limited experiences with criminals and "the worst of the worst" and the frequent witnessing of the aftermath of violence, shapes an interpretative bubble which has the potential to mislead.[21] Thus, an officer who has been hardened by the limited experiences, will ignore, minimize or dismiss symptoms of post-traumatic stress in its various forms and thereby fail to employ alternative communication techniques to de-escalate any situation.

The nature of historical trauma experienced may vary whether their ancestors were voluntary immigrants who chose to come to the United States or involuntary enslaved persons who were kidnapped and forced to serve others without free will.[22] The descendants of enslaved persons in this country have endured significant and repetitive harms as a consequence of abuse and discrimination. In many instances throughout history, abuse to Black and brown persons came at the hands of law enforcement who began as slave patrols and evolved into inconsistent enforcement of laws. Photographs and other published imagery of abuses by law enforcement throughout history, ranging from lynching, water hoses on children and physical beatings have provided impetus for stories and warnings passed down from generation to generation. While it may seem unfair that actions of today's law enforcement officers are viewed through the interpretative bubble of the worst actors, such stories of trauma at the hands of law enforcement continue to plague Black and brown citizens. (Carter 2007, 2009) In 2015, former Oklahoma city police officer, Daniel Holtzclaw, was convicted of multiple rape and other assault charges, and sentenced for 268 years in prison, for the systematic selection of thirteen African American women for the purpose of sexually assaulting them.[23] Whereas it could be argued that the targeting and rape of African American women in Oklahoma is an isolated incident, its occurrence is reminiscent of the systematic kidnapping and rape of African American women throughout the South from 1940–1979, all too often, committed by members of law enforcement. Those historical occurrences of targeted rape of African American women are recounted in the book, *On the Dark Side of the Street* by Danielle McGuire.[24] Indeed, historical trauma is exacerbated by fatal encounters toward Black and brown men, such as Eric Gardner, Freddie Gray, Walter Scott, Trayvon Martin, Jordan Davis and Philando Castile, to name a few. The systematic murder of African American worshipers by a radicalized White man revives fears and latent trauma within families which experienced similar atrocities in the 1960s.[25] In 1999, the public learned of the scandal within the Los Angeles Police Department, Rampart CRASH Division, in which police officers within the Unit were alleged to have planted evidence in a targeted manner on Black and brown citizens, further eroding community trust toward law enforcement which continues to this day.[26] Moreover, recent reports by the US Department of Justice on the use of excessive force by law enforcement and seemingly predatory policing practices in Baltimore, Chicago, Cleveland, Ferguson and New Orleans, add to the vicarious trauma for Black and brown persons.[27] In addition, new research which has identified the consequence of historical trauma in the form of PTSD has been documented and is subject to further inquiry.[28] (Carter 2007, 2009; Geller et al. 2014) However, what is recognized is that news coverage of such events contributes to the interpretative bubble within our communities.

Where Do We Go From Here? Mindful Conversations

If the stated goal is to provide a community with effective policing by law enforcement, then such policing must be provided with a deep understanding of historical trauma and a deliberate infusion of cultural competence.[29] Three approaches worthy of consideration for mindful conversations where historical trauma exists within a community include: (1) The Peacemaking Program of the Judicial Branch of the Navaho Nation;[30] (2) The Truth and Reconciliation Commissions of South Africa;[31] and (3) The Art of Mindful Facilitation for Difficult Conversations developed by Lee Mun Wah.[32] Each program offers an opportunity for traumatized parties and communities to give voice to their experience with the guidance of a moderator trained in mindfulness techniques, and guides parties to consider alternative approaches to address conflicts between individuals or communities plagued by trauma in various forms. While current programs such as Citizen Review Panels are helpful, such review panels are plagued with the perception of chaotic presentations of perspectives and marginally influence changes in a community which would be deemed trust-building.[33] In the end, the cost of systemic engagement of mindful conversations does not exceed the costs associated with excessive policing versus informed management of historical trauma, and vicarious trauma by law enforcement. "To whom much is given, much is required."[34] Much is required of law enforcement to effectively engage with communities and individuals plagued by historical trauma, post-traumatic stress and vicarious trauma, lest interpretative bubbles burst, and chaos and injury ensues.

CONCLUSION

Historical, direct and vicarious trauma facing law enforcement and members of our communities cannot be ignored. Trauma, whether direct or indirect, has a direct impact on opportunities to advance the conversation and healing process for community relations with law enforcement. Healing must occur, but healing comes with a price. That price involves acknowledgement and understanding of present and historical trauma which influence the interpretative bubbles of our human interaction. In addition, continued investment in the mental and emotional health of law enforcement and the citizens of the communities they protect is nonnegotiable. Being accountable for the actions and events which have brought us to this time and space, and actively investing in the mindful processes of healing and growth, lead to a system of community policing which is trustworthy and, above all, humane.

NOTES

1. Black, M. C., Basile, K. C., Breiding, M. J., Smith, S. G., Walters, M. L., Merrick, M. T., Chen, J., & Stevens, M. R. (2011). "The National Intimate Partner and Sexual Violence Survey (NISVS): 2010 Summary Report." Atlanta, GA: National Center for Injury Prevention and Control, Centers for Disease Control and Prevention, 17–26, Accessed July 21, 2017, http://www.cdc.gov/violenceprevention/pdf/NISVS_Report2010-a.pdf

2. "Culture." Merriam-Webster.com. Accessed July 21, 2017. https://www.merriam-webster.com/dictionary/culture

3. Human Impact Partners. December 2015. Stress on the Streets (SOS): Race, Policing, Health, and Increasing Trust not Trauma. Oakland, CA. 29–36, Accessed July 21, 2017, www.trustnottrauma.org/downloads/

4. Arnsten, Amy F. T., "Stress Signaling Pathways the Impair Prefrontal Cortex Structure and Function." *Nature Reviews Neuroscience* 10, no. 6 (2009): 410, doi:10.1038/nrn2648.

5. Goldman-Rakic, P. S., A. R. Cools, and K. Srivastava. "The Prefrontal Landscape: Implications of Functional Architecture for Understanding Human Mentation and the Central Executive [and Discussion]." *Philosophical Transactions of the Royal Society B: Biological Sciences* 351, no. 1346 (1996): 1445–1453. doi:10.1098/rstb.1996.0129.

6. J. Deebiec, "Noradrenergic Signaling in the Amygdala Contributes to the Reconsolidation of Fear Memory: Treatment Implications for PTSD." *Annals of the New York Academy of Sciences* 1071, no. 1 (2006): 521–24, doi:10.1196/annals.1364.056.

7. A. P. Levin, S. B. Kleinman, J. S. Adler, J. S., "DSM-5 and Posttraumatic Stress Disorder." *Journal of the American Academy of Psychiatry and the Law Online* 42, no. 2, June (2014): 146–158, Accessed July 21, 2017, jaapl.org/content/jaapl42/2/146.full.pdf

8. J. A. Chu and D. L. Dill, "Dissociative symptoms in relation to childhood physical and sexual abuse." *American Journal of Psychiatry* 147, no. 7 (1990): 887–92, doi:10.1176/ajp.147.7.887.

9. K. L. Humphreys, C. L. Sauyder, E. K. Martin, B. P. Marx, "Tonic Immobility in Childhood Sexual Abuse Survivors and Its Relationship to Posttraumatic Stress Symptomatology," *Journal of Interpersonal Violence* 25 no. 2, (2010): 358–9. Accessed July 21, 2017, www.kathrynhumphreys.com/uploads/4/3/0/6/43065295/humphreys_2010_tonic_immobility.pdf

10. Martin, G., Cromer, L. D., DePrince, A. P. and Freyd, J. J., "The Role of Cumulative Trauma, Betrayal and Appraisals in Understanding Trauma Symptomatology." *Psychological Trauma: Theory, Research, Practice and Policy* 5, no. 2, (2011): 110–118.

11. Grossman, D. 2008, *On Combat: The Psychology and Physiology of Deadly Conflict in War and In Peace-3rd ed.*

12. Grossman, On Combat, 278–301.

13. Grossman, On Combat, 278–301.

14. American Psychiatric Association. (2013). *Diagnostic and statistical manual of mental disorders*, (5th ed.). Washington, DC: Author.

15. *Diagnostic and Statistical Manual of Mental Disorders: DSM-5.* 5th ed. Arlington, VA: American Psychiatric Association, 2013.

16. Friedman M. J, Resick P. A, Bryant R. A, *et al.*: Considering PTSD for DSM-5. Depress Anxiety 28 (2011): 750–69.

17. Human Impact Partners, Stress On the Streets (SOS): Race, Policing, Health, and Increasing Trust Not Trauma (2015): 29–36.

18. Vanessa Rocha-Rego *et al.*, "Decreased Premotor Cortex Volume in Victims of Urban Violence with Posttraumatic Stress Disorder." *PLoS ONE*7, no. 8 (2012). doi:10.1371/journal.pone.0042560.

19. Human Impact Partners, Stress On the Streets (SOS): Race, Policing, Health, and Increasing Trust Not Trauma (2015): 11, 16–17.

20. Human Impact Partners, Stress On the Streets (SOS): Race, Policing, Health, and Increasing Trust Not Trauma (2015): 29–36.

21. *Investigation of the Baltimore City Police Department,* report, United States Department of Justice, Civil Rights Division, August 10, 2016, 3–24, accessed July 25, 2017, http://www.justice.gov/crt/file/883296/download; *Investigation of the Chicago Police Department*, report, United States Department of Justice, Civil Rights Division & United States Attorney's Office, Northern District of Illinois, January 13, 2017, 22–45, accessed July 25, 2017, http://www.justice.gov/opa/file/925846/download; *DOJ Investigation of Cincinnati Police Department—Findings Letter—Re: Investigation of the Cincinnati Police Division*, report, United States Department of Justice, Civil Rights Division, October 23, 2001, University of Michigan Law School, 1–15, accessed July 25, 2017, http://www.clearinghouse.net/chDocs/public/PN-OH-0006—0001.pdf; *Investigation of the Cleveland Division of Police*, report, United States Department of Justice, Civil Rights Division & United States Attorney's Office, Northern District of Ohio, December 4, 2014, 3–59, accessed July 25, 2017, https://www.justice.gov/sites/default/files/opa/press-releases/attachments/2014/12/04/cleveland_division_of_police_findings_letter.pdf; *Investigation of the Ferguson Police Department,* report, United States Department of Justice, Civil Rights Division, March 4, 2015, 15–90, accessed July 25, 2017, https://www.justice.gov/sites/default/files/opa/press-releases/attachments/2015/03/04/ferguson_police_department_report.pdf; *Investigation of the New Orleans Police Department*, report, United States Department of Justice, Civil Rights Division, March 16, 2011, 31–43, accessed July 25, 2017, https://www.justice.gov/sites/default/files/crt/legacy/2011/03/17/nopd_report.pdf

22. Howard Zinn, *A People's History of the United States* (New York: Harper Perennial Modern Classic, 2010), 22–38, 171–210, 443–467.

23. Matt, Ford, "A Guilty Verdict for Daniel Holtzclaw." *The Atlantic*, December 11, 2015. Accessed July 26, 2017. https://www.theatlantic.com/politics/archive/2015/12/daniel-holtzclaw-trial-guilty/420009/

24. Danielle L. McGuire, *At the Dark End of the Street: Black Women, Rape, and Resistance—A New History of the Civil Rights Movement from Rosa Parks to the Rise of Black Power* (New York: Vintage Books, 2011).

25. Matt Zapotosky, "Charleston Church Shooter: 'I would like to make it crystal clear, I do not regret what I did,'" *The Washington Post*, January 4, 2017, accessed July 26, 2017, https://www.washingtonpost.com/world/national-security/charleston-church-shooter-i-would-like-to-make-it-crystal-clear-i-do-not-regret-what-i-did/2017/01/04/05b0061e-d1da-11e6-a783-cd3fa950f2fd_story.html?utm_term=.ab11ddc78a32

26. U.S. v. City of Los Angeles—Report of the Rampart Independent Review Panel, report, Rampart Independent Review Panel, November 16, 2000, 1–33, accessed July 25, 2017, http://www.clearinghouse.net/chDocs/public/PN-CA-0002—0008.pdf

27. Investigation of the Baltimore City Police (2016); Investigation of the Chicago Police Department (2017); DOJ Investigation of the Cincinnati Police Department-Findings Letter-Re: Investigation of the Cincinnati Police Division (2001); Investigation of the Cleveland Department of Police (2014); Investigation of the Ferguson Police Department (2015); Investigation of the New Orleans Police Department (2011).

28. Robert T. Carter, "Racism and Psychological and Emotional Injury," *The Counseling Psychologist*35, no. 1 (2007). doi:10.1177/0011000006292033; Robert T. Carter and Jessica M. Forsyth. "A Guide to the Forensic Assessment of Race-Based Traumatic Stress Reactions." *The Journal of the American Academy of Psychiatry and The Law* 37, no. 1 (2009): 28–40.

29. Sharlene Graham Boltz, J. D., "Mindful Conversations: Historical Trauma, Policing, and Cultural Competence." *The Police Chief, International Association of Chiefs of Police*, September 2015, 42–43.

30. *Peacemaking Program of the Judicial Branch of the Navajo Nation.* Report. July 30, 2012. Accessed July 25, 2017. http://www.navajocourts.org/Peacemaking/Plan/PPPO2013—2-25.pdf

31. Michal Ben-Josef Hirsch, Megan Mackenzie, and Mohamed Sesay, "Measuring the impacts of truth and reconciliation commissions: Placing the global 'success' of TRCs in local perspective," *Cooperation and Conflict* 47, no. 3 (September 22, 2012): 386–403, doi:10.1177/0010836712454273.

32. Lee Mun Wah. *The Art of Mindful Facilitation.* CA: Stir Fry Seminars and Consulting, 2004.

33. Human Impact Partners, Stress On the Streets (SOS): Race, Policing, Health, and Increasing Trust Not Trauma (2015): 37–53.

34. Luke 12:48. Scripture taken from THE AMPLIFIED BIBLE, Old Testament copyright ©1965, 1987 by the Zondervan Corporation. The Amplified New Testament copyright ©1958, 1987 by The Lockman Foundation. Used by permission.

REFERENCES

Arnsten, Amy F.T. "Stress signalling pathways that impair prefrontal cortex structure and function." *Nature Reviews Neuroscience* 10, no. 6 (2009): 410–22. doi:10.1038/nrn2648.

Black, M.C., Basile, K.C., Breiding, M.J., Smith, S.G., Walters, M.L., Merrick, M.T., Chen, J., & Stevens, M.R. (2011). The National Intimate Partner and Sexual Violence Survey (NISVS): 2010 Summary Report. Atlanta, GA: National Center for Injury Prevention and Control, Centers for Disease Control and Prevention, Accessed July 21, 2017, http://www.cdc.gov/violenceprevention/pdf/NISVS_Report2010-a.pdf

Boltz, Sharlene Graham, J.D. "Mindful Conversations: Historical Trauma, Policing, and Cultural Competence." *The Police Chief, International Association of Chiefs of Police*, September 2015, 42–43.

Bryant-Davis, Thema, and Carlota Ocampo. "A Therapeutic Approach to the Treatment of Racist-Incident-Based Trauma." *Journal of Emotional Abuse* 6, no. 4 (2006): 1–22. doi:10.1300/j135v06n04_01.

Carter, Robert T. "Racism and Psychological and Emotional Injury." *The Counseling Psychologist* 35, no. 1 (2007): 13–105. doi:10.1177/0011000006292033.

Carter, R.T., and J. M. Forsyth. "A Guide to the Forensic Assessment of Race-Based Traumatic Stress Reactions." *The Journal of the American Academy of Psychiatry and The Law* 37, no. 1 (2009): 28–40.

Chu, J.A., and D.L. Dill. "Dissociative symptoms in relation to childhood physical and sexual abuse." *American Journal of Psychiatry* 147, no. 7 (1990): 887–92. doi:10.1176/ajp.147.7.887.

Comas-Díaz, Lillian. "Racial trauma recovery: A race-informed therapeutic approach to racial wounds." *The cost of racism for people of color: Contextualizing experiences of discrimination*. Washington, DC: American Psychological Association, 2016, 249–72. doi:10.1037/14852—012.

Deebiec, J. "Noradrenergic Signaling in the Amygdala Contributes to the Reconsolidation of Fear Memory: Treatment Implications for PTSD." *Annals of the New York Academy of Sciences* 1071, no. 1 (2006): 521–24. doi:10.1196/annals.1364.056.

Diagnostic and Statistical Manual of Mental Disorders: DSM-5. 5th ed. Arlington, VA: American Psychiatric Association, 2013.

DOJ Investigation of Cincinnati Police Department—Findings Letter—Re: Investigation of the Cincinnati Police Division. Report. United States Department of Justice, Civil Rights Division, s, University of Michigan Law School. Accessed July 25, 2017. http://www.clearinghouse.net/chDocs/public/PN-OH-0006—0001.pdf

Friedman, M.J., Resick, P.A., Bryant, R.A., and Brewin, C.R. "Considering PTSD for DSM-5." *Depression and Anxiety* 28, no. 9 (2010): 750–69. doi:10.1002/da.20767.

Geller, Amanda, Jeffrey Fagan, Tom Tyler, and Bruce G. Link. "Aggressive Policing and the Mental Health of Young Urban Men." *American Journal of Public Health* 104, no. 12 (2014): 2321–327. doi:10.2105/ajph.2014.302046.

Goldman-Rakic, P.S. "The prefrontal landscape: implications of functional architecture for understanding human mentation and the central executive." *Philosophical transactions of the Royal Society of London. Series B, Biological sciences* 351, no. 1346 (1996): 1445.

Grossman, Dave, and Loren W. Christensen. *On combat: the psychology and physiology of deadly conflict in war and in peace*. 3rd ed. Illinois: Warrior Science Pub., 2008.

Hirsch, Michal Ben-Josef, Megan Mackenzie, and Mohamed Sesay. "Measuring the impacts of truth and reconciliation commissions: Placing the global 'success' of TRCs in local perspective." *Cooperation and Conflict* 47, no. 3 (September 22, 2012): 386–403. doi:10.1177/0010836712454273.

Human Impact Partners.December 2015. Stress on the Streets (SOS): Race, Policing, Health, and Increasing Trust not Trauma. Oakland, CA. Accessed July 21, 2017, www.trustnottrauma.org/downloads/

Humphreys, K.L., Sauyder, C.L., Martin, E.K., Marx, B.P. "Tonic Immobility in Childhood Sexual Abuse Survivors and Its Relationship to Posttraumatic Stress Symptomatology." *Journal of Interpersonal Violence* 25 no. 2, (2010): 358–73. Accessed July 21, 2017, www.kathrynhumphreys.com/uploads/4/3/0/6/43065295/humphreys_2010_tonic_immobility.pdf

Investigation of the Baltimore City Police Department. Report. United States Department of Justice, Civil Rights Division. August 10, 2016. Accessed July 25, 2017. http://www.justice.gov/crt/file/883296/download

Investigation of the Chicago Police Department. Report. United States Department of Justice, Civil Rights Division & United States Attorney's Office, Northern District of Illinois. January 13, 2017. Accessed July 25, 2017. http://www.justice.gov/opa/file/925846/download

Investigation of the Cleveland Division of Police. Report. United States Department of Justice, Civil Rights Division & United States Attorney's Office, Northern District of Ohio. December 4, 2014. Accessed July 25, 2017. https://www.justice.gov/sites/default/files/opa/press-releases/attachments/2014/12/04/cleveland_division_of_police_findings_letter.pdf

Investigation of the Ferguson Police Department. Report. United States Department of Justice, Civil Rights Division. March 4, 2015. Accessed July 25, 2017. https://www.justice.gov/sites/default/files/opa/press-releases/attachments/2015/03/04/ferguson_police_department_report.pdf

Investigation of the New Orleans Police Department. Report. United States Department of Justice, Civil Rights Division. March 16, 2011. Accessed July 25, 2017. https://www.justice.gov/sites/default/files/crt/legacy/2011/03/17/nopd_report.pdf

Lee Mun Wah. *The Art of Mindful Facilitation.* Berkeley, CA: Stir Fry Seminars and Consulting, 2004.

Martin, C.G., Cromer, L.D., DePrince, A.P., & Freyd, J.J. "The Role of Cumulative Trauma, Betrayal, and Appraisals in Understanding Trauma Symptomatology." *Psychological Trauma: Theory, Research, Practice and Policy* 52, no.2, (2013): 110–118. Accessed July 21, 2017, https://www.ncbi.nlm.nih.gov/pmc/articles/PMC3608140/

McGuire, Danielle L. *At the Dark End of the Street: Black Women, Rape, and Resistance-- A New History of the Civil Rights Movement from Rosa Parks to the Rise of Black Power.* New York: Vintage Books, 2011.

Peacemaking Program of the Judicial Branch of the Navajo Nation. Report. July 30, 2012. Accessed July 25, 2017. http://www.navajocourts.org/Peacemaking/Plan/PPPO2013—2-25.pdf

Rocha-Rego, V., Pereira, M.G., Oliveira, L., Mendlowicz, M.V., Fiszman, A., Marques-Portella, C., Berger, W., Chu, C., Mateus Joffily, Jorge Moll, Jair J. Mari, Ivan Figueira, and Eliane Volchan. "Decreased Premotor Cortex Volume in Victims of Urban Violence with Posttraumatic Stress Disorder." *PLoS ONE* 7, no. 8 (2012). doi:10.1371/journal.pone.0042560.

U.S. v. City of Los Angeles—Report of the Rampart Independent Review Panel. Report. Rampart Independent Review Panel. November 16, 2000. Accessed July 25, 2017. http://www.clearinghouse.net/chDocs/public/PN-CA-0002—0008.pdf

Zinn, Howard. *A People's History of the United States.* New York: Harper Perennial Modern Classic, 2010.

Chapter 9

Assessing Racial and Ethnic Differences in the Consequences of Police Use of Force

Jared Ellison and Benjamin Steiner

Police use of force has been described as the most volatile issue facing police departments (Olsen 2004), and there has been considerable research aimed at understanding the factors that influence officers' decisions to use force (e.g., Alpert and Dunham 2004; Garner et al. 2002; Hickman et al. 2008; Paoline and Terrill 2007; Ryderg and Terrill 2010; Terrill et al. 2008). Yet very little is known about the consequences of exposure to police use of force (Klahm, Steiner, and Meade In Press), or whether these consequences differ for individuals with different racial or ethnic backgrounds.

While there is no agreed-upon definition of police use of force (Adams 1999), if officers use physical, less-than-lethal, and/or deadly tactics to subdue or control suspects, use of force has taken place (Garner et al. 1995; Alpert and Dunham 2004). Because these encounters involve physical or psychological violence, force, or coercion, researchers have drawn comparisons between the National Academy of Science's definition of violence—individual behaviors that intentionally threaten, attempt, or inflict physical harm on others—and police use of force (e.g., Garner et al. 1995). Exposure to violence has been linked to behavioral problems such as hostility, aggression, and criminal offending (Eitle and Turner 2002; Finkelhor et al. 2009; Thornberry et al. 2001; Widom and Maxfield 2001), and so it is reasonable to infer that police use of force may result in similar consequences.

Police use of force differs from other forms of violence because it is typically applied legitimately during an arrest (Adams 1999; Terrill 2005), but if officers use force when it is not legally prescribed or when individuals consider it unnecessary, then the use of force (and the police) might be considered illegitimate (Klahm et al. In Press; Tankebe 2013; Tyler 2003). Perceptions of unfair treatment by the police and other government officials have been linked to cynical and/or defiant attitudes toward authority figures (Paternoster et al. 1997; Sherman 1993; Vigoda-Gadot 2007), and individuals who believe they were treated undeservedly may display adverse cognitive and behavioral responses, such as reduced levels of trust and confidence in government officials (Van Ryzin et al. 2004), less participation in conventional behaviors (Niemi et al. 1991; Vigoda-Gadot 2007), and higher odds of assaultive behavior (e.g., Sherman et al. 1997). Perceptions of illegitimate force might be especially likely to elicit negative responses among Black and Hispanic offenders because minority groups are disproportionately exposed to violence (Buka et al. 2001; Crouch et al. 2000; Selner-O'Hagan et al. 1998) and police use of force (Terrill 2005; Terrill and Reisig 2003; Worden 1996). Moreover, minorities tend to view the police more negatively relative to Whites (Mastrofski et al. 2002; Rosenbaum et al. 2005; Van Ryzin et al. 2004).

The purpose of this study is to examine whether offending behavior in jail is more common among inmates who had force used against them during their arrest, and in particular, those inmates who experienced force but did not resist arrest. The force-offending behavior relationship is then compared among Black, Hispanic, and White inmates. Recent incidents of police use of force (e.g., the death of Eric Garner) have stimulated discussions about the consequences of police use of force, but most of the empirical studies to date have focused on the factors that precipitate force. An examination of whether defiant or offending behavior in jail is more common among persons exposed to police use of force relative to those not exposed is important because such an examination contributes to a better understanding of the nonlethal consequences of police force for recipients. Institutional safety and order are also evaluated to some extent based on the level of offending behavior within a correctional facility (DiIulio 1987), and inmates who violate institutional rules are more likely to reoffend upon release (Cochran et al. 2012). Thus, understanding the effects of exposure to force on offending in jail has implications for the police, jail administrators, and public safety.

EXPOSURE TO VIOLENCE AND SUBSEQUENT ANTISOCIAL BEHAVIOR

There is considerable evidence of a link between exposure to violence and subsequent problem behaviors among both the general and incarcerated populations (e.g., Boxer et al. 2009; Eitle and Turner 2002; Meade and Steiner 2013; Steiner et al. 2014; Thornberry et al. 2001; Widom 1989; Widom and Maxfield 2001). If police use of force is similar to other forms of violence (e.g., assault, physical abuse) (Garner et al. 1995), then individuals who experience force at arrest may react aggressively toward others and/or use purposeful violence as a means of dispute resolution (Klahm et al. In

Press). Hostile attribution theory and learning theories offer relevant explanations for the link between exposure to violence and subsequent antisocial behavior. For instance, researchers have suggested that individuals exposed to violence may develop hostile attribution biases, or cognitive deficits (e.g., depression, hyperarousal) that preclude their ability to interpret social situations effectively (Dodge 1980; Dodge et al. 1990). These deficits in social information processing can make individuals hypervigilant toward aggressive cues, whereby they begin to subconsciously infer hostile intent during benign interactions with others (Todorov and Bargh 2002), and as a result, react aggressively (Dodge et al. 1990; Dodge et al. 1990; De Castro et al. 2002). Individuals exposed to police use of force at arrest may develop hostile attributional biases, subsequently resulting in aggressive responses toward others.

Individuals who experience violence may also use aggression as a way to settle disputes because such behavior was modeled by influential persons (e.g., the police) as a way to achieve self-interests (Anderson 1999; Bandura 1973). That is, individuals who experience violence could begin to use it as a means of conflict resolution because they have *learned* that aggressive responses are associated with desired outcomes, such as status attainment, the removal of the aversive stimuli, or control over a situation (Matsuda et al. 2012; Mears et al. 2013). Thus, exposure to violence may be linked to purposeful aggression if the behaviors have become part of an individual's behavioral repertoire (Dodge et al. 1990), which is largely developed through vicarious or direct experience with the rewarding nature of such behaviors (Bandura 1973; Huesmann 1988). Individuals exposed to police use of force might therefore perceive violence as an acceptable way to achieve their goals, and replicate these behaviors when threatened or challenged by others.

Perceptions of (Il)Legitimate Force and Offending Behavior

Police use of force represents a form of violence, but it is a unique form of violence because officers tend to use force in order to affect a lawful arrest (Adams 1999; Garner et al. 2002). That is, officers use lawful force—the minimal amount of effort that is required to compel a suspect to comply—in the vast majority of police-citizen encounters that involve the use of force (Garner et al. 2002; Terrill 2005). Yet the legality of police use of force may be largely irrelevant for shaping individuals' *perceptions* of police legitimacy. Rather, citizens' evaluations of police are often based on their appraisals of whether officers acted within minimum expectations of justice and fairness (Tankebe 2013; Tyler 1990; Van Ryzin et al. 2004; Vigoda-Gadot 2007). If officers use force that falls short of citizens' expectations, then recipients might perceive their treatment undeserving, and therefore, illegitimate (Klahm et al. In Press).

Researchers have found that individuals who believe police officers treated them unfairly or undeservedly are more likely to view the treatment they received, and ultimately the police, as illegitimate (Clarkson et al. 2010; Sunshine and Tyler 2003; Tankebe 2013; Tyler 1990).This is because individuals' perceptions of legitimacy are largely based upon whether they were treated in an honest, unbiased, and ethical manner (Tyler 2003), and will cooperate with authorities when they believe their treatment was consistent with legal and moral expectations (Tankebe 2013; Tyler 1990; Tyler and Wakslak 2004). In other words, police officers need to demonstrate what Brown, Tevino, and Harrison (2005) called "ethical leadership," and garner legitimacy and credibility by acting in a normatively appropriate manner (i.e., treat people as they feel they should be treated); power-holders that exhibit these qualities are more likely to be perceived as effective (Bottoms and Tankebe 2013; Kirkpatrick and Locke 1991), garner satisfaction and/or trust (Van Ryzin et al. 2004), and elicit prosocial rather than deviant behavior from their subordinates (Hassan et al. 2014; Tyler and Huo 2003). By contrast, if individuals feel that their normative desires were ignored by authority figures, they may become defiant because their rights and their desire for dignified and respectful treatment were seemingly ignored (Hassan et al. 2014; Sherman 1993; Tyler and Huo 2003).

The preceding discussion suggests that police officers, like many public officials, garner legitimacy by exercising power in ways that recipients perceive is within legal boundaries and appropriate or deserving (Klahm et al. In Press); such perceptions may be the critical difference between legitimate force and unwarranted violence. As Klahm and colleagues noted, one way to measure these aspects of police use of force is to examine whether individuals believed they resisted arrest, which is a precursor of lawful and legitimate force (Alpert et al. 2004; Engel et al. 2000; Garner et al. 2002; Terrill 2005). When a suspect resists arrest, and an officer responds with force, the suspect may be more likely to view the officer's behavior as legitimate. If the suspect had force used against them but did not perceive that they resisted arrest, they might consider their treatment undeserving and illegitimate, which may lead to defiant or retaliatory behavior toward the police and/or other sanctioning representatives (e.g., correctional officers) (Paternoster et al. 1997; Sherman 1993). In support of these ideas, Klahm and colleagues (In Press) found that inmates exposed to police use of force were more likely to violate prison rules, and this relationship was strongest among those who did not resist arrest.

Racial and Ethnic Differences in the Effect of Exposure to Force

The effects of exposure to police use force may be greater among Blacks and Hispanics because minority groups are disproportionately represented in urban areas plagued by violence, concentrated disadvantage, and/or the absence of prosocial opportunities (Clear 2007; Crouch et al. 2000; Krivo and Peterson 2000; Western 2006). Routine exposure to violence and a lack of conventional opportunities may cause individuals to develop a negative view of themselves, the world, and their futures (Mrug and Windle 2010). Such perceptions may contribute to hostile attributional biases (Vitale et al. 2005), and result in aggressive responses to benign stimuli. In addition, minority groups tend to have fewer options than Whites that would prevent or counter the learning of aggression as an acceptable way to respond to a violent experience, and may be more likely to adopt violence as a way to achieve normative desires (Anderson 1999; Spaccarelli et al. 1995).[1]

Mistrust of the criminal justice system and government officials is also more pervasive in areas where minority groups are disproportionately represented (Berman 1997; Hurwitz and Peffley 2005; Sampson and Bartusch 1998), which could affect the way non-whites view and interpret police behavior. For example, Blacks and Hispanics experience a disproportionate amount of negative contact with police (Fagan and Davies 2000; Mastrofski et al. 2002; Weitzer 1999), police use of force (Terrill 2005; Terrill and Reisig 2003; Worden 1996), arrests (Tonry 1995), and incarceration (Clear 2007; Western 2006), which may lead to perceptions of racial profiling and less favorable views of law enforcement and the criminal justice system (Rosenbaum et al. 2005; Sherman 2002; Weitzer and Tuch 2002; Walker and Myers 2000). Moreover, Black and Hispanic communities tend to have higher rates of poverty, lower rates of economic growth, and higher rates of crime (Krivo and Peterson 2000; Western 2006), all of which are associated with greater levels of mistrust and dissatisfaction with government officials (Berman 1997; Van Ryzin et al. 2004). Taken together, disproportionate exposure to adverse experiences with the criminal justice system and government services may undermine minority perceptions of the police (Paternoster et al. 1997; Tyler 1990), and result in more defiant responses to use of force, regardless of whether individuals resisted arrest.

Relevant Controls

To isolate the police use of force-offending behavior relationship and examine the racial/ethnic differences in these effects, it was necessary to consider variables linked to both use of force and institutional misconduct. For instance, researchers have found that legal factors such as criminal history or offense type are linked to police use of force (Engel et al. 2000; Garner et al. 2002; Worden 1996) and institutional misbehavior (Harer and Langan 2001; Steiner et al. 2014). Individuals with antisocial peers and those who use drugs and/or alcohol are also more likely to experience force (Adams 1999; Alpert and

Dunham 2004; Engel et al. 2000; Garner et al. 2002; Terrill and Mastrofski 2002) and commit more institutional misconduct (Drury and DeLisi 2008; Griffin and Hepburn 2006). A disrespectful demeanor is a salient predictor of use of force (Garner et al. 2002; Kaminski et al. 2004), and may be an indicator of antisocial attitudes that lead to institutional rule-breaking. Mental health problems have been related to both offending behavior in prison (Steiner et al. 2014; Steiner and Wooldredge 2009a; 2009b) and police use of force (Worden 1996), while an individual's age and sex affect the odds of being exposed to police use of force (Alpert and Dunham 2004; Hickman et al. 2008) and their likelihood of institutional rule-breaking (Harer and Langan 2001; Steiner et al. 2014).

Researchers have also found that involvement in conventional behaviors (i.e., marriage, education, employment) is associated with lower rates of offending among those in the general population (Laub and Sampson 2001), and among those who are incarcerated (Meade and Steiner 2013; Wooldredge et al. 2001). Such attachments may act as a buffer to the adverse effects of exposure to violence (e.g., Chapman et al. 2006), and deter inmates from violating rules (Wooldredge et al. 2001). Finally, researchers have determined that the chronicity of violence exposure (including other forms of violence) may influence the likelihood and rate of adverse outcomes (Fagan and Mazerolle 2011).

Current Study

The purpose of this study is to examine whether offending behavior in jail is more common among individuals who had force used during their arrest, and more specifically, those exposed to force who did not resist arrest.[2] This study extends existing research (e.g., Klahm et al. In Press) by examining the force-misconduct relationship among jail inmates rather than prison inmates. Jail inmates are a more heterogeneous group of individuals, and would have experienced police use of force more recently than prison inmates. In addition, this study extends prior research by considering whether the exposure to police use of force-offending relationship differs for Blacks, Hispanics, and Whites. Three primary hypotheses are considered:

1. Offending behavior in jail will be more common among inmates who experienced police use of force during their arrest than among those who did not experience force.
2. The effect of exposure to police use of force on offending behavior will be greater among inmates who did not resist arrest compared to those who did resist arrest.
3. The exposure to police use of force-offending behavior relationship (with and without resistance) will be stronger among Blacks and Hispanics versus Whites.

Data and Measures

The data used in this study was collected as part of the most recent (2002) Survey of Inmates in Local Jails (SILJ), which is a nationally representative sample of individuals detained in local jails. A two stage sampling design was used, such that a representative sample of facilities was first selected from the jails listed in the 1999 National Jail Census, followed by a systematic random sample of inmates housed within those jails. For this study, inmates were removed if they were housed in jails with a rated capacity of fewer than fifty inmates given that small jails face unique issues (Kerle 1998). The study was also restricted to inmates who were arrested and convicted because only those inmates were asked questions pertaining to police use of force. Finally, inmates were removed if they had missing data on time served or offense of commitment (n=120), or were not Black, Hispanic, or White (n=397). These restrictions yielded a final sample of 4,305 inmates in 377 facilities. Descriptive statistics for the outcomes, inmate demographic characteristics, and main predictor variables were compared before and after missing data were removed and no differences were revealed. Normalized sample weights derived by the US Census Bureau were applied to all analyses to account for sample effects and represent the population distribution from which the sample was drawn.

The measures included in the analyses are described in Table 9.1. Outcome measures were created from inmates' responses to questions regarding whether they were written up or charged with assault on an inmate or staff member or nonviolent misconduct (e.g., disrespecting staff, refusal to work) since their admission.[3] Because some factors predict whether inmates may engage in misconduct (i.e., prevalence), while others predict the frequency at which they engage in misconduct (i.e., incidence), both were examined. Self-report data may be limited by under/over exaggeration as well as recall error, but scholars have found that both official and self-report data produce valid estimates of inmate misconduct (Steiner and Wooldredge 2014; Van Voorhis 1994) and arrests (Maxfield et al. 2000).

Exposure to use of force is a dichotomous measure based on several survey items that asked inmates if the police pushed, grabbed, kicked or hit them, unleashed a dog on them, sprayed chemical/pepper spray in their direction, pointed a gun but did not shoot, or fired a gun at them during arrest. Exposure to use of force was further distinguished by whether inmates resisted arrest—*police use of force-resistance* and *police use of force-no resistance*—based on inmates' responses to survey questions that asked whether they (1) resisted being handcuffed or arrested, (2) resisted having their person or vehicle searched, (3) attempted to run away or escape, (4) grabbed, hit, or fought with police, (5) used a weapon to threaten officers, or (6) assaulted police with a weapon during arrest.

Table 9.1   Description of Sample and Measures

	Proportion/Mean	(SD)
Outcome Variables		
Prevalence of assaults	.07	
Incidence of assaults	.14	(.69)
Prevalence of nonviolent offenses	.12	
Incidence of nonviolent offenses	.29	(1.52)
Predictor Variables		
Police used force during arrest-resistance	.05	
Police used force during arrest-no resistance	.15	
Natural log of the number of times arrested	1.18	(.91)
Incarcerated for a violent offense	.20	
Used drugs daily before arrest	.44	
Used alcohol daily before arrest	.25	
Antisocial peers or associates	.74	
Disrespectful demeanor during arrest	.07	
Mental health problems	.34	
Prior abuse	.25	
Conventional behaviors	1.17	(.83)
Age	32.83	(10.05)
Female	.30	
Black	.41	
Hispanic	.19	
Natural log time served	3.96	(1.35)
N=	4,305	

Notes. With the exception of the incidence outcomes, the natural log of times arrested, the natural log time served, conventional behaviors, and age, all variables were dummy coded. In order to avoid making conclusions based on artificially inflated coefficients and unreliable estimates, incidence responses were top coded at the 99th percentile.

Potential covariates of both police use of force and institutional misconduct that were included were criminal history (*incarceration for a violent offense, number of times arrested*), *daily drug use, daily alcohol use, disrespectful demeanor at arrest, antisocial peers or associates, mental health problems, prior abuse, conventional behaviors, age* (in years), sex (*female*), race/ethnicity (*Black, Hispanic*), *and time served* (in days). Most of these measures are intuitive, but a few require explanation. *Antisocial peers or associates* is a measure derived from a series of questions that asked inmates whether they had friends growing up who engaged in various criminal behaviors (e.g., drug use, vandalism). *Disrespectful demeanor at arrest* assesses whether inmates reported cursing at, insulting, or calling the police a name during their arrest. *Mental health problems* is a measure of whether inmates reported that they had been admitted to a mental hospital, received mental health counseling/services, or were prescribed psychotropic medication in the year prior to arrest (see James and Glaze 2006). *Prior abuse* taps whether inmates were physically/sexually abused prior to their arrest. *Conventional behaviors* is an additive scale created by summing three survey items that asked inmates whether they were married, had at least a high school diploma, and were employed prior to their arrest (Wooldredge et al. 2001). For the analyses, White inmates and those incarcerated for a nonviolent offense were treated as reference groups. Similar to the outcome variables, the measures indicating whether the police used force during an individual's' arrest, whether the individual resisted arrest, and all of the control variables were based on inmates' self-reports, and are therefore subject to potential limitations related to recall error and/or under or over reporting.

Analysis

Given the hierarchical data structure (i.e., inmates within facilities), the analysis involved multilevel modeling techniques to (1) control for facility characteristics that may affect misconduct rates across facilities and, (2) adjust for correlated error among inmates housed within the same jail. By applying this strategy and group mean centering all the predictor variables, the results of the analyses are independent of facility-level influences (Raudenbush and Bryk 2002). Facility-level effects were not examined because the study hypotheses only involved the examination of individual level relationships. The prevalence outcomes were examined using Bernoulli regression while the incidence measures were examined using Poisson regression with a correction for over-dispersion (see Table 9.1 for means and standard deviations). All measures were assessed for (multi)collinearity, which was determined not to be a problem here.

Unconditional models were estimated in order to determine how much variance in the dependent variables existed within and between facilities. Next, random effects models were estimated by permitting the slopes to vary randomly across facilities, showing whether any of the relationships were stronger in some facilities versus others. Any effects that did not vary across facilities (p ≤ .05) were fixed, or treated as if they had a common slope across facilities. All of the predictor variables were group-mean centered in order to remove any similarities among the inmate populations that might have contributed to variation in levels of misconduct across facilities (Raudenbush and Bryk 2002). Finally, to examine the racial and ethnic differences in the force-misconduct relationship, race and ethnic-specific measures of exposure to force with and without resistance (e.g., force used during arrest-no-resistance (Black)) were added to the models and individually compared to a reference group that did not experience force.

Findings

The results from the analysis of assaults on inmates or staff are displayed in Table 9.2, while the results from the analysis of nonviolent misconduct are

Table 9.2 Inmate Effects on Assaults

	Prevalence		Incidence	
	β	(SE)	β	(SE)
Intercept	-3.14	(.09)	-.69	(.11)
Police used force during arrest-resistance	.31	(.28)	-.34	(.36)
Police used force during arrest-no resistance	.06	(.21)	1.71**	(.26)[a]
Natural log of the number of times arrested	.22**	(.08)	.12	(.14)
Incarcerated for a violent offense	.19	(.17)	.64*	(.30)
Used drugs daily before arrest	.29*	(.15)	.37	(.20)[a]
Used alcohol daily before arrest	.06	(.17)	.27	(.21)
Antisocial peers or associates	.19	(.19)	.76**	(.24)
Disrespectful demeanor during arrest	.72**	(.24)	1.30**	(.24)
Mental health problems	.65**	(.16)	.68**	(.17)
Prior abuse	.38*	(.19)	.84**	(.25)[a]
Conventional behaviors	-.07	(.08)	-.34*	(.14)
Age	-.05**	(.01)	-.04**	(.01)
Female	.03	(.21)	.43	(.32)
Black	.33**	(.18)	.60*	(.26)[a]
Hispanic	.28	(.22)	.27	(.47)
Natural log of time served	.60**	(.07)	.32**	(.09)[a]
Proportion variation within facilities	.91		.64	
Proportion variation within facilities explained	.28		.90	

Notes. Maximum likelihood coefficients reported with robust standard errors in parentheses.
[a] Relationship varies across facilities (p ≤ .05).
*p ≤ .05; **p ≤ .01.

contained in Table 9.3. Descriptive statistics for the outcomes and use of force measures generated from race/ethnic-specific samples are displayed in Table 9.4, followed by the results of the analyses pertaining to the racial and ethnic differences in the exposure to police use of force-jail offending relationship in Tables 9.5 (assaults) and 13.6 (nonviolent). Prior to the discussion of the findings, it is worth noting that about twenty percent of the inmates in this national sample were exposed to police use of force during their arrest—a figure reflective of other national estimates (Hickman et al. 2008); seventy-five percent of these inmates indicated they did not resist arrest.

Table 9.3   Inmate Effects on Nonviolent Offenses

	Prevalence		Incidence	
	β	(SE)	β	(SE)
Intercept	-2.32	(.07)	-.21	(.07)
Police used force during arrest-resistance	.07	(.22)	-.04	(.27)
Police used force during arrest-no resistance	.05	(.15)	1.21**	(.15)[a]
Natural log of the number of times arrested	.12	(.06)	.18*	(.08)[a]
Incarcerated for a violent offense	.13	(.12)	.73**	(.21)
Used drugs daily before arrest	.21	(.11)	.30*	(.14)[a]
Used alcohol daily before arrest	.14	(.12)	.73**	(.13)[a]
Antisocial peers or associates	.50**	(.14)	.42**	(.16)
Disrespectful demeanor during arrest	.14	(.21)	-.14	(.18)
Mental health problems	.39**	(.12)	.63**	(.14)[a]
Prior abuse	.49**	(.14)	.33	(.22)
Conventional behaviors	-.02	(.07)	-.12	(.09)
Age	-.04**	(.01)	-.05**	(.01)
Female	-.12	(.14)	.83**	(.19)[a]
Black	.03	(.13)	-.002	(.17)
Hispanic	.05	(.17)	-.16	(.28)
Natural log of time served	.60**	(.04)	.61**	(.06)[a]
Proportion variation within facilities	.85		.72	
Proportion variation within facilities explained	.27		.92	

Notes. Maximum likelihood coefficients reported with robust standard errors in parentheses.
[a] Relationship varies across facilities (p ≤ .05).
*p ≤ .05; **p ≤ .01.

Assaults

The analysis of assaults (Table 9.2) showed that exposure to force (with or without resistance) had no effect on the odds an inmate committed an assault on another inmate or staff member. Exposure to force with resistance also had no effect on the incidence of assaults. However, inmates who experienced force but did not resist arrest committed *more* assaults than those who did not experience use of force. Based on the event rate ratios generated from the analysis, inmates exposed to force that did not resist arrest committed a 452 percent higher rate of assaults than inmates not exposed to force.

Several of the control variables were related to both the likelihood and frequency of assaults, including a disrespectful demeanor, mental health

Jared Ellison and Benjamin Steiner

Table 9.4 Description of Outcomes and Main Predictor Variables by Racial Group

	White (W)		Black (B)		Hispanic (H)		Difference of Means Test		
	Mean	SD	Mean	SD	Mean	SD	W-B	W-H	B-H
Outcome Variables									
Prevalence of assaults	.05	(.23)	.08	(.27)	.06	(.24)	**		
Incidence of assaults	.12	(.67)	.16	(.73)	.12	(.63)	*		*
Prevalence of nonviolent offenses	.13	(.34)	.10	(.30)	.12	(.33)	*		
Incidence of nonviolent offenses	.34	(1.69)	.24	(1.36)	.29	(1.45)	*		
Predictor Variables									
Police used force during arrest-resistance	.04	(.21)	.06	(.24)	.04	(.16)	*		*
Police used force during arrest-no resistance	.11	(.31)	.19	(.39)	.15	(.36)	**	*	*
N=	1,750		1,758		797				

Notes. *p ≤ .05; **p ≤ .01.

Table 9.5   Relationship between Use of Force and Assaults by Race/Ethnicity

	Prevalence		Incidence	
	β	(SE)	β	(SE)
Intercept	−3.14	(.09)	−1.99	(.08)
Force during arrest-resistance (Black)	.54	(.34)	−.06	(.41)
Force during arrest-no resistance (Black)	−.12	(.26)	−.18	(.22)
Force during arrest-resistance (Hispanic)	.18	(.76)	−.05	(.73)
Force during arrest-no resistance (Hispanic)	−.13	(.35)	−.06	(.28)
Force during arrest-resistance (White)	.07	(.48)	.25	(.37)
Force during arrest-no resistance (White)	.50	(.33)	.55**	(.17)

Notes. Models include also include the control variables: number of time arrested, offense type (incarcerated for a violent offense), used drugs daily before arrest, used alcohol daily before arrest, antisocial peers or associates, disrespectful demeanor during arrest, mental health problems, prior abuse, conventional behaviors, age, sex (female).
*$p \leq .05$; **$p \leq .01$.

problems, prior abuse, age, Black, and time served. Inmates who had more arrests and a daily drug habit were more likely to have committed an assault, while those who were incarcerated for a violent offense, had antisocial peers, and those who participated in fewer prosocial behaviors committed more assaults. The inmate characteristics that did not predict the likelihood or the frequency of assaults were a daily alcohol habit, female, and Hispanic. The significant predictors variables accounted for twenty-seven percent of the within facility variation in the odds of assault and ninety percent of the within facility variation in the frequency of assaults.

Nonviolent Offenses

The results of the analysis of nonviolent offenses (Table 9.3) portrayed a similar pattern with regard to exposure to police use of force. While inmates who had force used against them (with and without resistance) did not have higher odds of nonviolent misconduct, those who experienced force but did not resist arrest committed more nonviolent offenses than those who did not experience force. Exposure to force with resistance had no effect on the frequency of nonviolent misconduct. On average, inmates exposed to police use of force that did not resist arrest committed a 236 percent higher rate of nonviolent offenses than inmates not exposed to force.

Inmates who had antisocial peers, mental health problems, more time served, or were younger were more likely to violate rules, and do so more often. Inmates with more previous arrests, a violent commitment offense, a daily drug habit, a daily alcohol habit, and female inmates committed more misconducts; only prior abuse predicted the prevalence but not the incidence of misconduct. A disrespectful demeanor at arrest, conventional behaviors, Black, and Hispanic had no effect on the prevalence or the incidence of nonviolent rule violations. The significant predictors in the models explained twenty-seven percent of the within facility variation in the odds of nonviolent rule violations and ninety-two percent of the within facility variation in the frequency of these offenses.

Racial/Ethnic Differences in the Force-Misconduct Relationship

Before delving into the racial and ethnic differences in the force-misconduct relationship, it is worth noting that the incidence of assaults was highest among Black inmates, as was exposure to use of force by police (with and without resistance).[4] White and Hispanic inmates, by contrast, shared a similar propensity to violate jail rules, but Hispanics were more likely than Whites to experience police use force without resistance. It is also important to note that the models presented in Tables 9.5 and 9.6 include all of the control variables incorporated in the analyses of the main effects of exposure to force and race/ethnicity. The effects of these variables are not presented, however, because they were not substantively different from those displayed in Tables 9.2 and 9.3.

With regard to the racial and ethnic differences in the relationship between exposure to police use of force and assaults (Table 9.5), there was no meaningful difference in the odds of perpetrating an assault among individuals exposed to force versus those not exposed to force; these findings held across the racial and ethnic groups examined here. In contrast, Whites exposed to force in the absence of resistance committed more assaults than individuals not exposed. Based on the event rate ratios generated from the analysis, White inmates exposed to force who did not resist arrest committed a seventy-three percent higher rate of assaults than inmates not exposed to force. The remainder of the race and ethnic-specific effects of exposure to police use of force on the incidence of assaults were nonsignificant.

Turning to the racial and ethnic differences in the relationship between use of force and nonviolent rule infractions (Table 9.6), both Hispanics and Whites exposed to force in the absence of resistance committed more rule infractions than individuals not exposed to force. White inmates exposed to police use of force that did not resist arrest committed a 70 percent higher rate of nonviolent offenses than inmates not exposed to force, whereas Hispanic inmates exposed to police use of force that did not resist arrest committed a 126 percent higher rate of nonviolent offenses than inmates not exposed

Table 9.6   Relationship between Use of Force and Nonviolent Offenses by Race/Ethnicity

	Prevalence		Incidence	
	β	(SE)	β	(SE)
Intercept	−2.32	(.07)	−.84	(.06)
Force during arrest-resistance (Black)	−.03	(.32)	−.22	(.20)
Force during arrest-no resistance (Black)	−.05	(.20)	.25	(.20)
Force during arrest-resistance (Hispanic)	−.21	(.47)	−.58	(.37)
Force during arrest-no resistance (Hispanic)	.46	(.25)	.82*	(.34)
Force during arrest-resistance (White)	.26	(.34)	.08	(.28)
Force during arrest-no resistance (White)	−.09	(.25)	.53*	(.21)

Notes. Models include also include the control variables: number of times arrested, offense type (incarcerated for a violent offense), used drugs daily before arrest, used alcohol daily before arrest, antisocial peers or associates, disrespectful demeanor during arrest, mental health problems, prior abuse, conventional behaviors, age, sex (female).
*p ≤ .05; **p ≤ .01.

to force. Exposure to use of force, both with and without resistance, had no effect on the prevalence or incidence of misconduct among Black inmates. The remainder of the race/ethnic-specific exposure to use of force-nonviolent misconduct relationships were nonsignificant.

DISCUSSION

Police use of force is a critical issue facing police departments (Olsen 2004), and yet the consequences of exposure to police use of force for recipients remain largely unknown (Klahm et al. In Press). This study involved an examination of the effect of exposure to police use of force on offending behavior in jail, and an assessment of the racial and ethnic difference in these effects. Examination of these questions among jail inmates is informative because an incarcerated sample is inclusive of a disproportionate amount of persons who experienced police use of force (Hickman et al. 2008), and a disproportionate amount of racial/ethnic minorities (Western 2006).

The first hypothesis stated that inmates exposed to police use of force would be more likely to violate jail rules, and do so more frequently, than those who did not experience force during their arrest. This is because police use of force is a form of violence (Garner et al. 1995), and researchers have found that individuals exposed to violence are subsequently more likely to exhibit antisocial behaviors (e.g., Thornberry et al. 2001; Widom 1989). This hypothesis was not supported, however; exposure to legitimate police use of force (with resistance) had no effect on jail rule-breaking. These findings contradict those observed by Klahm and colleagues (In Press) in their analysis of this relationship among prison inmates.

The second hypothesis—that inmates exposed to police use of force who did not resist arrest would share a greater propensity to violate jail rules than those not exposed to force—was partially supported. While inmates exposed to police force at arrest without resistance were not more *likely* to violate jail rules than those who did not experience force, they did commit *a greater frequency* of assaults and nonviolent rule infractions when force was applied without resistance. That is, similar to Klahm and colleagues' (In Press) results, the findings from this study show that inmates exposed to police force who did not resist arrest committed more assaults and nonviolent misconduct than those who did not experience police use of force.

Taken together, these results suggest that a physical encounter with police does not necessarily have a negative impact on individuals' future behavior. Experiencing force in a manner that may be perceived as unwarranted and/or unfair (i.e., force-no resistance), however, may have adverse consequences as recipients subsequently act aggressively and defy authority (e.g., institutional rules). Therefore, the findings from this study suggest that the behavioral consequences of police use of force may be tied to perceptions of deservedness, although an assessment of the relationship between individuals' perceptions regarding whether police use of force was deserved and their subsequent behavior would be needed to support this notion.

Recall that the primary difference between exposure to force and other forms of violence is that police officers are legally justified to use physical restraint to affect an arrest (Adams 1999; Alpert and Dunham 2004; Terrill 2005). Yet regardless of whether the police acted in a lawful manner, perceptions of legitimacy strongly depend on individuals' appraisals of deservedness (Brunson and Miller 2006; Clarkson et al. 2010; Tankebe 2013; Tyler 1990), and/or the extent to which government officials behaved according to normative expectations (Van Ryzin et al. 2004; Van Ryzin 2006; Vigoda-Gadot 2007). Thus, recipients who feel that force was applied deservedly (i.e., when they resisted arrest) may not exhibit the adverse effects of exposure to violence because they believe officers acted legitimately. If police use force in a way that is perceived as undeserving or outside of normative expectations (i.e., force without resistance), however, recipients might associate their treatment with unwarranted aggression, and exhibit behavioral effects that are more similar to exposure with other forms of undeserved violence (e.g., child abuse, domestic assault) (Eitle and Turner 2002; Dodge et al.

1990; Thornberry et al. 2001; Widom and Maxfield 2001). Perceptions of unfair treatment may also breed feelings of hostility, resentment, and defiance (Fogler 1986; Paternoster et al. 1997; Sherman 1993), and lead to involvement with misconduct. It is important to reiterate, however, that these findings are based on an assessment of the effect of an antecedent of legitimate force, rather than direct measures of recipients' attitudes regarding police fairness and legitimacy. Future research should include direct measures of these concepts.

Regarding the racial and ethnic differences in the police use of force-jail offending relationship (Hypothesis 3), the analyses revealed that exposure to force has largely similar effects among Blacks, Hispanics, and Whites. A few notable differences did emerge, however, such as the stronger adverse effects of exposure to force without resistance on the incidence of offending in jail among Whites versus Blacks or Hispanics. These results run counter to those hypothesized, and suggest that the effect of undeserved treatment by police is strongest among Whites compared to Hispanics or Blacks.

At the risk of post hoc hypothesizing, it could be that the disproportionate amount of violence and police use of force that Blacks and Hispanics experience relative to Whites generates a gradual desensitization to violence (Boxer and Sloan-Power 2013; Ng-Mak et al. 2004), coping strategies to deal with this exposure (Coker et al. 2014; Fowler et al. 2009), and/or the expectation of police mistreatment (Brunson and Miller 2006; Woolard et al. 2008). Repeated exposure to general forms of violence, for example, may cause minorities to reach a saturation point where they become desensitized to these experiences, and therefore, do not exhibit the pathological effects associated with exposure to violent events (Fitzpatrick 1993; Fowler et al. 2009). In addition, non-whites may become so cynical that they actually come to expect physical maltreatment by police (see Brunson and Miller 2006); perceptions of undeserved force may have weaker effects among minorities because unethical treatment by the police has become normal to some extent. Whites, on the other hand, hold stronger expectations of fair treatment by police (Rosenbaum et al. 2005), and the quality of police services plays a more significant role in their perceptions of police satisfaction and legitimacy (Berman 1997; Schuck et al. 2008; Sunshine and Tyler 2003; Van Ryzin et al. 2004). Thus, unfair treatment by police may have a stronger effect on the behavior of Whites because they enter police interactions with stronger expectations regarding fair treatment than Blacks and Hispanics. A critical next step may be to assess racial and ethnic differences in individuals' expectations from the police, not to mention their appraisals of whether particular police action (e.g., use of force) was deserved.

While these findings are informative, and potentially highlight the racial and ethnic differences in the consequences of police use of force, it is important to remain mindful of the limitations of this study. First, the sample was restricted to jail inmates who were arrested and convicted, which limits the generalizability of the study. However, the use of an incarcerated sample is also advantageous because it is inclusive of the persons most likely to experience force and those who experience the most serious forms of force given that (1) police use force almost exclusively in the context of an arrest (Adams 1999), (2) individuals exposed to force are more likely to be incarcerated, and (3) inmates experience the most serious forms of force (Hickman et al. 2008; Klahm et al. In Press). Second, this data may contain some degree of error because it are based on self-reports, which are vulnerable to under/over exaggeration as well as recall error. However, given the lack of self-reported use of force studies (Adams 1999), as well as the validity of self-reported indicators of institutional misbehavior (Steiner and Wooldredge 2014) and arrest (Maxfield et al. 2000), there is little reason to suggest that the current estimates are invalid. Third, this data did not include measures of inmates' attitudes regarding police legitimacy, but a potential antecedent upon which these appraisals are made. Fourth, this study examines inmate behavior since their most current arrest, and so it was not possible to account for the effects of prior forceful encounters with police and/or involvement with rule-breaking during prior jail commitments. To be sure, prior exposure to police use of force and degree of familiarity with the jail routine may explain the racial and ethnic differences in the effects of forceful encounters with police noted above. Fifth, the data used here is somewhat dated (i.e., 2002), and thus, the findings and corresponding implications from this study should be interpreted with some degree of caution. Contemporary racial/ethnic tensions and high-profile police killings involving men of color (e.g., Freddie Gray), for example, may alter the relationships described above (Weitzer and Tuch 2004; Weitzer 2015). Finally, the binary measure of police use of force may obscure differences that correspond with the seriousness of the tactic used. However, the purpose of this study was to compare the effects of violent police encounters to that of nonviolent encounters, and so the extent to which these effects differed depending on the seriousness of the violent encounter was beyond the scope of this study.

Practitioner Points

Despite the limitations of this study, the results discussed above offer some important insights for police and jail administrators. Police departments, for example, should be aware of the consequences of using force, and encourage or perhaps require officers to provide timely explanations to suspects in the event that physical restraint was necessary. This transparency might improve how individuals view the nature of their treatment at arrest (i.e., unwarranted violence versus justified restraint), and reduce resentment among arrestees and other community members who witness the incident. Jail administrators might also encourage intake staff to gather information from both the arresting officer(s) and the detainee regarding the circumstances that resulted in arrest. For example, knowing whether the arresting officer(s) used force, whether the individual resisted arrest, and how the recipient defined their treatment might permit the jail staff to identify individuals who pose a greater security risk (i.e., persistent rule violators) and utilize counseling services to alleviate some of the anger and resentment that may lead to violations of institutional rules (Klahm et al. In Press). Finally, jail staff must be careful not to exacerbate these effects by treating inmates in a way that might be perceived as undeserving, and instead, emphasize that inmates will be treated with dignity and respect regardless of what took place during arrest (Irwin 2013; Reisig and Mesko 2009).

CONCLUSION

In sum, the findings from this study indicate that individuals exposed to police use of force who did not resist arrest tend to commit more assaults and nonviolent rule violations in jail. While these findings are consistent with the broader literature on exposure to violence and perceptions of police fairness, the nuances of the consequences of police use of force remain largely unknown. When the effects of exposure to police use of force were examined across race and ethnicity, for example, only White inmates exhibited a consistent propensity to violate jail rules after such encounters. Thus, the consequences of police use of force may depend on the shared experiences of recipients, and researchers should continue to dissect these effects more thoroughly. For instance, it might be useful to consider the number of times individuals have interacted with police, and more importantly, how they perceived the nature of such encounters (e.g., positive, negative). It might also be important to explore how other groups (e.g., women, the indigent) interpret police behavior differently. A series of direct inquiries concerning whether individuals felt police acted fairly and/or legitimately during their arrest, the duration of the use of force incident, and the characteristics of the officer might also be a useful endeavor. Only through continued inquiry might scholars gain a more contextualized understanding of how violations of fairness and legitimacy might influence subsequent behavior.

NOTES

1. The use of an inmate sample raises the possibility that Whites have experienced similar levels of violence and disadvantage as minorities. However, researchers have found that minorities are overrepresented in racially/ethnically heterogeneous neighborhoods plagued by disadvantage and violence, and there are a greater number of the racially/ethnically homogenous minority neighborhoods that are disadvantaged relative to White neighborhoods (Krivo and Peterson 1996; Rose and Clear 1998; Sampson and Bean 2006). Therefore, within racial/ethnic groups a greater proportion of Black and Hispanic inmates (as opposed to White inmates) have likely been exposed to violence and disadvantage.

2. Preliminary analyses of the data showed that there were no substantive differences between the effects of exposure to force and exposure to force with injury on the prevalence or incidence of misconduct.

3. The decision to combine assaults on inmates and staff into a single measure was based on Steiner and Wooldredge's (2013) finding that there is no meaningful difference in the predictors of assaults on inmates versus staff.

4. Differences based on results of bivariate hypotheses tests (p < .05).

REFERENCES

Adams, Kenneth. "What we know about police use of force." *Use of Force by Police: Overview of National and Local Data* (1999): 1.

Alpert, Geoffrey P., and Roger G. Dunham. *Understanding Police Use of Force: Officers, Suspects, and Reciprocity.* New York, NY: Cambridge University Press, 2004.

Alpert, Geoffrey P., Roger G. Dunham, and John M. MacDonald. "Interactive police-citizen encounters that result in force." *Police Quarterly* 7, no. 4 (2004): 475.

Anderson, Elijah. *Code of the Street: Decency, Violence, and the Moral Life of the Inner City.* New York, NY: WW Norton and Company, 2000.

Bandura, Albert. *Aggression: A Social Learning Analysis.* Prentice-Hall, 1973.

Berman, Evan M. "Dealing with cynical citizens." *Public Administration Review* (1997): 57, 105–112.

Boxer, Paul, Keesha Middlemass, and Tahlia Delorenzo. "Exposure to violent crime during incarceration: Effects on psychological adjustment following release." *Criminal Justice and Behavior* 36, no. 8 (2009): 793.

Boxer, Paul, and Elizabeth Sloan-Power. "Coping with violence: A comprehensive framework and implications for understanding resilience." *Trauma, Violence, and Abuse* 14, no. 3 (2013): 209.

Brown, Michael E., Linda K. Treviño, and David A. Harrison. "Ethical leadership: A social learning perspective for construct development and testing." *Organizational Behavior and Human Decision Processes* 97, no. 2 (2005): 117–134.

Brunson, Rod K., and Jody Miller. "Young black men and urban policing in the United States." *British Journal of Criminology*, 46, no. 4 (2006): 613.

Bottoms, Anthony, and Justice Tankebe. "Beyond procedural justice: A dialogic approach to legitimacy in criminal justice." *The Journal of Criminal Law and Criminology* 102, (2012): 119–170.

Buka, Stephen L., Theresa L. Stichick, Isolde Birdthistle, and Felton J. Earls. "Youth exposure to violence: prevalence, risks, and consequences." *American Journal of Orthopsychiatry* 71, no. 3 (2001): 298.

Chapman, J.F., Desai, R.A., Falzer, P.R. and Borum, R. "Violence risk and race in a sample of youth in juvenile detention: The potential to reduce disproportionate minority confinement." *Youth Violence and Juvenile Justice* 4, no. 2 (2006): 170.

Clarkson, Joshua J., Edward R. Hirt, Lile Jia, and Marla B. Alexander. "When perception is more than reality: The effects of perceived versus actual resource depletion on self-regulatory behavior." *Journal of Personality and Social Psychology* 98, no. 1 (2010): 29.

Clear, Todd R. *Imprisoning Communities: How Mass Incarceration Makes Disadvantaged Neighborhoods Worse.* Oxford University Press, 2007.

Coker, Kendell L., Uduakobong N. Ikpe, Jeannie S. Brooks, Brian Page, and Mark B. Sobell. "The Effect of Social Problem Solving Skills in the Relationship between Traumatic Stress and Moral Disengagement among Inner-City African American High School Students." *Journal of Child and Adolescent Trauma* 7, no. 2 (2014): 87.

Cochran, Joshua C., Daniel P. Mears, William D. Bales, and Eric A. Stewart. "Does inmate behavior affect post-release offending? Investigating the misconduct-recidivism relationship among youth and adults." *Justice Quarterly* 31, no. 6 (2014): 104.

Crouch, Julie L., Rochelle F. Hanson, Benjamin E. Saunders, Dean G. Kilpatrick, and Heidi S. Resnick. "Income, race/ethnicity, and exposure to violence in youth: Results from the national survey of adolescents." *Journal of Community Psychology* 28, no. 6 (2000): 625.

De Castro, Bram Orobio, Jan W. Veerman, Willem Koops, Joop D. Bosch, and Heidi J. Monshouwer. "Hostile attribution of intent and aggressive behavior: A meta-analysis." *Child Development* (2002): 73, 916.

DiIulio, John J. *Governing Prisons.* Free Press, 250, 1990.

Dodge, Kenneth A. "Social cognition and children's aggressive behavior." *Child Development* (1980): 162.

Dodge, Kenneth A., John E. Bates, and Gregory S. Pettit. "Mechanisms in the cycle of violence." *Science* 250, no. 4988 (1990): 1678.

Dodge, Kenneth A., Joseph M. Price, Jo-Anne Bachorowski, and Joseph P. Newman. "Hostile attributional biases in severely aggressive adolescents." *Journal of Abnormal Psychology* 99, no. 4 (1990): 385.

Drury, Alan J., and Matt DeLisi. "Gangkill: An exploratory empirical assessment of gang membership, homicide offending, and prison misconduct." *Crime and Delinquency* 57, no. 1 (2008): 130.

Eitle, David, and R. Jay Turner. "Exposure to community violence and young adult crime: The effects of witnessing violence, traumatic victimization, and other stressful life events." *Journal of Research in Crime and Delinquency* 39, no. 2 (2002): 214.

Engel, Robin Shepard, James J. Sobol, and Robert E. Worden. "Further exploration of the demeanor hypothesis: The interaction effects of suspects' characteristics and demeanor on police behavior." *Justice Quarterly* 17, no. 2 (2000): 235.

Fagan, Jeffrey, and Garth Davies. "Street stops and broken windows: Terry, race and disorder in New York City." *Fordham Urban Law Journal* 28 (2000): 457.

Fagan, Abigail A., and Paul Mazerolle. "Repeat offending and repeat victimization: Assessing similarities and differences in psychosocial risk factors." *Crime and Delinquency* 57, no. 5 (2011): 732.

Finkelhor, David, Heather Turner, Richard Ormrod, Sherry Hamby, and Kristen Kracke. "National survey of children's exposure to violence." *Juvenile Justice Bulletin* (2009): pp. 1–12.

Fitzpatrick, Kevin M. "Exposure to violence and presence of depression among low-income, African-American youth." *Journal of Consulting and Clinical Psychology* 61, no. 3 (1993): 528.

Fogler, R. (1986). Rethinking equity theory: A referent cognitions model. In H. Bierhoff, R. Cohen and J. Greenberg (Eds.), *Justice in Social Relations* (pp. 145–162). New York: Plenum Press.

Fowler, Patrick J., Carolyn J. Tompsett, Jordan M. Braciszewski, Angela J. Jacques-Tiura, and Boris B. Baltes. "Community violence: A meta-analysis on the effect of exposure and mental health outcomes of children and adolescents." *Development and Psychopathology* 21, no. 1 (2009): 259.

Garner, Joel H., Christopher D. Maxwell, and Cedrick G. Heraux. "Characteristics associated with the prevalence and severity of force used by the police." *Justice Quarterly* 19, no. 4 (2002): 705.

Garner, Joel H., Thomas Schade, John Hepburn, and John Buchanan. "Measuring the continuum of force used by and against the police." *Criminal Justice Review* 20, no. 2 (1995): 146.

Griffin, Marie L., and John R. Hepburn. "The effect of gang affiliation on violent misconduct among inmates during the early years of confinement." *Criminal Justice and Behavior* 33, no. 4 (2006): 419.

Harer, Miles D., and Neal P. Langan. "Gender differences in predictors of prison violence: Assessing the predictive validity of a risk classification system." *Crime and Delinquency* 47, no. 4 (2001): 513.

Hassan, Shahidul, Bradley E. Wright, and Gary Yukl. "Does ethical leadership matter in government? Effects on organizational commitment, absenteeism, and willingness to report ethical problems." *Public Administration Review* 74, no. 3 (2014): 333–343.

Hickman, Matthew J., Alex R. Piquero, and Joel H. Garner. "Toward a national estimate of police use of nonlethal force." *Criminology and Public Policy* 7, no. 4 (2008): 563–604.

Huesmann, L. Rowell. "An information processing model for the development of aggression." *Aggressive Behavior* 14 (1988): 13.

Hurwitz, Jon, and Mark Peffley. "Explaining the great racial divide: Perceptions of fairness in the US criminal justice system." *Journal of Politics* 67, no. 3 (2005): 762.

Irwin, John. *The Jail: Managing the Underclass in American Society.* University of California Press, 2013.

James, Doris J., and Lauren E. Glaze. *Mental health problems of prison and jail inmates.* Washington, DC: US Department of Justice, Office of Justice Programs, Bureau of Justice Statistics, 2006.

Kaminski, Robert J., Clete Digiovanni, and Raymond Downs. "The use of force between the police and persons with impaired judgment." *Police Quarterly* 7, no. 3 (2004): 311.

Kerle, Kenneth E. *American Jails: Looking to the Future.* Burlington MA: Butterworth-Heinemann, 1998.

Kirkpatrick, Shelley A., and Edwin A. Locke. "Direct and indirect effects of three core charismatic leadership components on performance and attitudes." *Journal of Applied Psychology* 81, no. 1 (1996): 36.

Klahm, Charles F., Benjamin Steiner, and Benjamin Meade. "Assessing the Relationship Between Police Use of Force and Inmate Offending (Rule Violations)." *Crime and Delinquency* (In Press): 0011128714558291.

Krivo, Lauren J., and Ruth D. Peterson. "The structural context of homicide: Accounting for racial differences in process." *American Sociological Review* 65, (2000): 547–599.

Laub, John H., and Robert J. Sampson. "Understanding desistance from crime." *Crime and Justice* 23, (2001): 1–69.

Mastrofski, Stephen D., Michael D. Reisig, and John D. McCluskey. "Police disrespect toward the public: An encounter-based analysis." *Criminology* 40, no. 3 (2002): 519.

Matsuda, Kristy N., Chris Melde, Terrance J. Taylor, Adrienne Freng, and Finn-Aage Esbensen. "Gang membership and adherence to the "code of the street." *Justice Quarterly* 30, no. 3 (2013): 440.

Maxfield, Michael G., Barbara Luntz Weiler, and Cathy Spatz Widom. "Comparing self-reports and official records of arrests." *Journal of Quantitative Criminology* 16, no. 1 (2000): 87–110.

Meade, Benjamin, and Benjamin Steiner. "The effects of exposure to violence on inmate maladjustment." *Criminal Justice and Behavior* 40, no. 11 (2013): 1228.

Mears, Daniel P., Eric A. Stewart, Sonja E. Siennick, and Ronald L. Simons. "The code of the street and inmate violence: Investigating the salience of imported belief systems." *Criminology* 51, no. 3 (2013): 695.

Mrug, Sylvie, and Michael Windle. "Prospective effects of violence exposure across multiple contexts on early adolescents' internalizing and externalizing problems." *Journal of Child Psychology and Psychiatry* 51, no. 8 (2010): 953–961.

Ng-Mak, Daisy S., Suzanne Salzinger, Richard S. Feldman, and C. Stueve. "Pathologic adaptation to community violence among inner-city youth." *American Journal of Orthopsychiatry* 74, no. 2 (2004): 196.

Niemi, Richard G., Stephen C. Craig, and Franco Mattei. "Measuring internal political efficacy in the 1988 National Election Study." *American Political Science Review* 85, no. 4 (1991): 1407–1413.

Olsen, Robert K. PERF to Identify Best Practices in Police Use of Force and Managing Mass Demonstrations (Press Release). Police Executive Research Forum, Washington, DC, 2004.

Paoline, Eugene A., and William Terrill. "Police education, experience, and the use of force." *Criminal Justice and Behavior* 34, no. 2 (2007): 179.

Paternoster, Raymond, Robert Brame, Ronet Bachman, and Lawrence W. Sherman. "Do fair procedures matter? The effect of procedural justice on spouse assault." *Law and Society Review* (1997): 31, no. 1, pp. 163–204.

Raudenbush, Stephen W., and Anthony S. Bryk. *Hierarchical Linear Models: Applications and Data Analysis Methods*. Vol. 1. Sage, 2002.

Reisig, Michael D., and Gorazd Mesko. "Procedural justice, legitimacy, and prisoner misconduct." *Psychology, Crime and Law* 15, no. 1 (2009): 41.

Rose, Dina R., and Todd R. Clear. "Incarceration, social capital, and crime: Implications for social disorganization theory." *Criminology* 36, no. 3 (1998): 441.

Rosenbaum, Dennis P., Amie M. Schuck, Sandra K. Costello, Darnell F. Hawkins, and Marianne K. Ring. "Attitudes toward the police: The effects of direct and vicarious experience." *Police Quarterly* 8, no. 3 (2005): 343.

Sampson, Robert J., and Dawn Jeglum Bartusch. "Legal cynicism and (subcultural?) tolerance of deviance: The neighborhood context of racial differences." *Law and Society Review* (1998): 32, no. 4, pp. 777–804.

Sampson, Robert J., and Lydia Bean. 2006. "Cultural mechanisms and killing fields: A revised theory of community-level racial inequality." *The Many Colors of Crime: Inequalities of Race, Ethnicity and Crime in America* edited by Ruth Peterson, Lauren Krivo, and John Hagan. New York: New York University Press.

Schuck, Amie M., Dennis P. Rosenbaum, and Darnell F. Hawkins. "The influence of race/ethnicity, social class, and neighborhood context on residents' attitudes toward the police." *Police Quarterly* 11, no. 4 (2008): 496.

Selner-O'Hagan, Mary Beth, Daniel J. Kindlon, Stephen L. Buka, Stephen W. Raudenbush, and Felton J. Earls. "Assessing exposure to violence in urban youth." *Journal of Child Psychology and Psychiatry* 39, no. 2 (1998): 215.

Sherman, Lawrence W. "Defiance, deterrence, and irrelevance: A theory of the criminal sanction." *Journal of Research in Crime and Delinquency* 30, no. 4 (1993): 445.

Sherman, Lawrence W. "Trust and confidence in criminal justice." *National Institute of Justice Journal* 248 (2002): 22.

Spaccarelli, Steve, J. Douglas Coatsworth, and Blake Sperry Bowden. "Exposure to serious family violence among incarcerated boys: Its association with violent offending and potential mediating variables." *Violence and Victims* 10, no. 3 (1995): 163.

Steiner, Benjamin, and John Wooldredge. "Individual and environmental effects on assaults and nonviolent rule breaking by women in prison." *Journal of Research in Crime and Delinquency* 46, no. 4 (2009a): 437.

Steiner, Benjamin, and John Wooldredge. "The relevance of inmate race/ethnicity versus population composition for understanding prison rule violations." *Punishment and Society* 11, no. 4 (2009b): 459.

Steiner, Benjamin, and John Wooldredge. "Implications of different outcome measures for anunderstanding of inmate misconduct." *Crime and Delinquency* 59, no. 8 (2013): 1234.

Steiner, Benjamin, and John Wooldredge. "Comparing self-report to official measures of inmate misconduct." *Justice Quarterly* 31, no. 6 (2014): 1074.

Steiner, Benjamin, H. Daniel Butler, and Jared M. Ellison. "Causes and correlates of prison inmate misconduct: A systematic review of the evidence." *Journal of Criminal Justice* 42, no. 6 (2014): 462.

Sunshine, Jason, and Tom R. Tyler. "The role of procedural justice and legitimacy in shaping public support for policing." *Law and Society Review* 37, no. 3 (2003): 513.

Tankebe, Justice. "Viewing things differently: The dimensions of public perceptions of police legitimacy." *Criminology* 51, no. 1 (2013): 103.

Terrill, William. "Police use of force: A transactional approach." *Justice Quarterly* 22, no. 1 (2005): 107.

Terrill, William, Fredrik H. Leinfelt, and Dae-Hoon Kwak. "Examining police use of force: A smaller agency perspective." *Policing* 31, no. 1 (2008): 57.

Terrill, William, and Stephen D. Mastrofski. "Situational and officer-based determinants of police coercion." *Justice Quarterly* 19, no. 2 (2002): 215.

Terrill, William, and Michael D. Reisig. "Neighborhood context and police use of force." *Journal of Research in Crime and Delinquency* 40, no. 3 (2003): 291.

Thornberry, Terence P., Timothy O. Ireland, and Carolyn A. Smith. "The importance of timing: The varying impact of childhood and adolescent maltreatment on multiple problem outcomes." *Development and Psychopathology* 13, no. 4 (2001): 957.

Todorov, Alexander, and John A. Bargh. "Automatic sources of aggression." *Aggression and Violent Behavior* 7, no. 1 (2002): 53.

Tonry, Michael. *Malign Neglect: Race, Crime, and Punishment in America.* Oxford University Press, 1995.

Tyler, Tom R. *Why People Obey the Law: Procedural Justice, Legitimacy, and Compliance.* Princeton University Press, 1990.

Tyler, Tom R. "Procedural justice, legitimacy, and the effective rule of law." *Crime and Justice* 30 (2003): 283.

Tyler, Tom R., and Yuen Huo. *Trust in the Law: Encouraging Public Cooperation with the Police and Courts.* Russell Sage Foundation, 2002.

Tyler, Tom R., and Cheryl J. Wakslak. "Profiling and Police Legitimacy: Procedural Justice, Attributions of Motive, and Acceptance of Police Authority." *Criminology* 42, no. 2 (2004): 253.

Van Ryzin, Gregg G. "Testing the expectancy disconfirmation model of citizen satisfaction with local government." *Journal of Public Administration Research and Theory* 16, no. 4 (2006): 599–611.

Van Ryzin, Gregg G., Douglas Muzzio, and Stephen Immerwahr. "Explaining the race gap in satisfaction with urban services." *Urban Affairs Review* 39, no. 5 (2004): 613–632.

Van Ryzin, Gregg G., Douglas Muzzio, Stephen Immerwahr, Lisa Gulick, and Eve Martinez. "Drivers and consequences of citizen satisfaction: An application of the American customer satisfaction index model to New York City." *Public Administration Review* 64, no. 3 (2004): 331–341.

Van Voorhis, Patricia. "Measuring prison disciplinary problems: A multiple indicators approach to understanding prison adjustment." *Justice Quarterly* 11, no. 4 (1994): 679–709.

Vigoda-Gadot, Eran. "Citizens' perceptions of politics and ethics in public administration: A five-year national study of their relationship to satisfaction with services, trust in governance, and voice orientations." *Journal of Public Administration Research and Theory* 17, no. 2 (2007): 285–305.

Vitale, Jennifer E., Joseph P. Newman, Ralph C. Serin, and Daniel M. Bolt. "Hostile attributions in incarcerated adult male offenders: An exploration of diverse pathways." *Aggressive Behavior* 31, no. 2 (2005): 99.

Walker, Samuel, and Richard W. Myers. *Police Interactions with Racial and Ethnic Minorities: Assessing the Evidence and Allegations.* Washington, DC: Police Executive Research Forum, 2000.

Weitzer, Ronald. "American policing under fire: Misconduct and reform." *Society* 52, no. 5 (2015): 475–480.

Weitzer, Ronald, and Steven A. Tuch. "Perceptions of racial profiling: Race, class, and personal experience."*Criminology* 40, no. 2 (2002): 435.

Weitzer, Ronald, and Steven A. Tuch. "Race and perceptions of police misconduct." *Social Problems* 51, no. 3 (2004): 305–325.

Western, Bruce. *Punishment and Inequality in America.* Russell Sage Foundation, 2006.

Widom, Cathy S. "Does violence beget violence? A critical examination of the literature." *Psychological bulletin* 106, no. 1 (1989): 3.

Widom, Cathy S., and Michael G. Maxfield. "An Update on the Cycle of Violence." *Research in Brief.* (2001).

Woolard, Jennifer L., and M. P. P. Harvell. "Anticipatory injustice among adolescents: Age and racial/ethnic differences in perceived unfairness of the justice system." *Behavioral Sciences and the Law* 26, no. 2 (2008): 207.

Wooldredge, John, Timothy Griffin, and Travis Pratt. "Considering hierarchical models for research on inmate behavior: Predicting misconduct with multilevel data." *Justice Quarterly* 18, no. 1 (2001): 203.

Worden, Robert E. *The Causes of Police Brutality: Theory and Evidence on Police Use of Force.* National Academies of Sciences, Engineering and Medicine (Washington, DC), 1996.

Chapter 10

Bridging the Safety Divide through Technology to Improve the Partnership between Students and Campus Law Enforcement

An "App" Opportunity

Edward C. Dillon, Brian N. Williams, Seong C. Kang, Juan E. Gilbert, Julian Brinkley, and Dekita Moon

The President's Task Force on 21st Century Policing under the Obama Administration encouraged the development, implementation, and replication of best practices to improve efforts to reduce crime and build public confidence and trust (Washington, DC: Office of Community Oriented Policing Services 2015). The establishment of the Task Force itself reflects the significant role that law enforcement plays in contemporary American society—to serve and protect the community by maintaining peace and order through the enforcement of laws. With approximately 18,000 local, state, and federal police agencies, officers who serve a range of people and populations, from college campuses, counties or parishes, and urban places, as well as state and federal spaces, safeguard American communities (Washington, DC: Office of Community Oriented Policing Services 2015). Within these disparate jurisdictions, law enforcement agencies, both large and small, are called to be transparent, responsive, and accountable to the public they serve, in spite of the dystopian historical legacies of police-community relations that impact contemporary perceptions of certain demographics, especially African Americans. Today's public safety organizations operate within a new type of problem environment—a wicked one. This environment is filled with *wicked problems*, like opioid addiction and sex trafficking—problems that defy clear resolutions due to the vastness of interdependencies, complexities, and uncertainties, as well as the increasing and often inherent conflicts among stakeholders (Rittel and Webber 1973). Yet, to address these wicked problems, law enforcement is expected to do more with less due to fiscal stress and budgetary constraints.

Recently, scholars and practitioners alike called for a more active involvement of citizens in the design and delivery of police services. This approach to engaging the public with the police and collaborating in the provision of public order and safety is referred to as coproduction (Alford 1998). The framework for coproduction is offered below.

THEORETICAL FRAMEWORK: THE COPRODUCTION OF PUBLIC SERVICES

Coproduction is commonly associated with the expanding role that citizens as clients, volunteers, or members of a community play in assisting public agencies and their agents in developing, implementing, and delivering public services (Bovaird 2007; Parks et al. 1981; Whitaker 1980). As the collective action between entities of government, citizens, or residents who work or reside in a jurisdiction, and nongovernmental institutions and organizations, coproduction entails a series of steps that are dependent upon the willingness of all parties to collaborate, cooperate, and coordinate. In theory, these collective efforts are necessary to better understand, address, and prevent public problems as well as enhance the delivery of public services.

Coproduction is often connected to the practice of local law enforcement (Percy 1984; Parks et al. 1981; Whitaker 1980; Ostrom et al. 1978). In response to the evolution of American society and many of the challenges facing the government in general, and local governments in particular, local law enforcement agencies have increasingly utilized citizens to assist in the production and delivery of police services. This arrangement integrates service recipients from the community with civilian and sworn employees of local police departments, to coproduce public safety and public order. This method highlights a postmodern effort to realize a premodern society principle, first articulated by Sir Robert Peel (1829), which equates the public with its police (Reith 1948). Most police organizations in the United States have embraced this ethos through the inculcation of the philosophy of community-oriented policing. At its core, community-oriented policing is about civic engagement and community partnerships that seek to have police departments partner with individuals, institutions, and other organizations to prevent crime and solve problems that impact communities (Kappeler and Gaines 2012).

Coproduction is being lauded for its potential to increase the efficiency and effectiveness of providing public services while also enhancing the morale of public sector employees and engendering support from citizen coproducers (Needham 2008). Vital to the success of coproduction efforts are the interactions between the providers of services (professionals), and the recipients of those services (users). Bovaird (2007) has provided a conceptual framework, which we have adapted in Figure 10.1 that highlights the range of user and community relationships with professionalized public services. These forms of interaction and engagement range from traditional professional service provision with users and communities involved in the planning and design-ing, to user codelivery of professionally designed services where profession-als dictate service plans and designs, to relationships where users are sole deliverers of coplanned or codesigned services.

Yet, within this range of professional-user relationships and interactions in the coproduction of public safety and public order, many challenges are evident. One basic challenge is the inevitable problem of conflict that impacts all group processes (Follett 1918). Other challenges include issues related to trust, incentives, transparency, conflicting value orientations, role ambiguity, burnout by community coproducers, and cocontamination (Williams, Kang, and Johnson 2016; Taylor 2011; Bovaird 2005; Birchall and Simmons 2003; Mayo and Moore 2002). These can be especially problematic for members of minority groups when considering the historical legacy of disparate police services and discriminatory criminal justice policies and resulting practices.

Research suggests that minority groups are victims of the *group threat theory* (Blalock 1967; Blumer 1958), in which they are recipients of prejudice and relative hostilities due to a perception of them as "threatening" toward dominant groups (King and Wheelock 2007; Liska 1997; Liska 1992). Those groups are, consequently, prone to formal and informal *social control* as a way to preserve a social order (Tolnay, Deane, and Beck 1996; Liska 1992; Jackson 1989). Such behaviors are found to be more prevalent in areas where minority populations are relatively large (Quillian 1995; Blalock 1967).

		SERVICE DESIGN		
		Professionals as sole planners	Professionals / Users as co-planners	No professional input
	Professionals as sole deliverers	1. Traditional professional service delivery	2. Professional service delivery, but user involvement in design	3. Professionals as sole deliverers
SERVICE DELIVERY	Professionals / Users as co-delivers	4. User co-delivery of professionally designed services	5. Full Coproduction	6. User delivery of services with minimal professional involvement
	Users as sole deliverers	7. User delivery of professionally designed services	8. User delivery of co-designed services	9. Self-organized community delivery

Figure 10.1   **Conceptual Framework of Co-Production.** *Source.* Adapted from Boivard (2007) and Ryan (2012).

Within the minority group population, African Americans are found to exhibit more negative perceptions about law enforcement than their racial minority and majority counterparts (Horowitz 2007; Weitzer and Tuch 2005; Tuch and Weitzer 1997; Decker 1981; Bayley and Mendelsohn 1968). In particular, African Americans tend to experience a higher frequency of racial profiling, unwarranted neighborhood stops, verbal abuse/insults, and excessive force from law enforcement agents (Johnson 2003; Weitzer 1999; Larrabee 1997). These experiences impact public confidence as noted by the results of recent Gallup poll surveys (Figure 10.2 and Figure 10.3) that aggregate data on the confidence in the police in general, and confidence in police by race and place of residence, in particular.

The results from these surveys reinforce the obstacles to coproduction efforts related to enhancing public safety and public order. These highly nuanced challenges go beyond mere engagement and participation and can result in a "crowding out," "crowding in," or "glass ceiling" effect on citizen participation and ultimately the success of coproduction efforts (Pestoff 2009; Needham 2008; Bovaird 2007).

In institutional settings, police departments are faced with the challenge of becoming more inclusive, especially in urban areas, including densely populated college environments. The Virginia Commonwealth University's police chief, John Venuti, notes that inclusion is critical for policing urban institutions because these campuses are typically located in the heart of a municipality, thus making it a challenge to distinguish students from local residents (Gray 2015). An inclusive approach could also help alleviate certain views portrayed about minority groups, in particular, young African American men. Brunson and Miller (2006), for instance, conducted a qualitative study on forty young African American men and gathered feedback about their experiences and perceptions, as inhabitants in an urban community. This study notes how the participants perceived themselves to be "symbolic assailants in the eyes of the police" (Brunson and Miller 2006).

To explore and engage in a deeper understanding of the current relations between students and campus law enforcement, our study conducted four focus group discussions at two institutions in the state of Georgia. The target population for these assessments was African American male undergraduates. The purpose for soliciting this particular group for these assessments was to gather further insight about their individual experiences as college students and as African American men based upon the contemporary backdrop of police-community relations. After a brief presentation of the context of the study, the research methodology, and an overview of the data breakdown and analytical process precede a description of the findings. These findings

	A great deal/ Quite a lot	Some	Very little/None
	%	%	%
National adults	56	30	14
Whites	59	29	12
Blacks	37	37	25

Gallup poll aggregate from surveys conducted in June 2011, June 2012, June 2013, and June 2014

GALLUP

Figure 10.2   Police Confidence (Overall).

have implications for employing technology to enhance relations and develop partnerships between students and campus law enforcement.

Context of Study

This study took place at two universities in the state of Georgia: The University of Georgia (UGA) in Athens and Albany State University (ASU) in Albany. Both universities are located in central cities in metropolitan statistical areas that serve as economic hubs for their respective regions. ASU is a historically Black, master's granting (or M2) institution that serves the southwest portion of the state of Georgia. At the time of data collection, ASU had an enrollment in excess of 4,000 students. UGA is a predominately White, research-intensive (or R1) institution that serves as the flagship institution for the state of Georgia. At the time of data collection, UGA had an enrollment in excess of 34,000 students.

Confidence in Police, by Race and Place of Residence

Figures are percentages saying they have a great deal or quite a lot of confidence in the police

	All Americans	Non-Hispanic whites	Non-Hispanic blacks	Hispanics
	%	%	%	%
Total	57	61	34	57
Live in urban area	54	62	26	54
Live in non-urban area	58	60	38	59

2006-2014 aggregated data

GALLUP

Figure 10.3   Police Confidence (by Race and Location).

Research Methodology

The study was composed of focus group discussions—a non-directive interviewing technique to uncover the concerns, needs, and feelings that underlie people's opinions and preferences (Krueger 2014). Previous research highlighted the ability of focus groups to get in touch with the lived and perceived realities of participants, including college (Williams et al. 2015; Williams 1999; Williams 1997). Four focus groups—two male groups at ASU (n = 21) and two male groups at UGA (n = 11)—were assembled across both campuses. This method allowed the exploration of the following four main questions:

1. What does it mean to be a student on campus (*the self-assessment*)?
2. From your perspective, what does it mean to be a police officer on our campus (*the assessment of the other*)?
3. From your perspective, how would you describe the relationship between students and campus law enforcement (*the relationship assessment*)?
4. Are there any barriers or obstacles that inhibit the development and functioning of an effective and productive relationship between students and campus law enforcement (*the obstacles assessment*)?

Data Breakdown and Analysis

As illustrated in Figure 10.4, key words and phrases from students' responses were identified and content analyzed to achieve data breakdown. Illustrative quotes were then used to highlight and reinforce the emergent perceptions.

Findings

From the data analysis, three converging perceptions and one diverging perception emerged across the focus groups and college campuses. The first point of convergence revolved around the roles and responsibilities of students and officers. Participants at both institutions voiced the need for students to be *campus keepers* and *contingent informants* while the role of officers was to *maintain order* on campus. As *campus keepers,* students have a role and responsibility, as noted by one ASU participant, "to police ourselves so that the police won't have to." Similarly, students expressed the need for students to serve as informants, but contingent upon certain situations. ASU students shared a nuanced position related to serving as a *contingent informant* best articulated by the comments of one participant—"They say 'if you see something, say something.' But it depends on what you see." This sentiment was shared by participants at UGA as encapsulated by the comments of

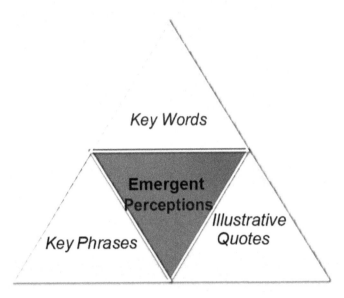

Figure 10.4   Emergent Perceptions.

one participant, "If it [a student's action or behavior] is only impacting him, that's one thing, but if it could impact others that may be different." Focus group participants at both institutions saw the vital role that officers play in maintaining order on their respective campuses. As one ASU student mentioned, "if there weren't any officers here, I could only imagine the kind of chaos that would happen on campus."

Perceptions across groups and campuses also converged around barriers and obstacles. These include cultural and generational barriers, lack of personal relationships, and an "us versus them" perspective. Participants at both institutions highlighted cultural and generational barriers that prevent an effective and productive relationship between students and campus law enforcement. In each discussion at ASU and UGA, students mentioned the present-day stigma attached to "snitching" and the subsequent consequence whereby "snitches get stitches." This cultural and generational barrier reinforced the emergent perceptions of the lack of personal relationships as summarized by the comments of an ASU participant—"I describe our relationship as nonexistent"—and virtually fortified the perceived notion of "us versus them" as embedded in the comments of an UGA participant—"It is not an adversarial type of thing but there is an 'us versus them' tension that exists."

The final converging perception centers on developing a strategic response to improve the relationship between students and campus law enforcement—the need for more personal, positive, and informal interactions between students and officers to build trust. Participants at both institutions recognized "we need to get to know them beyond the uniform," as expressed by a UGA participant, and "they need to get to know me as a person and not just as a student," as expressed by an ASU participant.

One diverging perception emerged from this analysis. This divergence was related to enforcement actions. UGA participants perceived law enforcement actions as protective. One participant mentioned, "We are transitioning into adulthood...we are away from home for the first time without parental support but we have that police supervision to guide and watch over us." ASU participants, on the other hand, perceived enforcement actions as punitive. This perception is best summarized by the statement of an ASU student, "They sweat the small stuff...I was walking back to my dorm and I got stopped for a random backpack check. I had 1 bottle...one bottle in my backpack and they took me to jail. I was of age!"

Our analyses of focus group data highlight obstacles, real and perceived, that impact building, maintaining, and sustaining a meaningful and productive relationship between campus law enforcement and the focal demographic of our study. The chasm reflected by the "us versus them" theme is supported by cultural and generational differences, and often exacerbated not only by historical legacies but also is based upon contemporary instances of negative police-citizen interactions. These instances, especially those involving African American males, have garnered media attention—like the 2015 encounter between University of Virginia student Martese Johnson with Alcoholic Beverage Control agents in Charlottesville, Virginia—at the national, regional, and local, inclusive campus, levels. When considering the lost opportunities of the past, how do we begin bridging the gap between some segments of our community with law enforcement? This question is a pertinent one that we address below.

Implications for Employing Technology

Technological systems can be developed with the purpose of improving relations and partnerships between students and campus law enforcement. A common form of technology that has been employed is social media (Meijer and Thaens 2013; Olivera and Welch 2013). Twitter, for instance, has been reported as a strategically resourceful platform for civilians to communicate with law enforcement regarding suspicious activity, missing persons, and other notable instances within a neighborhood (Kim, Park, and Rho 2015; Bonson et al. 2012). Moreover, this platform has been noted to possess some potential for strengthening police legitimacy in the eyes of civilians (Grimmelikhuijsen and Meijer 2015).

Software applications (or *software apps*) are another form of technology that has been utilized for law enforcement related purposes. Many of these apps have been developed for the purpose of accommodating civilians, law enforcement, and even legal professionals as primary users. These apps can provide information ranging from knowing *Police Miranda Warnings* to *the US Constitution*. There is also a subset of apps that assist with providing information pertaining to the law and how it should be enforced. Furthermore, a smaller subset of apps has been developed with the intent of promoting stronger police-community relations. Nevertheless, apps of this nature have also been prone to lacking reliability, being underdeveloped, and containing bugs and other errors.

Taking Advantage of an App Opportunity: Bridging the Hi-Tech with the Hi-Touch

When laws are developed and authorized in our society, the interpretation of such policies and ordinances is critical. It is also possible that finding some common entity between civilians and law enforcement could help promote coproduction and strengthen relations between both parties. Laws are designed to be interpreted by both civilians and law enforcement agents. Specifically, it is important that civilians understand the law and know their rights. It is equally important for law enforcement agents to understand the law and uphold it appropriately. From this perspective, it can be inferred that law interpretation imposes a common entity that connects both the civilian and law enforcement communities.

To better study law interpretation and its potential, we are currently undertaking an opportunity to develop a computational application that possesses the sophistication, intelligence, and reliability of informing civilians and law enforcement respectively with how laws should be interpreted and enforced. An application of this type—one that bridges the hi-tech with the hi-touch—has the potential to improve how civilians understand the law and assist law enforcement with avoiding behaviors, judgments, or procedures, that contradict their position for upholding the law.

From a technological standpoint, the nature of this application will consist of current technological advances that enable the use of computational processing, natural language interpretation, and content extraction. Specifically, this application will be implemented as an automated conversational agent system, allowing the user to ask questions in a natural language and receiving intelligent answers regarding law interpretations. Figure 10.5 illustrates an example scenario for how this particular application would work.

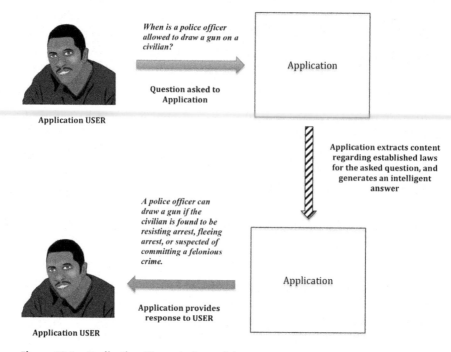

Figure 10.5   Application (Example Scenario).

CONCLUSION

Overall, the effective use of technology could have a bridging effect—by assisting in improving public trust and confidence amongst police-community partners, thus enhancing efforts to more effectively and efficaciously coproduce public safety and public order. This technology can be transferrable to all jurisdictions or settings like institutional settings—inclusive of college campuses—to improve partnerships between the user of services like students and professional providers of services like campus law enforcement; especially institutions located in urban areas with diverse, high population densities. Through the lens of law interpretation, our current application system will also be applicable and transferrable in a similar capacity.

Taking advantage of an "app opportunity" fits with the overall objective of the President's Task Force on 21st Century Policing as it directly relates to four of the six pillars (*building trust and legitimacy, technology and social media, community policing and crime reduction,* and *officer wellness and safety*) and indirectly has connections to the remaining two (*policy and oversight* and *training and education*). In parallel, the evolution of technology throughout the twenty-first century provides the potential platforms, such as social media, intelligent apps, and other relative technologies, to assist with the aforementioned pillars of the 21st Century Policing Initiative; in particular the education of civilians and also the building of trust and legitimacy toward policing. Moreover, the recent climate between police and civilians welcomes the necessity for implementing strategies to equip civilians and law enforcement agents with ways to improve such relations.

REFERENCES

Alford, John. 1998. A Public Management Road Less Travelled: Clients as Co-Producers of Public Services. *Australian Journal of Public Administration* 57 (4): 128–37.

Bayley, David H., and Harold A. Mendelsohn. 1968. *Minorities and the Police: Confrontation in America.* New York: Free Press; London: Collier-MacMillan.

Birchall, Johnston, and Richard Simmons. 2004. *User Power: The Participation of Users in Public Services.* A report prepared for the National Consumer Council, October 2004, London (UK).

Blalock, Hubert M. 1967. Toward a Theory of Minority-Group Relations. Edison, NJ: John Wiley & Sons, 1967.

Blumer, Herbert. 1958. Race Prejudice as a Sense of Group Position. *Pacific Sociological Review* 1 (1): 3–7.

Bonsón, Enrique, Lourdes Torres, Sonia Royo, and Francisco Flores. 2012. Local e-Government 2.0: Social Media and Corporate Transparency in Municipalities. *Government Information Quarterly* 29 (2): 123–32.

Bovaird, Tony. 2007. Beyond Engagement and Participation: User and Community Coproduction of Public Services. *Public Administration Review* 67 (5): 846–60.

Bovaird, Tony. 2005. Public Governance: Balancing Stakeholder Power in a Network Society. *International Review of Administrative Sciences* 71 (2): 217–28.

Brunson, Rod K., and Jody Miller. 2005. Young Black Men and Urban Policing in the United States. *British Journal of Criminology* 46 (4): 613–40.

Decker, Scott H. 1981. Citizen Attitudes Toward the Police: A Review of Past Findings and Suggestions for Future Policy. *Journal of Police Science and Administration* 9 (1): 80–7.

Follett, Mary Parker. 1918. *The New State: Group Organization the Solution of Popular Government.* University Park, PA: Penn State Press.

Grimmelikhuijsen, Stephan G., and Albert J. Meijer. 2015. Does Twitter Increase Perceived Police Legitimacy? *Public Administration Review* 75 (4): 598–607.

Hattersley-Gray, Robin. How an Urban University Police Department Changed Its Culture. October 19, 2015. *Campus Safety.*

Horowitz, Jake. 2007. Making Every Encounter Count: Building Trust and Confidence in the Police. *National Institute of Justice Journal* 256 (1): 8–11.

Jackson, Pamela Irving. 1989. *Minority Group Threat, Crime, and Policing: Social Context and Social Control.* Santa Barbara, CA: Greenwood Publishing Group.

Johnson, Kevin R. 2003. The Case for African-American and Latina/O Cooperation in Challenging Racial Profiling in Law-enforcement. *Fla.L.Rev.* 55: 341.

Kappeler, Victor E., and Larry K. Gaines. 2012. *Community Policing: A Contemporary Perspective.* New York, NY: Routledge.

Kim, Suk Kyoung, Min Jae Park, and Jae Jeung Rho. 2015. Effect of the Government's Use of Social Media on the Reliability of the Government: Focus on Twitter. *Public Management Review* 17 (3): 328–55.

King, Ryan D., and Darren Wheelock. 2007. Group Threat and Social Control: Race, Perceptions of Minorities and the Desire to Punish. *Social Forces* 85 (3): 1255–80.

Krueger, Richard A. 2014. *Focus Groups: A Practical Guide for Applied Research.* Thousand Oaks, CA: Sage publications.

Larrabee, Jennifer A. 1997. DWB (Driving While Black) and Equal Protection: The Realities of an Unconstitutional Police Practice. *JL & Pol'y* 6: 291.

Liska, Allen E. 1997. Modeling the Relationships Between Macro Forms of Social Control. *Annual Review of Sociology* 23 (1): 39–61.

Liska, Allen E. 1992. *Social Threat and Social Control.* Albany, NY: SUNY Press.

Mayo, Ed, and Henrietta Moore. 2002. Building the Mutual State: Findings from the Virtual Thinktank.

Meijer, Albert, and Marcel Thaens. 2013. Social Media Strategies: Understanding the Differences between North American Police Departments. *Government Information Quarterly* 30 (4): 343–50.

Needham, Catherine. 2008. Realising the Potential of Co-Production: Negotiating Improvements in Public Services. *Social Policy and Society* 7 (2): 221–31.

Office of Community Oriented Policing Services. 2015. President's Task Force on 21st Century Policing: *"Final Report of the President's Task Force on 21st Century Policing."* Washington, DC: Office of Community Oriented Policing Services.

Oliveira, Gustavo Henrique Maultasch, and Eric W. Welch. 2013. Social Media Use in Local Government: Linkage of Technology, Task, and Organizational Context. *Government Information Quarterly* 30 (4): 397–405.

Ostrom, Elinor, Roger B. Parks, Gordon P. Whitaker, and Stephen L. Percy. 1978. The Public Service Production Process: A Framework for Analyzing Police Services. *Policy Studies Journal* 7 (s1): 381.

Parks, Roger B., Paula C. Baker, Larry Kiser, Ronald Oakerson, Elinor Ostrom, Vincent Ostrom, Stephen L. Percy, Martha B. Vandivort, Gordon P. Whitaker, and Rick Wilson. 1981. Consumers as Co-producers of Public Services: Some Economic and Institutional Considerations. *Policy Studies Journal* 9 (7): 1001–11.

Percy, Stephen L. 1984. Citizen Participation in the Co-production Of Urban Services. *Urban Affairs Quarterly* 19 (4): 431–46.

Pestoff, Victor. 2009. Towards a Paradigm of Democratic Participation: Citizen Participation and Co-Production of Personal Social Services in Sweden. *Annals of Public and Cooperative Economics* 80 (2): 197–224.

Quillian, Lincoln. 1995. Prejudice as a Response to Perceived Group Threat: Population Composition and Anti-Immigrant and Racial Prejudice in Europe. *American Sociological Review*: 60, no. 4, 586–611.

Reith, Charles. 1948. *A Short History of the British Police.* New York, NY: Oxford Univ. Press.

Rittel, Horst W.J, and Melvin M. Webber. 1973. Dilemmas in a General Theory of Planning. *Policy Sciences* 4 (2): 155–69.

Ryan, Bill. "Co-Production: Option or Obligation?." *Australian Journal of Public Administration* 71, no. 3 (2012): 314–324.

Taylor, Marilyn. 2011. *Public Policy in the Community.* New York, NY: Palgrave Macmillan.

Tolnay, Stewart E., Glenn Deane, and Ellwood M. Beck. 1996. Vicarious Violence: Spatial Effects on Southern Lynchings, 1890–1919. *American Journal of Sociology* 102 (3): 788–815.

Tuch, Steven A., and Ronald Weitzer. 1997. Trends: Racial Differences in Attitudes toward the Police. *The Public Opinion Quarterly* 61 (4): 642–63.

Weitzer, Ronald. 1999. Citizens' Perceptions of Police Misconduct: Race and Neighborhood Context. *Justice Quarterly* 16 (4): 819–46.

Weitzer, Ronald, and Steven A. Tuch. 2005. Determinants of Public Satisfaction with the Police. *Police Quarterly* 8 (3): 279–97.

Whitaker, Gordon P. 1980. Coproduction: Citizen Participation in Service Delivery. *Public Administration Review*: May/June 1980: 240–6.

Williams, Brian N. 1999. Perceptions of Children and Teenagers on Community Policing: Implications for Law-enforcement Leadership, Training, and Citizen Evaluations. *Police Quarterly* 2 (2): 150–73.

Williams, Brian N. 1998. *Citizen Perspectives on Community Policing: A Case Study in Athens, Georgia.* Albany, New York: SUNY Press.

Williams, Brian N., Seong-Cheol Kang, and Japera Johnson. 2016. (Co)-Contamination as the Dark Side of Co-Production: Public Value Failures in Co-Production Processes. *Public Management Review* 18 (5): 692–717.

Williams, Brian N., Megan LePere-Schloop, P. Daniel Silk, and Alexandra Hebdon. 2016. The Co-Production of Campus Safety and Security: A Case Study at the University of Georgia. *International Review of Administrative Sciences* 82 (1): 110–30.

Chapter 11

Community Policing as a Solution

What is the Evidence?

Lauren Hamilton Edwards and Ian Klein

Sandra Bass begins her 2001 essay in *Social Justice* with the understanding that the relationship between policing and race is a persistent problem in the United States, occasionally reaching the level of crisis that consumes the country at the national level. Recent media coverage of officer-involved deaths of African American men and the protests following these events have once again put a spotlight on the relationship between policing and racial and ethnic minorities. This spotlight is not new. Protests and race riots in the late 1960s were often reactions to police actions, as were the riots after the acquittal of officers involved in deadly beating Rodney King in 1993 (Barlow and Barlow 2000).

With a few exceptions, most histories of policing paint an incomplete picture of the field (Bass 2001; Alexander 2012), by leaving out how groups other than White citizens potentially view the police differently. Barrow and Barrow (2000) write, "The personal experiences of racial and ethnic minorities, abused children, immigrants, and battered women who have frequently failed to find a safe haven among the police expose the ethnocentrism and the assumption that the role of police is to fight crime and thus protect the citizenry from harm" (12).

Community policing was an idea that began as a way to build trust between the police and communities, particularly minority communities, in the 1970s and 1980s after protests and riots in the previous decade (see Fisher-Stewart 2007, Spelman, and Eck 1987, Thomas and Burns 2005). The reaction to the current protests of police actions had led to a predictable call for a return to community policing. President Obama's Task Force on 21st Century Policing proposed six pillars of reform (2015). The fourth pillar is "Community Policing and Crime Reduction." This task force discussed the movement from zero tolerance policing, or broken windows policing, to community policing requires officers to "enforce the law *with* the people not just *on* the people" (Task Force 2015, 41, emphasis original).

Though community policing is routinely recommended by the Department of Justice to improve departments with a history of racism,[1] the evidence is less clear that the philosophy is effective. This study is a systematic review of the research that specifically examines the outcomes of community policing after defining the philosophy. We end with a discussion of the current practices in the most well-known police department in the United States, New York City, as well as another with its own struggles, Oakland, California.

COMMUNITY POLICING: A PRACTICE AND A PHILOSOPHY

No work on community policing can begin without recognizing how difficult the innovation is to explain. In a review of *Citizen, Cops, and Power: Recognizing the Limits of Community*, the reviewer admits that "Everybody knows about community policing, but nobody really knows what it is or what it accomplishes" (Deflem 2007). Herbert (2006) begins with a discussion on defining community as a starting point for discussing community policing. He states that community can be an elusive ideal with social and political dimensions that make it difficult to grasp. What are the boundaries of community? Who has the right to speak for and represent a community?

Defining community policing can be equally difficult because the strategy is both a set of practices and a philosophy. The Office of Community Oriented Policing Services (COPS) in the US Department of Justice defines community policing as promoting "organizational strategies that support the systematic use of partnerships and problem-solving techniques to proactively address the immediate conditions that give rise to public safety issues such as crime, social disorder, and fear of crime" (*Community Policing Defined*, 2014). Likewise, Herbert (2006) defines community policing as a set of practices to improve connections with citizen groups by decentralizing policing operations.

In addition to a set of practices, community policing is also defined as a philosophy. Kappeler and Gaines write that this type of policing is a "philosophy that turns traditional policing on its head by empowering the community rather than dictating to the community (2009, 1). This philosophical change is reflected in the language used to describe community policing, including references to respectful or sensitive policing with the community at the heart (Hanniman 2008, Meliala 2001).

Guided by the first director of COPS, three aims are at the center of most community policing definitions (Goldstein 1987, Herbert 2006, Roth, Roehl, and Johnson 2004). The first is to build partnerships with community groups to build better connections with citizens. This is likely the most recognizable to those who know the minimum about community policing. The second is to adopt problem-oriented policing. Problem-oriented policing requires that departments define and focus on particular problems. Some researchers see problem-oriented policing as separate but not distinct from community policing (see Weisburd and Eck 2004). The overlap in the two approaches is in how departments define and work to solve community problems. Done well, both actions require input from community groups. The third goal is to decentralize decision-making.

To achieve the philosophy of community policing, departments have a potential toolbox in which policing departments can use what best fits the needs of the community (Skogan 2006). However, this can also mean that departments can claim they do community policing with minimal effort. For example, departments can have one community police officer that attends community meetings and argue that they are following the strategy. Meanwhile, little actually changes in the department because the philosophy of community policing does not infuse the rest of the department though training or other means.

The goals of community policing relate primarily to citizen satisfaction and police legitimacy (Kelling and Moore 1988), though crime prevention and reduction remains a goal (Herbert 2006). From the citizen perspective, one of the main goals is to shorten the distance between them and police (Zhao, Lovrich, and Thurman 1999, McKee 2001). Another goal is to alleviate fear in communities (Herbert 2006, McKee 2001). The logic of the goal is that better relationships with the police will lead to less fear and more trust on both sides.

The improved relationships and trust between citizens is at the heart of why community policing is often the suggested solution to issues between racial and ethnic minorities and the police. The reasoning is rarely made explicit but is based on the idea that citizens and police would trust each other more if they knew each other (Task Force 2017). This can be done practically through advisory groups from specific communities, like an advisory committee focused on the particular needs of race or ethnic minorities. Other methods are more informal such as foot patrols that get officers out of their cars or meet-ups with community groups. The intent is that officers not only meet citizens when they respond to emergencies but build relationship with citizens before the emergency or need for information.

The potential benefits are not one-sided. Police also need to understand the communities and citizens they police. In the recent use of force incident that resulted in the death of Philando Castillo in Minneapolis, Minnesota, Officer Jeronimo Yanez recounted being afraid when Castillo told the officer that he was legally carrying a firearm. A recent article in Slate magazine links the fear of officers to fear of the other, particularly African American men (Bouie 2017). This is likely also the case with Muslim men.

COMMUNITY POLICING AND OTHER PRACTICES

Community policing as a practice and a philosophy cannot be defined in isolation. Other practices, as well as the events of September 11, 2001, have had major impacts on policing. To illustrate, we will focus particularly on the changes beginning in the police department in New York (hereafter NYPD) under the leadership of Bill Bratton, beginning in 1994. As part of the era known as broken windows or zero tolerance policing, the philosophy of policing in New York began with an understanding that any small infraction could lead to more serious crimes. To lower crime, every minor crime and even the suspicion of crime had to be taken seriously (Wilson and Kelling 1982). Two reforms came out of this era of policing. First, CompStat revolutionized how the department accounted for crimes and held each precinct accountable.[2] Second, stop and question tactics, more commonly known as stop and frisk, were implemented.

That both practices led to lower crime rates is widely documented but the impact on minority communities overshadows the gains.[3] CompStat, at least in popular literature, is linked with an intense focus on minority, immigrant, and low-income neighborhoods (Hayes 2017). Stop and question tactics have an interesting congruence with foot patrols, which had regained popularity as an element of community policing. About half of these stops were African American citizens and a third were Hispanic citizens, though this does not reflect the general population (Bass 2001). Furthermore, few of these stops resulted in arrest. A Federal District Court found these stops unlawful in 2013; and the election of Mayor Bill de Blasio formally closed out the practice. The Brennan Center at New York University found that the end of the practice did not result in a spike in crime (Cullen 2016).

This era also saw an increased focus not only on racial minorities but on ethnic minorities and immigrants, as well. Some refer to the era after 9–11 as the Homeland Security era in policing. Local departments, especially in New York City, were asked to take on the additional role of protecting the public by preventing terrorism. This led to increased profiling of Middle Eastern individuals (Jones and Supinski 2010). Therefore, in addition to the call for a new focus on community policing in response to current issues between racial minorities and police, there are also calls for community policing to help with mistrust between Middle Eastern individuals and police (for an example see Jones and Supinski 2010).

POLICING STRATEGY EFFECTIVENESS

How do we know a strategy is working? Performance measurement in policing is well documented and researched, given the rise of evidence-based policing and CompStat-like programs. Most research studies that look at the impact of policing strategies rely solely on crime reports. These measures are regularly gathered and analyzed for the Uniform Crime Report (UCR) and are reported by departments in annual reports and by the Federal Bureau of Investigation (FBI). With the data readily available, the research on the impact of various policing strategies, such as hot spot policing and problem-oriented policing, is increasingly rigorous and the results are impressive.

A study from this year, for example, used experimental modeling to determine what would have occurred in actual incidents to determine differences between using hot spot policing and not using the strategy (Weisburd, Braga, Groff, and Wooditch 2017). The authors are able to manipulate the data to determine different contexts to understand different outcomes. This type of experiment, and others like it, are very useful in determining the impact of policing strategies, specifically on crime rates. Few studies are this sophisticated that look at community policing.

Furthermore, police do far more than crime reduction activities and citizen perception is an important component of how well the police are doing. Police departments are advised to collect performance information for different purposes (Moore and Braga 2003, based on an earlier book by Moore). These authors lay out seven purposes for measuring performance for policing: (1) reducing crime, (2) holding offenders accountable, (3) reducing fear, (4) maintaining civility in public, (5) efficient and fair use of resources, (6) fair use of force and authority, and (7) providing quality services and maintaining customer satisfaction/legitimacy.

For the purpose of this study, we suggest some additions to the original list from Moore and Braga (2003) to understand the impact of any policing strategy. We suggest the following:

1. Reducing crime
2. Holding offenders accountable
3. Reducing fear
4. Maintaining civility
5. Efficient and fair use of resources
6. Fair use of force and authority
7. Providing quality services
8. Maintaining citizen satisfaction
9. Increasing and maintaining legitimacy in community
10. Maintaining a robust police force

These are not in a particular order and the first six remain unchanged. However, how these are measured and checked likely requires revision. For example, some of the cities reviewed in the original piece track for use of force incidents and have early warning systems for officers who seem problematic. How departments determine when use of force is problematic or unfair is unclear. The transparency with the public is also unclear.

We divided the seventh purpose into three purposes and changed the language. Treating citizens like customers was common in the early part of the 2000s due to the new public management movement but more recent research acknowledges that this is problematic (for a review see Thomas 2016). Citizens are customers at times; but the label is not clear in the policing context. We also split out the purpose of legitimacy. Satisfaction may lend to legitimacy; but this cannot be assumed. We then added a purpose to maintain a robust force. A satisfied group of officers who are willing to commit to the career is key for a successful department and better relationships with the community.

For the strategy of community policing, several purposes stand out as potentially more salient. Reducing fear, citizen satisfaction, and increased legitimacy (trust) are a stated goal of community policing. Though not a direct goal, fair use of force and authority has a heightened import in community policing as the strategy is a stated solution for problems between racial and ethnic minorities and police, including racial and ethnic profiling. And, finally, reduced crime and holding offenders accountable are the ultimate goal of any strategy, including community policing.[4]

COMMUNITY POLICING IMPACT: IN RESEARCH

To determine how researchers study the impact of community policing, we conducted a systematic review of criminal justice and policing peer-reviewed journals. The names of journals reviewed can be found in Appendix 1. The criteria for inclusion were that articles should primarily focus on the impacts of community policing in the United States. There are studies that are located in other countries but might not be comparable for this purpose. We searched article databases using search terms for community policing, community policing components (foot patrols, neighborhood/community meetings, and community engagement), and several terms for impact, including: impact, outcomes, and evaluation. We also searched additionally for the words race, ethnicity, and minority. To ensure that the primary focus of articles was the impact of community policing, we searched abstracts and key words rather than full text. We did not consider books or professional reports for the review.[5]

Overall, we found twenty articles that met our inclusion criteria. We classified each article using our revised framework for measuring policing performance. The largest number of articles looks specifically at the impact of community policing on police officers. None of the articles in our review study the impact on maintaining civility, efficient and fair use of resources, fair use of force or authority, and legitimacy. That the fair use of force or authority is not studied is disappointing given the import of decreasing racial and ethnic profiling in community policing. Below is an overview of the review.

REDUCING CRIME

Two articles specifically studied the impact of community policing on crime, which are summarized in Table 11.1. This low number is not surprising given that the stated aims for community policing do not directly include reducing crime. For community policing to logically impact crime rates, other objectives need to be met, such as building trust in the community. The authors operationalize community policing three ways: a dichotomous variable of having a plan for community policing, an index of activities, and three separate dimensions. The first article finds that community policing does not impact homicide rates (MacDonald 2002). The second article finds that all dimensions of community policing impact property and violent crime rates in small communities. Only the dimension of partnerships in problem-solving impact property crime rates in larger communities.

HOLDING OFFENDERS ACCOUNTABLE

Two articles researched the impact of community policing on arrest (see Table 11.2). Though this purpose is not a direct goal of community policing,

Table 11.1 Findings for Reducing Crime

Article	Community policing	Performance	Findings
MacDonald (2002)	• Dichotomous variable of having plan • Index of activities	Homicide rates	No impact
Sozer and Merlo (2013)	Three dimensions • community contributions • problem-solving partnerships • training and problem-solving	• Property crime rates • Violent crime rates	Improved rates in small communities, mixed results for larger communities

Table 11.2   Findings for Holding Offenders Accountable

Article	Community policing	Performance	Findings
Novak, Frank, Smith and Engel (2002) Tillyer (2017)	Classification of officer • Dichotomous variable of having a plan • Index of activities	Decision to arrest Violent crime: • Murder • Kidnapping • Robbery • Assault • Sexual offense	No impact for this purpose A greater number of activities and some specific activities increased arrests

the purpose is highly important in other types of policing. Novak and coauthors did not find a significant difference between community policing officers and traditional beat cops in the number of arrests; and noncompliance increases the likelihood of arrest for both groups. There are some notable differences. Community officers are more likely to arrest than beat officers when the victim requests an arrest or when the subject is a juvenile. Beat officers are more likely to arrest citizens who are male, not White, are intoxicated, or perceived as being hostile. A recent piece finds that when departments do more community policing activities and make their commitment explicit in their mission statement, violent crimes were more likely to end in an arrest (Tillyer 2017). The author finds the strongest relationship between community policing and arrest in cases of kidnapping. The author hypothesized that this finding is likely due to the nature of the crime involving children. An article by King (2007) was not included in the review because the author's focus was not on community policing but on departmental compliance with hate crime laws. The findings are interesting, nonetheless. The author found that departments are more likely to comply when they do community policing.

REDUCING FEAR

One of the main aims of community policing is to reduce citizen fear. The low number of articles in this portion of review was not expected; and the studies are very different (see Table 11.3). The first uses the results of a study about victimization and fear of crime in twelve cities, which was sponsored by COPS (Roh and Oliver 2005). The authors point out that reducing fear is not likely a direct impact of community policing but rather the result of other mediating factors, including: improved perceptions of community disorder and decreased concern for community. Another interesting piece looks at the mediating impact of community policing on perception of safety and other

Table 11.3   Reducing Fear

Article	Community policing	Performance	Findings
Reisig and Parks (2004)	Citizen perception of police bonds to neighborhood	Citizen perception of quality of life measures	Improves fear
Roh and Oliver (2005)	Citizen perception of whether or not community uses community policing	Fear of crime	Improves fear of crime
Rukus (2017)	• Trust in police • Engagement with other community groups • Neighborhood watch, formal and informal	Citizen perception of safety	No impact for this purpose

quality of life measures (Reisig and Parks 2004). Citizens from disadvantaged neighborhoods were more likely to have lower perceptions of quality of life measures and safety. However, stronger bonds with police at least partially improved feelings about safety. The last piece is much more comprehensive in aims but less conclusive due to method (Rukus 2017). This article studies the impact of community policing components on citizen perception of safety and does not find an impact. However, the data from the study is from a survey of chief executives in communities, not the citizens or police perceptions.

CITIZEN SATISFACTION AND IMPROVED PERCEPTION

We reviewed five articles that studied the impact of community policing on citizen satisfaction and improved perception of police (see Table 11.4). Citizen satisfaction may not clearly link to all policing activities; but it is very important for community policing. The logic is that satisfied citizens would be more likely to participate, as well as legitimize the police. Logic is not evidence, though! Future studies should determine whether satisfaction and legitimacy are linked.

These studies range from 1993 until 2005. Though one study did not find that community policing activities improve citizen perception in Thomasville, Georgia (Prine, Ballard, and Robinson 2002), most studies did. The first study evaluated the impacts of a community policing pilot program that targeted youth in Spokane, Washington (Thurman, Giacomazzi, and Bogen 1993). The authors demonstrate that the children and their parents improved their perception of police. Two studies specifically look at how community policing improves perceptions of police by race. One found that African American and Hispanic respondents had more favorable views of community

Table 11.4   Citizen Satisfaction

Article	Community policing	Performance	Findings
Thurman, Giacomazzi, and Bogen (1993)	Case: project in Spokane, Washington	Youth and parent perception of police	Improved perception
Prine, Ballard, and Robinson (2001)	Citizen perception of activities	Citizen perception of police	No impact
Davis and Miller (2002)	Case: Queens, New York City	Citizen awareness community policing	Citizens were aware
Ong and Jenks (2004)	Citizen perception of whether or not community uses community policing	Citizen perception of police	Black and Hispanic citizens more favorable than White citizens
Thomas and Burns (2005)	Citizen perception of whether or not community uses community policing	Citizen perception of police	Improved perceptions but only for White women

policing than White respondents (Ong and Jenks 2004). This favorable view of community policing was positively correlated with positive perceptions of police for Hispanic respondents. Another study, using the same data, studied the interaction of whether or not knowledge of community policing improved perceptions of police for White women but not for African American and Hispanic respondents (Thomas and Burns 2005). The final study in this set studied whether or not residents of an ethnic neighborhood in New York City were aware of the department's community policing practices (Davis and Miller 2002). Citizens were more aware of community policing if they lived in an established neighborhood than citizens who lived in neighborhoods made up of recently arrived immigrants.

INCREASED CITIZEN ENGAGEMENT

Three articles study the impact factors, including community policing, on citizens engagement. For a summary see Table 11.5. Two of these find that living in high-risk neighborhoods improve the likelihood that citizens will engage with police departments (Pattavina, Byrne, and Garcia 2006). This outcome is improved when citizens felt that police got to know their neighborhood. Another, which is also included in the purpose of reducing fear, found that city executive felt that citizens were more likely to engage when they trust the police (Rukus 2017). This type of study that determines why

Table 11.5 Citizen Engagement

Article	Community policing	Performance	Findings
Pattavina, Byrne, and Garcia (2006)	Case: Boston	Likelihood of citizen participation	Citizens from high-risk neighborhoods are more likely to engage
Wehrman and De Angelis (2011)	Case: a Midwestern city	Likelihood of citizen participation	Citizens from high-risk neighborhoods and African–American respondents are more likely to engage
Rukus (2017)	• Trust in police • Engagement with other community groups • Neighborhood watch, formal and informal	Citizen engagement	One component improves engagement

citizens participated in community policing is helpful. These also demonstrate the need for ensuring that community policing practices are leading to more trust and legitimacy.

MAINTAINING A ROBUST POLICE FORCE

Five articles were found that study the impact of community policing on police perception of community policing, abilities, and job satisfaction. This is surprising, given that police officer's feelings are not a major aim of community policing. However, the logic is that officers carry out the innovation and are on the front lines. Also, there is an assumption that police officers will be happier doing community policing activities. Furthermore, departments need officer buy-in for the best results.

One study found that police officers had largely favorable attitudes toward community policing (Adams, Rohe, and Arcury 2002, Pate and Shtull 1994, Paoline, Meyers, and Worden 2000, Rosenbaum, Yeh, and Wilkinson 1994), though others found that this varied by race and/or gender. One study found that White men were more favorable (Ammar, Kessler, and Kratcoski 2008), while another found that minority officers were more favorable (Paoline et al. 2000). Hispanic officers in another study were more likely to think that community meetings were important than African American and White officers (Jenkins 2016). There are mixed results on job satisfaction. Adams and coauthors (2002) found that community policing improved job satisfaction but Rosenbaum and coauthors (1994) did not. This last article does find that

Table 11.6   Police Force

Article	Community policing	Performance	Findings
Pate and Shtull (1994)	Case: New York City	Officer support	Officers were generally favorable
Rosenbaum, Yeh, and Wilkinson (1994)	Case: departments in Chicago	• Officer support • Job satisfaction	• More likely after training • No impact
Paoline, Myers, and Worden (2000)	Case: training Indianapolis and St. Petersberg	Officer perceptions of citizens and policing culture	Associations were weak
Adams, Rohe, and Arcury (2002)	Case: five cities in North Carolina	• Officer support • Job satisfaction	• Officers were favorable • Officers had higher job satisfaction than officers that did not do community policing
Ammar, Kessler, and Kratcoski (2008)	Case: Cleveland, Ohio	Officer support	Mixed findings by race
Black and Kari (2008)	COP in twelve city study	Officer abilities	Mixed findings by race and gender
Jenkins (2016)	Comparison of community and problem-oriented policing	Officer support for components	Mixed findings by race

community policing improves officer knowledge of the community. The final article reviewed for this purpose compares the community policing skills of officers and found that minority males in Arizona were most likely to adapt to community policing and best able to interact with diverse groups of people (Black and Kari 2008).

Though the results are mixed, breaking out these measures by race is an important first step. However, this does little to explain why minority officers feel differently about their jobs than their White counterparts. Clearly, more qualitative studies are needed.

DISCUSSION

To summarize, findings suggest that studies about the impact of community policing are not necessarily researching the stated goals of the innovation.

Surprisingly, the largest number of articles found for the review were related to the impact of community policing on police officers. This demonstrates the need for including a purpose of measurement for ensuring a robust police force. Measures that are related to the stated aims of community policing still require a lot of research to gauge the broader impact of the strategy.

A bright spot in the review is the approaches of some studies to break out respondents, or units of analysis, by race or ethnicity, as well as neighborhood risk levels. Similar to traffic stop data, this type of analysis is crucial for understanding different treatment, though it could go deeper with qualitative case studies like that found in a recent book, *Pulled Over* (Epps, Maynard-Moody, and Haider-Merkel 2015).

More to the point of this chapter, some evidence exists that community policing research uses some measures that begin to get at the impact of community policing on one of the problems it was created to help. Measures that determine whether policing impacts minority citizens differently partially highlights that policing impacts communities differently. In our rush for improved crime rates, departments often sacrifice other worthy goals, like equity (Radin 2015).

Another takeaway from this study is that researchers often use the data that they can get. Citizen satisfaction is easily obtained through surveys; and crime and victimization data are both collected by the federal government. As long as research relies on available data sets, we will barely scratch the surface of understanding the full impact of community policing and policing more broadly. In an age of big data, we are not optimistic that there will be additional measures that go below the surface on treatment differences and a better understanding of equity in this study.

COMMUNITY POLICING: IN PRACTICE

Many of these studies do not detail the quality of the community policing programs being studied, which could have a fairly large impact on the impact of the strategy. These studies do not show more recent trends in community policing. To that point, we conclude with some promising new developments in the department this study focused on as an exemplar, the NYPD, as well as the Oakland Police Department (hereafter OPD).

New York Police Department: Neighborhood Policing and Qualitative Performance

Once again under Bill Bratton until his retirement, the department published a plan for a new era in both community policing and CompStat. The *Plan of Action* is most notable for its stark admission of the latest issues in the city and the mistrust between minority community and police following the death of Eric Garner. In a candid narrative, former Commissioner Bratton acknowledges that community policing was not as successful as he would like and that having community policing officers separate from patrol officers is problematic. He writes:

> The NYPD has an excellent staff of community-focused officers working with everything from youth programs to block associations to crime prevention, and they have done important work in keeping the department connected with the neighborhoods we serve. They have been a bridge between the community and the police. But bridging the police/community divide is not enough. We want to close it. (2)

The plan to accomplish this task is the brainchild of James O'Neill, who replaced Bratton as the Police Commissioner of the NYPD last year when he retired. The new strategy organizes beats by neighborhoods rather than precincts. Even if this is a change in language only, it reflects an interesting change in thinking about the meaning of community. In addition, officers will be assigned to neighborhoods fulltime. Houston's department did this a few decades ago; and it has seemed to work well (Brown 1987). An even more innovative move has been to integrate policing with community functions. As pointed out by Goetz and Mitchell (2003), COP rarely changed a whole department. Instead, departments might have a community division or liaison. The NYPD wants to now get rid of specialized community officers and give all officers that responsibility. They desire to ensure that all officers spend thirty-three percent of their time with the community.

The inventors of CompStat are also changing what they measure in ways that are unclear to date but have the potential to shift CompStat. First, the NYPD wants to centralize data in a 'data warehouse' and make it more available to all officers, across boroughs and units. Second, and most important for this study, they want to rely less on quantitative measures than they have in the past. There is a recognition that focusing solely on certain performance measures have caused adverse behaviors. They will not get rid of these measures, like arrest data; but they will supplement these measures to evaluate officers with other, more qualitative measures, like leadership and timeliness of reports. These qualitative measures still do not go far enough; but is a step in the right direction.

Oakland Police Department: Community Policing

Another department in Oakland, California (OPD) more specifically addressed the current policing climate in their strategic plan, which was published in early 2016 under the former Chief Sean Whent. The plan is tied directly to former President Obama's Task Force on 21st Century Policing. The following is included in the introduction of the plan:

> The United States is continuing to face a crisis of confidence in law enforcement. Two recent and significant events where police officers in Ferguson, Missouri and New York City used deadly force on unarmed African American males. These two incidents—coupled with a long history of disparate treatment of African Americans by law enforcement—served as a catalyst that resulted in formation of the President's Task Force on 21st Century Policing. This strategic plan provides an opportunity to examine and incorporate task force recommendations and action items. (6)

The admission is admirable but does not address the local issues within the OPD. The OPD agreed to a consent decree with the Department of Justice in early 2000. In 2013, a federal judge appointed a special compliance director due to a decade of noncompliance. A recent study also found that officers treat African American residents very differently than White residents using body camera footage (Voigt et al. 2017). The study was made available on the OPDs website, though, with a plan for better training.

Under a newly appointed Chief, Anne E. Kirkpatrick after a scandal unrelated to race led to the firing of Sean Whent, the OPD has since carried out several items from the 2016 plan that other departments can learn from. The first is a citizen advisory board to assist with the implementation and review of community policing. Many departments have other types of review boards, especially citizen review boards that investigate use of force and other complaints. This type of citizen advisory board is particularly interesting because it demonstrates a willingness to include citizens from the beginning, rather than just give community policing lip service. Members represent each policing district.

Also, like the NYPD, the OPD requires all officers to engage with the community, not specialized community police officers. The structure is different, though. The OPD requires officers to attend a community meeting once a month. The department did have a plan to pilot more intimate meetings in resident's homes, which are called living room meetings. It is unclear if these have been implemented. The OPD also rewards officers that volunteer in the community, which can now included in promotion decisions.

However, the OPD has not included broader measures of performance. The only performance measure associated with community policing is citizen satisfaction. The plan states that community volunteer hours are recorded. Reporting these could help the community understand how many hours the police are giving back to the community they serve. A report of activities would also be advisable.

CONCLUSION

The findings from research may be inconclusive but we have provided examples of two police departments that are incrementally improving their community policing practices. Both researchers and practitioners need to continue to move forward incrementally, learning as we go to improve strategies and our understanding of how well those strategies work.

In the meantime, we need better information on how community policing is implemented as a set of practices and the extent to which it influences change in departments as a philosophy. Furthermore, broader data gathering practices in departments that include qualitative measures and racial differences in treatment like the Oakland study (Voigt et al. 2017) would help the public better understand if community policing is a worthy, even partial, solution to the long history of problems between racial and ethnic minorities and police in the United States.

NOTES

1. See the consent decrees for the cities of Baltimore and Ferguson following protests after highly publicized use of force incidents. Each specifically recommends community policing and different forms of community engagement.

2. Much has been written about COMPstat and similar programs, which I will not review here. For a good review of the literature, I suggest an article by Tiwana, Bass, and Farrell published in *Crime Science* that overviews the major works. It should be noted that there are more critical works. One book highlights evidence that the NYPD manipulated crime data by reclassifying crimes and, in some instances, cheating by reporting officers (Eterno and Silverman 2012).

3. For an in depth discussion of the crime rate decline in New York City, see the report from the Brennan Center at New York University released in 2015 by Oliver Roeder, Lauren-Brooke Eisen, and Julia Bowling.

4. One article suggests several measures for community policing but the suggestions are all based on crime statistics (Alpert, Flynn, and Piquero 2001).

5. A book by Wesley G. Skogan, a proponent of community policing has two excellent chapters on outcomes for both citizens and police (2004), though this was the only book I found in my search.

REFERENCES

*Adams, Richard E., William M. Rohe, and Thomas A. Arcury. "Implementing Community-Oriented Policing: Organizational Change and Street Officer Attitude." *Crime and Delinquency* 48, no. 3 (2002): 399–430.

Alexander, Michelle. *The New Jim Crow: Mass Incarceration in the Age of Color-blindness*. New York: The New Press, 2012.

Alpert, Geoffrey P., Daniel Flynn, and Alex P. Piquero. "Effective Community Policing Performance Measures." *Justice Research and Policy* 3, no. 2 (2001): 79–94.

*Ammar, Nawal, David Kessler, and Peter Kratcoski. "The Interaction between a Neighbourhood's Racial Composition and Officer Race in Community Policing: A Case Study from the Resident Area Policing Programme (RAPP), Cleveland, Ohio." *International Journal of Police Science and Management* 10, no. 3 (2007): 313–325.

Barlow, David E., and Melissa Hickman Barlow. *Police in a Multicultural Society: An American Story*. Long Grove, IL: Waveland Press, Inc., 2000.

Bass, Sandra. "Policing Space, Policing Race: Social Control Imperatives and Police Discretionary Decisions." *Social Justice* 28, no. 1 (2001): 156–176.

Black, Pamela J., and Camilla J. Kari. "Policing Diverse Communities: Do Gender and Minority Status Make a Difference? *Journal of Ethnicity in Criminal Justice* 8, (2010): 216–229.

Bratton, William J. *The NYPD Plan of Action and Neighborhood Policing Plan: A Realistic Framework for Connecting Police and Communities*. New York: NYPD, 2015.

Cullen, James. "Ending New York's Stop-and-Frisk Did not Increase Crime." Brennan Center for Justice (blog). Accessed June 2017. https://www.brennancenter.org/blog/ending-new-yorks-stop-and-frisk-did-not-increase-crime

*Davis, Robert C. and Joel Miller. "Immigration and Integration Perceptions of Community Policing among Members of Six Ethnic Communities in Central Queens, New York City." *International Review of Victimology* 9 (2002): 93–111.

Deflem, Mathieu. "Citizens, Cops, and Power: Recognizing the Limits of Community by Steve Herbert." *Law and Society Review* 41, no. 1 (2007): 255–257.

Department of Justice, Community Oriented Policing Services. *Community Policing Defined*. (2014). Accessed January 2016. https://cops.usdoj.gov/pdf/vets-to-cops/e030917193-CP-Defined.pdf

Epps, Charles R., Steven Maynard-Moody, and Donald P. Haider-Markel. *Pulled Over: How Police Stops Define Race and Citizenship*. Chicago, IL: The University of Chicago Press, 2014.

Eterno, John A.and Eli B. Silverman. *The Crime Numbers Game: Management by Manipulation*. Baco Raton, FL: CRC Press, 2012.

Fisher-Stewart, Gayle. *Community Policing Explained: A Guide for Local Governments*. Washington, DC: ICMA, 2007.

Goldstein, Herman. "Toward Community-Oriented Policing: Potential, Basic Requirements, and Threshold Questions." *Crime and Delinquency* 33, no. 1 (1987): 6–30.

Hanniman, Wayne. "Canadian Muslims, Islamophobia and national security." *International Journal of Law, Crime and Justice* 36, no. 4 (2008): 271–285.

Hayes, C. *A Colony in a Nation*. New York: W. W. Norton and Company, 2017.

Herbert, Steve. *Citizens, Cops, and Power: Recognizing the Limits of Community*. Chicago: University of Chicago Press, 2006.

Jones, Chapin and Stanley B. Supinski. "Policing and Community Relations in the Homeland Security Era." *Journal of Homeland Security and Emergency Management* 7, no. 1 (2010).

Kappeler, Victor E., and Larry K. Gaines. *Community Policing: A Contemporary Perspective* (5th ed.). Newark, NJ: Matthew Bender and Company, Inc, 2009.

Kelling, George L., and Mark H. Moore. 1988. "The Evolving Strategy of Policing." *Perspectives on Policing* 4 (November): 1–16.

*King, Ryan D. "The Context of Minority Group Threat: Race, Institutions, and Complying with Hate Crime Law." *Law and Society Review* 41, no. 1 (2007): 189–224.

*MacDonald, John M. "The Effectiveness of Community Policing in Reducing Violent Crime." *Crime and Delinquency* 48, no. 4 (2002): 592–618.

McKee, Adam J. "The Community Policing Evaluation Survey: Reliability, Validity, and Structure." *American Journal of Criminal Justice* 25, no. 2 (2001): 199–209.

Meliala, Adrianus. "The notion of sensitivity in policing." *International Journal of the Sociology of Law* 29, (2001):99–111.

*Novak, Kenneth J., James Frank, Brad W. Smith, and Robin Shephard Engel. "Revisiting the Decision to Arrest: Comparing Beat and Community Officers." *Crime and Delinquency* 48, no. 1 (2002): 70–98.

Oakland Police Department. *Strategic Plan 2016*. Oakland, CA: Oakland Police Department, 2016.

*Ong, Marcus and David A. Jenks. "Hispanic Perceptions of Community Policing: Is Community Policing Working in the City?" *Journal of Ethnicity in Criminal Justice* 2, no. 3 (2004): 53–66.

*Pate, Antony M. and Penny Shtull."Community Policing Grown in Brooklyn: An Inside View of the New York City Police Department's Model Precinct." *Crime and Delinquency* 40, no. 3 (1994): 384–410.

*Pattavina, April, James M. Byrne, and Luis Garcia. "An Examination of Citizen Involvement in High-risk versus Low- to Moderate-risk Neighborhoods." *Crime and Delinquency* 52, no. 2 (2006): 203–231.

*Paoline, Eugene A., Stephanie M. Myers,and Robert E. Worden."Police Culture, Individualism, and Community Policing: Evidence from Two Departments." *Justice Quarterly* 17, no. 3 (2000): 575–605.

President's Task Force on 21st Century Policing. *Final Report of the President's Task Force on 21st Century Policing*. Washington, DC: Office of Community Oriented Policing Services, 2015.

*Prine, Rudy K., Chet Ballard, and Deborah M. Robinson. "Perceptions of Community Policing in a Small Town." *American Journal of Criminal Justice* 25, no. 2 (2001): 211–221.

Radin, Beryl A. "Baltimore: When Good Intentions Bring Negative Consequences." *Public Administration Review* 75, no. 4 (2015): 511–512.

*Reisig, Michael D. and Roger Parks. "Can Community Policing Help the Truly Disadvantaged?" *Crime and Delinquency* 50, no. 2 (2004): 139–167.

Roeder, Oliver, Lauren-Brooke Eisen, and Julia Bowling. *What Caused the Crime Decline?* New York: Brennan Center for Justice, 2015. Accessed June 2017. https://www.brennancenter.org/publication/what-caused-crime-decline

Roh, Sunghoon and William M. Oliver. "Effects of Community Policing upon Fear of Crime: Understanding the Causal Linkage." *Policing: An International Journal of Police Strategies and Management* 28 (2005): 670–683.

*Rosenbaum, Dennis P., Sandy Yeh, and Deanna L. Wilkinson. "Impact of Community Policing on Police Personnel: A Quasi-experimental Test." *Crime and Delinquency* 40, no. 3 (1994): 331–353.

Roth, Jeffery A., Jan Roehl, and Calvin C. Johnson. "Trends in the Adoption of Community Policing." In *Community Policing: Can it Work?*, edited by Wesley G. Skogan, 3–24. Belmont, CA: Thomas Wadsworth, 2004.

Rukus, Joseph, Mildred E. Warner, and Xue Zhang. "Community Policing: Least effective where need is greatest." *Crime and Delinquency* (2017): 1–24. doi:10.1177/0011128716686339.

Skogan, Wesley, G. *Community Policing: Can it Work?* Belmont, CA: Wadsworth, 2004.

———. *Police and Community: A Tale of Three Cities.* New York: Oxford University Press, 2006.

*Sozer, Mehmet Alpert and Alida V. Merlo. (2013). "The Impact of Community Policing on Crime Rates: Roes the Effect of Community Policing Differ in Large and Small Law Enforcement Agencies?" *Police Practice and Research* 14, no. 6 (2013): 506–521.

Spelman, William and John E. Eck. *Problem-Oriented Policing.* Washington, DC: U.S. Department of Justice, 1987.

Thomas, J. C. (2015). *Citizen, Customer, Partner: Engaging the Public in Public Management.* New York: Routledge, 2015.

*Thomas, Matthew O. and Peter F. Burns. "Repairing the Divide: An Investigation of Community Policing and Citizen Attitudes toward the Police by Race and Ethnicity." *Journal of Ethnicity in Criminal Justice* 31, no. 1/2 (2005): 71–89.

Thurman, Quint C., Andrew Giacomazzi, and Phil Bogen. "Research Note: Cops, Kids, and Pommunity Policing—An Assessment of a Community Policing Demonstration Project." *Crime and Delinquency* 39, no. 4 (1993): 554–64.

*Tillyer, Rob. "Assessing the Impact of Community-oriented Policing on Arrest." *Justice Quarterly* (2017). doi: 10.1080/07418825.2017.1327609.

Tiwana, Neena, Gary Bass, and Graham Farrell. (2015). "Police Performance Measurement: An Annotated Bibliography." *Crime Science* 4, no. 1 (2015):1–28.

United States of America vs. Police Department of Baltimore City. *Consent Decree*, 2017. Accessed May 2017. https://www.justice.gov/opa/file/925056/download

United State of America vs. The City of Ferguson. *Consent Decree*, 2016. Accessed May 2017. https://www.justice.gov/opa/file/833431/download

Voigt, Rob, Nicholas P. Camp, Vinodkumar Prabhakaran, William L. Hamilton, Rebecca C. Hetey, Camilla M. Griffiths, David Jurgens, Dan Jurafskya, and Jennifer L. Eberhardt. "Language from Police Body Cameras Shows Racial Disparities in Officer Respect." *Proceedings from the National Academy of Sciences* 114, no. 25 (2017): 6521–6526.

*Wehrman, Michael M., and Joseph De Angelis. "Citizen Willingness to Participate in Police-community Partnerships: Exploring the Influence of Race and Neighborhood Context." *Police Quarterly* 14, no. 1 (2011): 48–69.

Weisburd, David, Anthony A. Braga, Elizabeth R. Groff, and Alese Wooditch. "Can Hot Spot Policing Reduce Crime in Urban Areas? An Agent-based Simulation." *Criminology* 55, no. 1 (2017): 137–173.

Wilson, James Q. and George L. Kelling. "Broken Windows." *Atlantic*, March 1982.

Zhao, Jihong, Nicholas P. Lovrich, andQuint Thurman. "The Status of Community Policing in American Cities: Facilitators and Impediments Revisited." *Policing: An International Journal of Police Strategies and Management* 22, no. 1 (1999): 74–92.

*indicates that the citation is included in review.

Chapter 12

Developing a Comparativist Ethics for the Evaluative Study of Racialized Police Violence

Mario A. Rivera and James D. Ward

There are prospective advantages to an adaptive analytical method drawing on public administration and policy traditions, in the evaluation of police violence and racism. A broadly construed comparative methodology relying on Comparative Public Administration would allow for cross-group study of police violence against African Americans, Latinos, and other groups in the United States, possibly incorporating cross-national analysis for the sake of a larger perspective. Comparative study would also allow for policy-specific studies, for example, on the racialization of healthcare (Tessler 2012; Jee-Lyn García & Sharif 2015), the ethics of social welfare policy (Ward & Rivera 2014), and the development of public-sector diversity competencies (Rice 2015). Social theory provides another disciplinary source, with analytical constructs such as "institutional racism," capable of integration into public administration and political science evaluative frames (Goldberg 2002; Adams & Balfour 2003; Gutmann 2003; King 2005; Abdelal, Herrera, Johnston & McDermott, 2006; Fong 2008; Lieberman 2008; Hooker 2009; Mitchell 2010; Sheth 2011).

Public Ethics, including the study of social equity, offers yet another value-analytical approach, one that is by its nature close to the grounding that we seek, in public administration and policy (Frederickson 1990). The present study aims to situate these questions in a broadly inclusive research context, pointing toward new paths for theoretical development in the study of policing and race, broadly within the bounds of public administration, public policy, and politics. It will suggest that one standpoint in particular—that of *public ethics*—offers an apt approach to inquiry along these lines. Nonetheless, we will consider whether prominent standpoints on public ethics—those tied to the liberal state in particular—can take us far enough to (literally) do

241

justice to questions of racism—in employment, education, and, in particular, policing.

PUBLIC ADMINISTRATION: EPISTEMOLOGY
AND EPISTEMIC COMMUNITY

A first step in this endeavor is to consider the *epistemic position* of public administration and policy scholars and practitioners, meaning (1) the scope of knowledge in the public administration/policy field(s) and the conditions for the acquisition of such knowledge (Raadschelders 2011; Fischer 2003), and (2) the context in which knowledge of this nature primarily applies (or where it has explanatory primacy—Axtell 2000; Hofweber 1999). Roughly defining these domains will also allow us to specify how best to address public-sector issues in those novel instances when there may be difficult knowledge-construction or knowledge-framing challenges involved, as is the case with police-involved shootings and other systemic violence against African Americans in the United States. As Frederickson (1999) suggests, it is public administration as an epistemic community, in the context of political science, "that is responding to the modern challenges of high fragmentation and the disarticulation of the state" and to related "structural and contextual dynamics—the problems of jurisdictions and system disorder, unpredictability, and instability," in short to systemic shortcomings and breakdowns (p. 15). In other words, public administration research represents an epistemic break with political science in connection with the contemporary liberal state, with its premises of human equality and social equity, insofar as these are often violated, specifically in regard to systemic racism (Frederickson 1990). Put differently, racialized police violence in the United States may amount to state failure, given its virulence and persistence (Miller 2015), and the disciplines of public administration and public policy (including public ethics) may offer greater insight into the subject at various levels of analysis than does political science as such.

Using constructs like *representative bureaucracy*, public administration scholars have distinctly probed institutional roles, thereby accounting for racialized police violence, by positing that police often come to identify with their organizations—police forces—to such an extent that they are blinded to their unwarrantedly aggressive responses to individual citizens (Wilkins & Williams 2009). Others have extended the range of contextual influences from police departments to the communities and neighborhoods in which police operate, referencing those attitudes toward race, police discretion, and response to crime that are prevalent in those sociodemographic spheres (Gaines & Kappeler 2003). It is these variegated forms of inquiry that

singularly allow public administration/policy disciplines to probe an extensive range of influences on these subjects, from the cognitive/developmental
to the cultural, organizational, and institutional.

Sources for the Study of Institutional Racism

In their recent text (Ward & Rivera 2014), the authors addressed a conundrum in the public administration/policy literature with regard to the study
of systemic racism: On the one hand, the literature is (by its very nature)
eclectic and seemingly all-embracing; on the other hand, notwithstanding its
integration of vast streams of multidisciplinary theoretical and methodological sources, it has largely failed to address the institutional embeddedness
of racism. In our text, we posited that institutional racism is often found in
the spaces between (1) avowed commitments to diversity and (2) regressive,
discriminatory practices—as found, among other places, in the prevalence of
police-involved violence against African American and other communities
of color.

These gaps in knowledge may obtain because the concept of racism forces
research emphasis on hidden factors—operating at every level of analysis—
that are as difficult to define operationally as they are to acknowledge in practice. The failure of the otherwise well-suited public administration literature
to address racism in its entrenched manifestations forces reliance on other
sources and ways of knowledge—that is, epistemologies. We in fact relied on
a synthesis of far-ranging theoretical and methodological sources in our text,
in our effort to define institutional racism in conceptual and practical terms,
which brings us back to the need for definition of discipline-specific grounding for the study of police violence, profiling, and other persistent forms of
racism in policing, in the United States and elsewhere. We principally relied
on the following conceptual schema and sources:

1. 'Cognitive complexity,' 'intersectionality,' and Critical Race Theory
   (CRT), constructs in the main from psychology and sociology. Building
   on these sources, we considered *integrative complexity* to be a requirement for cultural competency in the public service, including policing.
   Integrative complexity entails cognitive differentiation and assimilation
   of multiple outlooks, a way of perceiving, thinking, and acting that allows
   individuals to take expansive perspectives on issues and problems while
   regarding their own as only one among many (Antonio, Chang, Hakuta,
   Kenny, Levin, & Milem 2004; see also Tuckman 1966 and Ortiz & Jani
   2010). Integrative complexity involves openness to different races, eth-
   nicities, cultures, and ways of life on the part of public officials. For a
   comparative, CRT-based treatment of police violence against Blacks and

other racial minorities, premised on such a cosmopolitan outlook, see Chaney (2015).

2. Contributions from contextual historical analysis, including legal history and legal theory, on racial exclusion in the provision for human services, for instance in public housing and mortgage refinance programs. Critical Race Theory itself relies on contextual/historical analysis (Heinze 2006), and it was frequently relied upon in our text, which considered a wide range of subjects, as indicated by the following chapter headings: Religious Institutions, Race, and Belief Systems; Institutions of Higher Learning; Nonprofits, Community Service Organizations, and Philanthropy; Racial Profiling and Law Enforcement Agencies; Employment Equity and Institutional Racism; and Transformative Leadership and Public Ethics. In adapting CRT to these various studies, we incorporated it in a larger, historical policy analysis that was consistent with our public administration and public policy focus (Cf. Hamilton 2009). On CRT, higher education, and the use of contextual/historical method, see Morfin, Perez, Parker, Lynn, and Arona (2006). For a legal-analytical application of Conflict Theory to police-initiated racial profiling, see Petrocelli, Piquero, and Smith (2003).

3. Cultural analysis and the politics of cultural identity. Of special interest to us was the devaluation of minority cultural identity, involving the imputation of blame for poverty and crime on the cultural norms, traditions, values, and behaviors of racial and ethnic minorities. Here we examined how jaundiced cultural outlooks of this kind impact people of color, in various organizational and policy domains that include policing. Cultural identity is bound up with what Kwame Anthony Appiah (2004) calls the "irreducibly plural nature of human [and cultural] values"; and, as Jürgen Habermas argues (1993, pp. 130–131), "identity formation depends upon relations of reciprocal recognition." Anyone denied recognition because of sheer prejudice is also denied communicative competence—access to community and polity, and therefore even to recognition of her or his personhood. Identity is plural, multiperspective, transactional, social, and dialogical. As Evangelia Tastsoglou suggests, rather than an imputed quality, identity must be regarded as "other-referenced, relational and comparative," contextual, historically situated, and as "constructed and subject to ongoing negotiation and reconstruction" in the push-and-pull of social relations (Tatsoglou 2001, p. 3). For a treatment of racism and identity as constructed categories that are nonetheless irreducibly political and public in nature, see Abdelal, Herrera, Johnston, and McDermott (2006); and as necessarily contextual, historical, and discursive phenomena, in legal-critical analysis, see Coyle (2010).

4. Institutional/organizational analysis of ingrained practices that predictably exclude people of color from economic and social opportunity—for instance, in the insularity of professional recruitment and hiring networks. The lack of diversity among police departments is often cited as a cause for police-involved shootings and other violence against African Americans and other populations of color. Here we relied on the construct of institutional racism, which refers to both intentional and unintentional, overt, and covert forms of racial prejudice that become manifest in established social and organizational practices, for instance in employment and promotion processes that disadvantage racial and ethnic minorities (Price 1997). Braham (1992, p. 106) suggests that widening the definition of discrimination to include indirect institutional racism would give one a much better understanding of the formidable obstacles faced by racial and ethnic minorities in their everyday lives, including the experience of *de facto* state-sanctioned violence. We also relied in this connection on the economic construct of 'hysteresis,' or socioeconomic historicity, which points to the entrenchment of privilege in the historic development of racist policies and practices, and the normalization of racism and impunity.

5. We drew as well on professional and public ethics, relying heavily on the public administration and policy literature streams. We considered ethical dimensions of racism at various levels of analysis, from public ethics to situated ethics—for instance, in encounters between police and Black citizens which seem especially conducive to racial profiling and unfettered violence. Here we explicitly articulated methods and epistemic positions that ultimately relied on an ethics bound to political philosophy—it was the vantage point of politico-philosophical ethics that would allow us to consider "how racial profiling illuminates the nature, justification, and reproduction of hierarchies of power and privilege" based on (mis)perceptions of people of color (Lever 2016, p. 1). For a research synthesis concerning a 'unified theory' of philosophical and public ethics, public policy and administration, and policing and race, see FitzPatrick (2006). For a consideration of the limits and possibilities of statistical method in the study of disparate racial outcomes in policing, see Leung, Woolley, Tremblay and Vitaro (2005). For a political science treatment of the complex and 'immutable' racialization of identity and related research and analytical methods, see Sen and Wasow (2016).

In all of these analytical efforts, we probed the interplay of social and political interests with settled institutional agendas, what Pinderhughes (1989) calls "power-assigning structures," so as to assess the reasons for the perpetuation of racial inequity and propose new frameworks for its remediation. In this connection, there is considerable indication in the academic and periodical literatures that racial profiling (singling out of individuals on the basis of race for traffic stops, frisking, and the like) occurs to victims of color irrespective of social class and gender (Harris 1999; Ward 2002). It is literally the subject's racial profile—young Black man walking, wearing a hoodie—that seems to prompt stops, interrogations, and—much too often—police-involved shootings and other forms of violence. The stereotyping involved—the projection of dangerousness and menace onto African American men—is deeply embedded in American history and society, dating to the days of slavery. Rather than attribute related police abuses to individual misconduct, Luna points to "a systemic disorder within the institution of law enforcement" and in many departments (Luna 2003, p. 186). An indication that racial profiling is systemic to law enforcement culture rather than simply a matter of individual White police officer bias, such behavior is demonstrated by Black and Latino officers as well, with minority motorists and pedestrians still the primary targets. This phenomenon speaks to the hyperidentification of officers with police culture and their departments, and generally to institutional factors rather than mere cognitive and attitudinal ones (Ward 2002; Ward & Rivera 2014, p. 106).

Notwithstanding this evidence of systemic factors at work, analysis of racial profiling through the lens of individual behaviors may suggest ways to bring method back to public administration and policy. Writing for the *Washington Post*, Erin Texeira (2006) addressed the topic with respect to African American men and the daily challenges they face in facing stereotypes. Texeira presents the story of Black attorney Keith Borders and the lengths to which he goes to avoid being regarded as dangerous—trying to somehow diminish his six-foot-seven frame, choosing physical stances (placement of hands and feet) that might be seen as nonthreatening, dressing conservatively, and using a soft voice and deferential speech, especially in encounters with police. Of this kind of defensive posturing, Borders says: "It's all about surviving, and trying to thrive, in a nation where biased views of Black men stubbornly hang on decades after segregation and where statistics show a yawning gap between the lives of White men and Black men." (Texeira 2006, p. 1)

Miller (2015) notes the wide prevalence of this sort of defensive behavior among people of color, including that of avoiding 'abrupt' movements, in confrontations with police. Here we need to bring our critical analysis to a more encompassing level—that of the larger culture in which offending police officers have been socialized—personally as well as professionally. By way of illustration, Johnson and Rivera (2007) have found in empirical classroom studies that African American men are subject to threatening stereotypes much more often than their White male counterparts, even among graduate and undergraduate University students (see Garcia & Johnston-Guerrero

2016, on campus experiences of racism nationally). Police bias based on stereotyped threat makes for the unwarranted use of force in situations involving police discretion (Friedrich 1980; McElvain & Kposowa 2008); however, this kind of abuse has many formative sources, as we have just noted.

Social Equity and Public Ethics

Over several decades, public administration scholars such as Rice, Wooldridge, Gooden and Borrego, and Norman-Major and Haynes have come to address concerns such as stereotyping under the social equity as well as cultural competency frames (Johnson 2012). More than any other single researcher in the discipline, however, it is George Fredrickson (2005) who is most closely associated with the study of social equity. Fredrickson has long argued that the public administration field has insufficiently considered social equity when it concerns race and gender, for instance in regard to disparate educational opportunities (Frederickson 2010). Frederickson and other researchers just noted have cast the subjects of race and gender equity as social and political ones, while laying stress on ways to implement corrective public policy. These authors have also grounded social equity analysis in public and philosophical ethics. We find, for example, that Wooldridge and Gooden (2009), Norman-Major (2011), and Rivera, Johnson, and Ward (2010) all draw directly or indirectly on the contractarian proposals of John Rawls (1971), in *A Theory of Justice*, with his definition of fairness as the maximally equitable extension of public goods, consistent with the maximization of liberty (see also Rivera & Johnson 2015; Rice 2015; Shelby 2004). These authors would reposition the *equipoint* between liberty and social justice, and between discretionary police authority and its regulatory constraint, in light of the persistence of institutional racism. We will propose later in this study, however, that Rawlsian ethics fall short in this context.

From Ferguson to Baltimore, police-involved violence against African Americans, in particular African American young men, has become a matter of almost daily news reports in the US (see Rothstein 2015, for a summary account that turns on government-sanctioned segregation; on the so-called "Ferguson Effect," on the purported chilling effect on policing of an anti-police backlash, see Pyrooz, Decker, Wolfe, & Shjarback 2016). For Frederickson and Ghere (2013), police violence in these contexts is a matter for consideration under the rubric of social and public ethics, beyond the headlines. This is the case for a number of reasons. The patterned frequency of abuses erodes the perceived legitimacy of government, of state power, especially among communities of color victimized by police violence; and it makes for a perception of ethical failure on the part of government officials, particularly police and their overseers. Only "ethics reform [then] promises to restore political legitimacy" and public trust (Frederickson & Ghere 2013, p. 4). While these authors argue that a restorative emphasis on normative ethics has become necessary, they also emphasize that, in a postpositivist public administration field, interpretation, perception, expectation, and in general the social construction of meaning are the fulcrums for ethical responses to abuses of power (p. 7).

Disciplinary, professional, and normative considerations now coincide: "In this regard, it appears important to direct as much attention to what ethics *do* or *can do* for the professional as to what ethics *are* or *can be* as a unified body of theory and research," for public administration as an epistemic community (Frederickson & Ghere 2013, p. 11). The current scope of research must be broadened to issues of social equity even as research turns more deliberately toward public ethics. Public administration ethics by definition and inclination lays stress on the constraining effects of legislation and policy, and by extension on administrative and regulatory limits on governmental discretion, including discretionary police power *as* state power.

A central argument in this study is that the comparative study of policing in relation to the restoration of governmental legitimacy is essential at this juncture—consider Light, Mota Prado, and Wang on 'redemocratization' in Russia, Brazil, and China in relation to policing (2015), and Pollit and Bouckaert (2004) and Ferraro and Garofalo(2010) on government reform in relation to public ethics. Our probe of comparative public ethics may also point toward a disciplinary synthesis suited to the analysis of police violence (Rivera & Ward 2013). We thereby return to the need for the integration or reintegration of epistemic positions and methodological streams in the analysis of racialized police violence, proposing that public ethics—and in particular a *comparativist* public ethics—offers the best disciplinary approach for an apt synthesis in relation to subjects related to racism and violence.

To give one example of the singular applicability of public ethics, it is the case globally that the state must ultimately assume *remedial responsibility* for the righting of the wrongs it sanctions, even when individuals or organizations are held responsible for the same instances of oppression (Pearson 2011), since it is the state that must bear ultimate *causal responsibility* (from a legal/normative viewpoint) for the wrongs it permits. Remediation could come to include national reparations programs, although that discussion is outside the scope of this study (for an authoritative treatment, of individual versus collective reparations, see Feagin 2004). The settlements that many American cities have had to pay to remedy police-involved shootings and other violence against African Americans are worth noting here—we address Cincinnati's Collaborative Agreement in our text (Ward & Rivera 2014); Copeland (2013) considers the same compact in relation to settlements by other cities. Changing public moral discourse and political agenda-setting on racism and police violence is another remedial course but one that may be as difficult to approach as reparations. On former President Obama's apparent reticence on the subject of police violence against African Americans, see Dyson (2016, pp. 180–202); on "racially divisive appeals" and the current GOP Presidential debate, see Brown (2016); on anti-immigrant discourse and the criminalization of immigration, see Sellers and Arrigo (2016) and Pickett (2015). Current developments on the hypernationalist policy proposals often emanating from the White House are constantly in the news.

Remedies

The concluding chapter of our text (Ward & Rivera 2014) addressed several lesser-scale practices worthy of adoption, including San Antonio's Fear Free Environment (SAFFE) program and Cincinnati's community policing initiative, part of a forced settlement resulting from the just-referenced 2001 Collaborative Agreement, which was prompted by a National Association for the Advancement of Colored People (NAACP) lawsuit. Standard remedial interventions elsewhere include the following:

1. Increasing diversity in police departments through affirmative action recruitment and promotion initiatives, for the sake of greater representativeness and community rapport (Hong 2016).
2. Training in community policing and operational, ethical, and legal constraints on the use of force in the same vein (Stum 2016).
3. Cultural Competence or Diversity training, building on foundations of postsecondary education—as either a hiring requirement for police officers or a continuing education opportunity.
4. "Culture Audits" of police departments; introducing *bias-reducing* policies and practices (Stum 2016).
5. Strengthening line supervision and administrative investigation capacities (Stum 2016).
6. Developing Administrative Review Databases to identify officers with a history of complaints or actions relating to racial encounters; greater data generation and use so as to promote of transparency and accountability (Rushin 2016).
7. Developing more thorough background investigation procedures focused on pertinent behavioral histories among candidates for employment as police officers, supervisors, and chiefs, especially as to commitment to community engagement (Stum 2016).
8. Mandating continuous and consistent use of body-worn cameras so as to capture incidents of police violence for the purposes of investigation; securing funding for these cameras.

9. Strengthening citizen complaint procedures in general as well as in racial encounter contexts; fostering citizen involvement in bolstered police oversight functions.
10. And, in general, strengthening policies and procedures pursuant to a new culture of integrity and the adoption of an accountable "guardian" rather than "warrior" approach to policing.

The authors, however, found through extensive research synthesis that two interventions seldom considered critical were the most impactful—with regard to increasing cognitive or integrative complexity, the previously-noted capacity for accepting differences in race, ethnicity, culture, religion, and ways of life (Rivera & Ward 2017). One is postsecondary education: A college degree is the strongest predictor of openness toward others found in the literature. The second is the just-mentioned mandated use of body-worn cameras, which seem to increase officers' self-awareness as well as mindfulness of possible monitoring of their behavior (Rivera & Ward 2017, p. 246). The other types of interventions just listed appear to work only when they are designed to serve, and actually serve, to develop cognitive/integrative complexity among police officers. These remedies are for the most part administrative in nature. This brings our inquiry back to the practice of public administration, since these ameliorative initiatives are frequently the consequence of governmental intervention—Justice Department receivership actions in offending communities (like Ferguson), Homeland Security mandates, and other binding policy, statutory, or regulatory actions.

It is important to underscore here what sets the cognate professional as well as academic fields of public administration and public policy apart. It is their orientation toward effective practice, toward both remedial and proactive action under governmental mandate—legislation, regulation—that characterizes these fields. Whetsell (2013) casts this distinctive disciplinary perspective as "progressive, pragmatic problem resolution" (p. 609). The questions that remain in the framing of public-administrative responses to race-related police violence are ones of conceptual as well as practical integration: How do we promote an effective synthesis of policy and administrative analysis, including consideration of historical context and patterned sociocultural behaviors, with workaday changes in policies and procedures such as those just outlined? Is there reason to expect that synergies will obtain among these kinds of interpretation (epistemologies, constructions of knowledge), and that there will be consequential state action, so as to make for sufficient reform, given the history of racial violence in the United States? To what extent are the framing issues involved, such as the dilemmas entailed in the balancing of privacy and law enforcement, of police discretion and imposed constraint, and of liberty and social justice, capable of enduring resolution? And can we learn from the experience of other nations, and from our best experience and national sources, in these same connections, if we take a specifically comparative ethical perspective?

Developing a Comparativist Ethics

In the end, policy interventions must stem from fundamental attitudinal and ethical as well as institutional changes, in the building of national community where fragmentation and conflict now prevail. From the perspective of traditional political philosophy, a liberal public ethics is founded upon interest-based competition, political conflict, bargaining, compromise, and consent—when consent obtains at all, following from discourse that routinely excludes much of the citizenry. However, the connection between individual subjects and public institutions—the regulative ways in which institutions as such condition moral deliberation and agency—provides a firmer grounding for public ethics, and for substantive concerns relating to public values such as racial justice.

Whatever the scope and level of analysis, or its starting and endpoints, any exercise in public ethics needs to land squarely in the encounter between citizen and state, especially the victimized citizen and the state. As Hooker (2015) forcibly argues, scholarship has to approach Michael Brown dying in a Ferguson street and only then try to address that reality (Hooker 2015, p. 1). It is there, literally at street level, that the kind of police violence of concern in this study is most palpably evident. Critical ethical analysis in public administration in such situated contexts necessarily involves both ethical justification and epistemic definition (Whetsell 2013): While it may be policy-oriented and programmatic in its essential focus, public ethics has to consider the complex interplay of the raw and personal, on the one hand, and the more distantly institutional or systemic, on the other, in any approach to horrific encounters such as these.

The prominent social theorist Giorgio Agamben (1998) has developed an analytical construct, "Bare Life" (roughly, depoliticized life), that fits the Brown/Ferguson example well. As Agamben describes it, Bare Life is the lot of persecuted people (he focuses particularly on stateless persons, and refugees). Persecution implicates the state in that the state is complicit, either by omission or by commission, in the exercise of power (Foucault 2000), in stripping these of a dignified life, and in excluding them from full membership in polity and society. What results is the *denaturalization* of the oppressed (Guttmann 2003, p. 120), who are denied recognition, or who are left with only those acknowledged configurations of identity that are ascribed to them. And good response options are few: Racial and ethnic minorities need to guard against purely reactive assertions of identity, since these can mean surrender to negative ascriptions of identity (Rivera & Ward 2008). Meanwhile, Agamben's Bare Life intrudes, diminishing the possibility of a larger sociopolitical engagement around identity.

Constructivist (interpretive) frameworks are now dominant in much of political and social theory, including liberal theories of justice, as well as in Critical Race Theory. However, constructivist theories, which turn on definitions and interpretations of situations, account for only half of an interrogatory—what race is *not* about (i.e., not about inherent differences, only ascriptive ones)—and not the other half, what race *is*, if anything (Guttmann 2003). The denial of recognition and the often political dynamics of reasserted identity therefore need attention in public-administrative scholarship, which urgently requires real-life grounding in this regard (Fraser & Honneth 2003), since the adverse experiences of people of color we consider are so alien to those of most public administration and policy scholars.

Agamben and those who have developed his work in this grounded direction (for instance, Astor 2009, writing about Operation Wetback), race is the unwarranted sentence inflicted on those, like Michael Brown, who have been effectively denied power and denuded of identity. For Critical Race Theory, the corollary may be that the oppressed can carve out a space of freedom by rejecting imposed identity, by asserting their own identities as they choose. However, for our purposes in this study, the corollary is that current disciplinary approaches to the problem of race and violence are inadequate. The absolutism of violence, including racialized police violence, requires a much less compromising response than is offered by most public administration/ policy sources we might consult.

Returning to the previously-cited work of John Rawls (1971) may allow us to briefly consider the difficulties involved. Rawls is virtually silent on race, and on the overwhelming impediments racism places in the way of the realization of a just society. There's no accounting for this gap in his body of work, which turns on the establishment of constitutive societal rules behind his famous "veil of ignorance." Although it is argued that this originalist "blindness" would obviate race as a factor, as it would physical disability or any other individual endowment, racism in particular is distinct. It revisits its harm continually and chronically, beyond what any contractarian arrangement of political rules could provide for. The idea of a hypothetical negotiation of constitutive rules among a congregation of equals seems untenable when so many are denied access to the political discourse of rulemaking and rule enforcement.

It is interesting to note, in passing, that Rawls's Harvard colleague and sometime rival Richard Rorty did address race in his works only to dismiss it as a philosophical problem, insisting on a "discontinuity" between philosophy and politics, and on remedial analysis and tactical policymaking in dealing with problems of race and inequality (Craig 2014). Whether it is Rawls, Rorty, Thomas Scanlon (2000), or others in or near the contractualist camp, moreover, another problem arises, that of the incommensurability or incomparability of nonnegotiable values (Chang 2015). Racism, and especially racist violence, presents irreducible value claims—restoration (including reparation) of loss, elimination of invidious bias—that, it may be argued, are not subject to a balancing project. Rather, the value propositions involved are not properly subject to epistemic or normative exchange at all. It therefore seems that liberal philosophical ethics simply does not take us far enough in our efforts at addressing the implications of a fully equity-based—not to say affirmatively counter-racist—scholarship or practice in the public administration and policy fields. Ironically enough, this argument coincides with Rorty's insistence on the discontinuity between philosophy and politics: not on conceptual grounds, in our case, but due to a lack of philosophical frames applicable to a thoroughgoing change project.

A final, related concern with these approaches to public ethics is the unacceptability of market-modeled analytical/evaluative frames when dealing with racism and race-based violence. One of the authors (Ward) has conducted research that demonstrates the adverse effects of privatization (a cornerstone of the New Public Management, NPM) on communities of color, and in particular African Americans. A study entitled "Privatization and Social Equity: A Research Note" (Ward 2008) provides exploratory data from a survey concerned with the relationship between increased use of privatization and minority employment in the public sector; its findings suggest that the marketization of public service is gravely detrimental to minorities across the spectrum of public employment. Fattore et al. (2012) make a significant effort to take the measure of the New Public Governance (NPG) perspective—sometimes called Public Value Governance—that is supplanting NPM, especially in the United States and English-speaking countries. NPG harkens back to the so-called New Public Administration and Frederickson's work of dating to the Minnowbrook conferences (Rivera & Ward 2008; Ward 2017 p. 1–8). There is less than advertised that would differentiate the two approaches (NPM and NPG)—which Fattore et al. argue fall short of being paradigmatic. Both have lent themselves to rough admixture in practice, and to political use by contending parties worldwide. More to the point, the NPM and NPG are both transactional, although the latter is more directly based on public value. Again, the issues attendant to racism should not be subject to the relative equivalence presumed of value positions under either framework. If realized, Frederickson's (1999) New Public Administration perspective would have avoided this conundrum, since it posited social equity as a meta-ethical criterion that is—or should be—largely exempt from such balancing equations, and from the tussle of political bargaining and compromise.

Concluding Analysis: Reinforcing the Case for a Comparative and Integrative Public Ethics

Consequently, we might return one last time to consideration of methods and analytical frameworks drawn more closely from the public administration/ policy disciplines. Fitzpatrick et al. (2011) posit that the study of administrative reform (including police reform) in an era of intensified and increasingly complex intercultural and cross-group problems requires public administration scholarship to take up comparative method. Results of a comprehensive research synthesis lead these authors to conclude that comparative research is uniquely promising in these contexts, building as it does on theory-based and empirical research using a mix of causal, descriptive, and exploratory methods, in what should be a mixed-method, multilevel approach to normative research. The argument in part is that comparativism allows for effective consideration of the complexities involved.

Some caution is warranted at this juncture. In an article entitled "The Future of the Study of Public Administration: Embedding Research Object and Methodology in Epistemology and Ontology," Raadschelders (2011) warns against reductive, methodologically driven research, arguing that the "wickedness" (or intractable complexity) of administrative challenges such as racialized police violence requires correspondingly nuanced epistemic stances and evaluative conceptual and methodological applications. Comparative value analysis is among these promising, postpositivistic, integrative approaches, warranting the consideration we are giving it here.

Wright (2011) proposes that while Public Administration continues to properly rely on comparative scholarship in the disciplines of law, management, and political science, its scholarly and applied research has become isolated from this value-critical foundation, making for insufficient capacity to frame questions in normatively and methodologically apt ways. Whether researchers are pulled toward empiricism or interpretivism, they should not try to reduce complex policy and administrative challenges to the constraints of particular methodologies. Comparativism is uniquely suited to a nonreductionist approach to the very difficult normative questions connected to racism and racist violence, in its expansive approach to evaluative analysis.

Comparative method is at the heart of all evaluation, in setting what actually obtains against a norm—a particular democracy against the democratic ideal, for instance. Ethical evaluation of racism requires a stern assessment of what is found in the bare reality of daily life when compared with undiluted conceptions of justice. An essentially comparativist public ethics would allow our experience with racism and violence to be set against other experiences globally as well as historically. One might look, for instance, to the Nuremburg codal principles of crimes against humanity and the inherent worth of the human person, which underlie the United Nations Charter. The Universal Declaration of Human Rights, which is well known was directly modeled on the American Declaration of Independence, would serve as a comparative ideal of our own, notwithstanding its incomplete realization from the time of the founding of the United States to this day.

Welfare Economist and Nobel Laureate Amartya Sen is the most prominent proponent of comparativist ethics, or comparative justice, as an analytical approach, posed in his work against any form of transcendentalist ethics (Thaler 2011). A comparative ethics compels us to consider the lived reality of others while acknowledging the limitations of our own cognitive and cultural perspectives, along with the shortcomings of present circumstances considered against our moral ideals. Such an exercise would be consistent with our earlier consideration of integrative complexity as a prerequisite in regard to efforts at overcoming institutional forms of prejudice.

Consistent with these observations, we argue for a nondualistic, integral approach to research on race and police violence—research analysis that reconciles theory with practice, as well as advocacy with the analytic neutrality that befits Public Administration scholarship. This proposed line of research would need to bridge levels of analysis (individual, community, organizational, institutional, and governmental) even as it spans disciplinary traditions. A comparative ethical lens allows for the prior definition of research questions and the eventual determination of analytical conclusions—be these based on quantitative, qualitative, or mixed-method inquiry, all of which can be empirically rigorous. Such a lens would allow for a moral position that Verran (2011) has called "comparison as [a] participant," or comparison as participation. Verran posits that "we need to understand comparison not as a practice or method, 'a sieve or filter,' but as an event: the creation of "a rapport or logos;" she calls these encounters with the bare reality encountered by others "participant-comparisons" (p. 65).

Racialized police violence represents a failure of public administration and therefore of the state itself, as we have proposed following Fredrickson (1999, 2005, 2010). Public administration as an epistemic community and community of practice is obliged to address the multilayered, complex, and daunting problems involved, in the interest of social equity and justice, in the public interest. It needs to do so integrally, nonreductively, and also in a way that rejects the equivalency of value positions when it comes to human rights claims. This kind of evaluation—whether rooted in Public Administration and Policy or not, dispassionate or not—also needs to be cognizant of the way anyone can be implicated in the institutional and processual forces that oppress others (Pedwell 2016). We hold, with the great American social historian and Pan–Africanist W. E. B. DuBois (1903), as the Tunisian novelist Albert Memmi has phrased it (2000, pp. 163–165), that resisting racism is the highest ethical duty, and that concessions to the exclusion of African Americans and others based on race corrupts public ethics, entrenching systems of violence—police-involved violence included.

REFERENCES

Abdelal, Rawi, Yoshiko Herrera, Alastair Johnston, and Rose McDermott. 2006. "Identity as a Variable." *Perspectives on Politics* 4(4):695–711.

Adams, Guy B. and Danny Balfour. 2003. "Public Service Ethics and Administrative Evil: Prospects and Problems." Available at: http://academic.udayton.edu/richardghere/MPA%20524/Adams.doc

Abdelal, Rawi, Yoshiko Herrera, Alastair Johnston, and Rose McDermott. 2006. "Identity as a Variable." *Perspectives on Politics* 4(4):695–711.

Agamben, Giorgio. 1998. *Homo Sacer: Sovereign Power and Bare Life*. Meridian: Crossing Aesthetics.

Antonio, A.L., Chang, M.J., Hakuta, K., Kenny, D.A., Levin, S. and Milem, J.F., 2004. "Effects of racial diversity on complex thinking in college students." *Psychological Science* 15(8): 507–510.

Appiah, Kwame A. 2004. *The Ethics of Identity*. Princeton: Princeton University Press.

Astor, Avi. 2009. "Unauthorized immigration, securitization and the making of Operation Wetback." *Latino studies* 7(1): 5–29.

Axtell, Guy (ed). 2000. *Knowledge, Belief, and Character*. Lanham: Rowman and Littlefield.

Braham, P., Rattansi, A., and R. Skellinton. 1992. *Racism and Antiracism: Inequalities, Opportunities and Policies*. London: Sage Publications.

Brown, Jessica Autumn. 2016. "Running on Fear: Immigration, Race and Crime Framings in Contemporary GOP Presidential Debate Discourse." *Critical Criminology*: 24, no. 3, pp. 315–331.

Chaney, Cassandra, and Ray V. Robertson. 2015. "Armed and Dangerous? An Examination of Fatal Shootings of Unarmed Black People by Police." *The Journal of Pan African Studies (Online)* 8(4): 45.

Chang, Ruth. 2015. "Value incomparability and Incommensurability." In *The Oxford Handbook of Value Theory*. Oxford: Oxford University Press: 205–225.

Copeland, M. Shawn. 2013. "Listening to the Struggle of Cincinnati." *Proceedings of the Catholic Theological Society of America 58*, pp. 83–86.

Coyle, Michael J. 2010. "Notes on the Study of Language: Towards a Critical Race Criminology." *Western Criminology Review 11*(1):11–19.

DuBois, William Edward Burghardt. 1903. *The Souls of Black Folk*. New York: New American Library.

Durant, Robert F., and David H. Rosenbloom. 2016. "The Hollowing of American Public Administration." *The American Review of Public Administration*: 0275074015627218.

Dyson, Michael E. 2016. *The Black Presidency: Barack Obama and the Politics of Race in America.* New York: Houghton Mifflin Harcourt Publishing Company.

Fattore, Giovanni, Hans FW Dubois, and Antonio Lapenta. 2012. "Measuring new public management and governance in political debate." *Public Administration Review 72* (2): 218–227.

Feagin, Joe R. 2004. "Documenting the Costs of Slavery, Segregation, and Contemporary Racism: Why Reparations Are in Order for African Americans." *Harvard BlackLetter Law Journal 20*: 49.

Ferraro, Agustin Ferraro, and Charles Garofalo. 2010. "A Positive Ethics for Public Administration. Altruism, Self-Interest and the Concept of the State." *Dilemata 2*: 33–47.

Fischer, Frank. 2003. *Reframing Public Policy: Discursive Politics and Deliberative Practices.* New York: Oxford University Press.

FitzPatrick, Daniel P. 2006. "Moving Beyond the Noble Cause Paradigm: Providing a Unified Theory of Ethics for 21st Century American Policing." In *Forum on Public Policy: A Journal of the Oxford Round Table*: 1–25. Fall 2006.

Fitzpatrick, Jody, Malcolm Goggin, Tanya Heikkila, Donald Klingner, Jason Machado and Christine Martell. 2011. "A New Look at Comparative Public Administration: Trends in Research and an Agenda for the Future." *Public Administration Review 71* (6): pp. 821–830.

Fong, Edmund. 2008. "Reconstructing the 'Problem' of Race." *Political Research Quarterly 61*(4): 660–670.

Foucault, Michel. 2000. *Power: Essential Works of Foucault, Vol. 3.* New York: The New Press.

Fraser, Nancy, and Axel Honneth. 2003. *Redistribution or Recognition?: A Political-Philosophical Exchange.* New York: Verso Books.

Fredrickson, H. George. 2005. "The State of Social Equity in American Public Administration." *National Civic Review* (Winter 2005): 31–38. Available at: http://oied.ncsu.edu/selc/wp-content/uploads/2013/03/The-State-of-Social-Equity-in-American-Public-Administration.pdf

Fredrickson, H. George. 2010. *Social Equity and Public Administration: Origins, Developments, and Applications.* Armonk, NY: M.E. Sharp Publishing.

Frederickson, H. George. 1999. "The Repositioning of American Public Administration." *PS, Political Science & Politics*, December 1999, 701–711 (1–22 online). Available at: https://www.google.com/url?sa=t&rct=j&q=&esrc=s&source=web&cd=1&cad=rja&uact=8&ved=0ahUKEwibsqDOnYzLAhXotIMKHcQ6BjEQFggdMAA&url=http%3A%2F%2Fwww.speters.net%2FPrincipalAgent%2Fshort%2520principal%2520agent%2Ffrederickson.doc&usg=AFQjCNFYQroOjCGHqV-U4LAYS2BxDgmuFA&sig2=RTHp7V_Z7EXWSoPrvagaNQ

Frederickson, H. George. 1990. "Public Administration and Social Equity." *Public Administration Review 50*(2): 228–37.

Frederickson, H. George and Ghere, Richard K. 2013. "Ethics in Public Management: Political Science Faculty Publications." *Paper 43.* Available at: http://ecommons.udayton.edu/pol_fac_pub/43

Friedrich, R. J. 1980. "Police Use of Force: Individuals, Situations, and Organizations." *The Annals of the American Academy of Political and Social Science 452*(1): 82–97.

Gaines, L. K., & Kappeler, V. E. 2003. *Policing in America* (4th ed). Cincinnati, OH: Anderson Publishing.

Garcia, Gina A., and Marc P. Johnston-Guerrero. 2016. "Challenging the Utility of a Racial Microaggressions Framework Through A Systematic Review of Racially Biased Incidents on Campus." *Journal of Critical Scholarship on Higher Education and Student Affairs 2* (1): 4.

Goldberg, David Theo. 2002. *The Racial State*. Oxford: Blackwell.

Gutmann, Amy. 2003. *Identity in Democracy*. Princeton: Princeton University.

Habermas, J. (1992). *Justification and Application: Remarks on Discourse Ethics*. Translated by Ciaran Cronin. Cambridge, MA: MIT Press.

Hamilton, L. 2009. "Human Needs and Political Judgment." In *New Waves in Political Philosophy* (pp. 40–62). Palgrave Macmillan UK.

Heinze, Eric. 2006. "Truth and Myth in Critical Race Theory and Latcrit: Human Rights and the Ethnocentrism of Anti-Ethnocentrism." *National Black Law Journal* 20: 107 ff.

Hofweber, Thomas. 1999. "Contextualism and the Meaning-Intention Problem." In *Cognition, Agency and Rationality*, edited by K. Korta, E. Sosa and J. Arrozola, Kluwer, 93–104.

Harris, David. 1999. "The Stories, the Statistics, and the Law: Why "Driving While Black"Matters. *Minnesota Law Review 84*(2): 265–326.

Hong, S. 2016. "Representative Bureaucracy, Organizational Integrity, and Citizen Coproduction: Does an Increase in Police Ethnic Representativeness Reduce Crime?" *Journal of Policy Analysis and Management 35*(1): 11–33. Available at: https://www.researchgate.net/profile/Sounman_Hong2/publication/280560973_ Representative_Bureaucracy_Organizational_Integrity_and_Citizen_Coproduc- tion_Does_an_Increase_in_Police_Ethnic_Representativeness_Reduce_Crime/ links/55b9911108aec0e5f43c3910.pdf

Hooker, Juliet. 2009. *Race and the Politics of Solidarity*. Oxford: Oxford University.

Hooker, Juliet. 2015. "Black Politics after Ferguson: From Democratic Sacrifice/ Suffering to Abolition Democracy." *Paper delivered at the Annual Meeting of the Western Political Science Association*, Las Vegas, NV, April 1–4, 2015.Avail- able at: http://wpsa.research.pdx.edu/papers/docs/Hooker_Ferguson_WPSA%20 2015%20paper.pdf

King, Desmond and Rogers Smith. 2005. "Racial Orders in American Political Devel- opment." *American Political Science Review 99*: 75–92.

Jee-Lyn García, J. and M.Z. Sharif. 2015. "Black Lives Matter: A Commentary on Racism and Public Health." *American Journal of Public Health 105*(8):.e27–e30.

Johnson III, Richard Greggory. 2012. "Promoting Social Equity in Public Adminis- tration: A Much-needed Topic in the 21st Century." *Public Administration Review 72*(3): 471–473.

Johnson III, Richard Greggory and Rivera, M. 2007. "Refocusing Graduate Public Affairs Education: A Need for Diversity Competencies in Human Resource Man- agement." *Journal of Public Affairs and Education 13*(1): 15–27.

Leung, Ambrose, Frances Woolley, Richard E. Tremblay, and Frank Vitaro. 2005. "Who Gets Caught? Statistical Discrimination in Law Enforcement." *The Journal of Socio-Economics 34*(3): 289–309.

Lever, Annabelle. 2016. "Racial Profiling and the Political Philosophy of Race." Available at: file:///C:/Users/faculty/Desktop/unige_78934_attachment01%20(1).pdf

Lieberman, Robert. 2008. "Legacies of Slavery? Race and Causation." In *Race and American Political Development*. Joseph Lowndes et al., eds. New York: Routledge.

Light, M., Prado, M.M. and Wang, Y., 2015. "Policing Following Political and Social Transitions: Russia, Brazil, and China Compared." *Theoretical Criminology 19*(2): 216–238.

Luna, Eric. 2003. Race, "Crime, and Institutional Design." *Law and Contemporary Problems 66*: 183–220.

Memmi, Albert. 2000, *Racism*. Minneapolis: U of Minnesota Press.

McElvain, J. P. and Kposowa, A. J. 2008. "Police Officer Characteristics and the Likelihood of Using Deadly Force." *Criminal Justice and Behavior 35*(4): 505–521.

McGinnis, Michael D., and Elinor Ostrom. "Reflections on Vincent Ostrom, Public Administration, and Polycentricity." *Public Administration Review 72* (1): 15–25.

Miller, Eric J. 2015. "Police Encounters with Race and Gender." 5 U.C. Irvine Law Review: 735–758. Available at: http://scholarship.law.uci.edu/ucilr/vol5/iss4/4

Miller, Lisa L. 2015. "What's Violence Got to do With it? Inequality, Punishment, and State Failure in US Politics." *Punishment & Society 17*(2): 184–210.

Mitchell, Gladys. 2010. "The Politics of Skin Color in Brazil." *Review of Black Political Economy 37*: 25–41.

Morfin, O.J., Perez, V.H., Parker, L., Lynn, M. and Arrona, J. 2006. "Hiding the Politically Obvious: A Critical Race Theory Preview of Diversity as Racial Neutrality in Higher Education." *Educational Policy 20*(1): 249–270.

Norman-Major, K.(2011). "Balancing the Four Es: Or Can We Achieve Equity for Social Equity in Public Administration?" *Journal of Public Affairs Education 17*(2): 233–252.

Ortiz, L. and J. Jani. 2010. "Critical Race Theory: A Transformational Model for Teaching Diversity." *Journal of Social Work Education 46*(2): 175–193.

Pearson, John. 2011. "National Responsibility, Global Justice and Exploitation: a Preliminary Analysis." *Journal of Global Ethics 7*(3): 321–335.

Pinderhughes, E. 1989. *Understanding Race, Ethnicity, and Power*. New York: Free Press.

Pollit, Christopher and Geert Bouckaert. 2004. *Public Management Reform. A Comparative Analysis*. Oxford: Oxford University Press.

Pyrooz, D.C., Decker, S.H., Wolfe, S.E. and Shjarback, J. A. 2016. "Was There a Ferguson Effect on Crime Rates in Large US Cities?" *Journal of Criminal Justice 46*: 1–8.

Pedwell, Carolyn. 2016. "De-Colonising Empathy: Thinking Affect Transnationally." *A Journal of Women's Studies (Online) 16*(1).

Petrocelli, Matthew, Alex R. Piquero, and Michael R. Smith. 2003. "Conflict Theory and Racial Profiling: An Empirical Analysis of Police Traffic Stop Data." *Journal of Criminal Justice 31*(1): 1–11.

Pickett, J.T., 2015. "On the Social Foundations for Crimmigration: Latino Threat and Support for Expanded Police Powers." *Journal of Quantitative Criminology*: 32, pp. 103–132.

Price, A. J. 1997. *Human Resource Management in a Business Context*. London: International Thomson Business Press.

Raadschelders, Jos. 2011. "The Future of the Study of Public Administration: Embedding Research Object and Methodology in Epistemology and Ontology." *Public Administration Review 71* (6): 916–924.

Rawls, John. 1971. *A Theory of Justice*. Cambridge, MA: Harvard University Press.

Rice, Mitchell. 2015. *Diversity and Public Administration: Theory, Issues, and Perspectives*, Edition 2. New York: Routledge.

Rivera, Mario A., and Richard Greggory Johnson III. 2015. "Intersectionality, Stereotypes of African American Men, and Redressing Bias in the Public Affairs Classroom." *Journal of Public Affairs Education 21*(4).

Rivera, Mario A., Richard Greggory Johnson III and James D. Ward. 2010. "The Ethics of Pedagogical Innovation in Diversity and Cultural Competency Education," *The Innovation Journal: The Public Sector Innovation Journal 15*(2): 511–522.

Rivera, Mario A., and James D. Ward. 2013. "Prospects for Public Ethics Focused on Claims to Equity: A Tentative Comparison of the United States and China." (pp. 219–231). In *Studies on Administrative Reform: Building Service-oriented Government and Performance Evaluation Systems*, edited by Allen Rosenbaum and Wei Liqun. Beijing, China: Jiuzhou Press and the American Society for Public Administration.

Rivera, Mario A., and James D. Ward. 2008. "Symposium Editors' Introduction: Social Equity, Diversity, and Identity: Challenges for Public Affairs Education and the Public Service." *Journal of Public Affairs Education 14* (1): ii–viii.

Rivera, Mario A., and James D. Ward. 2017. "Toward an analytical framework for the study of race and police violence." *Public Administration Review 77*(2): 242–250.

Rothstein, Richard. 2015. "From Ferguson to Baltimore: The Fruits of Government-Sponsored Segregation." Available at: http://blogs.lse.ac.uk/usappblog/2015/04/30/from-ferguson-to-baltimore-the-fruits-of-government-sponsored-segregation/

Rushin, Stephen. 2016. "Using Data to Reduce Police Violence." *Boston College Law Review 1*: 117. Available at: file:///C:/Users/faculty/Desktop/racial%20 profilng%20and%20the%20pol%20philo%20of%20race%20unige_78934_attachment01%20(1).pdf

Scanlon, Thomas M. 2000. "A Contractualist Reply1." *Theoria, 66*(3): 237–245.

Sellers, Brian G. and Bruce A. Arrigo. 2016. "Economic Nomads: A Theoretical Deconstruction of the Immigration Debacle."Available at: http://www.jtpcrim.org/2016February/Sellers.pdf

Sen, Maya, and Omar Wasow. 2016. "Race as a 'Bundle of Sticks': Designs That Estimate Effects of Seemingly Immutable Characteristics." *Annual Review of Political Science 19*.

Shelby, Tommie. 2004. "Race and Ethnicity, Race and Social Justice: Rawlsian Considerations."*72 Fordham Law Review*: 1697–1714.Available at: http://ir.lawnet.fordham.edu/flr/vol72/iss5/15

Sheth, Falguni. 2011. "The War on Terror and Ontopolitics." *Foucault Studies 12*: 51–76.

Stum, Blaine. 2016. *Recommendations, Part 1 of 2, to Spokane Mayor David Condon From the Police Leadership Advisory Committee (PLAC) January 26, 2016.* Available at: https://www.google.com/url?sa=t&rct=j&q=&esrc=s& source=web&cd=1&cad=rja&uact=8&ved=0ahUKEwjG5YXA9pPLAhVBGW MKHRTFCwgQFggdMAA&url=http%3A%2F%2Fmedia.spokesman.com%2Fd ocuments%2F2016%2F01%2FPLAC_Recommendations_Part_1_1_26_2016_2. pdf&usg=AFQjCNEP0kpoo4zyxkhCrz-66BU-Kcghbw&sig2=sP36fTG64L48NT kG8M3VNA

Tastsoglou, Evangelia. 2001. *Re-appraising Immigration and Identities: A Synthesis and Directions for Future Research.* A study commissioned by the Department of Canadian Heritage for the Ethnocultural, Racial, Religious, and Linguistic Diversity and Identity Seminar. Halifax, Nova Scotia, November 1–2, 2001. Available at: http://canada.metropolis.net/events/ethnocultural/publications/tastsoglou_e.pdf

Tuckman, B.W. 1966. "Interpersonal Probing and Revealing and Systems of Integrative Complexity." *Journal of Personality and Social Psychology 3*(6): 655–664.

Tessler, Michael. 2012. "The Spillover of Racialization into Health Care." *American Journal of Political Science 56*(3): 690–704.

Texeira, Erin. 2006. "Black men quietly combating stereotypes." *Washington Post*, July 1.

Thaler, Mathias. 2011. "Comment on Wilfried Hinsch. Ideal Justice and Rational Dissent: A Critique of Amartya Sen's." *The Idea of Justice. Analyse & Kritik 33*(2): 387–394.

Verran, Helen. 2011. "Comparison as participant." *Common Knowledge17*(1): 64–70.

Ward, James D. 2002. "Race, Ethnicity and Law Enforcement Racial Profiling: Implications for Public Policy." *Public Administration Review 62*(6): 726–735.

Ward, James D. 2008. "Privatization and social equity: A research note." *Journal of Public Affairs Education* (1): 111–114.

Ward, James D. and Mario a. Rivera. 2014. *Institutional Racism, Organizations and Public Policy.* New York: Peter Lang.

Ward, James D. (2017) "Beyond Reform: Leadership, Change, and the Role of Innovation," In *Leadership and Change in Public Sector Organizations: Beyond Reform,* edited by James D. Ward. New York: Routledge.

Whetsell, Travis A. 2013. "Theory-Pluralism in Public Administration Epistemology, Legitimacy, and Method." *The American Review of Public Administration 43*(5): 602–618.

Wilkins, Vicky M. and Brian N. Williams. 2009. "Black or Blue: Racial Profiling and Representative Bureaucracy." *Public Administration Review 68*(4): 654–664.

Wooldridge, B. and Susan. G. 2009. "The Epic of Social Equity: Evolution, Essence, and Emergence." *Administrative Theory and Praxis 31*(2): 222–234.

Wright, Bradley E. 2011. "Public Administration as an Interdisciplinary Field: Assessing its Relationship with the Fields of Law, Management, and Political Science." *Public Administration Review 71* (1): 96–101.

Wright, Bradley E. 2015. "The Science of Public Administration: Problems, Presumptions, Progress, and Possibilities." *Public Administration Review 75* (6): 795–805.

Conclusion

Reflection on Realities, Challenges, and Ramifications

James D. Ward

To what extent do racial disparities in police-community relations result in economic, political, and social inequities? As argued by Rivera and Ward (2017), and as postulated by Frederickson et al. (1999, 2010; Frederickson and Ghere 2013), race-related police violence represents a failure of public governance and thus a failure of the state itself. We may now expand on this acknowledgement and include economic, political, and social inequities as being part and parcel to government failure.

As noted earlier, employer attitudes compared to actual employer hiring decisions of Black versus White ex-offenders (Pager and Quillian 2005) is one example of the economic inequities which negatively impact Black ex-offenders at higher levels. Thus, one may argue, and rightly so, that if persistent racial disparities in police-community relations result in higher rates of arrests and imprisonment of African Americans, such cannot be lost on the economic realities associated with impoverished communities, along with the implicit bias. Furthermore, and although racial profiling takes place irrespective of social class (Ward 2002), one cannot ignore how the label of ex-offender reduces even further the job opportunities for an already employment challenged demographic.

According to Samuel L. Myers, Jr., and as noted in chapter 6 in this volume, the economic consequences of disproportionately imprisoning African Americans is enormous, as convicted felons are in many states prevented from acquiring occupational licenses and are therefore excluded from numerous jobs. In Minnesota, he writes that *convicted felons cannot be employed as mortgage originators, insurance agents, nursing or home care assistants, audiologists, physical therapists, dentists or veterinarians.* He adds that in Texas, *convicted felons cannot be employed in work with children (childcare, education), with the elderly (home care) and cannot hold licenses as locksmiths, barbers, electricians, or pharmacists.* In addition, and as cited in an earlier study by Darity and Myers (1998), a disproportionate incarceration of Black males also contributed to an even greater widening of the family income gap between 1980 and 2000, during the height of the government's War on Drugs, perhaps also a result of heavier sentencing laws for crack versus powder cocaine.

In explaining how economic disparities are further linked to law enforcement behavior, Friedman and Albo (chapter 8) closely identified how perceptions of impoverished communities may influence interactions between members of those communities and law enforcement. The authors highlight cases wherein persons were arrested and convicted for using poor judgment, and calling 911, in an effort to resolve nonemergency disputes. Friedman and Albo take the position that punishing the callers, who thought they were acting lawfully, further degrades the relationship between police and these minority communities.

In further examining the relationship between economic conditions and crime, Ronald Zullo (chapter 7) found that the size of regional public workforce has a crime-deterring role, especially in regions with "higher proportions of racial and ethnic minorities." One possible explanation is that public sector jobs are generally more stable, and often provide more generous benefits, compared to those in the private sector. Zullo also found that government spending on education is more closely associated with reducing crime in these communities than spending on law enforcement, social welfare, and other services.

Thus, it has been shown through evidenced-based research that racial disparities in police-community relations result in economic inequities that are tied to a higher level of arrests and convictions. In addition, there appears to be a cycle where those arrests and convictions reinforce and exacerbate attitudinal biases, thereby further reducing employment prospects.

What about political inequities? How do racial disparities in police-community relations result in political inequities? If we accept the fact that states including Alabama, Arizona, Delaware, Florida, Iowa, Kentucky, Mississippi, Nevada, Tennessee, Virginia, and Wyoming prohibit convicted felons from voting, then we must respond in the affirmative for these particular states. Furthermore, and in spite of calls for community policing to reduce the prevalence of racially motivated pretextual stops, there appears to be disagreement within the political arena regarding more proactive solutions.

Bearfield, Maranto, and Kingsbury (chapter 2) argued that incentives of the political system, for Black Lives Matter and for its conservative opponents, tend to devalue Black (and other) lives, mobilizing constituencies rather than solving problems. Although the authors recommend that law enforcement agencies build trust with Black communities through reinvention, they argue that such is less likely due to a nonreceptive political environment.

Bearfield, Maranto, and Kingsbury contend that the modern American political system is a source of the problem because it prevents innovation and reinvention. Although not discussed by Bearfield, Maranto, and Kingsbury, but expounded upon by Grandage, Aliperti, and Williams, such may be reflective of our Madisonian system of government, where checks and balances are built into the system to slow social movements and maintain a public policy process more amenable to the status quo.

Eterno and Barrow (chapter 3) contend that performance management systems should be de-emphasized in place of more civilian friendly approaches to policing and race. Democratic policing, simply put, they argue, is a difficult task, but one that is necessary if we are to successfully address the fallout of aggressive policing policies and help identify solutions for the problems caused by racial disparities in police-community relations. Eterno and Barrow's suggestions go to the heart of the law enforcement community in terms of innovative reforms from within. These suggestions also identify why communities of color may feel politically challenged when facing organizational and structural impediments that appear to devalue Black and other lives. Changing law enforcement agencies from within, through administrative reforms, would be in line with arguments made by Bearfield, Maranto, and Kingsbury, and skirt the *nonreceptive political system*.

Conversely, Grandage, Aliperti, and Williams contend that departmental centric or changing police departments from within cannot be properly understood apart from an historical analysis of their social and political environments. They argue that the *organizational or departmental centric focus misses the relevant unit of analysis, unnecessarily shrinks the scope of debate, and, more generally, lacks descriptive validity.* Any type of bureaucratic innovation that takes place under a departmental centric focus, they argue, would be at the expense of social innovation and thus confuse the means with the ends. The author's argument is based on the premise that police departments operate within open-systems or open political environments. Therefore, understanding those entities within the political environment, and how they interact with other elements in the environment, is essential in analyzing effective organizational change.

Research presented in all three chapters offers important implications for effective leadership, organizational change, and police department reform. Departmental centric or bureaucratic reform may successfully take place with full recognition of the greater political environment in which it operates, especially if utilizing a bottom up or backward mapping approach to reform and program implementation. Such emphasizes a negotiating as opposed to a top down approach, and reduces the likelihood of the goals of the department conflicting with those of politicians (Birkland 2016, pp. 337–340).

Another issue very germane to this volume is that of immigration and racial disparities in police-community relations. Vanessa Cruz Nichols, Alana M.W. LeBron, and Francisco I. Pedraza (chapter 5) point out that immigration enforcement has shifted away from being concentrated along the border states, particularly between the United States and Mexico, to an era of cross-jurisdiction coordination, meaning that immigration enforcement implicates a broader social group than healthcare policy designers had intended. The study by Cruz Nichols et al. supports findings by Armenta and Alvarez (2017) that policing practices that seem immigration-neutral are part of the immigration control machinery, in that pretextual stops encourages police officers to rely on their own implicit bias regarding who looks suspicious, putting officers disproportionately face to face with unauthorized Latino immigrants, as opposed to unauthorized non-Latino immigrants. Cruz Nichols et al. documented how the political inequity, centered on the politics of immigration and healthcare, enhanced racial profiling, and in the process, resulted in less access to vital healthcare information for unauthorized immigrants.

The social inequities caused by racial disparities in police-community relations are intrinsically related to economic and political inequities, and speak to perceptions of unfair treatment during interactions with members of law enforcement.

Sharlene Graham Boltz (chapter 9) presented research on how racially motivated pretextual stops may result in psychological trauma, stating that if the goal is to provide communities with effective policing, that policing must be provided with a deep understanding of historical trauma and a deliberate infusion of cultural competence. Boltz's contention is that earlier life experiences in individuals may trigger episodes of trauma when those individuals are subjected to forceful and disparate treatment at the hands of law enforcement. Those earlier trauma experiences, she contends, better explain the respondent's behavior than the perception that the person is voluntarily being noncooperative. Boltz recommends mindful conversations, guided by professionals trained in dealing with traumatized parties. She concludes that programs such as Citizen Review Panels, while helpful, are plagued with chaotic presentations and therefore only marginally influence change in police-community relations. Boltz's arguments support that of Davis (1997) who showed that *minority innocents* suffer embarrassment, humiliation, and psychological and emotional stress caused by the realization that they were targeted solely because of their race or ethnicity.

Ellison and Steiner (chapter 10) assess the relationship between police use of force and inmate behavior. Their findings reveal that individuals who were exposed to police use of force but did not resist are prone to commit more assaults and nonviolent rule violations while incarcerated. The study examined the effects of exposure to police use of force across race and ethnicity and found that only White inmates exhibited a consistent propensity to violate jail rules after such encounters. Thus, they conclude that the consequences of police use of force may depend on the shared experiences of recipients, and researchers should continue to dissect these effects more thoroughly. For instance, it might be useful to consider the number of times individuals have interacted with police, and more importantly, how they perceived the nature of such encounters (e.g., positive, negative). Needless to say, this is an interesting conclusion drawn by Ellison and Steiner, as it may shed light on the possibility of the existence of trauma, and if present, its relationship to racial disparities in police use of force.

Using technology to reduce racial disparities in police-community relations is offered by Dillon et al. in chapter 11. The authors conclude that software applications have been used for other law enforcement related purposes ranging from informing persons of their Maranda Rights to educating citizens about the US Constitution. What the authors suggest might reduce social inequities by finding some common entity between citizens and law enforcement which could help promote coproduction and strengthen relations between both parties.

Edwards and Klein (chapter 12) offer findings on the effectiveness of community policing programs compared to the popularity of this approach to policing both in the literature and in the field of practice. In doing so, the authors glean information from the case studies of two police departments that are gradually improving the ongoing implementation of their respective community policing programs. Edwards and Klein conclude that better information is needed on how community policing is implemented as a set of practices, and the extent to which it philosophically influences change at the department level. Whether or not community policing is the solution to the long history of problems that plague the relationship between law enforcement and racial and/or ethnic minorities in the United States remains to be seen.

Rivera and Ward (chapter 13) propose a nondualistic, integral approach to research on police violence—a comparativist public ethics stream that reconciles theory with practice, as well as advocacy with the analytic neutrality that befits Public Administration scholarship. In the end, Ward and Rivera conclude that racialized police violence represents a failure of public administration and therefore of the state itself.

To what extent is it the responsibility of government to address and eliminate the economic, political, and social inequities that are linked to racial disparities in police-community relations? From a societal and historical perspective, one may argue that racial disparities in police-community relations cannot be separated from the systemic, institutional, cultural, and other forms of racism that have helped to define current day economic realities, political challenges, and social ramifications. Historically, for example, the federal government played a key role in promoting economic and political inequities in regards to race. If we subscribe to the notion that for most American families, home ownership has been the primary means for building initial wealth, then we must also acknowledge that government policies which allowed for racial covenants, redlining, and the formation of urban public housing projects cannot be ignored. Government policies excluding African Americans from equal access to federal housing loans were first exercised in 1947 when the decision was made by developers to build economical, single-family, lot-sized housing for White only suburban communities with federal funding, while the government adopted policies that promoted the building of high-rise public housing projects in city centers to accommodate the influx of African Americans migrating to Northern cities from the rural South. African Americans who could afford the suburban homes were denied access to these communities. Although by no means the sole explanation for economic inequities in regards to race, the legacy of government sanctioned housing discrimination, including redlining and other discriminatory housing policies, has had lingering effects until this day, in the context of inherited wealth and social mobility. Even though these discriminatory policies and laws have long since been done away with (racial covenants were outlawed by the Supreme Court in the case of *Shelley v. Kraemer (1948)*; the 1968 *Fair Housing Act* made racial discrimination in housing illegal), it can be argued that today's hurdles regarding policing and race, implicit bias, and problems that go along with them are intrinsically tied to the past (Ward and Rivera 2014, pp. 17–19). As Grandage, Aliperti, and Williams demonstrated (in their study of organizational change in the police departments in Detroit, Los Angeles, and Atlanta), history and political environments cannot be ignored. Just as history and political environments were linked to government sanctioned housing discrimination policies, history and political environments are also linked to racial disparities in police use of force, whether it be in Baton Rouge, Ferguson, Baltimore, or New York.

What can government do? Constitutionally, the US Supreme Court ruled in *Whren v. United States* (1996) that any traffic offense committed by a driver is a legitimate basis for a stop, even if the officer's real motivation is to fish for evidence of criminal activity, thus allowing pretextual stops to remain legal. Although seventeen states have outlawed racial profiling altogether, and pretextual stops to a lesser degree, and thirty states have some form of racial profiling law, these laws are less clear when it comes to the practice of pretextual stops, which are legal under the US Constitution, and regarded as a legitimate law enforcement tool (Davenport 2017; NAACP Report 2014;

Ward and Rivera 2014, p. 111). However, the Washington State Supreme Court in 1999 outlawed pretextual stops based on a provision in the state constitution, as did the New Mexico State Supreme Court in 2008 (May, Duke, and Gueco 2017, p. 165). Because the US Supreme Court declared in *Whren* that prextetual stops do not violate the Fourth Amendment's protections against unreasonable search and seizure, it will more than likely require a lawsuit under the Fourteenth Amendment's Equal Protection Clause to bring the issue before the high court again.

Meanwhile, the National Urban League (Ward, 2017a) and other organizations have called for a national ban on racial profiling. *The End Racial Profiling Act of 2011*, if passed, would have made racial profiling illegal nationwide. However, like similar proposals before it, including those that would have only required a national data collection law, the bill fell short in the after math of 9/11. The *Traffic Stops Statistics Study Act of 2001* had been the third consecutive legislative proposal aimed at addressing racial profiling by requiring all law enforcement agencies (national, state, and local) to collect data on motorists stopped and detained to determine the extent of racially motivated pretextual stops. It would have had the same objectives as the city Houston's data collection program, but on a national scale. However, support for passing antiracial profiling laws at the national level, including data collection programs, waned in the after math of 9/11, as defeats came in 2001, 2004, 2007, and 2011. Evidence shows the proposed *Traffic Stops Statistics Study Act of 2001* had the best chance of becoming law because of support from President George W. Bush, Attorney General John Ashcroft, members of Congress, and the broader civil rights community. That is, support was widespread until the events of 9/11. To some Americans, racial profiling is a small price to pay in order to better secure the nation's safety from future terrorist attacks.

At the state and local levels of government, such states as Wisconsin and North Carolina no longer continue with their data collection programs that were put in place to ascertain the frequency of racially motivated pretextual stops within their jurisdictions. After the Wisconsin legislature repealed that state's program, a study revealed that African American motorists in Milwaukee were seven times more likely to be stopped than White motorists (Somanader 2011; Ward and Rivera 2014).

Beyond making pretextual stops and racial profiling illegal nationwide, other remedies are also available. Political solutions include expanding community policing programs and providing the necessary resources and incentives for supportive organizational and political environments. Enhancing diversity in police departments based on historical understandings of the social, political, and legal dynamics to effect transformative change. Or, building trust with the Black community by reinvention, establishing a more professional law enforcement workforce, and de-emphasizing performance management systems in favor of democratic policing. Economic solutions include more spending on educational programs to enhance the socioeconomic mobility for marginalized groups. Or, provide funding for government programs that provide training, expansion of jobs, and incentives for hiring returning ex-offenders. Social solutions include government-sponsored programs aimed at enhancing communication and understanding between law enforcement and communities of color, perhaps even a software application. To the extent that disparities in policing and race have caused psychological trauma, mindful conversations might be appropriate, as suggested by Boltz, when guided by professionals trained in dealing with traumatized parties. Regardless of which approach, or combination of approaches, that governments decide to take, it cannot be denied that race-related police violence represents a failure of public governance and thus a failure of the state itself.

REFERENCES

Birkland, Thomas A. (2016) *An Introduction to the Policy Process*, 4th ed. New York: Routledge.

Davenport, Vince E. (2017) "Investigative Police Stops—Necessary or Insidious? A Practitioners's Viewpoint," in *Public Administration Review*, Vol. 77, No. 2, pp. 179–180.

Davis, Angela J. (1997) "Race, Cops, and Traffic Stops," *University of Miami Law Review*, Vol. 51, U. Miami L. Rev. 425.

Frederickson, H. George and Richard K. Ghere, eds. (2013) *Ethics in Public Management*, 2nd ed. Armonk, NY: M.E Sharpe.

Frederickson, H. George (2010) *Social Equity and Public Administration: Origins, Development, and Applications*. Armonk, NY: M.E. Sharpe.

Frederickson, H. George (1999) "The Repositioning of American Public Administration.in PS" in *Political Science & Politics*, Vol. 32, No. 4: 701–12.

May, Jeff D., Rob Duke, and Sean Gueco (2017) "Pretext Stops and Seizures: In Search of Solid Ground," in *Alaska Law Review*, Vol. 30, No. 2: 152–188.

Pager, Davah and Lincoln Quillian (2005) "Walking the Talk? What Employers Say Versus What They Do," in *American Sociological Review*, Vol. 70 (June): 355–380.

NAACP Report (2014) "NAACP Report:20 States Do Not Forbid Racial Profiling," retrieved from http://www.griio.com/2014/09/27/20-state-no-ban-racial-profiling

Rattan, Aneeta and Jennifer L. Eberhardt (2010) "The role of social meaning in inattentional blindness: When the gorillas in our midst do not go unseen," in Journal of Experimental Social Psychology, Vol. 46:1085–1088.

Rivera, Mario A. and James D. Ward (2017) "Toward an Analytical Framework for the Study of Race and Police Violence," in *Public Administration Review*, Vol. 77, No. 2, 242–250.

Sampson, Rana (2004) *Misuse and Abuse of 911*.Washington, DC: Office of Community Oriented Policing Services, United States Department of Justice. August.

Somanader, T. (2011). "News flash—Racial Profiling: Police stop black drivers 7 times more than white drivers in Milwaukee," Center for American Progress Fund.

Ward, James D. (2017) "Local Government Reform, Convergence, and the Hybrid Model," in *Leadership and Change in Public Sector Organizations: Beyond Reform* edited by James D. Ward. New York: Routledge.

Ward, James D. (2017a) "Concrete Advice for Police Reform: An Interview with Marc Morial," in *Public Administration Review*, Vol. 77, No. 2: 166–167.

Ward, James D. and Mario A. Rivera (2014) *Institutional Racism, Organizations and Public Policy*. New York: Peter Lang Publishing.

Appendix 1

Determinants of Racial Differences in Incarceration Rates

MODEL SPECIFICATION

Equation 1

$$\ln\left[\frac{I_t^B}{I_t^W}\right] = \beta_0 + \sum \beta_{it-1} \ln\left[\frac{x_{it-1}^B}{x_{it-1}^W}\right] + \sum \gamma_{it} z_{it} + \varepsilon_t$$

Equation 2

$$\ln\left[I_t^B\right] = \beta_0^B + \sum \beta_{it-1}^B \ln\left[x_{it-1}^B\right] + \sum \gamma_{it}^B z_{it} + \varepsilon_t^B$$

Equation 3

$$\ln\left[I_t^W\right] = \beta_0^W + \sum \beta_{it-1}^W \ln\left[x_{it-1}^W\right] + \sum \gamma_{it}^W z_{it} + \varepsilon_t^W$$

Where:
I = incarceration rates (by race, by year)
X = unemployment rates (by race, gender, age-group and year); arrest rates by race by type
Z = offence rates by type, overall arrest rates, overall unemployment rates and overall drug incarceration rates.

DATA

Population data was obtained from Census Bureau Historical Data.

Number of violent and property crimes and violent and property crime rates was obtained from the Uniform Crime Reporting Statistic from the US Department of Justice Federal Bureau of Investigation website.

Number of arrests by race and type of crime (violent or property crime) was obtained from the ICPSR Inter-university Consortium for Political and

Table A1   OLS Estimates of Determinants of Racial Differences in Incarceration Rates

	(1)	(2)	(3)
	ln(b/w incarceration rate)		
ln(black unemployment rate)t-1/ white unemployment rate)t-1	-0.0193		
	(0.0708)		
ln(black arrest rate by property crimes)t-1/ (white arrest rate by property crimes)t-1	1.0629***		
	(0.1470)		
ln(black arrest rate by violent crimes)t-1/ (white arrest rate by violent crimes)t-1	-0.7859***		
	(0.1278)		
Property crime rate	0.0001		
	(0.0000)		
Violent crime rate	0.0002		
	(0.0001)		
Unemployment rate	-0.0084		
	(0.0066)		
Drug arrest rate	0.0001		
	(0.0001)		
ln(unemployment rate)		-0.1025*	-0.0764
		(0.0453)	(0.0640)
ln(violent crime rate)t-1		0.2549***	
		(0.0509)	
ln(drug arrest rate)t-1		0.0831	0.0744
		(0.0430)	(0.0460)
ln(unemployment Rate)t-1			-0.0383
			(0.0658)
ln(violent crime rate)t-1			0.2502***
			(0.0521)
_cons	1.6753***	-0.0358	0.0693
	(0.1734)	(0.5634)	(0.5978)
N	32	33	33
adj. R^2	0.8368	0.6266	0.6179

Standard errors in parentheses.

*p < 0.05, **p < 0.01, ***p < 0.001.

Table A2   OLS Estimates of Coefficients in Model of Black Incarceration Rates

	(1)	(2)	(3)
	ln(black incarceration rate)		
ln(black unemployment rate)t-1	0.1122		
	(0.1106)		
ln(black arrest by property crimes)t-1	-1.5452***		
	(0.3153)		
ln(black arrest by violent crimes)t-1	1.6384***		
	(0.3333)		
Black arrest rate	-0.0001		
	(0.0001)		
Black arrest by drugs	0.0006***		
	(0.0001)		
High Black unemployment rate		-0.0330	-0.0689
		(0.0491)	(0.0509)
ln(black drug arrest rate) t-1		0.7103***	0.3196**
		(0.0758)	(0.1151)
ln(offense rate)t-1		-0.6413***	
		(0.0999)	
ln(offense rate before 1990)t-1			-0.0528***
			(0.0083)
_cons	7.5814***	7.5673***	5.0740***
	(1.9219)	(1.1773)	(0.8500)
N	32	33	33
adj. R^2	0.9220	0.9086	0.9078

Standard errors in parentheses
*p < 0.05, **p < 0.01, ***p < 0.001.

Table A3   OLS Estimates of Coefficients in Model of White Incarceration Rates

	(1)	(2)	(3)
	ln(white incarceration rates)		
ln(white unemployment rate)t-1	0.0321		
	(0.1289)		
ln(white arrest rate by property crimes)t-1	-0.2637		
	(0.3988)		
ln(white arrest rate by violent crimes)t-1	0.8806***		
	(0.1984)		
White arrest rate	-0.0003		
	(0.0002)		
White arrest rate by drugs	0.0024***		
	(0.0006)		
High white unemployment rate		0.0932	0.0457
		(0.0596)	(0.0348)
ln(white drug arrest rate) t-1		1.2516***	0.8401***
		(0.1726)	(0.1054)
ln(offense rate)t-1		0.0519	
		(0.1974)	
ln(offense rate before 1990)t-1			-0.0283***
			(0.0064)
_cons	2.6195	-2.5527	0.3962
	(1.8665)	(2.6226)	(0.6401)
N	32	33	33
adj. R^2	0.9046	0.8883	0.9335

Standard errors in parentheses
*p < 0.05, **p < 0.01, ***p < 0.001.

Social Research. Uniform Crime Reporting Program [United States]: Arrests by Age, Sex, and Race for Police Agencies in Metropolitan Statistical Areas, 1960–1997 and from the Arrest Data Analysis Tool of the Bureau of Justice Statistics.

Persons incarcerated in state and federal prisons were obtained from National Prisoner Statistics, 1978–2013 archived within Inter-university Consortium for Political and Social Research.

Total arrests for drug offenses by race was obtained from Arrest Data Analysis Tool of the Bureau of Justice Statistics.

Unemployment rates were obtained from the Bureau of Labor Statistics and the Current Population Survey.[1]

NOTE

1. Data Sources:
United States Census Bureau, Population Estimates https://www.census.gov/popest/data/national/asrh/pre-1980/PE-11.html
   https://www.census.gov/popest/data/historical/1980s/county.html
   https://www.census.gov/popest/data/intercensal/st-co/characteristics.html
   https://www.census.gov/popest/data/intercensal/state/state2010.html
   United States Census Bureau, Vintage 2011: National Tables
   https://www.census.gov/popest/data/historical/2010s/vintage_2011/index.html
United States Census Bureau, QuickFacts United States
   http://www.census.gov/quickfacts/table/PST045214/00
   US Department of Justice, Federal Bureau of Investigation, Uniform Crime Reporting Statistics
   http://www.bjs.gov/ucrdata/Search/Crime/State/RunCrimeStatebyState.cfm
   ICPSR Inter-university Consortium for Political and Social Research. Uniform Crime Reporting Program [United States]: Arrests by Age, Sex, and Race for Police Agencies in Metropolitan Statistical Areas, 1960–1997 http://www.icpsr.umich.edu/icpsrweb/NACJD/studies/2538?paging.startRow=1&fundingAgency=United+States+Department+of+Justice.+Office+of+Justice+Programs.+Bureau+of+Justice+Statistics&keyword%5B0%5D=drug+abuse&fundingAgency%5B1%5D=United+States+Department+of+Justice.+Federal+Bureau+of+Investigation

Bureau of Justice Statistics, Arrest Data Analysis Tool http://www.bjs.gov/index.cfm?ty=datool&surl=/arrests/index.cfm#United States Department of Justice. Office of Justice Programs.

Bureau of Justice Statistics. National Prisoner Statistics, 1978–2013. ICPSR35608-v1. Ann Arbor, MI: Inter-university Consortium for Political and Social Research [distributor], 2015–01–09. http://doi.org/10.3886/ICPSR35608.v1

United States Department of Labor. Labor Force Statistics from the Current Population Survey http://www.bls.gov/cps/#data

Sarah Flood, Miriam King, Steven Ruggles, and J. Robert Warren. *Integrated Public Use Microdata Series, Current Population Survey: Version 4.0*. [Machine-readable database]. Minneapolis: University of Minnesota, 2015.

Appendix 2

List of Journals Included in Review

American Journal of Criminal Justice
Crime and Delinquency
Crime Prevention Studies
Criminal Justice and Behavior
Criminal Justice Policy Review
Criminology
International Criminal Justice Review
International Journal of Police Science and Management
International Review of Victimology
Journal of Contemporary Criminal Justice
Journal of Criminal Justice
Journal of Ethnicity in Criminal Justice
Journal of International Criminal Justice
Justice Policy Journal
Justice Quarterly
Law and Society Review
Police Practice and Research
Police Quarterly

Index

affirmative action, 61, 62, 66, 74, 77, 249
Allen Jr., Ivan, 72
Austin, Richard, 65

Baltimore city police department, 1, 20, 32, 171, 247, 268
black crime association, 4
Black Lives Matter, 1, 6, 7, 10, 17, 19, 21–24, 26, 264
de Blasio, Mayor Bill, 244
Bradley, Mayor Tom, 61, 69, 70
broken windows theory. *See* police performance management systems
Brown, Michael, 251, 252
Brown v. Board of Education (1954), 3
bureaucratic representation. *See* representation; representative bureaucracy

campaign zero, 22, 26
Castile, Philando, 1, 172
Cavanagh, Mayor Jerome, 65
Christopher Commission, 71, 147
Churchill, Winston, 35
Cincinnati, Ohio:
    collaborative agreement, 248;
    police department, 171, 249
citizen engagement, 230, 231

citizen review panels, 173, 266
Civil Rights Act (1964), 33, 61, 72
Cleveland police department, 72, 168, 171, 232
cognitive complexity, 243
Comey, James, 24
Committee on Accreditation of Law Enforcement, 34
community policing. *See* policing
Compstat. *See* police performance management systems
coproduction, 11, 208–10, 215
Craig, Chief James, 67
critical ethical analysis, 251
critical race theory, 4, 243, 244, 252
Crow, Jim, 32, 33, 35, 41
cultural competence, 173, 249, 266
cultural identity, 244

Davis, Jordan, 172
Detroit, Michigan:
    city of, 62–65, 69, 76, 77;
    police department, 7, 55, 61, 64, 65, 67, 68, 76
dissociative behavior/dissociation, 169

Eaves, Reginald, 73
Equal Employment Opportunity Commission, 33

ethics, 171, 241, 245, 287;
  comparative public, 248;
  comparativist, 243, 248, 254, 255, 267;
  liberal-philosophical, 253;
  liberal public, 251;
  normative, 248;
  politico-philosophical, 245, 247;
  public, 241, 242, 244, 245, 247, 248, 251, 253, 256;
  public administration, 248;
  Rawlsian, 247;
  situated, 245;
  transcendentalist, 255
explicit bias, 4, 5

Ferguson, Missouri, 8, 24, 123, 168, 171, 172, 247, 250, 251, 268
Ferguson effect, 247
Fraternal Order of Police, 24

Garner, Eric, 1, 182, 234
Gates, Chief Daryl, 70
Gray, Freddie, 1
Gribbs, Sheriff Roman, 65, 66
Griggs v. Duke Power Company (1971), 78
group threat theory, 209

Hartsfield, Mayor William, 72
Harvard, Chief Beverly, 74
Health Information National Trends Survey (HINTS), 87, 90, 95
Holtzclaw, Daniel, 172

immigration, 101, 266;
  authorities, 100;
  control machinery, 3, 266;
  enforcement, 95–102, 266
implicit bias, 3, 4, 5, 8, 10, 263, 266, 268
inattentional blindness, 4
incarceration, 9, 25, 111–20, 125, 153, 185, 188, 264
institutional misconduct, 185, 186, 188

institutional racism. *See* racism
International Association of Chiefs of Police, 24, 34
interpretative bubble, 165–68, 171–73
investigative stops. *See* pretextual stops

Jackson, Mayor Maynard, 61, 73, 74, 76, 77
Jenkins, Chief Herbert T., 72
Johnson, Micah Xavier, 1

King, Jr., Martin Luther, 21, 35
King, Rodney, 70, 221
Kirkpatrick, Chief Anne E., 235
ku klux klan, 72, 73, 171

law enforcement:
  behavior, 1, 4, 36, 264;
  culture, 2, 3, 9, 41, 42, 45, 48, 67, 71, 74, 75, 147, 171, 232, 249, 250;
  racial profiling, 6, 8, 246, 268, 269
Los Angeles, California:
  Christopher Commission, 71, 147;
  city of, 62, 63, 68, 69, 71, 76, 77, 268;
  CRASH division, 70;
  police department, 7, 32, 55, 61, 63, 67, 71, 76, 172

Maddox, Lester, 72
Mapp v. Ohio (1961), 33
Martin, Trayvon, 172
Maryland state police, 32
Miranda v. Arizona (1966), 33

New Jersey State Troopers, 32
New Orleans police department, 32, 171, 172
New Public Administration, 253
New Public Governance, 253
New Public Management, 226, 253
New York police department, 11, 18, 20, 25, 26, 32, 37–39, 41, 45, 222, 224, 230, 232, 233, 235, 268

Oakland police department, 11, 222, 233, 234, 236
Obama, President Barak, 21, 22, 86, 99, 101, 103, 207, 221, 235, 249
O'Neill, James, 234
open-system, 55, 56, 58, 59, 60, 77, 265
organizational change, 7, 25, 55, 56, 58, 60–62, 76–78, 265, 268

Parker, Chief Barnard, 71
Patient Protection and Affordable Care Act (ACA), 85
Peelian principle, 56
Pittsburgh police department, 32
police:
    legitimacy, 20, 47, 48, 56, 183, 198, 214, 223;
    management, 34, 283;
    use of force, 2–5, 11, 22, 24, 25, 67, 123, 181–99, 223, 225–27, 235, 247, 249, 266–68;
    violence, racialized, 10, 11, 241, 242, 248, 252, 254, 255, 267
police behavior. *See* law enforcement
police-community relations, 2, 12, 55, 56, 66, 68, 70, 207, 210, 215, 263, 264, 265, 266, 267
police culture. *See* law enforcement
police performance management systems, 32;
    broken windows theory, 7, 22, 31, 221, 224;
    Compstat, 7, 31, 38, 41, 42, 44, 45, 224, 225, 233, 234;
    zero tolerance, 7, 31, 221, 224
policing:
    community oriented, 7, 10, 11, 25, 31, 39, 49, 57, 74, 75, 165, 173, 216, 221–36, 249, 267, 269;
    democratic, 35, 50, 265, 270;
    of immigrants, 3;
    problem oriented, 223, 232
post-traumatic stress disorder (PTSD), 169, 170–73
power-assigning structures, 5, 245

President's Task Force on 21st Century Policing, 1, 2, 6, 55, 58, 207, 216, 235
pretextual stops, 1, 6, 8, 10, 264, 266, 268, 269
privatization, 253
procedural justice, 46, 47, 48, 149
public management approach, 17, 23
public sector performance, 7, 17

racial disparities:
    in drug arrests, 9, 117;
    in employment decisions, 8;
    in imprisonment, 112;
    in incarceration, 111, 112, 114–16;
    in police-community relations, 2, 12, 263–67;
    in police stops, 3;
    in police use of force, 4, 5, 267, 268;
    in sentencing of juvenile offenders, 8
racial profiling. *See* law enforcement
racism, 5, 33, 148, 241, 243, 248, 252, 253–55;
    concept of, 244;
    covert types of, 41;
    dimensions of, 245;
    ethical evaluation of, 254;
    evidence of, 34;
    experiences of, 247;
    forms of, 268;
    hidden, 41;
    history of, 19, 222;
    impediments of, 252;
    institutional, 5, 10, 20, 72, 76, 148, 149, 241, 243, 244, 245, 247;
    Jim Crow type, 41;
    normalization of, 245;
    police violence and, 249;
    policing and, 11, 35;
    questions of, 242;
    systemic, 242, 243;
    treatment of, 244;
    violence and, 241
reinvention literature, 7
representation, 63, 64, 67, 73–75, 117, 153, 169;

active, 57, 75, 76;
  Black, 5, 62, 72–74;
  explicit, 5;
  improving, 7, 17;
  minority, 5, 71;
  passive, 57;
  police force, 64, 65, 69, 75
representative bureaucracy, 56, 57, 74, 78, 242
reverse discrimination, 66

San Antonio Fear Free Environment (SAFFE) program, 249
Scott, Walter, 172
Secure Communities program, 7, 85
sharecropper finance, 9
Shaw, Mayor Frank, 68
Shumpert, Antwun "Ronnie," 1
slave patrols, 57, 172
social disorganization, 124, 137, 153
social equity, 2, 241, 242, 247, 248, 253, 255
social justice, 221, 247, 250
Sterling, Alton, 1
stop and frisk, 26, 31, 32, 37, 41, 44, 46, 147, 224
strain theory, 125, 137

Terry v. Ohio (1969), 32
tonic immobility. *See* dissociative behavior

transparency, 2, 7, 25, 199, 209, 226, 249
trauma, 10, 11, 165–73, 266, 267, 270
Trump, President Donald, 32

Uniform Crime Report, 114, 125
US Bureau of Immigration and Customs Enforcement (ICE), 85, 92, 93
US Department of Justice, 26, 66, 67, 71, 76, 168, 172, 222, 235;
  Office of Community Oriented Policing (COPS), 222
US Drug Enforcement Administration, 6
use of force. *See* police

VERA Institute of Justice, 46

Ward, Benjamin, 25
Watts Riots of 1965, 69
Whent, Chief Sean, 235
White, James, 67
White, Stephanie, 67
Whren v. United States (1996), 268, 269

Yanez, Jeronimo, 223
Young, Mayor Andrew, 61, 74
Young, Mayor Coleman, 61, 66, 77

About the Editor and Contributors

Maria J. Albo is Senior Lecturer in the Department of Political Science at the University of North Georgia. She teaches courses in American government, political science, and social science research methods, and has published several peer reviewed articles on the topic of illegal immigration and public policy. Prior to entering academia on a full-time basis, she worked as a special projects coordinator in commercial real estate where she specialized in planning, zoning, and land use. Albo has a MPA degree from the University of North Georgia.

Britt S. Aliperti is Project Manager for lowernine.org, a New Orleans based nonprofit dedicated to the long-term recovery of the Lower Ninth Ward following hurricanes Katrina and Rita. He previously worked with the Middle Georgia Regional Commission as a government services specialist, serving eleven counties and twenty cities in Georgia. Aliperti's primary area of interest includes community development and the reduction of disparity in access to resources for marginalized populations. He earned his MPA at the University of Georgia, with an emphasis on Nonprofit Management.

Christine S. Barrow is Assistant Professor in the Department of Criminal Justice at Molloy College. She spent several years performing qualitative research on how involvement in community organizations contributes to prosocial behavior among urban youth. Barrow teaches courses in criminology theories, juvenile justice, and corrections and women. She is also the author of two book chapters on delinquency and youth. She received her PhD in Criminal Justice from Rutgers University, Newark.

Domonic A. Bearfield is Associate Professor in the Bush School of Government and Public Service at Texas A&M University where he is Faculty Coordinator for the Good Governance Program of the Robert Mosbacher Institute for Trade, Economics, and Public Policy. Before joining Texas A&M University, he was an Assistant Professor at the University of New Hampshire. His research focuses on issues related to governance in public administration and on improving the understanding of public sector patronage. Bearfield's work has appeared in *Public Administration Review, Review of Public Personnel Administration*, and other leading journals. He is coeditor, with Melvin Dubnick, of the *Encyclopedia of Public Administration and Public Policy*. He received his PhD in Public Administration from Rutgers University, Newark.

Sharlene Graham Boltz is Professor of Law and former Associate Dean for Academic Affairs at Salmon P. Chase College of Law, Northern Kentucky University. Boltz serves on the Kentucky MultiDisciplinary Taskforce on Human Trafficking and as a board member and treasurer for the Ohio Alliance for Ending Sexual Violence. In 2011, she completed her training with Gavin DeBecker & Associates' Advanced Threat Assessment and Case Management Academy in Los Angeles, and in 2012, she graduated from the FBI Citizen's Academy. Boltz consults as a threat assessment analyst and strategic intervention specialist with expertise in abusive and controlling behavior and has published in *Police Chief Magazine* (September 2015), the official publication of the International Association of Chiefs of Police. She is currently leading the creation of a comprehensive human trafficking protocol for the Northern Kentucky region. A native of Ewing Township, New Jersey, Boltz received her BA from Brown University and her JD from the University of Michigan Law School.

Julian Brinkley is a PhD candidate in the Department of Computer and Information Science and Engineering at the University of Florida. He holds an MSc in Software Engineering from East Carolina University. He has authored papers on cloud computing, legacy system migration, software engineering education, and outline social networking accessibility, among other topics.

Edward C. Dillon is Assistant Professor in the Department of Computer Science at Morgan State University. His research interests include the use of interview technology to improve relations between civilians and law enforcement. He is also investigating the correlation between social networking sites and human behavior. He received his PhD in Computer Science from the University of Alabama.

Lauren Hamilton Edwards is Assistant Professor in the School of Public Policy at the University of Maryland, Baltimore County. Her research interests include nonprofit and public management, strategic management, planning and performance, public participation and coproduction, program evaluation, and diversity and gender issues. She has published in *Public Administration Review, Administration & Society*, and *Public Performance and Management Review*, among other journals. Edwards received her PhD in Public Administration jointly from Georgia State University and Georgia Institute of Technology.

Jared Ellison is Assistant Professor in the Department of Sociology and Criminal Justice at Old Dominion University where his research interests include corrections and court processing. His dissertation, titled "Identifying safety risks in jail: An opportunity model of the sources of violent victimization among inmates and staff," provides an analysis of the predictors of victimization among both inmates and staff in a Midwestern jail. He has published several articles and book entries related to these topics. Dr. Ellison received his PhD in Criminal Justice from the University of Nebraska at Omaha.

John A. Eterno is Professor, Associate Dean, and Director of Graduate Studies in Criminal Justice at Molloy College in Rockville Center, New York. He is also a retired Captain from the New York City Police Department. His accomplishments have been recognized with specific awards in various areas including research and publications, teaching, and service. He is the author of numerous books, book chapters, articles, and editorials. Examples of his most recent publications: an op-ed in the *New York Times* entitled "Policing by the Numbers," several peer-reviewed articles including one in *Justice Quarterly* titled "Police Manipulations of Crime Reporting: Insiders' Revelations" (with Arvind Verman and Eli B. Silverman), and editor/coeditor of three recent books including *The Crime Numbers Game: Management by Manipulation* (with Eli B. Silverman), *The New York City Police Department: The Impact of Its Policies and Practices*, and *The Detective's Handbook* (with Cliff Roberson). He has appeared on numerous television shows, radio programs, and other media as an expert on police, and has been recognized by the federal courts as an expert witness on police management. Eterno lives in a suburb of New York City with his wife JoAnn and two children, Julie and Lauren. He received his PhD in Criminal Justice from the State University of New York at Albany.

Barry D. Friedman is Professor and MPA Program Director in the Department of Political Science at the University of North Georgia. He teaches courses in American politics, public and nonprofit administration, and public policy. Friedman is author of *Regulation in the Reagan Bush-Era: The Eruption of Presidential Influence* (University of Pittsburgh Press, 1995). He received his PhD in Political Science from the University of Connecticut.

Juan E. Gilbert is the Andrew Banks Family Preeminent Endowed Professor and Chair of the Department of Computer and Information Science and Engineering at the University of Florida, where he leads the Human Experience Research Laboratory. Dr. Gilbert has published more than 140 articles, given more than 200 talks, and obtained more than $24 million in research funding. He is a Fellow of the American Association of Advancement for Science, and in 2012 he received the Presidential Award for Excellence in Science, Mathematics, and Engineering Mentoring from President Barack Obama. Gilbert received his PhD in Computer Science from the University of Cincinnati.

Andrew J. Grandage is a PhD candidate in the Department of Public Administration and Policy at the University of Georgia. His research focuses on issues concerning public budgeting and financial management, organizational theory and public policy. Prior to his doctoral studies, he spent several years working at the intersection of business and government, serving as a Financial Analyst for Harris Corporation and as a Research Assistant at the University of Georgia's Carl Vinson Institute of Government.

Seong C. Kang is a PhD candidate in the Department of Public Administration and Policy at the University of Georgia. His current research interests include organizational theory and behavior, coproduction, collaborative governance, and regulatory rulemaking.

Ian Kingsbury is a PhD candidate in the Department of Education Reform at the University of Arkansas. He received his BA in Government and History from the College of William and Mary and his MA in Education Policy from Teacher's College, Columbia University. Before joining the Department of Education Reform, Ian worked and lived with postgraduate high school students with learning differences, helping them to improve their independent living skills in preparation for college. His scholarly interests include civic outcomes and civic values.

Ian Klein is a PhD candidate in the School of Public Policy at the University of Maryland, Baltimore County. His research interests are in the areas of public management practices and policing.

Alana M. W. LeBrón is Assistant Professor in the Program in Health and the Department of Chicano/Latino Studies at the University of California at Irvine. Her research interests include: racial, ethnic, and socioeconomic health inequities; influence of social policies on the health of Latinas/os; contribution of racialization to psychosocial stress, health behaviors, and health inequities; community-based participatory research; and multilevel interventions. She received her PhD in Health Behavior and Health Education from the University of Michigan.

Robert Maranto is the 21st Century Chair in Leadership, Department of Education Reform, University of Arkansas in Fayetteville. He previously taught at Villanova University and served in government during the Clinton years. Maranto currently edits the *Journal of School Choice,* and serves on the Fayetteville School Board. His research addresses administrative reform generally, and school reform in particular. In concert with others, Bob has produced thirteen scholarly books which have sold dozens of copies and are so boring that his own mother refused to read them. Most recently, he coauthored *Education Reform in the Obama Era* (Palgrave/Macmillan, 2016) and the *End of the Experiment* (Transaction, 2016). He has also produced more than seventy refereed publications and more than a hundred newspaper op-eds. With April Gresham Maranto, he reports to Tony (b. 1999) and Maya (b. 2004), who attend Fayetteville public schools.

Dekita Moon is a PhD candidate in Human-Centered Computing and an Intel Gem Scholar at the University of Florida where her research interests include human-computer interaction and educational technologies, particularly on promoting meaningful learning through sociocultural intelligence tutoring systems. She has a BSc in Computer Information Systems from Fort Valley State University.

Samuel L. Myers, Jr. is Roy Wilkins Professor of Human Relations and Social Justice and directs the Roy Wilkins Center for Human Relations and Social Justice at the University of Minnesota's Hubert H. Humphrey School of Public Affairs, where he specializes in the impacts of social policies on the poor. Myers is a pioneer in the use of applied economic techniques to the examination of racial disparities in crime, the detection of illegal discrimination in credit markets, assessing the impacts of welfare on family stability, evaluating the effectiveness of government transfers in reducing poverty, determining the impacts of food pricing on low-income communities, and on detecting disparities and discrimination in government contracting. He is a national authority on the methodology of conducting disparity studies and has served as an expert witness in the groundbreaking federal case of GEOD v. New Jersey Transit (3rd Circuit Court of Appeals). He is cofounder of the Colorado Minnesota Disparity Study Consortium, which regularly provides technical assistance to state transportation departments, airport authorities, and local transit agencies. He received his PhD in Economics from Massachusetts Institute of Technology.

Vanessa Cruz Nichols is Postdoctoral Researcher in the Department of Political Science at Indiana University in Bloomington, where she specializes in American politics, as well as race and ethnicity. Cruz Nichols's research interests fall within the scope of political participation, public opinion, identity politics, and survey experiments. She is a two-time recipient of the NRC Ford Foundation Diversity Fellow (2011–2014) and (2014–2015) and was also selected for the American Political Science Association Minority Fellowship (2009–2011). She received her PhD in Political Science from the University of Michigan in Ann Arbor.

Francisco I. Pedraza is Assistant Professor in the Department of Political Science at the University of California at Riverside. His research focuses on political integration of marginalized communities in the United States, with an emphasis on minority groups and immigrants. Among his current projects is a large scale study of Latino public opinion of the U.S. Supreme Court, and the impact specific cases have on perceptions of American political institutions and civic engagement. His work has appeared in many academic venues including *Armed Forces and Society, Electoral Studies*, and *Latino Studies.* He has a PhD in Political Science from the University of Washington.

Mario A. Rivera is Regent's Professor of Public Administration at the University of New Mexico. Since his masters and doctoral studies in theology and political science at the University of Notre Dame, he has published extensively on the ethics of race and diversity and on issues of social equity, in contexts of international development, policy innovation and program evaluation. He received in PhD in Political Science from the University of Notre Dame.

Benjamin Steiner is Associate Professor in the School of Criminology and Criminal Justice at the University of Nebraska, Omaha. His research focuses on issues related to juvenile justice and corrections. He has published more than eighty journal articles and book entries related to these issues. Steiner is also the recipient of both the Outstanding Young Scholar award from the Juvenile Justice Section of the Academy of Criminal Justice Sciences and the Distinguished New Scholar award from the Division of Corrections and

Sentencing of the American Society of Criminology. He received his PhD in Criminal Justice from the University of Cincinnati.

James D. Ward teaches in the School of Public Affairs and Administration at Rutgers University, Newark. He is author or coauthor of more than seventy manuscripts, book chapters, journal articles, and books, including *Leadership and Change in Public Sector Organizations: Beyond Reform* (Routledge, 2017) and *Institutional Racism, Organizations and Public Policy* (Peter Lang Publishers, 2014). His current research interests include policing and race, local government reform, public sector performance (subnational, national, and transnational perspectives), and institutional commitments to diversity (including race and public policy). He is a former National Council member of the American Society for Public Administration, and served on the organization's Ethics and Standards Implementation Committee. Ward received his PhD in Political Science from the University of Cincinnati.

Brian N. Williams is Associate Professor of Public Administration and Public Policy in the School of Public and International Affairs at the University of Georgia. He has held previous academic appointments at Florida State University and Vanderbilt University. His research interests include coproduction of public safety and public order, community policing efforts within racial and ethnic communities, community-oriented governance, and the impact of personal and professional life experiences on the actions and inaction of pubic administrators. He received his PhD in Public Administration from the University of Georgia.

Roland Zullo is Associate Research Scientist at the Institute for Research on Labor, Employment, and the Economy at the University of Michigan. His work is broadly about the institutional conditions for socially responsible, politically viable, and environmentally sustainable economies. Toward that end, Zullo examines the role of nonmarket organizations, such as labor unions, religious organizations, and public services, and their effect on a variety of social indices, such as crime, political participation, and health. He received his PhD in Labor Relations from the University of Wisconsin in Madison.

Lightning Source UK Ltd.
Milton Keynes UK
UKOW04n1447191217
314738UK00010B/443/P